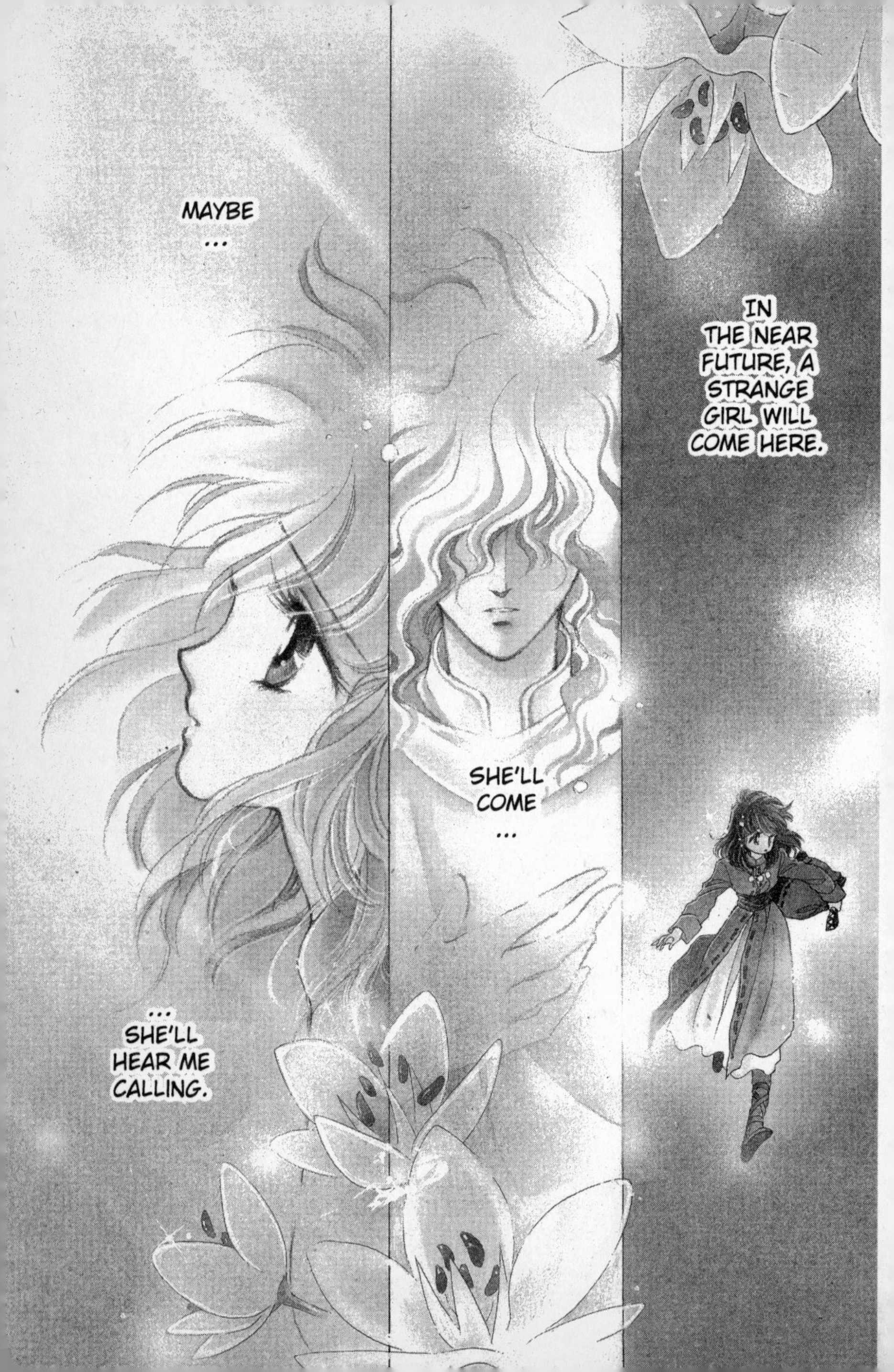
IN THE NEAR FUTURE, A STRANGE GIRL WILL COME HERE.
SHE'LL COME ...
MAYBE ...
... SHE'LL HEAR ME CALLING.

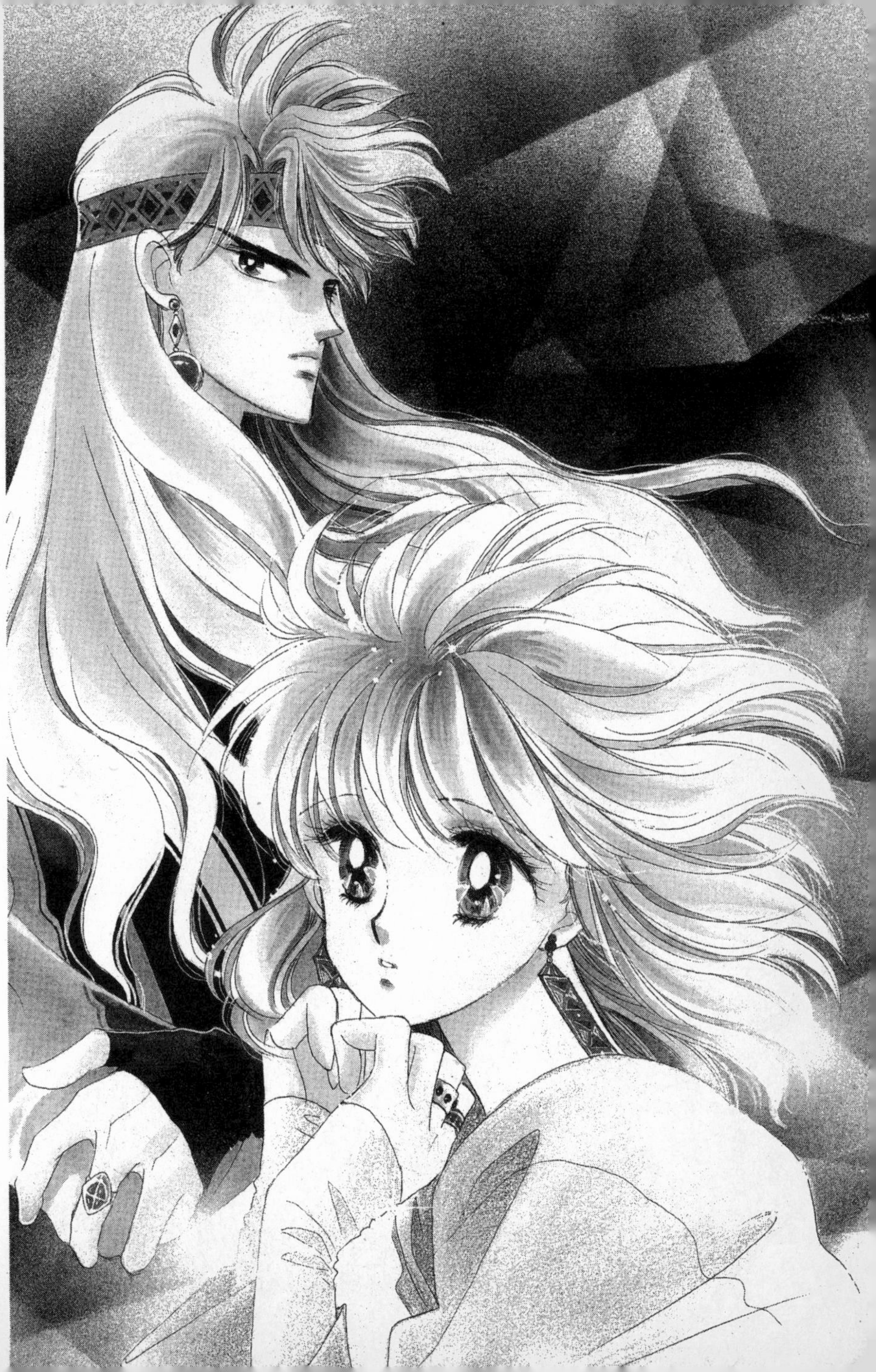

彼方から

FROM FAR AWAY
CHAPTER 2

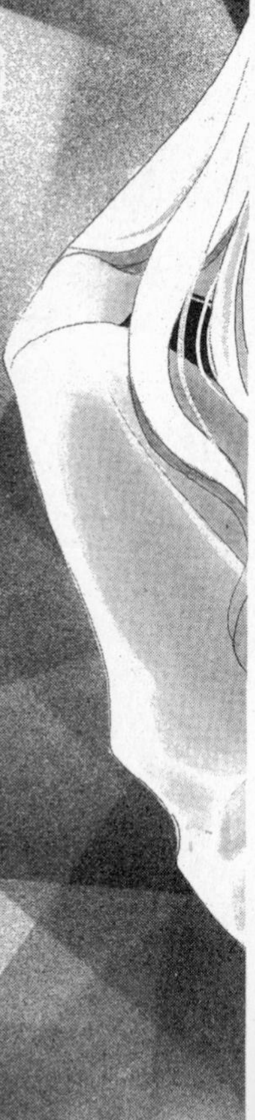

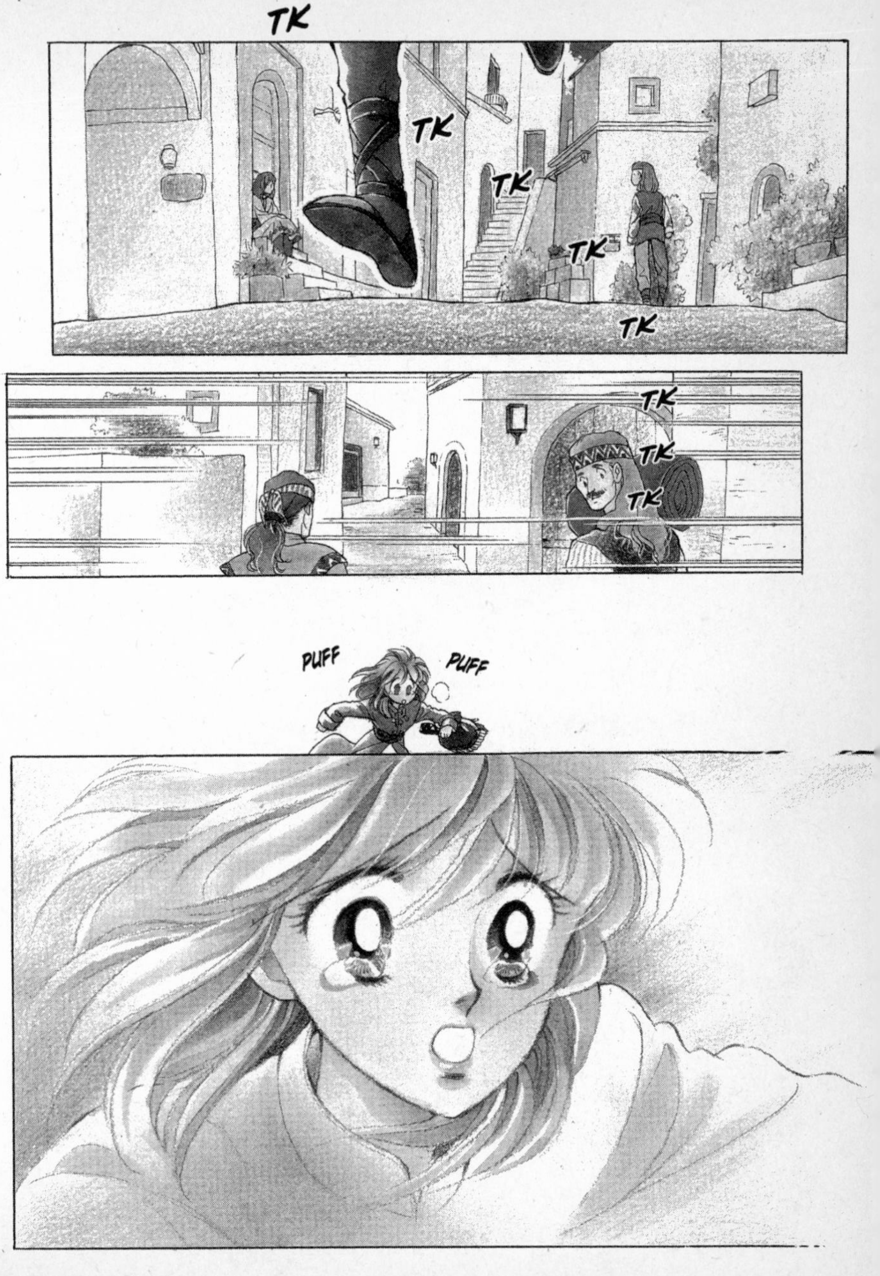
TK
TK
TK
TK
TK
TK
TK
TK
PUFF
PUFF

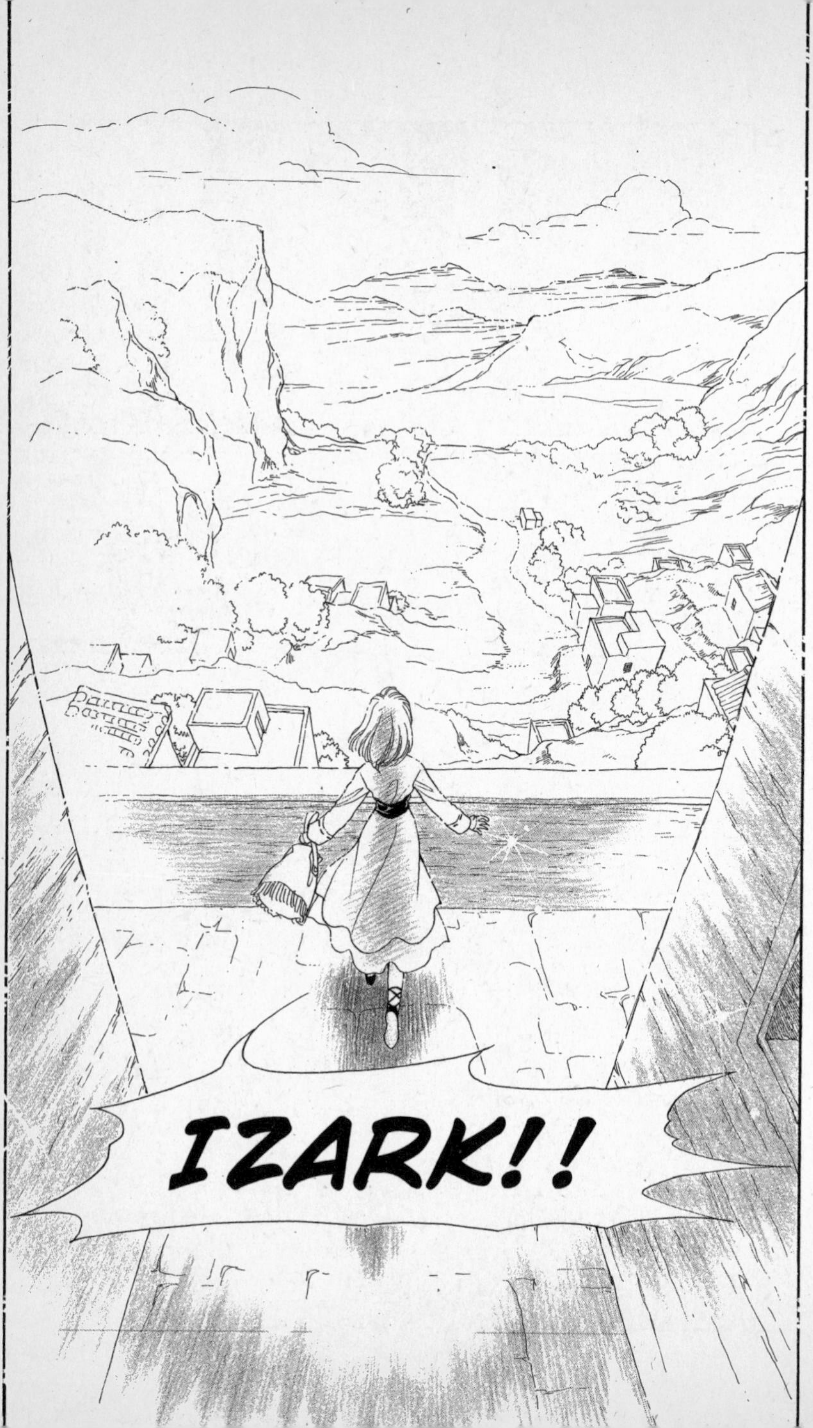
IZARK!!

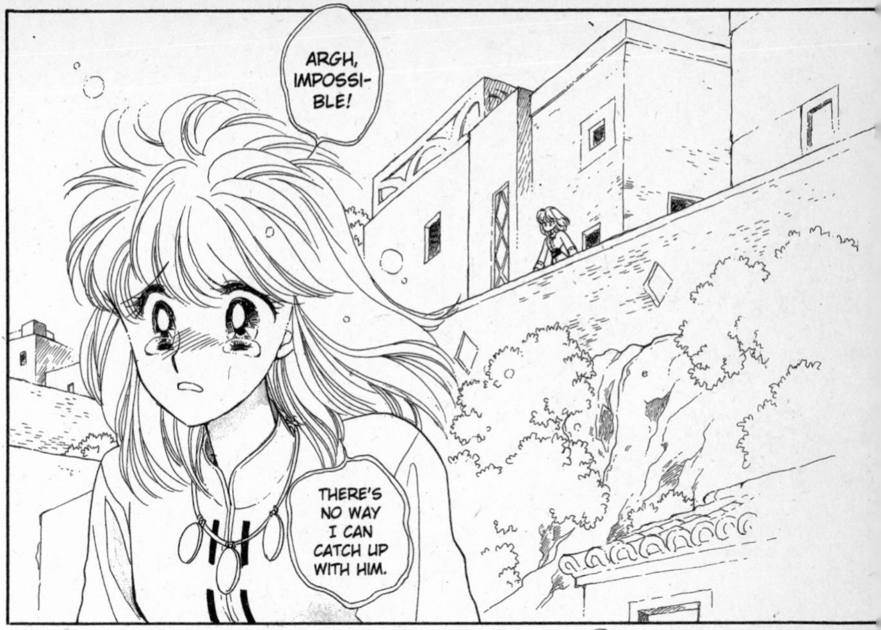
ARGH, IMPOSSI-BLE!
THERE'S NO WAY I CAN CATCH UP WITH HIM.

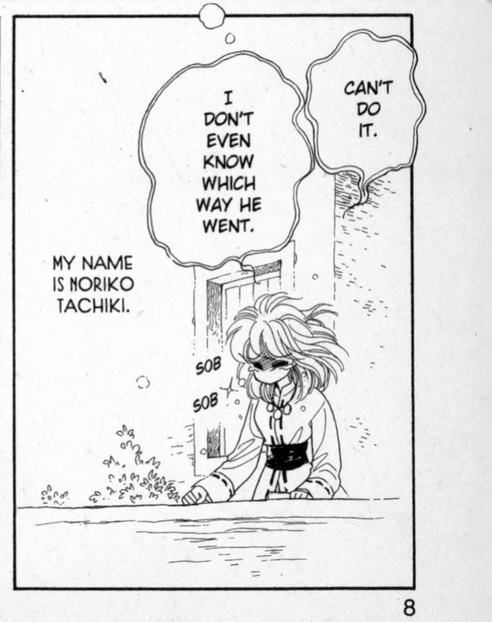
CAN'T DO IT.
I DON'T EVEN KNOW WHICH WAY HE WENT.
MY NAME IS NORIKO TACHIKI.
SOB
SOB

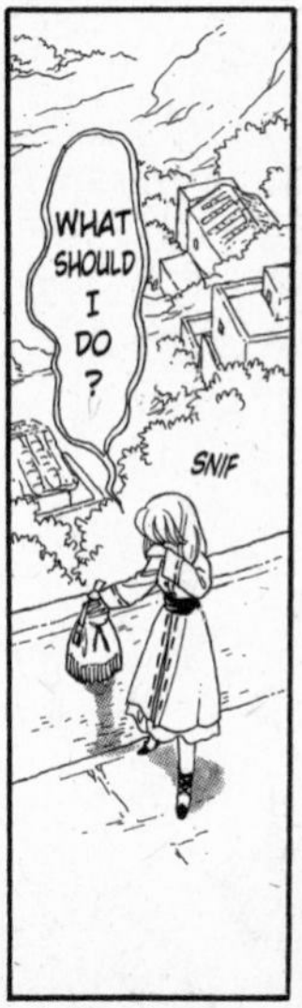
WHAT SHOULD I DO?
SNIF

I WAS JUST AN ORDINARY HIGH SCHOOL GIRL.

THEN SOMEHOW I WOUND UP IN THIS WORLD. THAT WAS THREE MONTHS AGO.

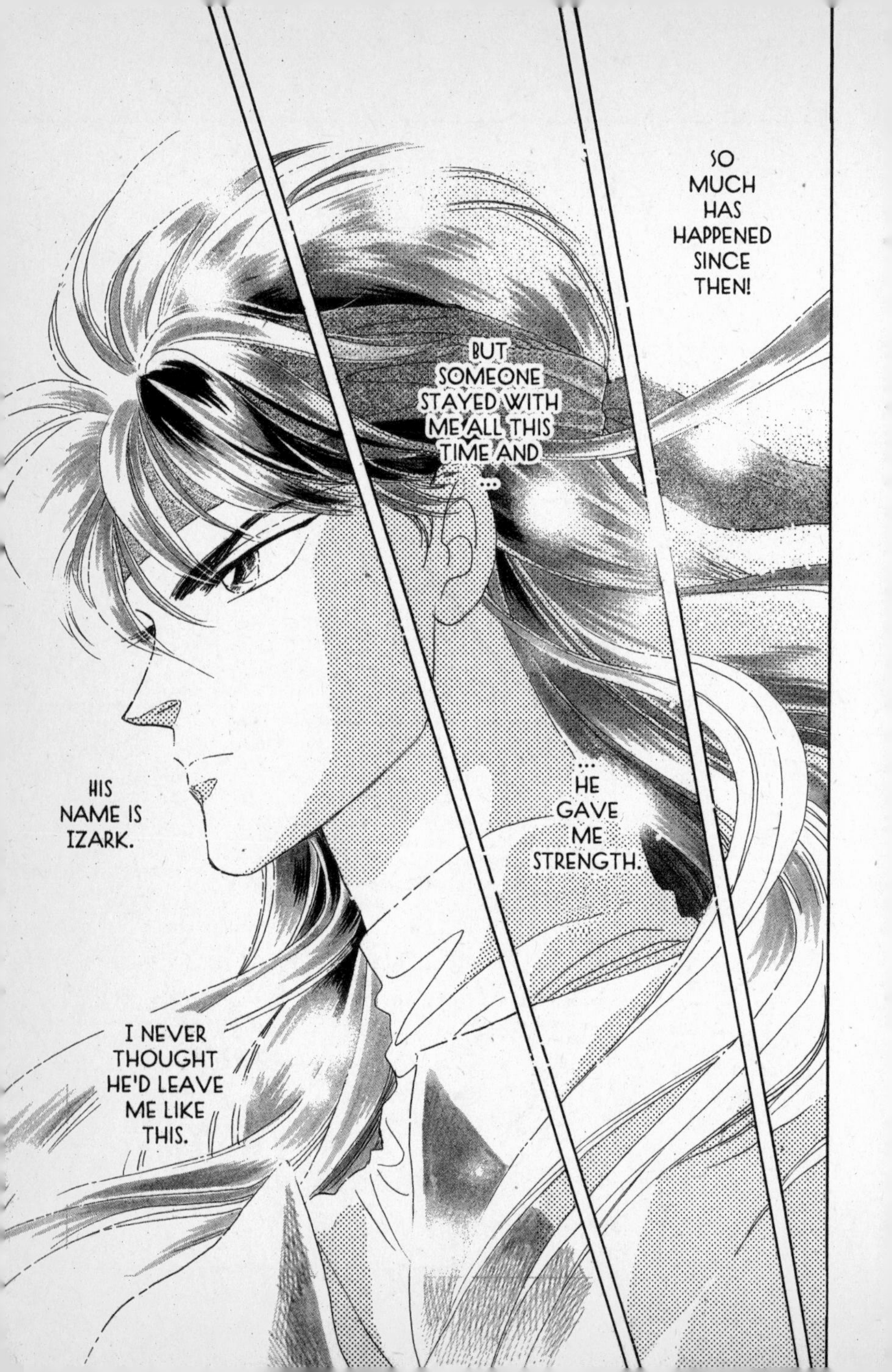
SO MUCH HAS HAPPENED SINCE THEN!
BUT SOMEONE STAYED WITH ME ALL THIS TIME AND ...
... HE GAVE ME STRENGTH.
HIS NAME IS IZARK.
I NEVER THOUGHT HE'D LEAVE ME LIKE THIS.

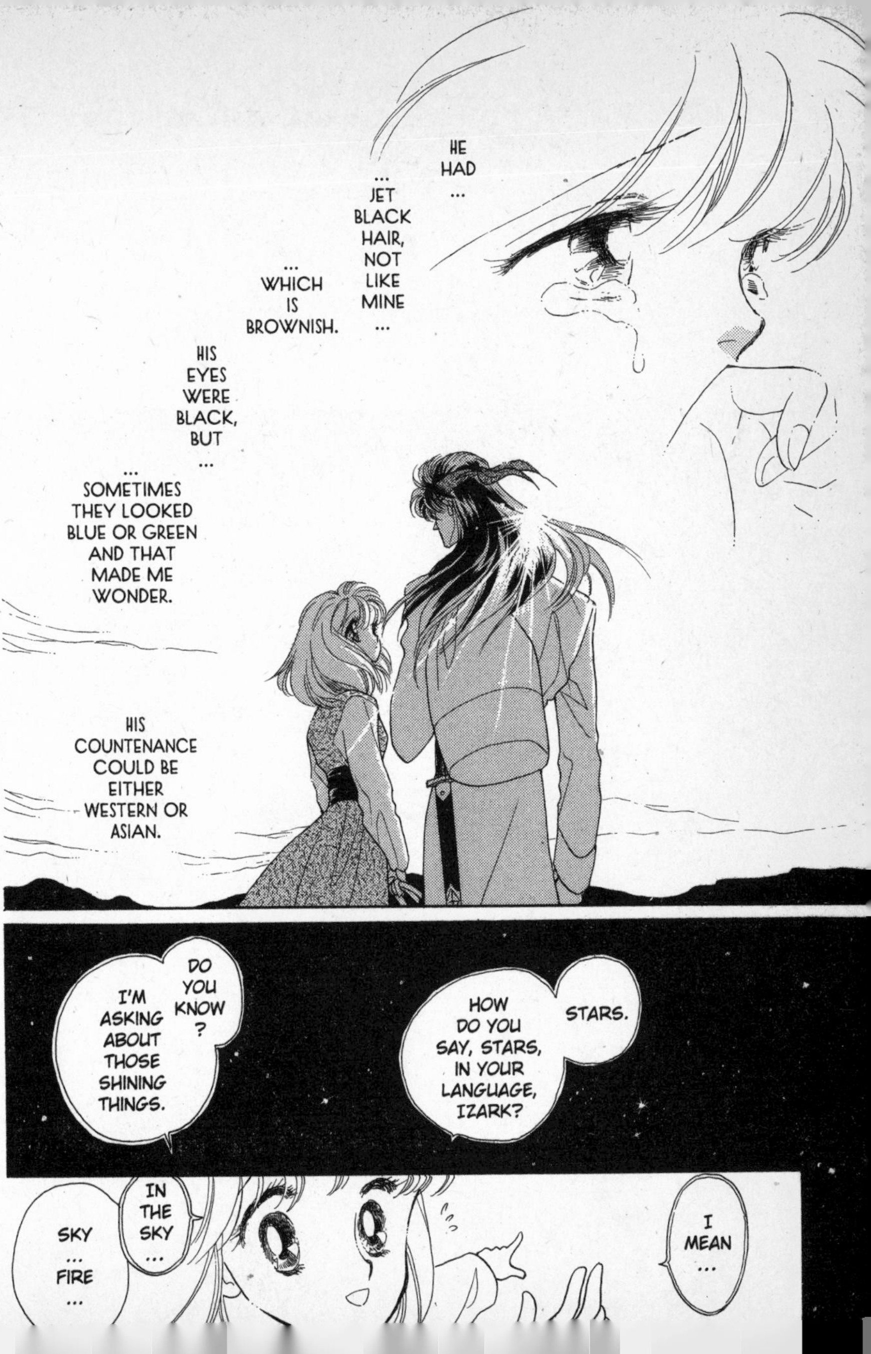
HE HAD ...
... JET BLACK HAIR, NOT LIKE MINE ...
... WHICH IS BROWNISH.
HIS EYES WERE BLACK, BUT ...
... SOMETIMES THEY LOOKED BLUE OR GREEN AND THAT MADE ME WONDER.
HIS COUNTENANCE COULD BE EITHER WESTERN OR ASIAN.
STARS.
HOW DO YOU SAY, STARS, IN YOUR LANGUAGE, IZARK?
DO YOU KNOW ?
I'M ASKING ABOUT THOSE SHINING THINGS.
I MEAN ...
IN THE SKY ...
SKY ... FIRE ...

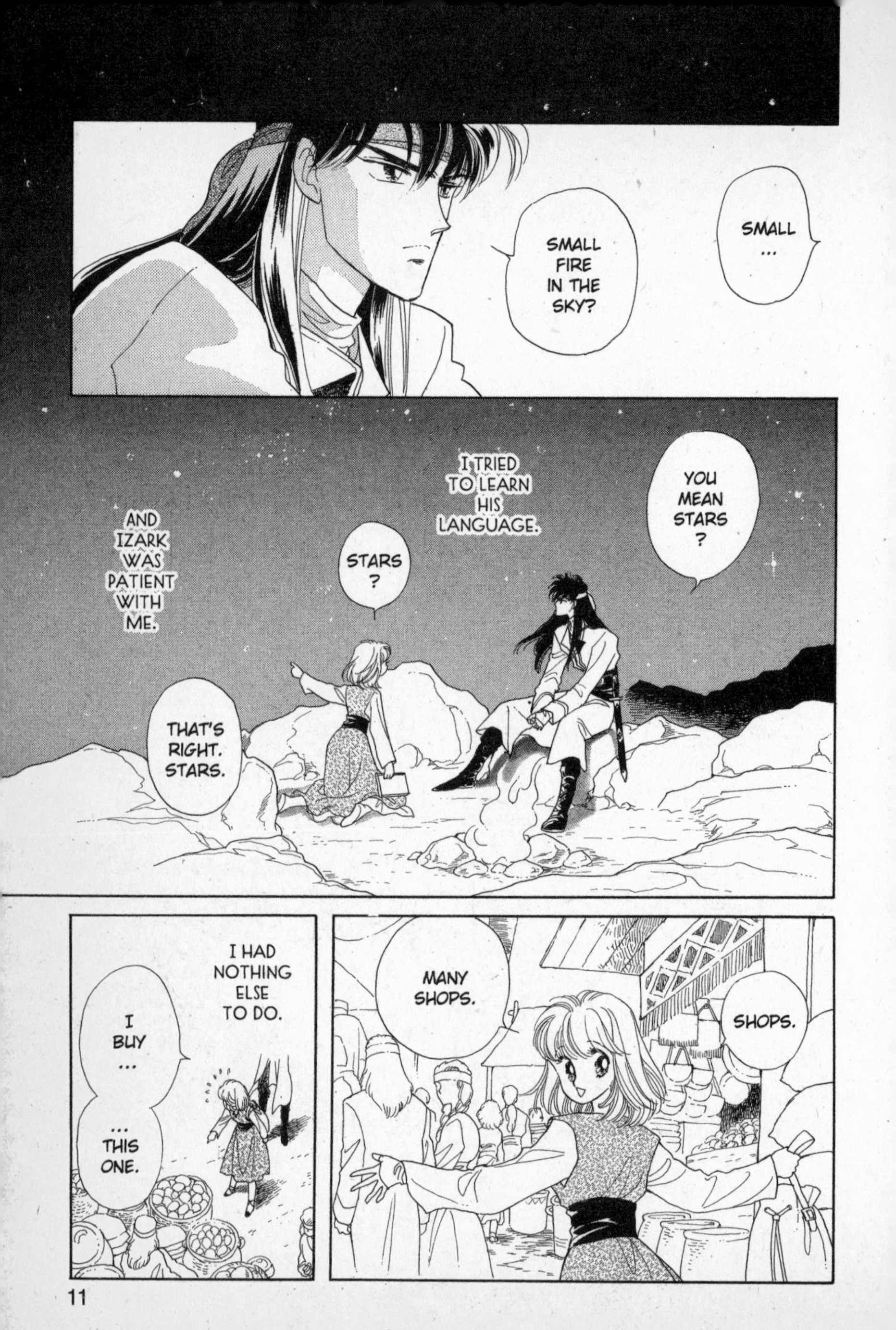
SMALL ...
SMALL FIRE IN THE SKY?
YOU MEAN STARS ?
I TRIED TO LEARN HIS LANGUAGE.
STARS ?
AND IZARK WAS PATIENT WITH ME.
THAT'S RIGHT. STARS.
SHOPS.
MANY SHOPS.
I HAD NOTHING ELSE TO DO.
I BUY ...
... THIS ONE.

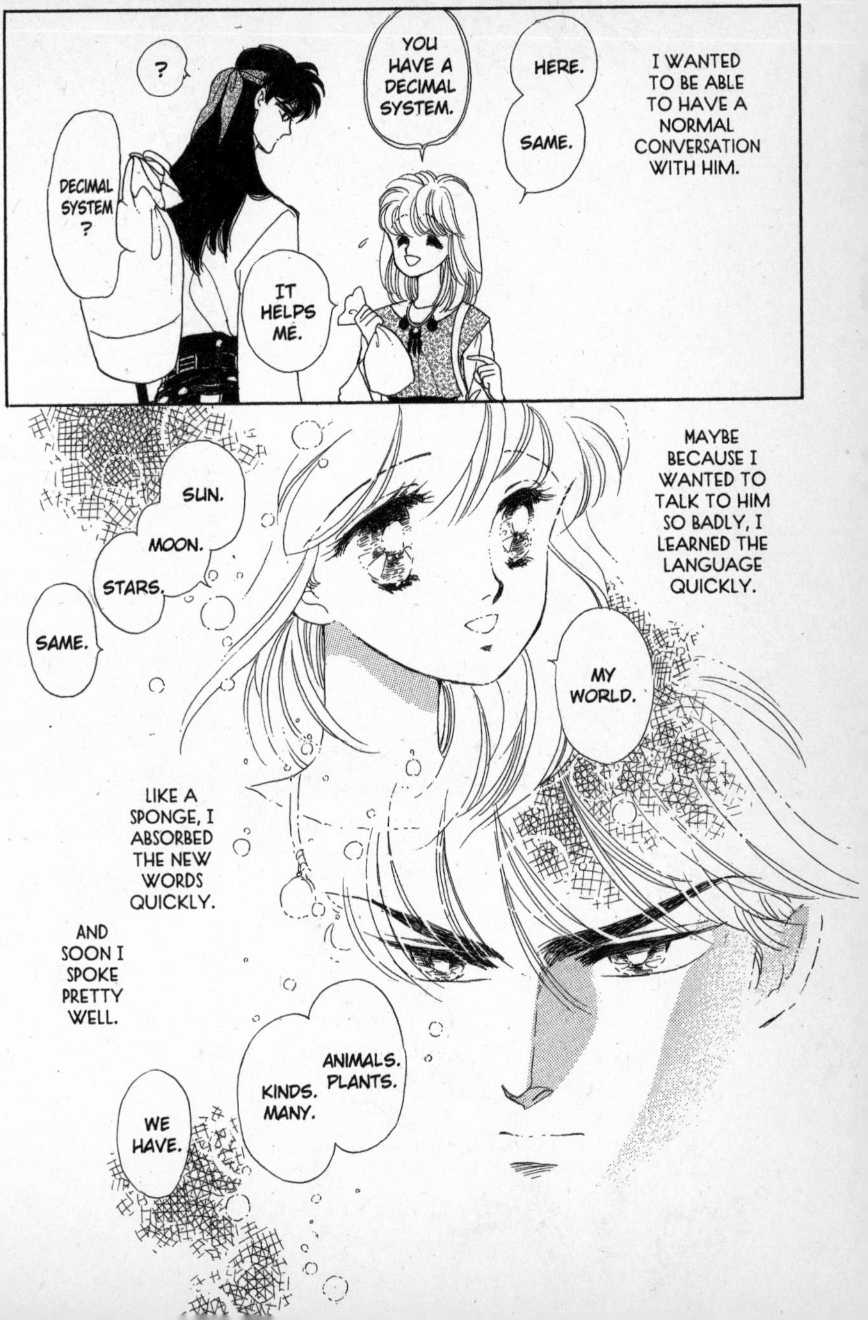
I WANTED TO BE ABLE TO HAVE A NORMAL CONVERSATION WITH HIM.
HERE.
SAME.
YOU HAVE A DECIMAL SYSTEM.
?
DECIMAL SYSTEM?
IT HELPS ME.
MAYBE BECAUSE I WANTED TO TALK TO HIM SO BADLY, I LEARNED THE LANGUAGE QUICKLY.
MY WORLD.
SUN.
MOON.
STARS.
SAME.
LIKE A SPONGE, I ABSORBED THE NEW WORDS QUICKLY.
AND SOON I SPOKE PRETTY WELL.
ANIMALS. PLANTS.
KINDS. MANY.
WE HAVE.

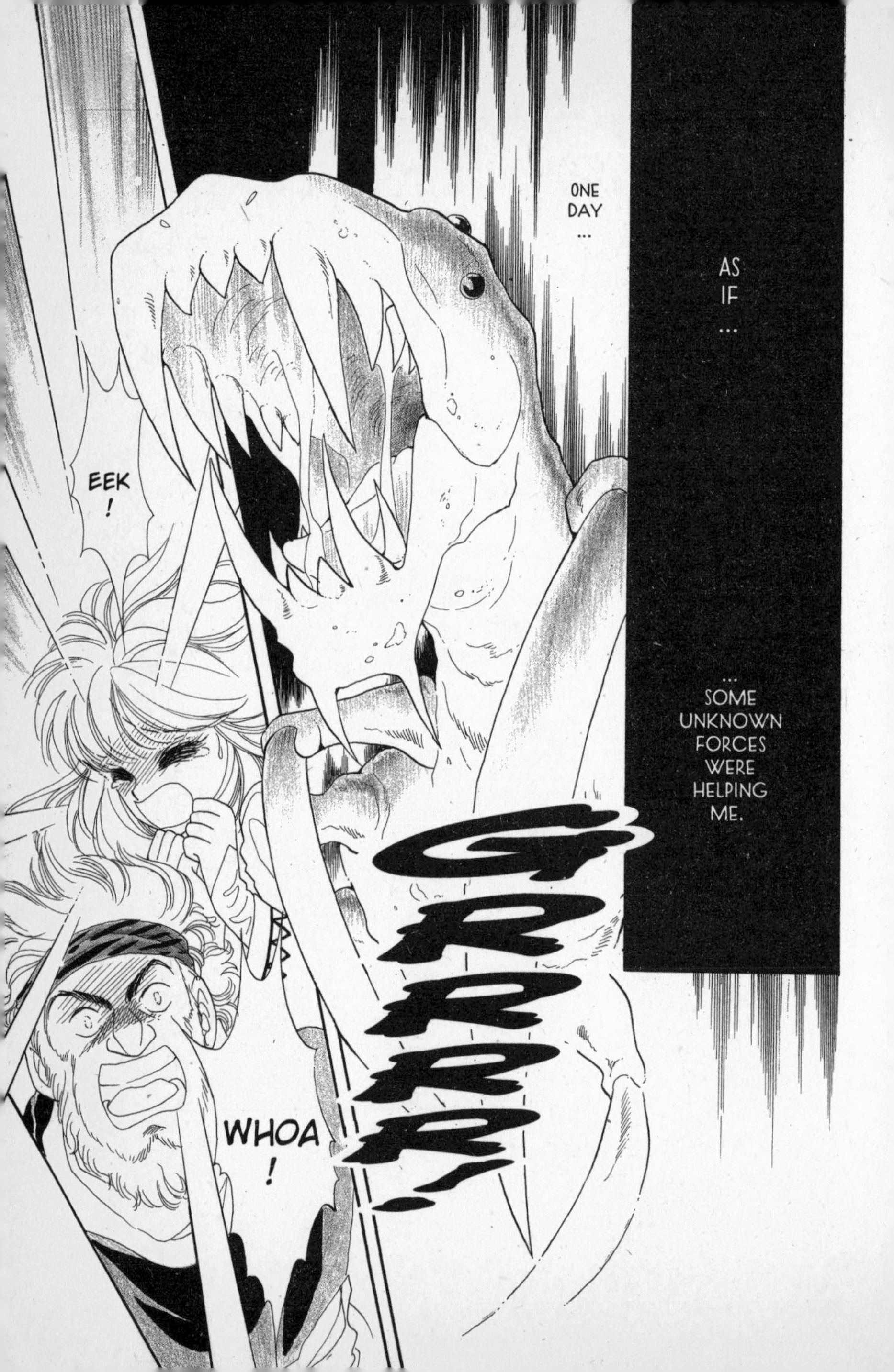

ONE DAY ...
AS IF ...
... SOME UNKNOWN FORCES WERE HELPING ME.
EEK !
GRRRR!
WHOA !

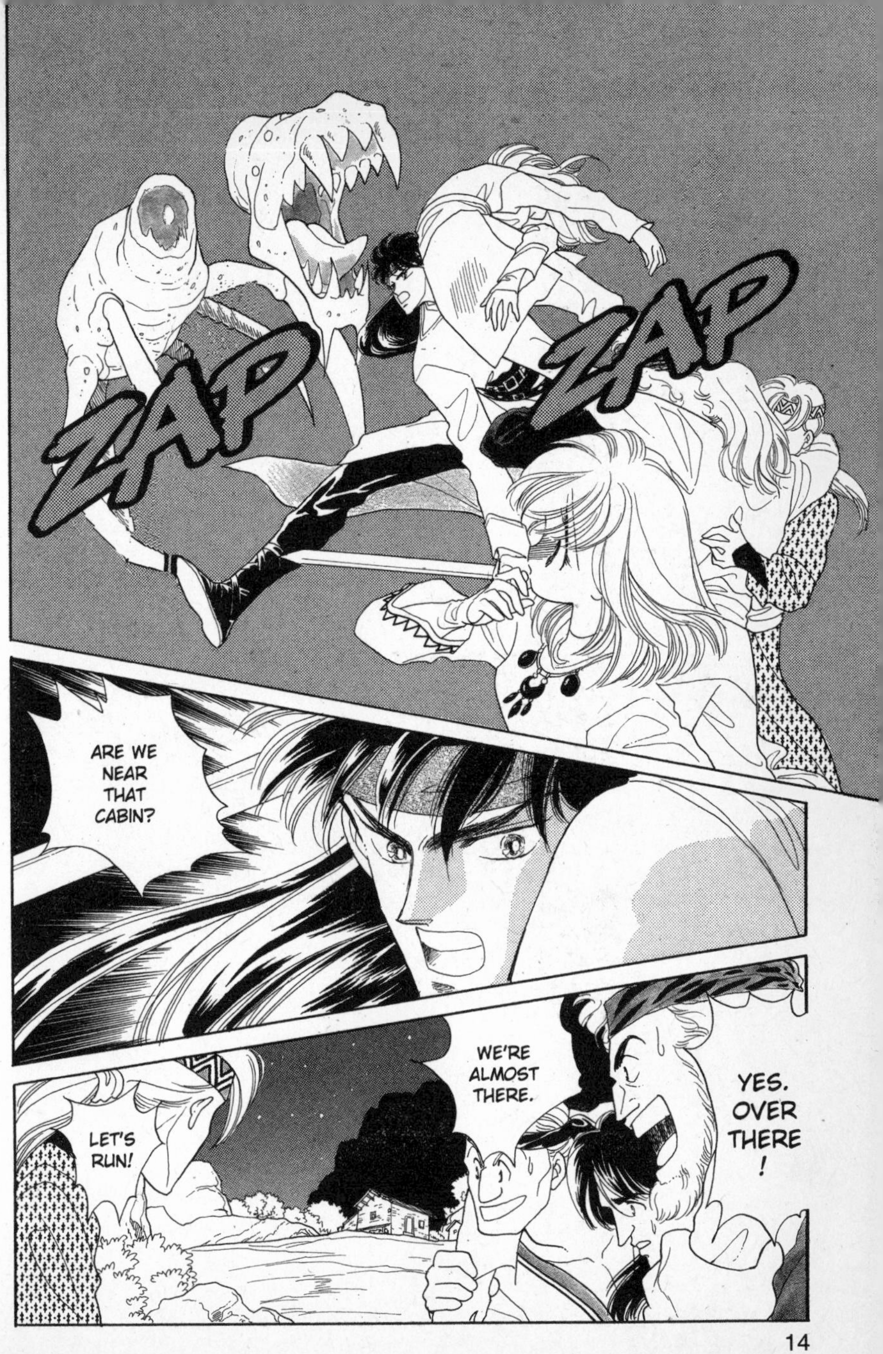
ZAP
ZAP
ARE WE NEAR THAT CABIN?
YES. OVER THERE!
WE'RE ALMOST THERE.
LET'S RUN!

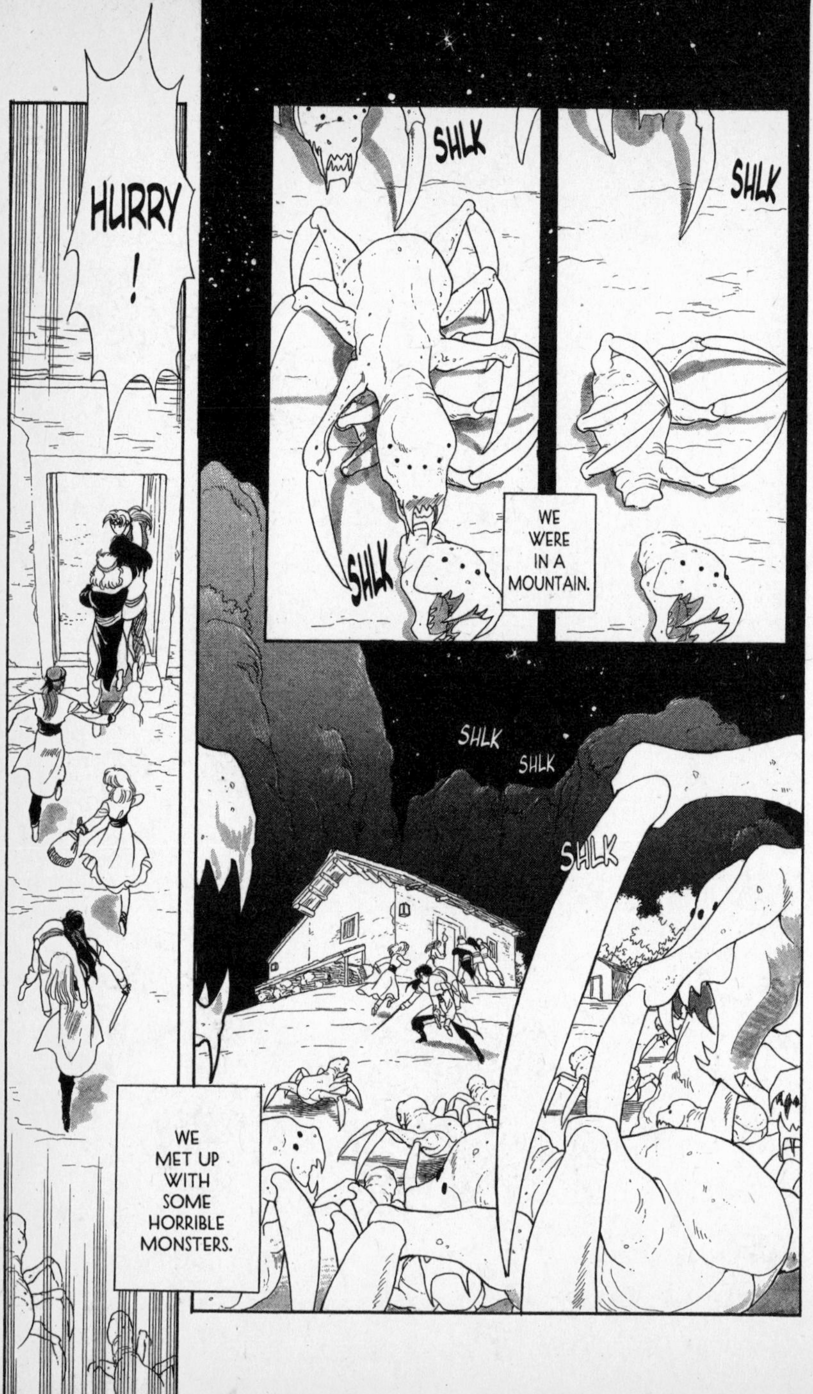
SHLK
SHLK
SHLK
WE WERE IN A MOUNTAIN.
SHLK
SHLK
SHLK
WE MET UP WITH SOME HORRIBLE MONSTERS.
HURRY!

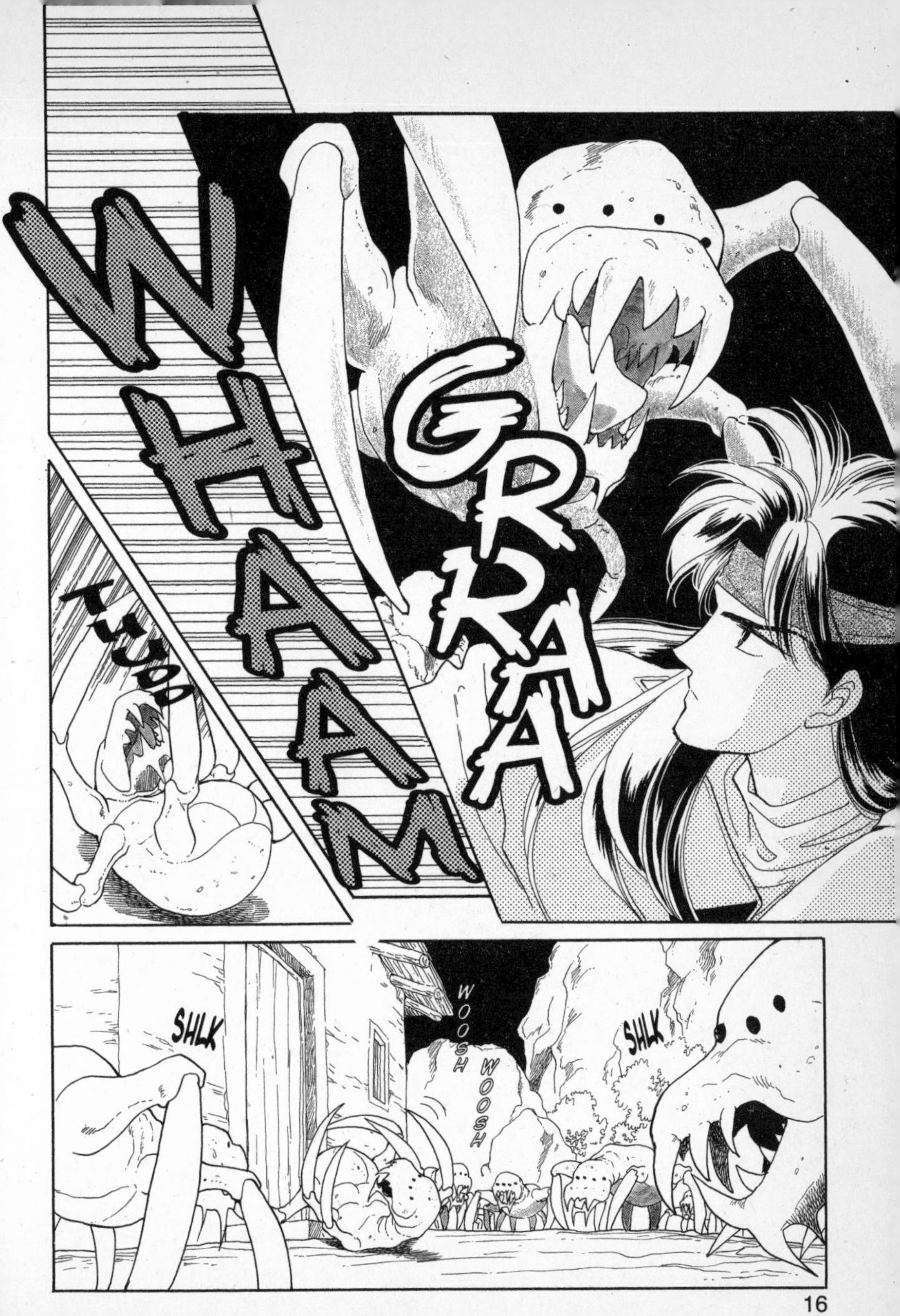
GRRAA
WHAAAM
THUDD
SHLK
WOOSH
WOOSH
SHLK

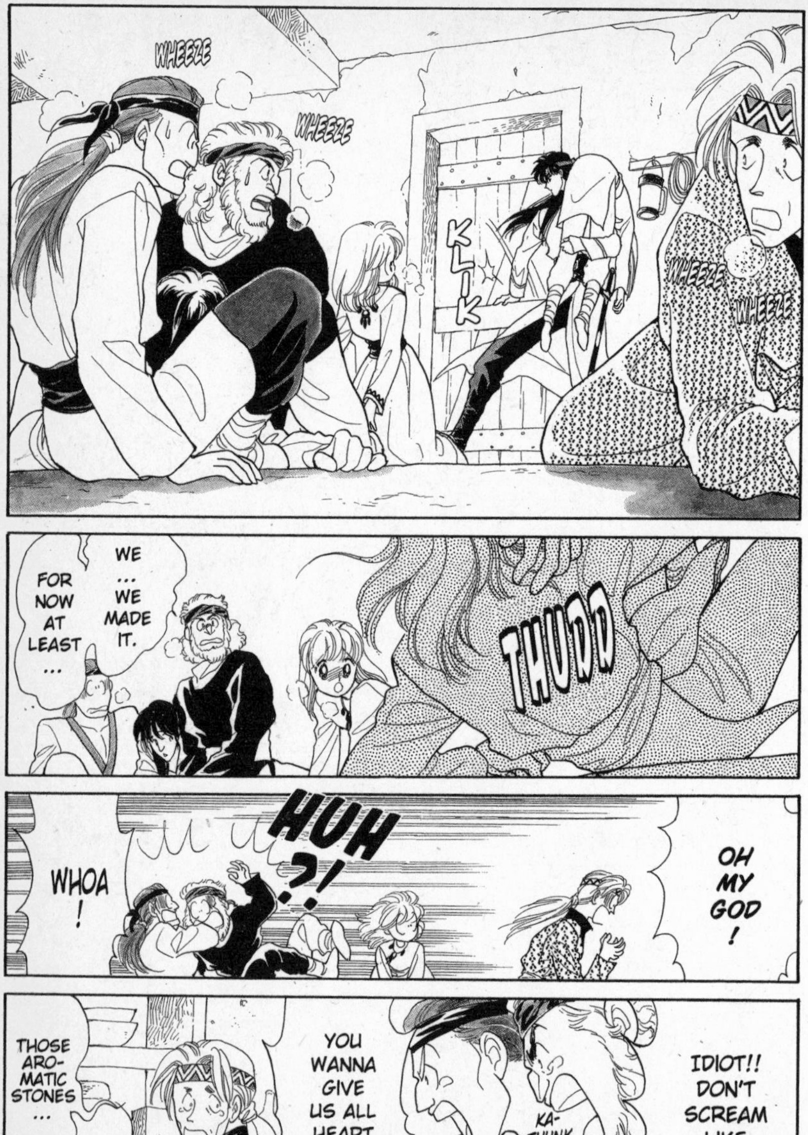
WHEEZE
WHEEZE
KLIK
WHEEZE
WHEEZE
THUDD
WE ... WE MADE IT.
FOR NOW AT LEAST ...
OH MY GOD!
HUH ?!
WHOA!
IDIOT!! DON'T SCREAM LIKE THAT!
KA-THUNK
KA-THUNK
KA-THUNK
YOU WANNA GIVE US ALL HEART ATTACKS?
THOSE ARO-MATIC STONES ...

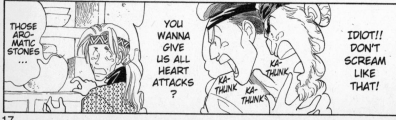

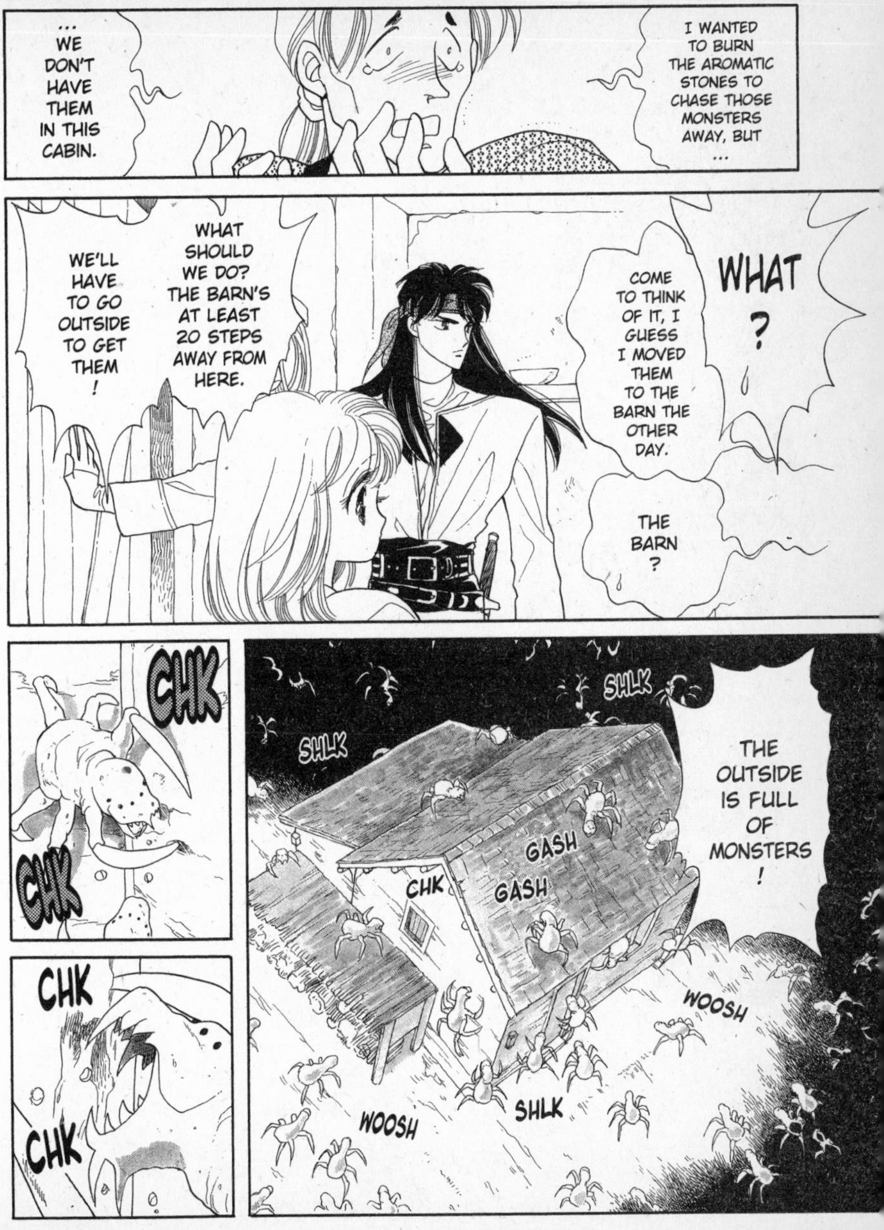
I WANTED TO BURN THE AROMATIC STONES TO CHASE THOSE MONSTERS AWAY, BUT ...
... WE DON'T HAVE THEM IN THIS CABIN.
WHAT?
COME TO THINK OF IT, I GUESS I MOVED THEM TO THE BARN THE OTHER DAY.
THE BARN?
WHAT SHOULD WE DO? THE BARN'S AT LEAST 20 STEPS AWAY FROM HERE.
WE'LL HAVE TO GO OUTSIDE TO GET THEM!
THE OUTSIDE IS FULL OF MONSTERS!
SHLK
SHLK
GASH
GASH
CHK
WOOSH
SHLK
WOOSH
CHK
CHK
CHK
CHK

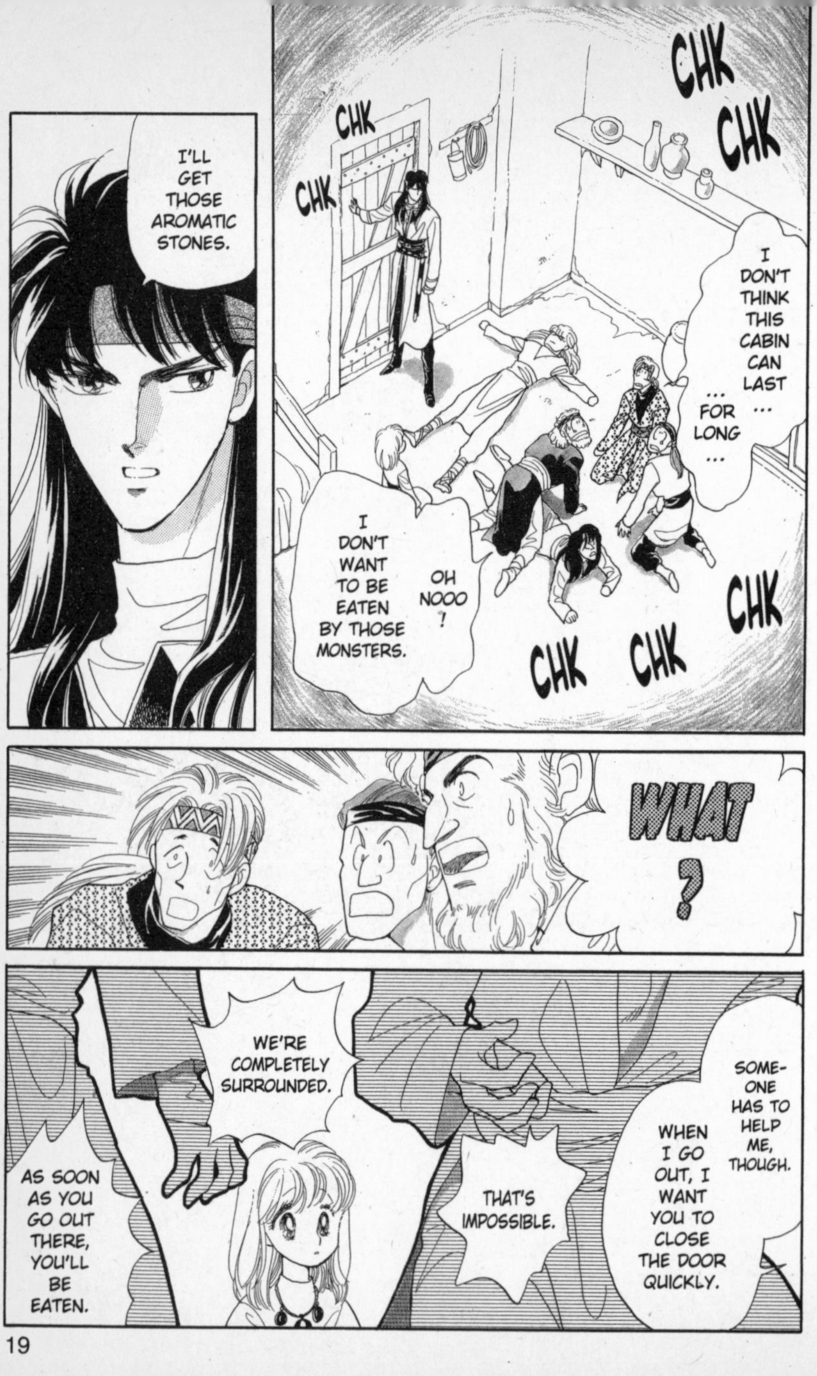
CHK
CHK
I DON'T THINK THIS CABIN CAN LAST ... ... FOR LONG ...
CHK
CHK
OH NOOO !
I DON'T WANT TO BE EATEN BY THOSE MONSTERS.
CHK
CHK
CHK
I'LL GET THOSE AROMATIC STONES.
WHAT ?
SOME-ONE HAS TO HELP ME, THOUGH.
WHEN I GO OUT, I WANT YOU TO CLOSE THE DOOR QUICKLY.
WE'RE COMPLETELY SURROUNDED.
THAT'S IMPOSSIBLE.
AS SOON AS YOU GO OUT THERE, YOU'LL BE EATEN.

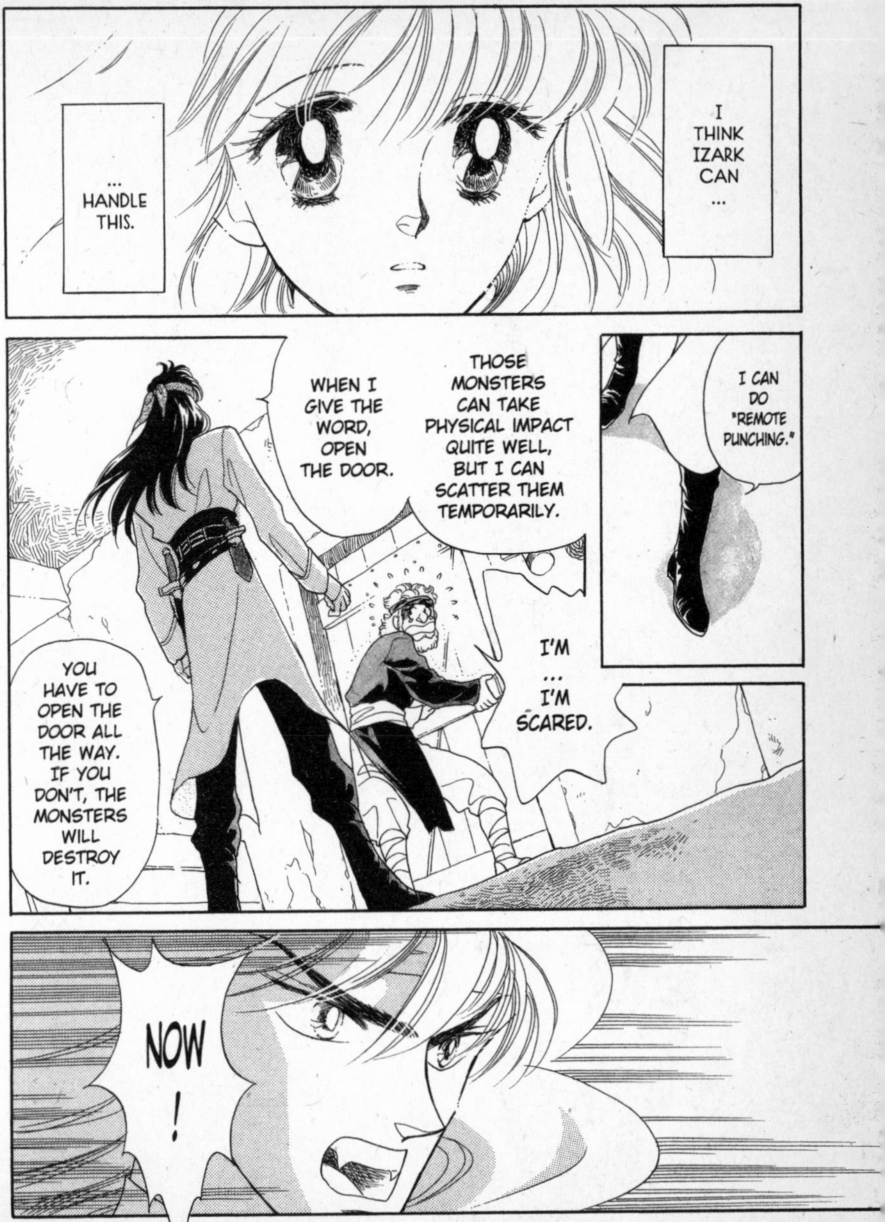
I THINK IZARK CAN ...
... HANDLE THIS.
I CAN DO "REMOTE PUNCHING."
THOSE MONSTERS CAN TAKE PHYSICAL IMPACT QUITE WELL, BUT I CAN SCATTER THEM TEMPORARILY.
WHEN I GIVE THE WORD, OPEN THE DOOR.
I'M ... I'M SCARED.
YOU HAVE TO OPEN THE DOOR ALL THE WAY. IF YOU DON'T, THE MONSTERS WILL DESTROY IT.
NOW !

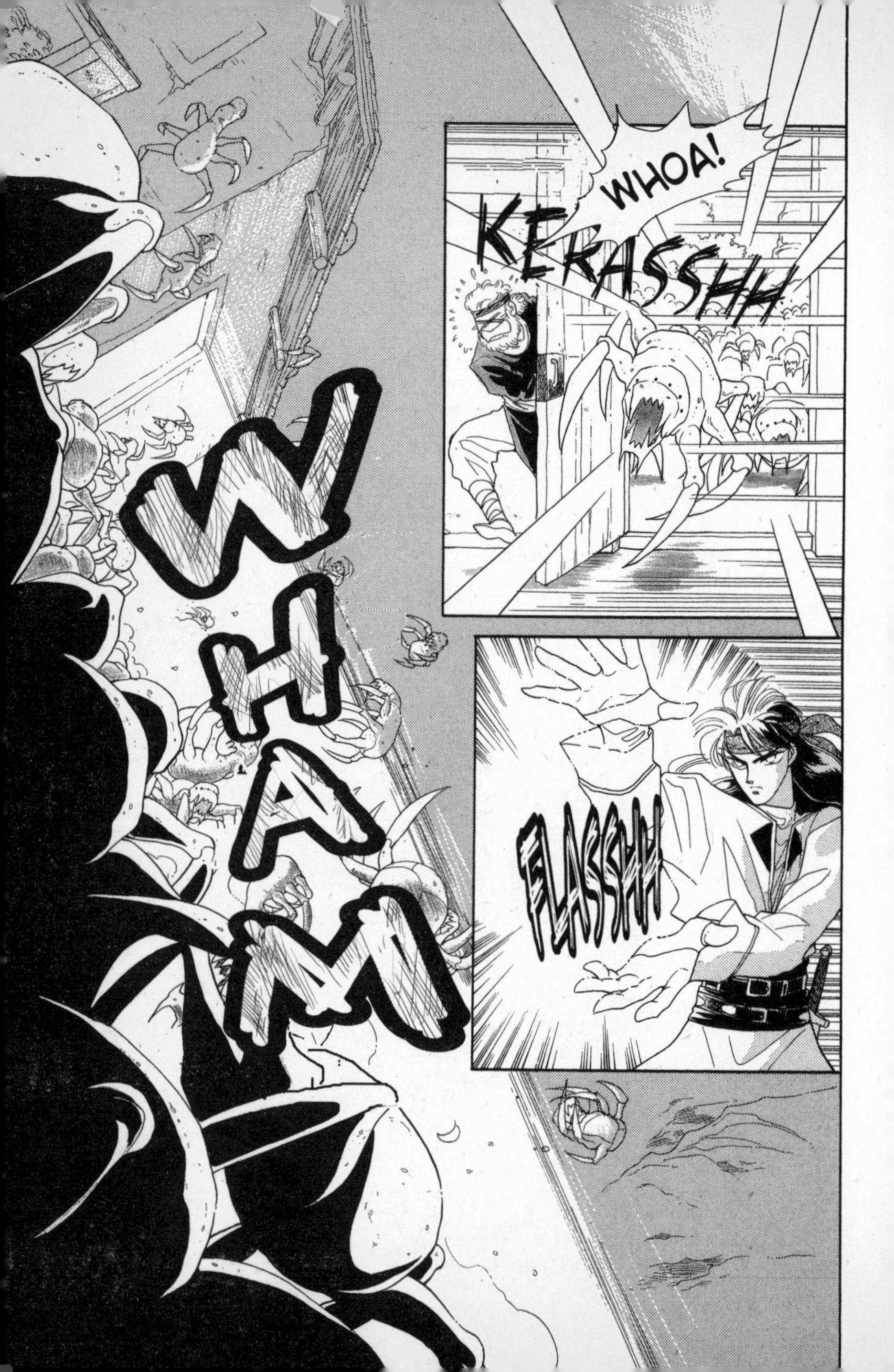
WHOA!
KERASSHH
FLASSHH
WHAM

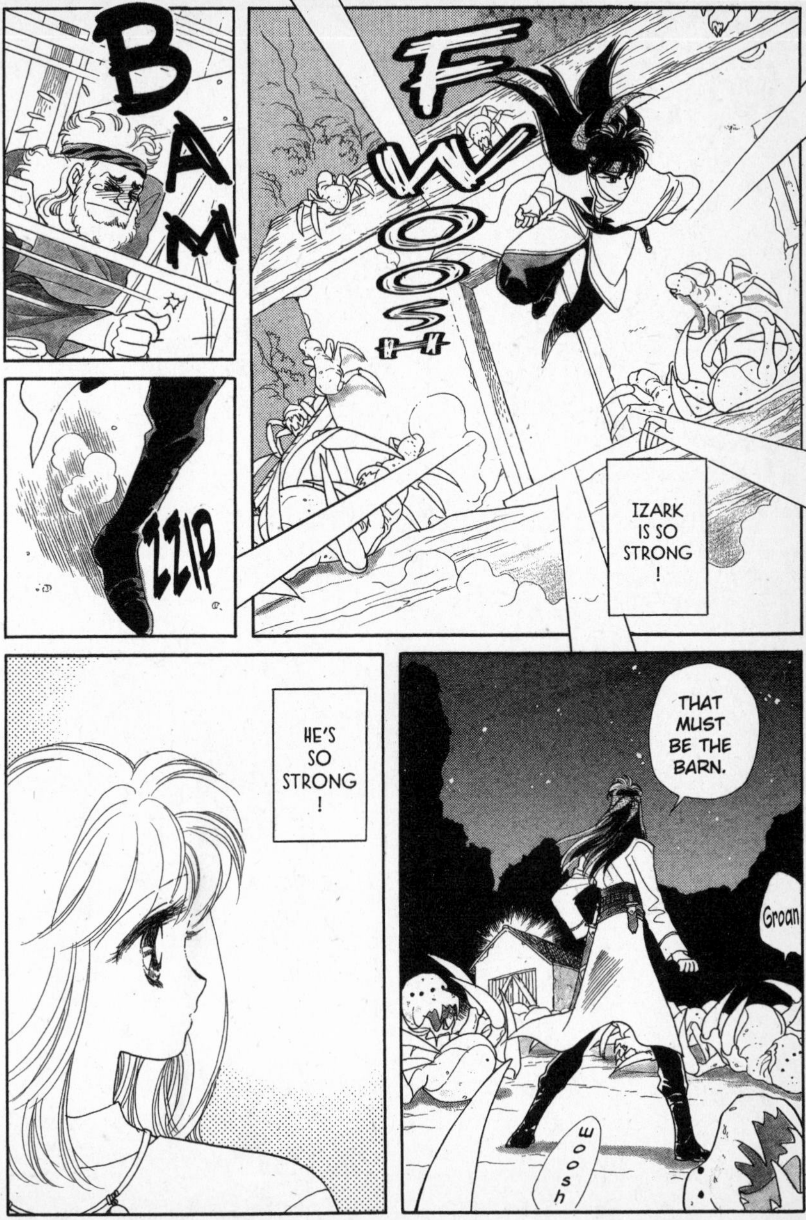
FWOOOSH!!
IZARK IS SO STRONG!
BAM
ZZIP
THAT MUST BE THE BARN.
Groan
Woosh
HE'S SO STRONG!

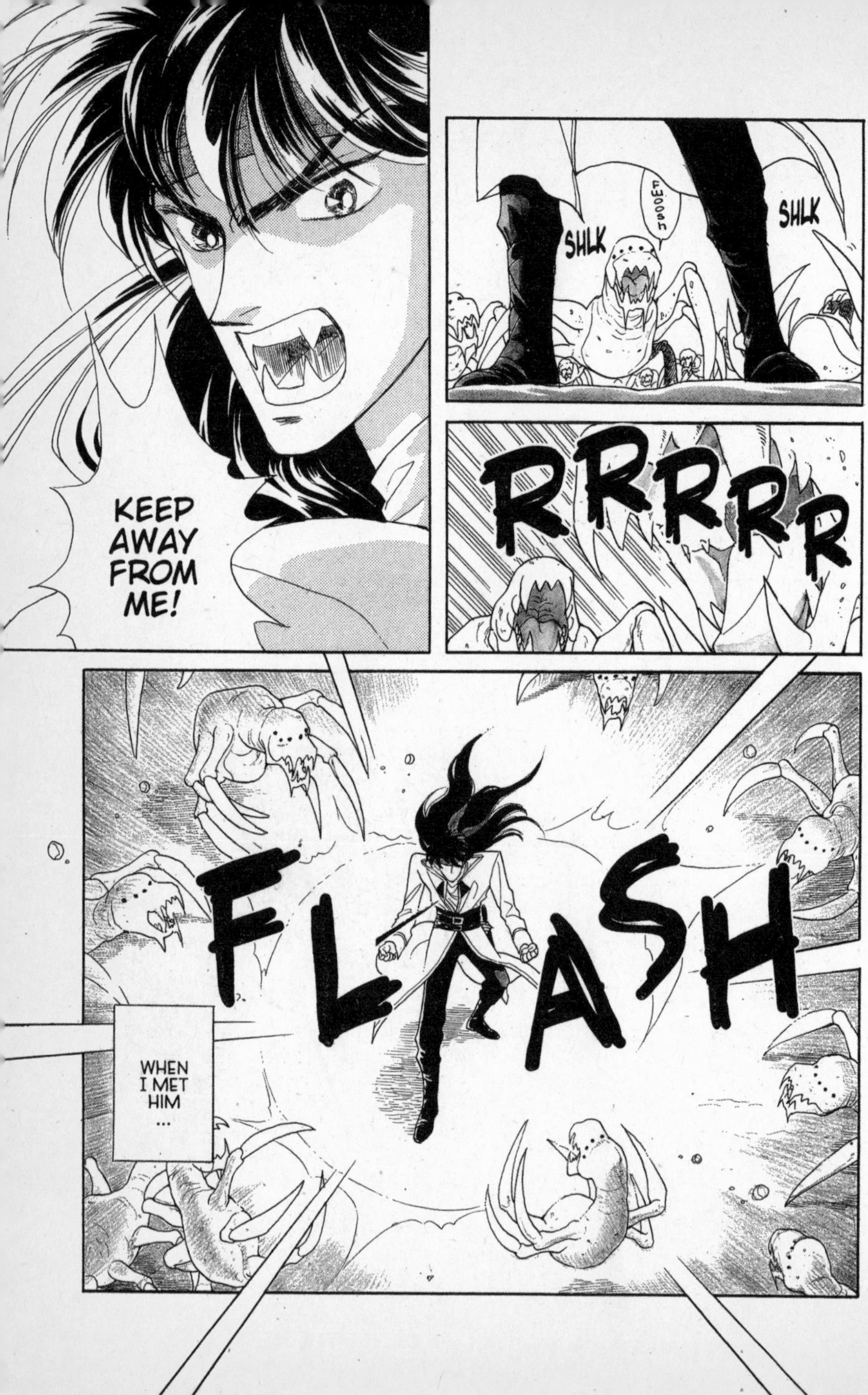
SHLK
Fwoosh
SHLK
RRRRRR
KEEP AWAY FROM ME!
FLASH
WHEN I MET HIM ...

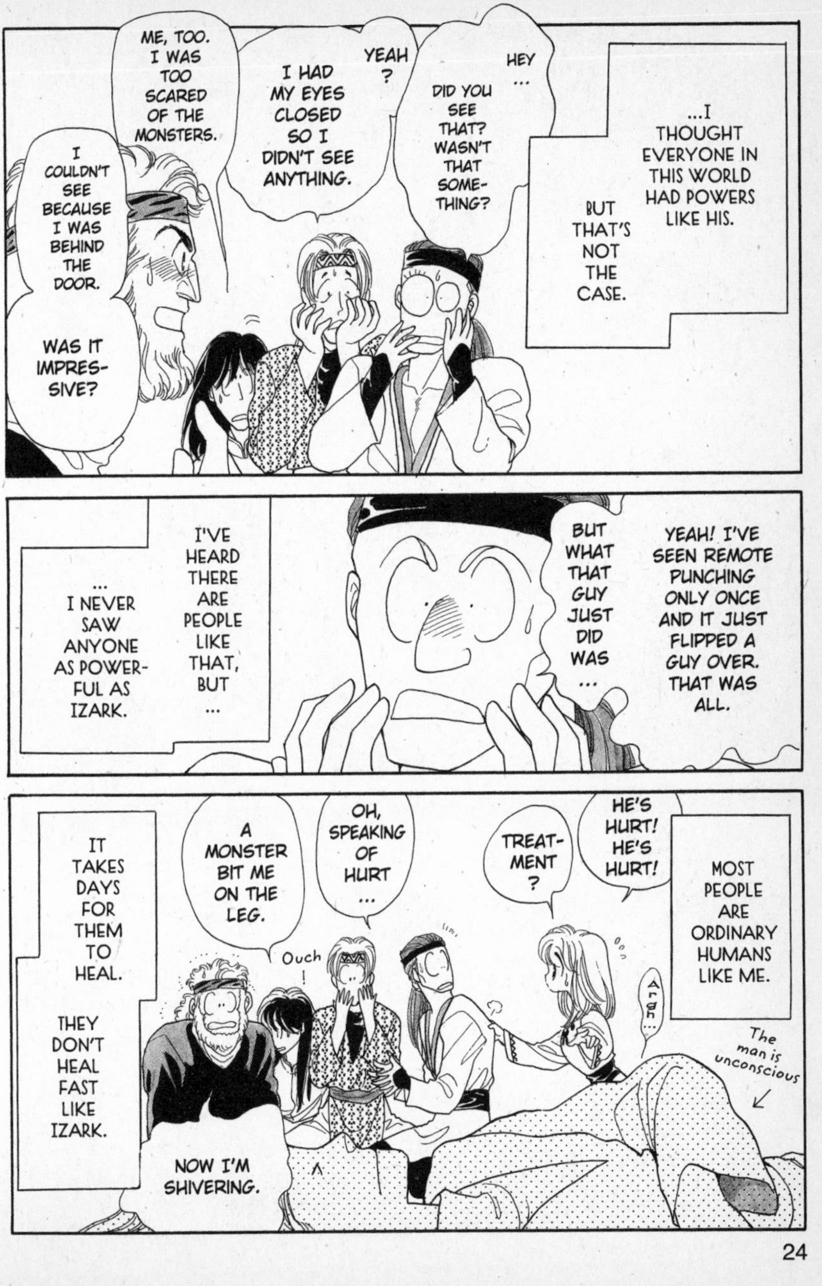
...I THOUGHT EVERYONE IN THIS WORLD HAD POWERS LIKE HIS.
BUT THAT'S NOT THE CASE.
HEY ...
DID YOU SEE THAT? WASN'T THAT SOME-THING?
YEAH ?
I HAD MY EYES CLOSED SO I DIDN'T SEE ANYTHING.
ME, TOO. I WAS TOO SCARED OF THE MONSTERS.
I COULDN'T SEE BECAUSE I WAS BEHIND THE DOOR.
WAS IT IMPRES-SIVE?
YEAH! I'VE SEEN REMOTE PUNCHING ONLY ONCE AND IT JUST FLIPPED A GUY OVER. THAT WAS ALL.
BUT WHAT THAT GUY JUST DID WAS ...
I'VE HEARD THERE ARE PEOPLE LIKE THAT, BUT ...
... I NEVER SAW ANYONE AS POWER-FUL AS IZARK.
MOST PEOPLE ARE ORDINARY HUMANS LIKE ME.
The man is unconscious
HE'S HURT! HE'S HURT!
Argh ...
TREAT-MENT ?
OH, SPEAKING OF HURT ...
A MONSTER BIT ME ON THE LEG.
Ouch !
NOW I'M SHIVERING.
IT TAKES DAYS FOR THEM TO HEAL.
THEY DON'T HEAL FAST LIKE IZARK.

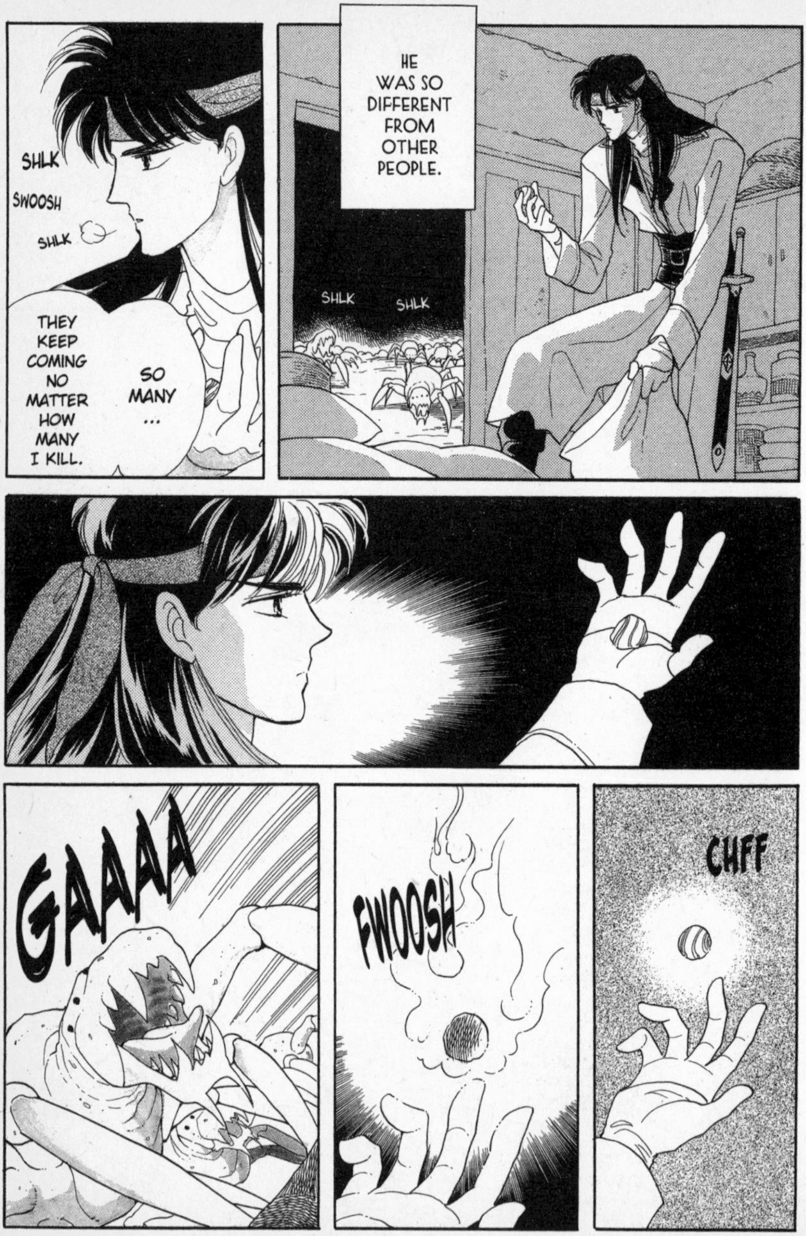
HE WAS SO DIFFERENT FROM OTHER PEOPLE.
SHLK
SHLK
SHLK
SWOOSH
SHLK
SO MANY ...
THEY KEEP COMING NO MATTER HOW MANY I KILL.
CHFF
FWOOSH
GAAAA

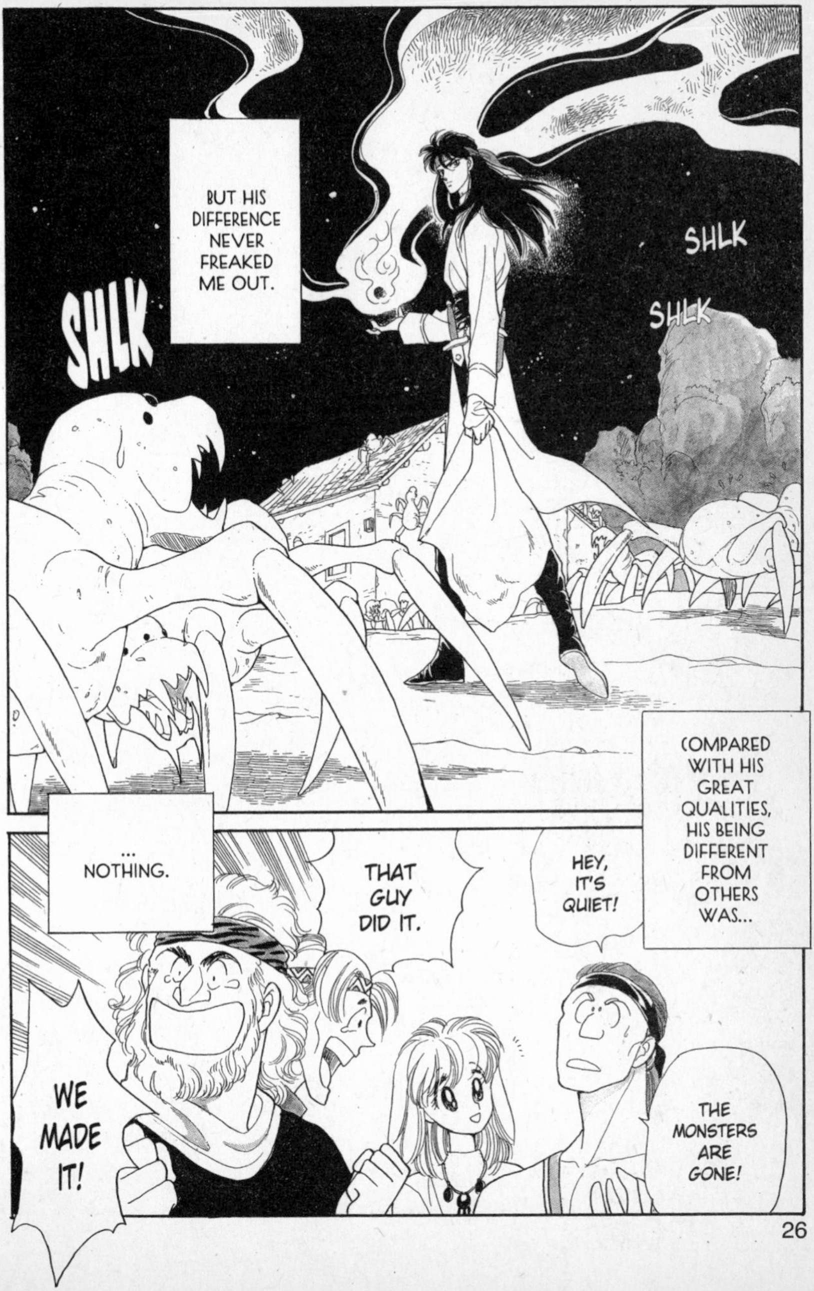
SHLK
SHLK
BUT HIS DIFFERENCE NEVER FREAKED ME OUT.
SHLK
COMPARED WITH HIS GREAT QUALITIES, HIS BEING DIFFERENT FROM OTHERS WAS...
... NOTHING.
HEY, IT'S QUIET!
THAT GUY DID IT.
THE MONSTERS ARE GONE!
WE MADE IT!

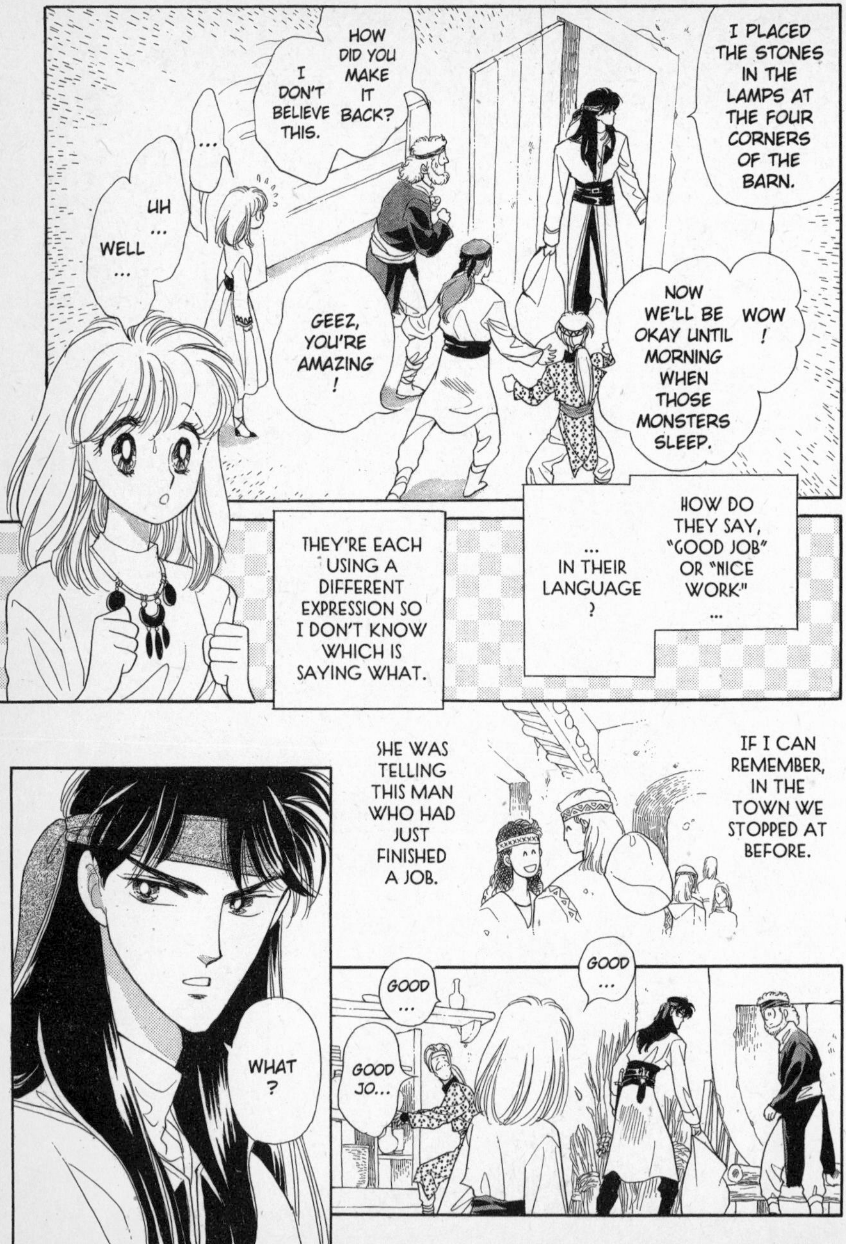
I PLACED THE STONES IN THE LAMPS AT THE FOUR CORNERS OF THE BARN.
HOW DID YOU MAKE IT BACK?
I DON'T BELIEVE THIS.
...
WOW!
NOW WE'LL BE OKAY UNTIL MORNING WHEN THOSE MONSTERS SLEEP.
GEEZ, YOU'RE AMAZING!
UH... WELL...
HOW DO THEY SAY, "GOOD JOB" OR "NICE WORK"...
... IN THEIR LANGUAGE?
THEY'RE EACH USING A DIFFERENT EXPRESSION SO I DON'T KNOW WHICH IS SAYING WHAT.
IF I CAN REMEMBER, IN THE TOWN WE STOPPED AT BEFORE.
SHE WAS TELLING THIS MAN WHO HAD JUST FINISHED A JOB.
GOOD...
GOOD...
GOOD JO...
WHAT?

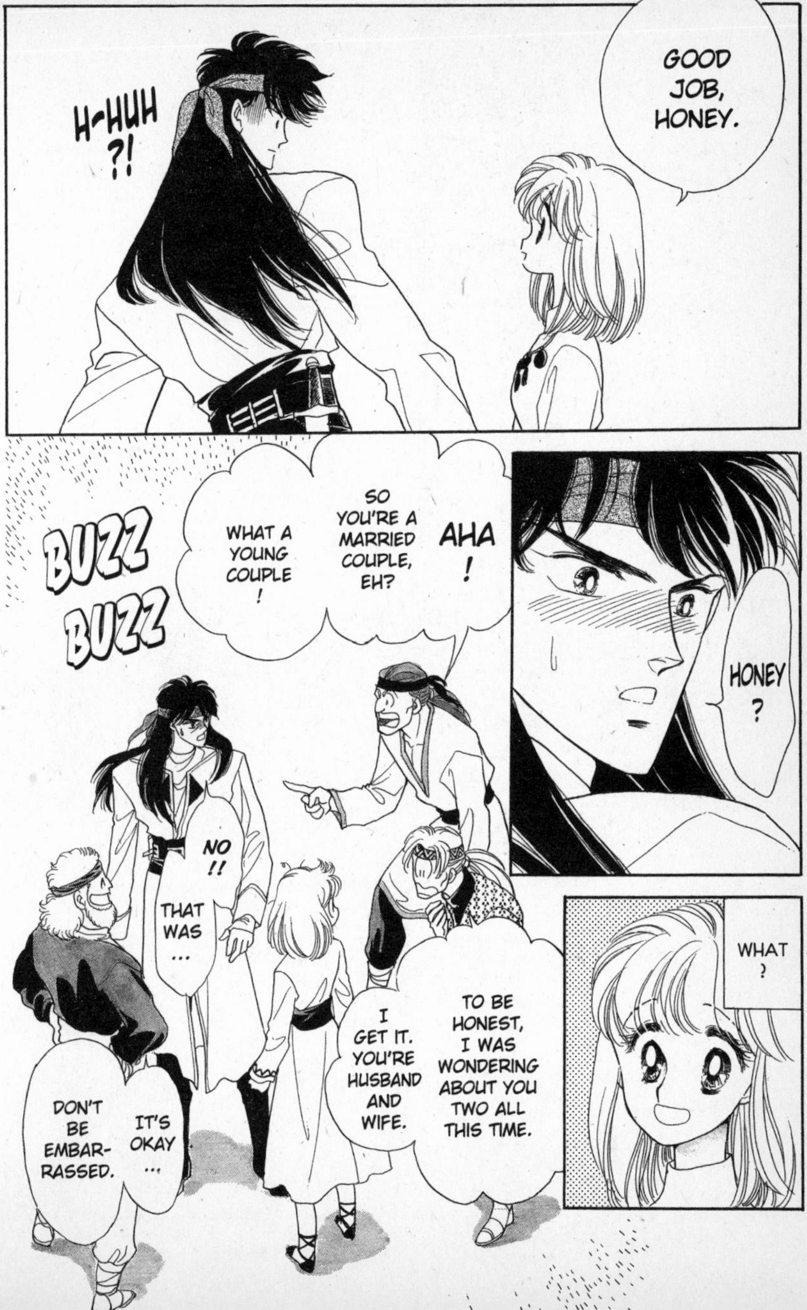
GOOD JOB, HONEY.
H-HUH ?!
HONEY ?
WHAT ?
AHA !
SO YOU'RE A MARRIED COUPLE, EH?
WHAT A YOUNG COUPLE !
BUZZ BUZZ
NO !! THAT WAS ...
TO BE HONEST, I WAS WONDERING ABOUT YOU TWO ALL THIS TIME.
I GET IT. YOU'RE HUSBAND AND WIFE.
IT'S OKAY ...
DON'T BE EMBARRASSED.

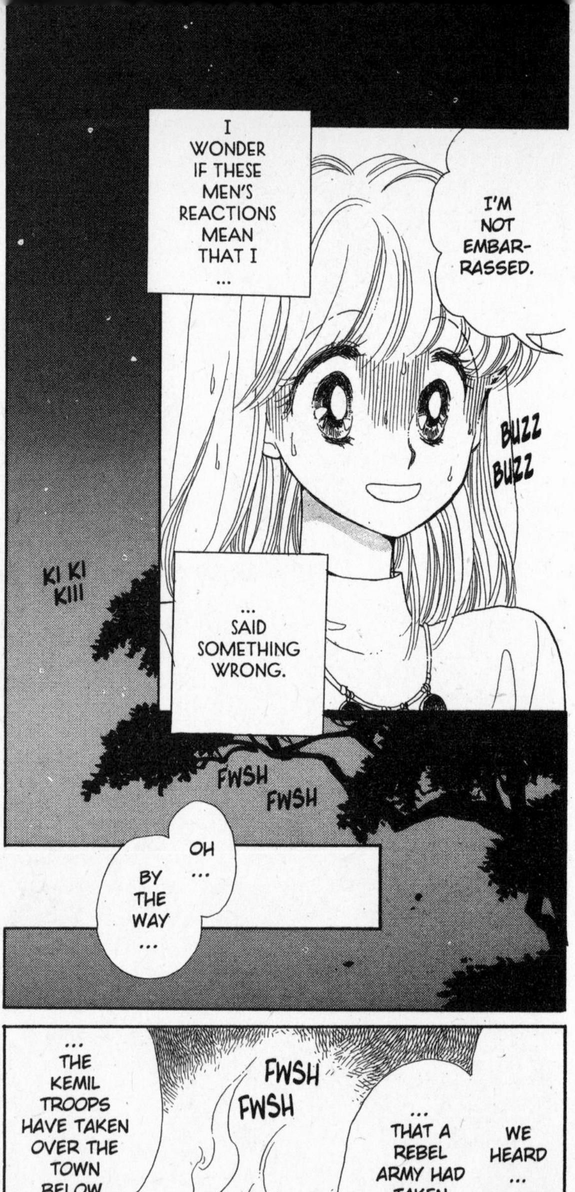
I'M NOT EMBARRASSED.
I WONDER IF THESE MEN'S REACTIONS MEAN THAT I ...
BUZZ BUZZ
... SAID SOMETHING WRONG.
KI KI KIII
FWSH FWSH
OH ...
BY THE WAY ...
WE HEARD ...
... THAT A REBEL ARMY HAD TAKEN REFUGE ON THE MOUNTAIN AND ...
FWSH FWSH
... THE KEMIL TROOPS HAVE TAKEN OVER THE TOWN BELOW.

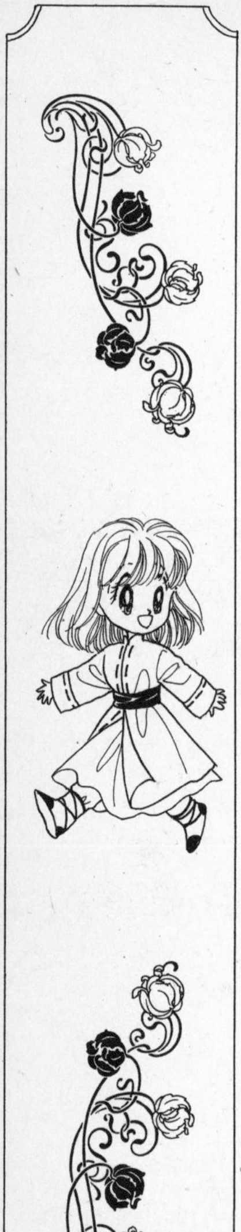

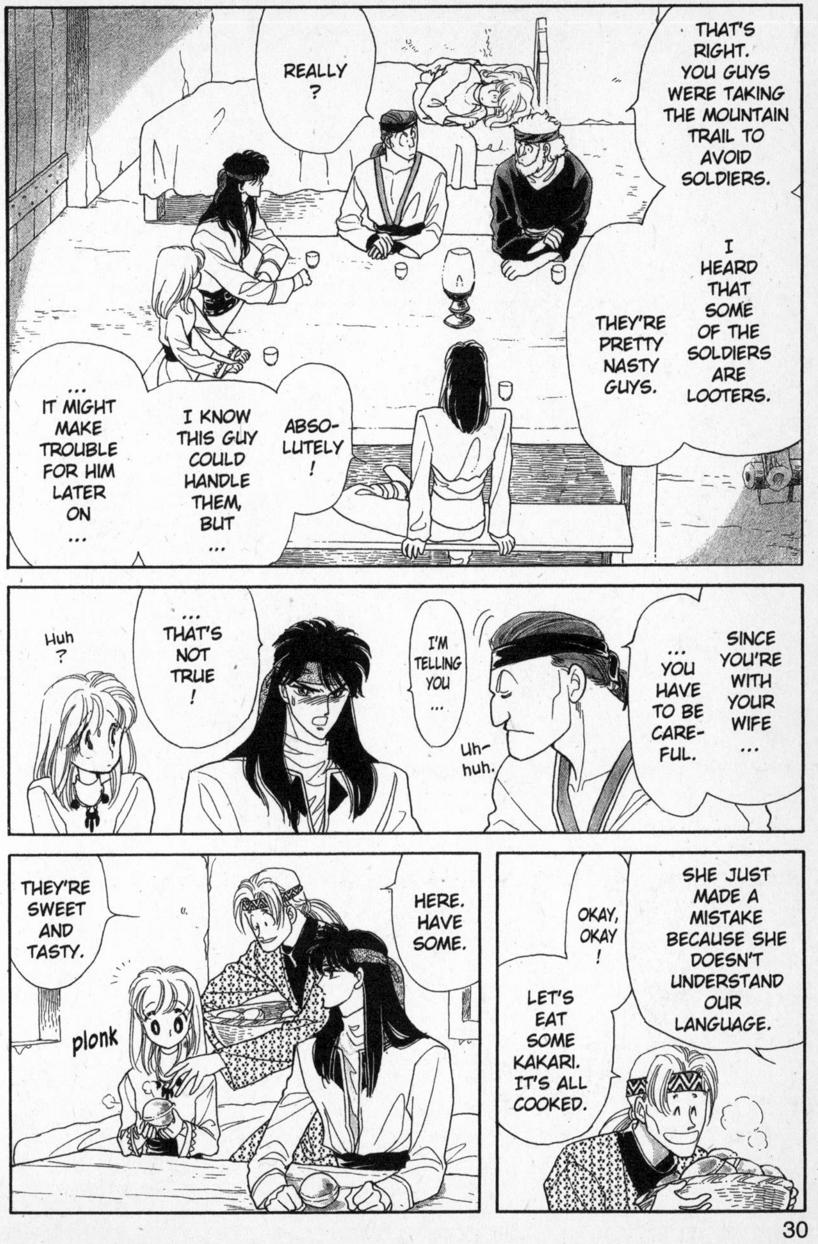
THAT'S RIGHT. YOU GUYS WERE TAKING THE MOUNTAIN TRAIL TO AVOID SOLDIERS.
I HEARD THAT SOME OF THE SOLDIERS ARE LOOTERS.
THEY'RE PRETTY NASTY GUYS.
REALLY?
ABSO-LUTELY!
I KNOW THIS GUY COULD HANDLE THEM, BUT ...
... IT MIGHT MAKE TROUBLE FOR HIM LATER ON ...
SINCE YOU'RE WITH YOUR WIFE ...
... YOU HAVE TO BE CARE-FUL.
Uh-huh.
I'M TELLING YOU ...
... THAT'S NOT TRUE!
Huh?
SHE JUST MADE A MISTAKE BECAUSE SHE DOESN'T UNDERSTAND OUR LANGUAGE.
OKAY, OKAY!
LET'S EAT SOME KAKARI. IT'S ALL COOKED.
HERE. HAVE SOME.
THEY'RE SWEET AND TASTY.
plonk

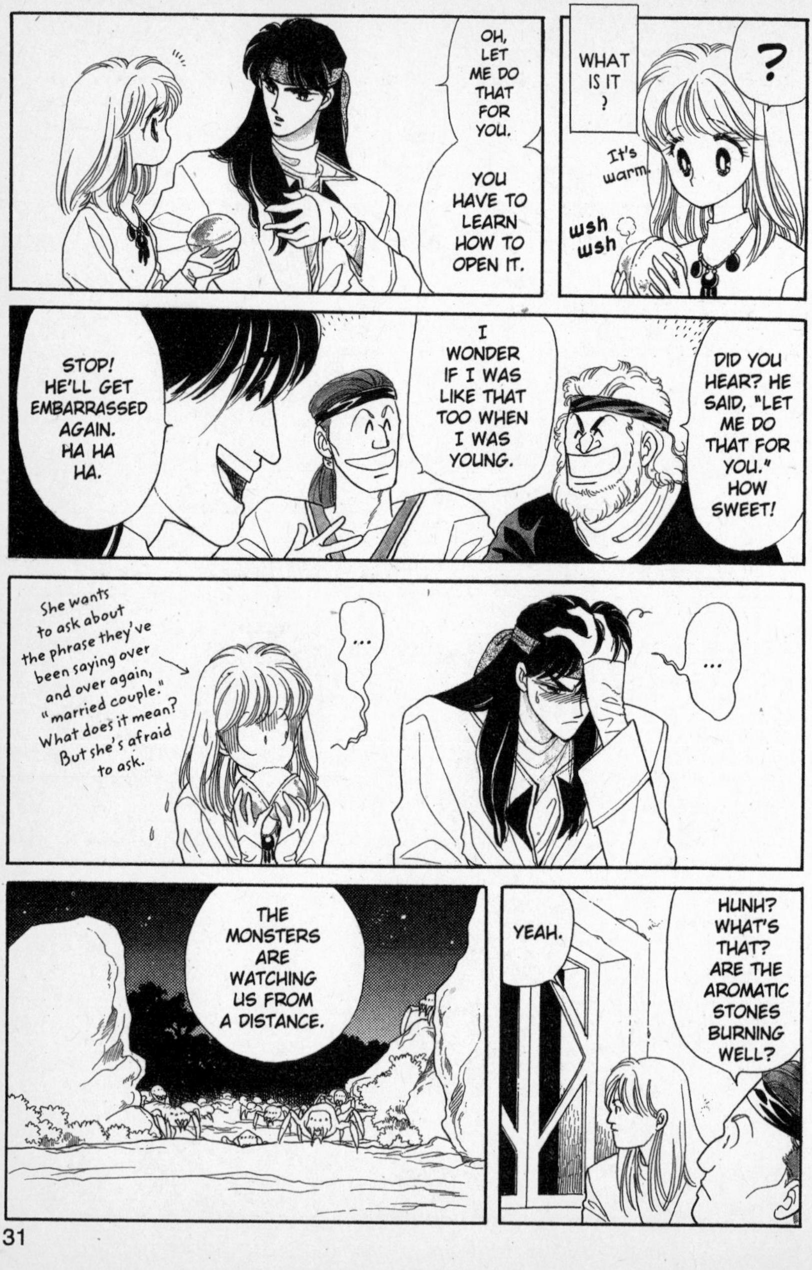
?
WHAT IS IT ?
It's warm.
wsh wsh
OH, LET ME DO THAT FOR YOU.
YOU HAVE TO LEARN HOW TO OPEN IT.
DID YOU HEAR? HE SAID, "LET ME DO THAT FOR YOU." HOW SWEET!
I WONDER IF I WAS LIKE THAT TOO WHEN I WAS YOUNG.
STOP! HE'LL GET EMBARRASSED AGAIN. HA HA HA.
...
...
She wants to ask about the phrase they've been saying over and over again, "married couple." What does it mean? But she's afraid to ask.
HUNH? WHAT'S THAT? ARE THE AROMATIC STONES BURNING WELL?
YEAH.
THE MONSTERS ARE WATCHING US FROM A DISTANCE.

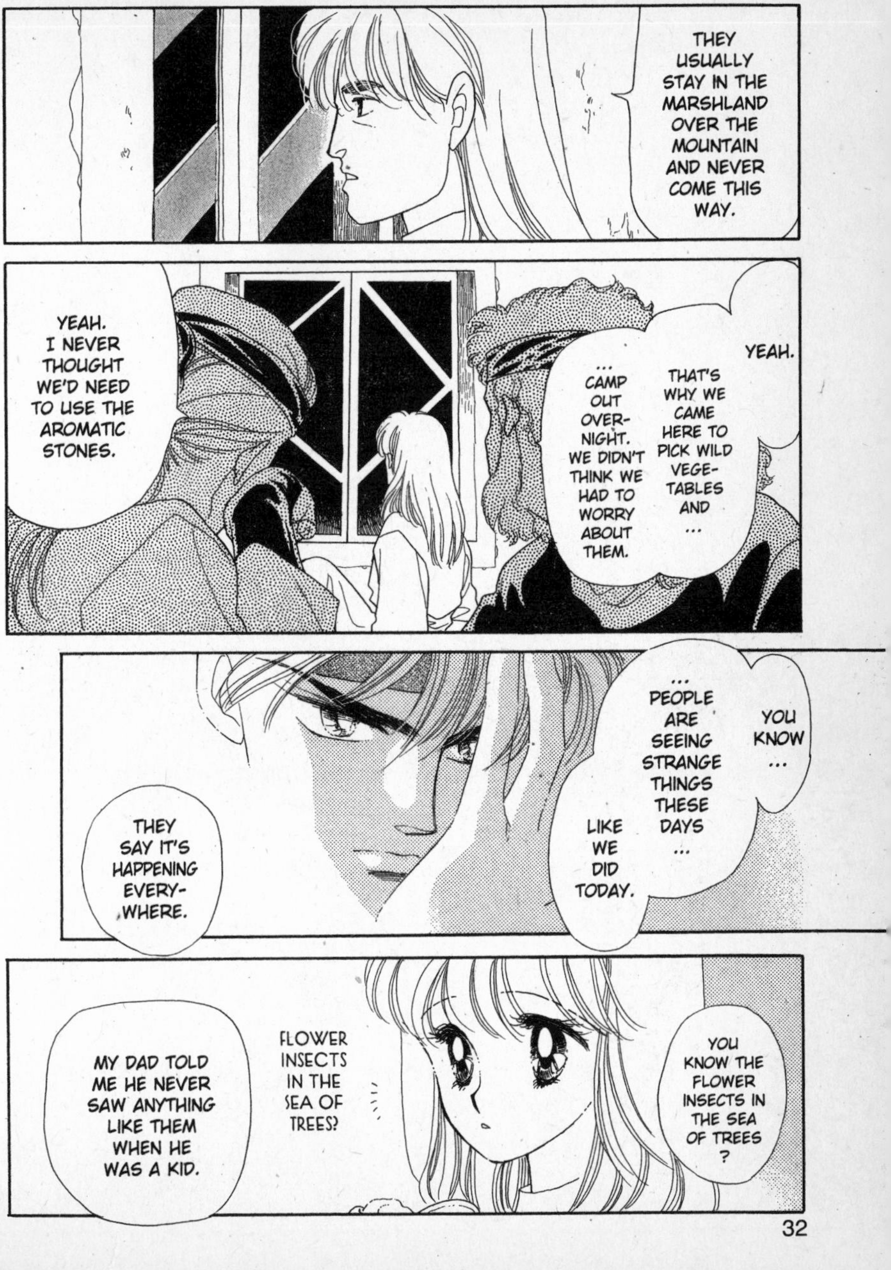
THEY USUALLY STAY IN THE MARSHLAND OVER THE MOUNTAIN AND NEVER COME THIS WAY.
YEAH.
THAT'S WHY WE CAME HERE TO PICK WILD VEGE-TABLES AND ...
... CAMP OUT OVER-NIGHT. WE DIDN'T THINK WE HAD TO WORRY ABOUT THEM.
YEAH. I NEVER THOUGHT WE'D NEED TO USE THE AROMATIC STONES.
YOU KNOW ...
... PEOPLE ARE SEEING STRANGE THINGS THESE DAYS ...
LIKE WE DID TODAY.
THEY SAY IT'S HAPPENING EVERY-WHERE.
YOU KNOW THE FLOWER INSECTS IN THE SEA OF TREES ?
FLOWER INSECTS IN THE SEA OF TREES?
MY DAD TOLD ME HE NEVER SAW ANYTHING LIKE THEM WHEN HE WAS A KID.

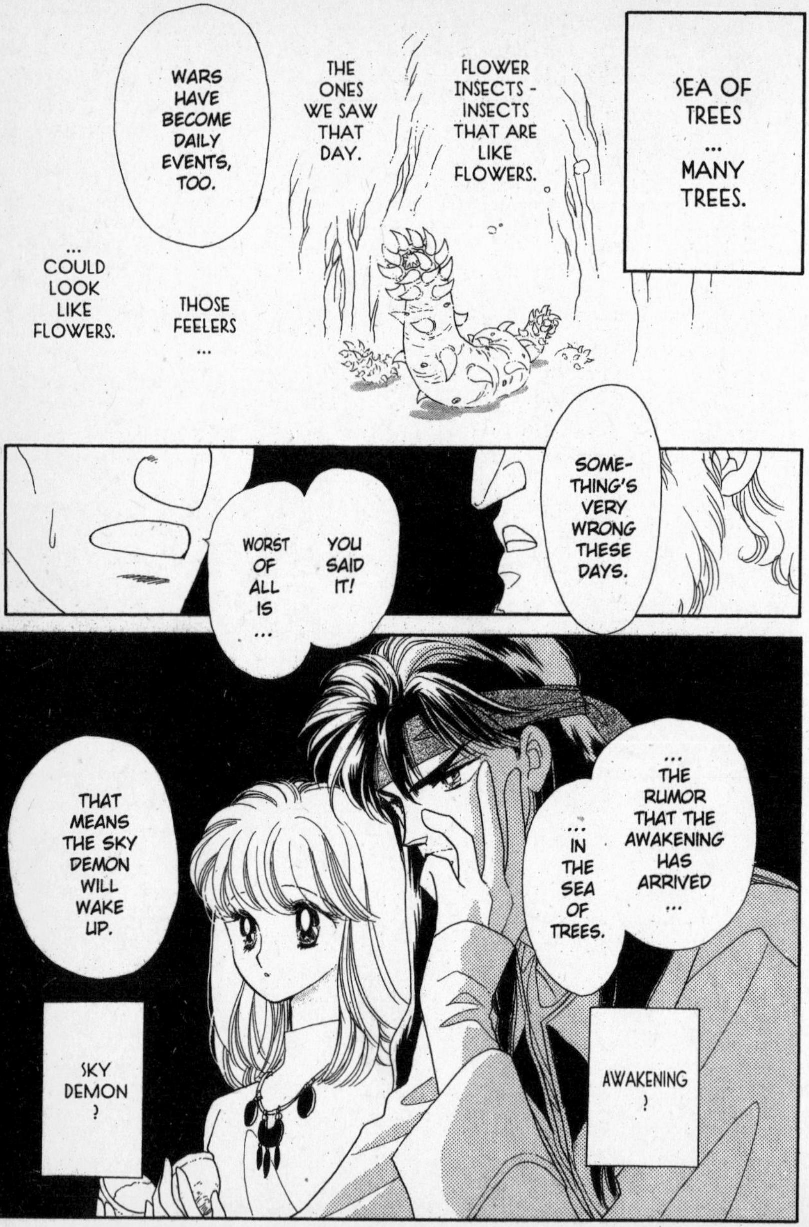
SEA OF TREES ... MANY TREES.
FLOWER INSECTS - INSECTS THAT ARE LIKE FLOWERS.
THE ONES WE SAW THAT DAY.
THOSE FEELERS ...
... COULD LOOK LIKE FLOWERS.
WARS HAVE BECOME DAILY EVENTS, TOO.
SOMETHING'S VERY WRONG THESE DAYS.
YOU SAID IT!
WORST OF ALL IS ...
... THE RUMOR THAT THE AWAKENING HAS ARRIVED ...
... IN THE SEA OF TREES.
THAT MEANS THE SKY DEMON WILL WAKE UP.
AWAKENING ?
SKY DEMON ?

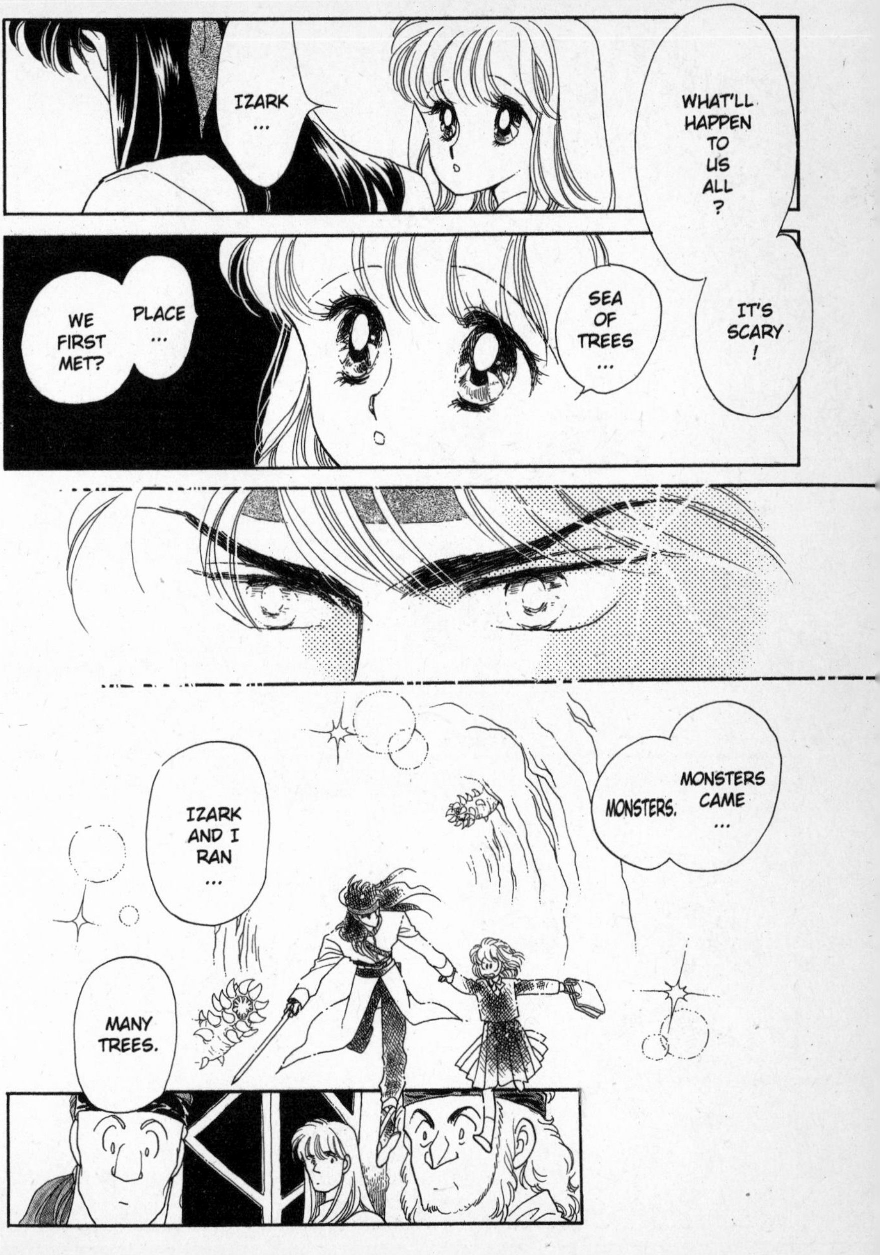
WHAT'LL HAPPEN TO US ALL?
IZARK ...
IT'S SCARY!
SEA OF TREES ...
PLACE ...
WE FIRST MET?
MONSTERS CAME ...
MONSTERS.
IZARK AND I RAN ...
MANY TREES.

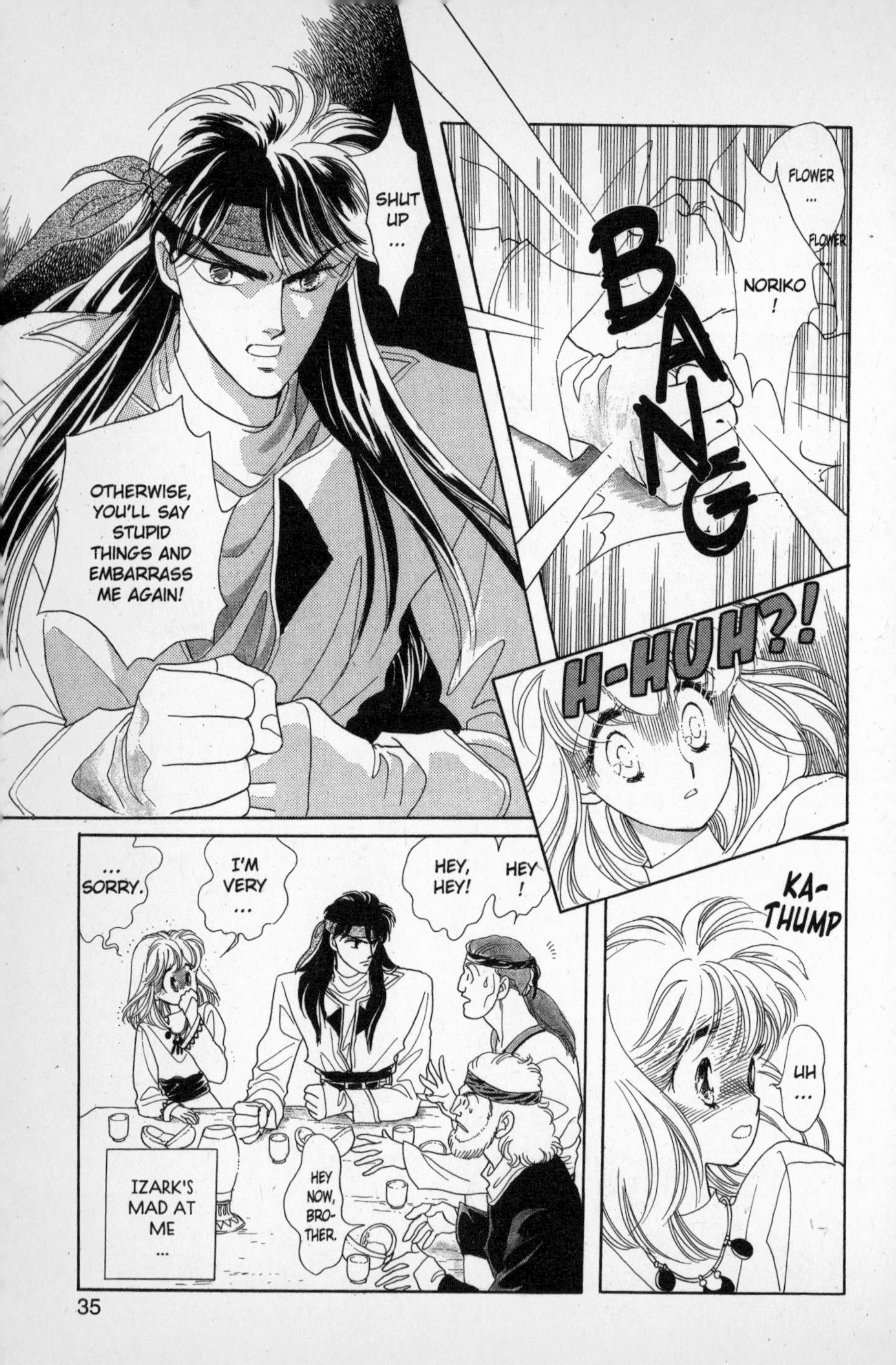
FLOWER ...
FLOWER ...
NORIKO !
BANG
H-HUH?!
SHUT UP ...
OTHERWISE, YOU'LL SAY STUPID THINGS AND EMBARRASS ME AGAIN!
KA-THUMP
UH ...
HEY !
HEY, HEY!
I'M VERY ...
... SORRY.
HEY NOW, BROTHER.
IZARK'S MAD AT ME ...

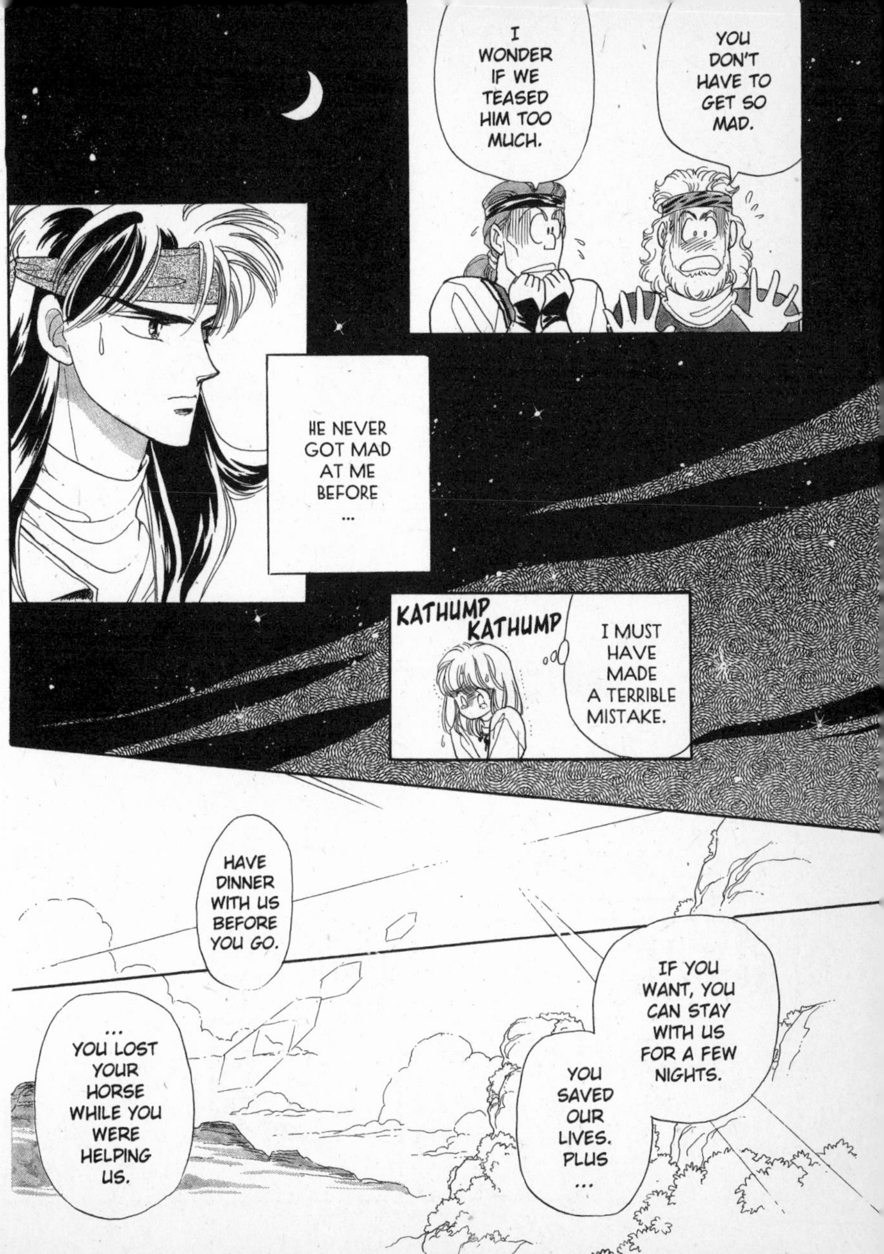
YOU DON'T HAVE TO GET SO MAD.
I WONDER IF WE TEASED HIM TOO MUCH.
HE NEVER GOT MAD AT ME BEFORE ...
KATHUMP KATHUMP
I MUST HAVE MADE A TERRIBLE MISTAKE.
IF YOU WANT, YOU CAN STAY WITH US FOR A FEW NIGHTS.
YOU SAVED OUR LIVES. PLUS ...
HAVE DINNER WITH US BEFORE YOU GO.
... YOU LOST YOUR HORSE WHILE YOU WERE HELPING US.

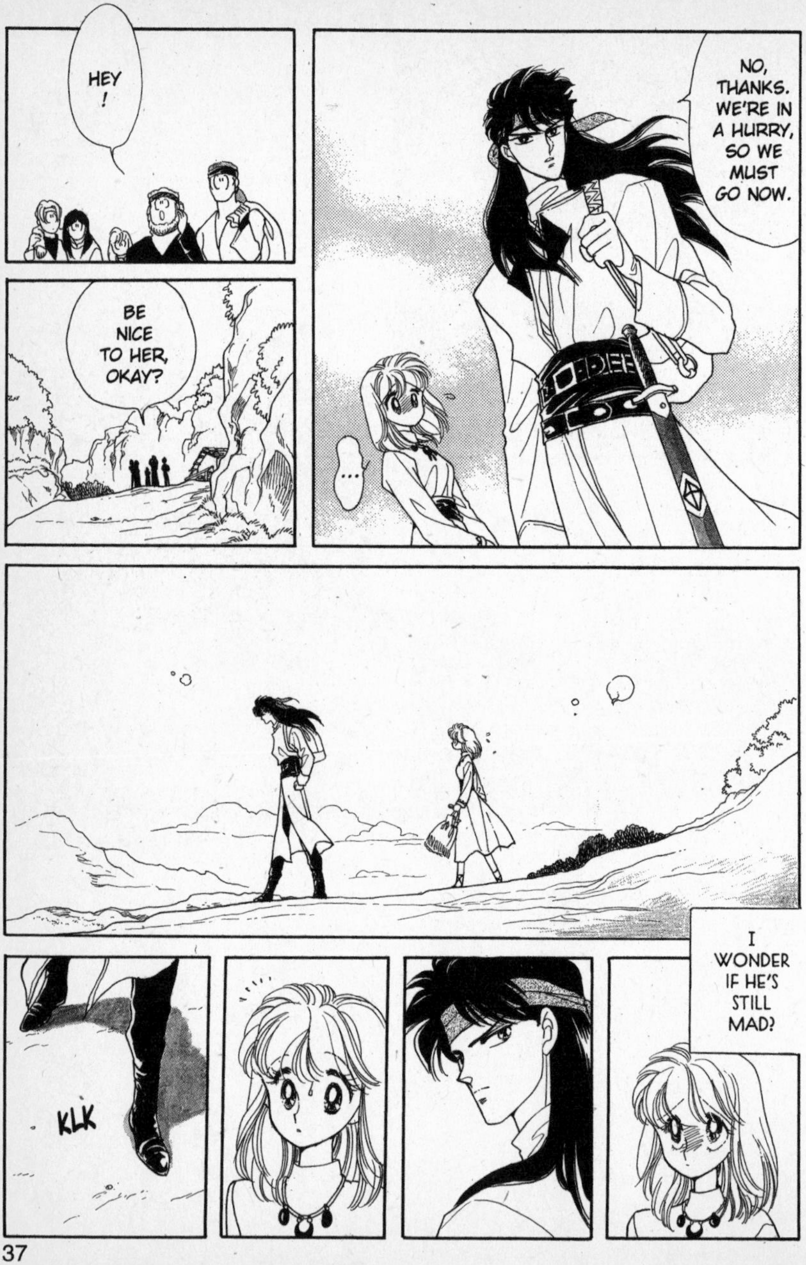
NO, THANKS. WE'RE IN A HURRY, SO WE MUST GO NOW.
...
HEY!
BE NICE TO HER, OKAY?
I WONDER IF HE'S STILL MAD?
KLK

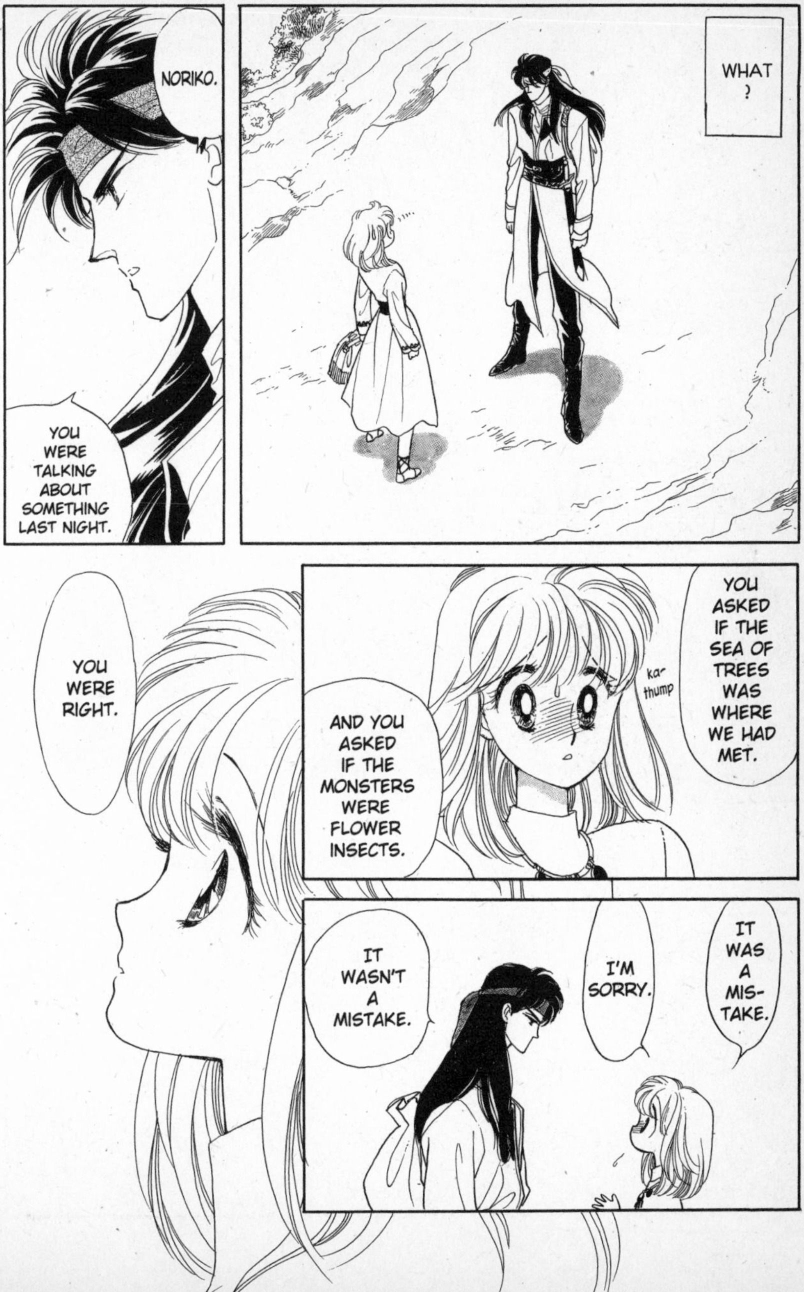
WHAT ?
NORIKO.
YOU WERE TALKING ABOUT SOMETHING LAST NIGHT.
YOU ASKED IF THE SEA OF TREES WAS WHERE WE HAD MET.
ka-thump
AND YOU ASKED IF THE MONSTERS WERE FLOWER INSECTS.
YOU WERE RIGHT.
IT WAS A MIS-TAKE.
I'M SORRY.
IT WASN'T A MISTAKE.

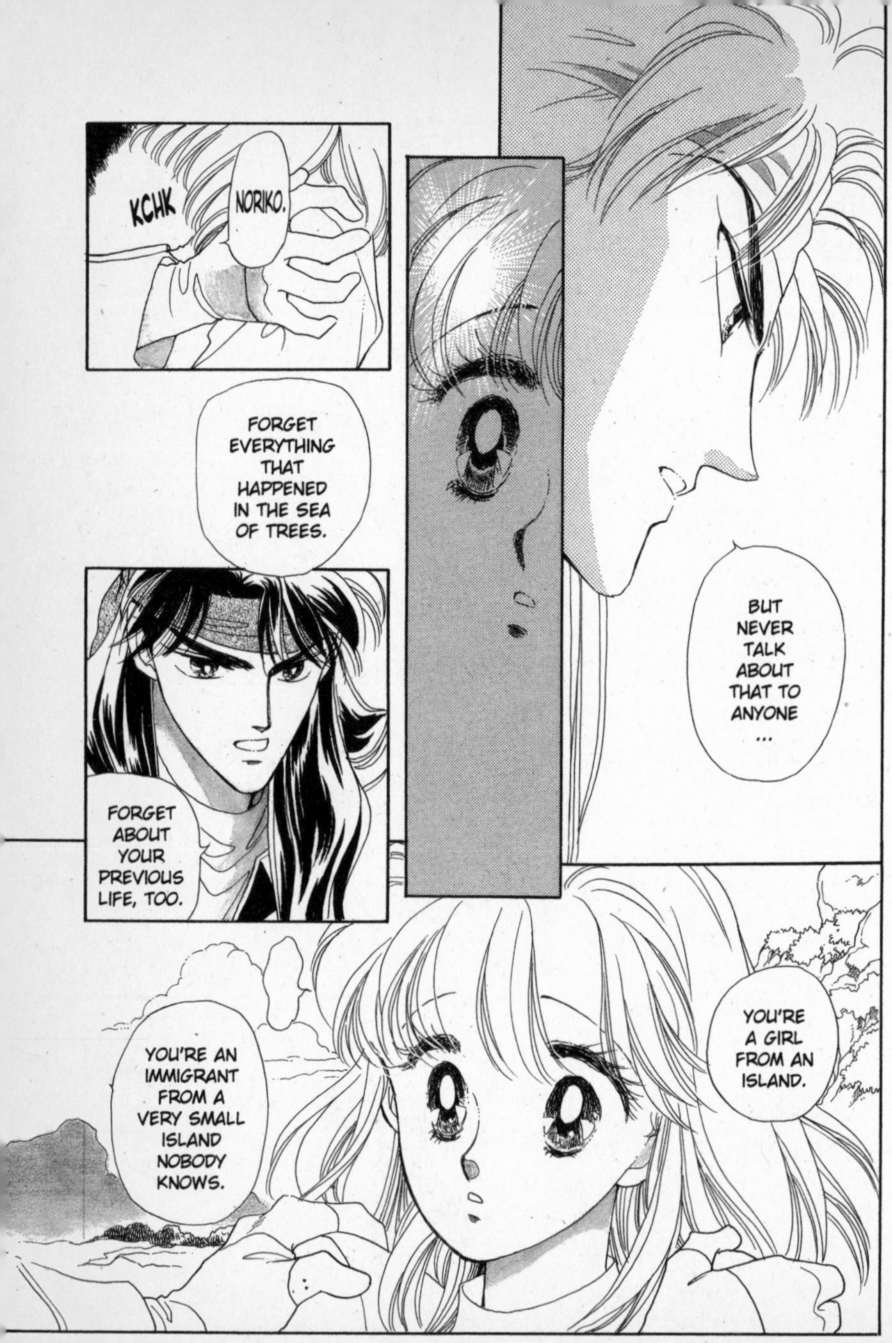
BUT NEVER TALK ABOUT THAT TO ANYONE ...
KCHK
NORIKO.
FORGET EVERYTHING THAT HAPPENED IN THE SEA OF TREES.
FORGET ABOUT YOUR PREVIOUS LIFE, TOO.
YOU'RE A GIRL FROM AN ISLAND.
YOU'RE AN IMMIGRANT FROM A VERY SMALL ISLAND NOBODY KNOWS.

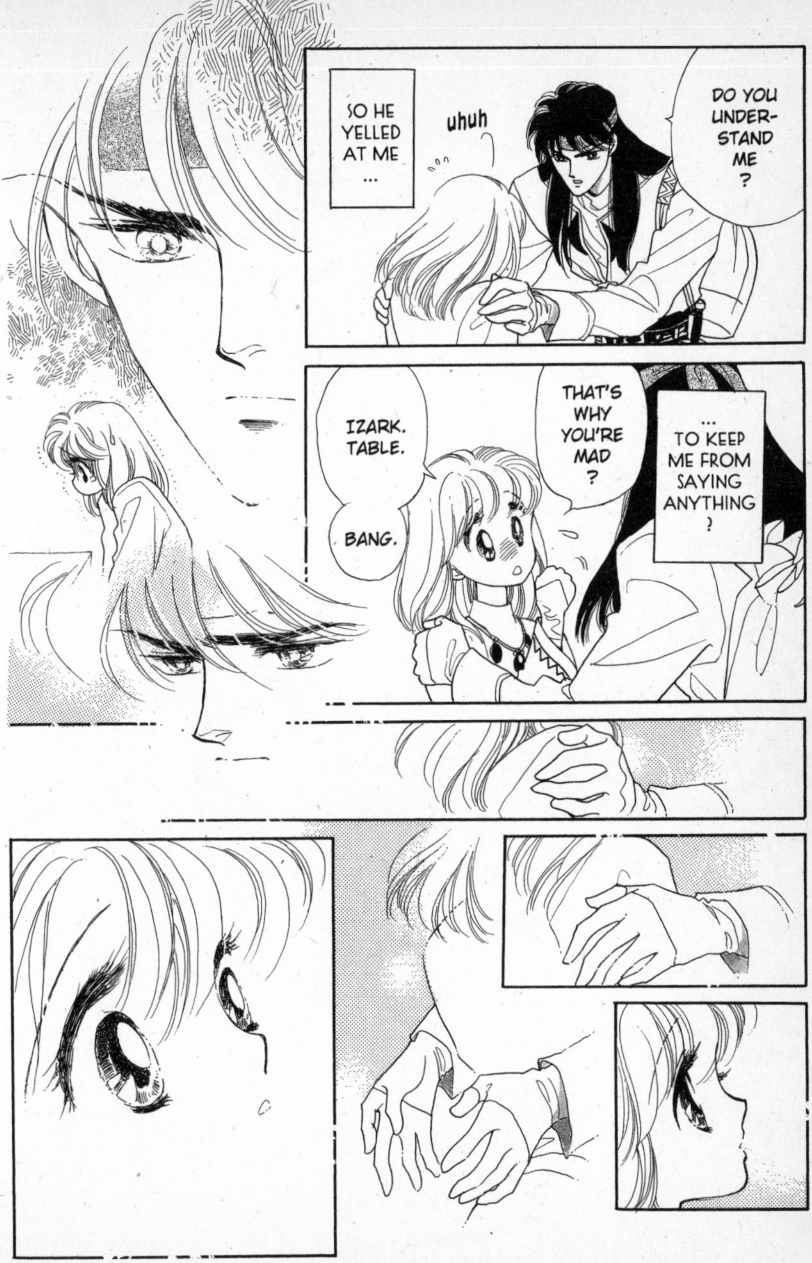
DO YOU UNDER-STAND ME ?
uhuh
SO HE YELLED AT ME ...
... TO KEEP ME FROM SAYING ANYTHING ?
THAT'S WHY YOU'RE MAD ?
IZARK. TABLE.
BANG.

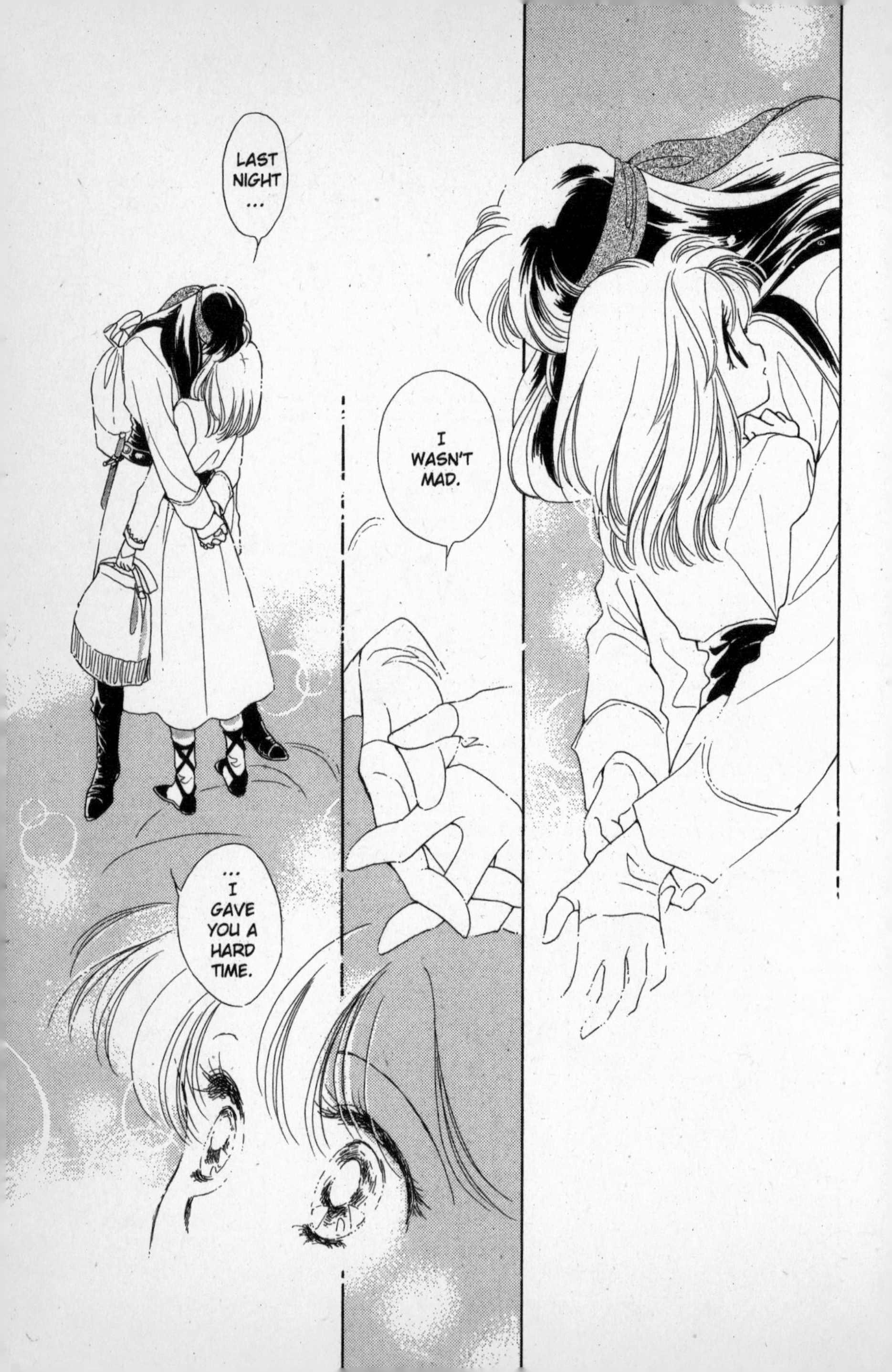
I WASN'T MAD.
LAST NIGHT ...
... I GAVE YOU A HARD TIME.

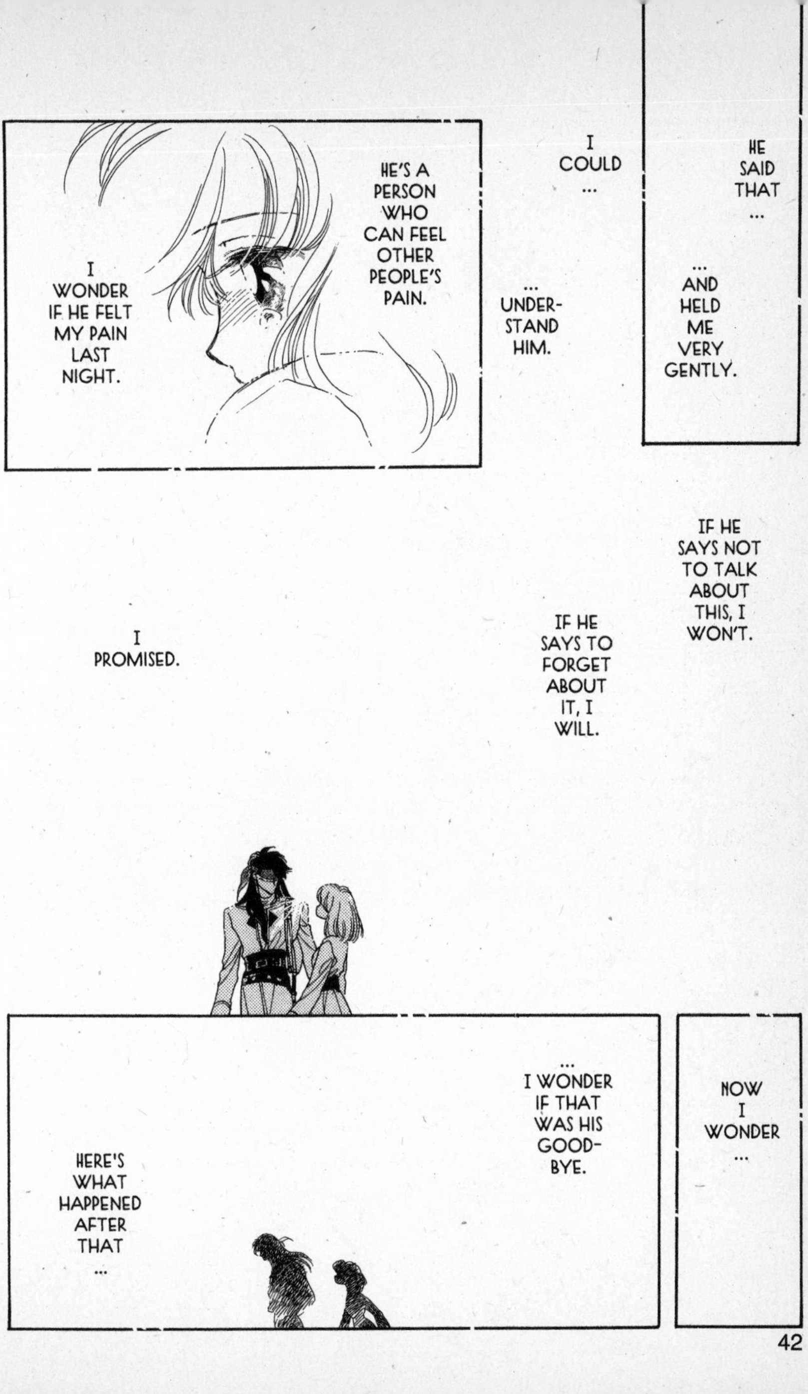
HE SAID THAT ...
... AND HELD ME VERY GENTLY.
I COULD ...
... UNDER-STAND HIM.
HE'S A PERSON WHO CAN FEEL OTHER PEOPLE'S PAIN.
I WONDER IF HE FELT MY PAIN LAST NIGHT.
IF HE SAYS NOT TO TALK ABOUT THIS, I WON'T.
IF HE SAYS TO FORGET ABOUT IT, I WILL.
I PROMISED.
NOW I WONDER ...
... I WONDER IF THAT WAS HIS GOOD-BYE.
HERE'S WHAT HAPPENED AFTER THAT ...

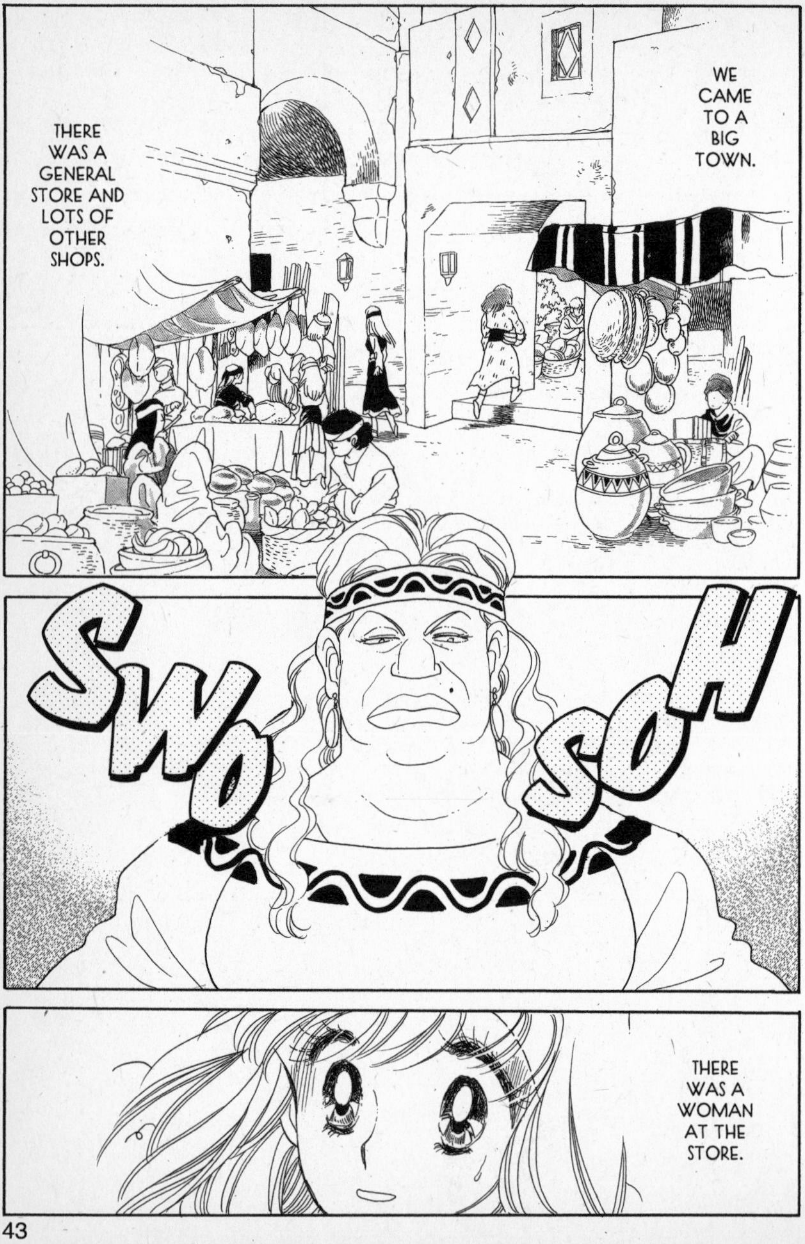
WE CAME TO A BIG TOWN.
THERE WAS A GENERAL STORE AND LOTS OF OTHER SHOPS.
SWO SOH
THERE WAS A WOMAN AT THE STORE.

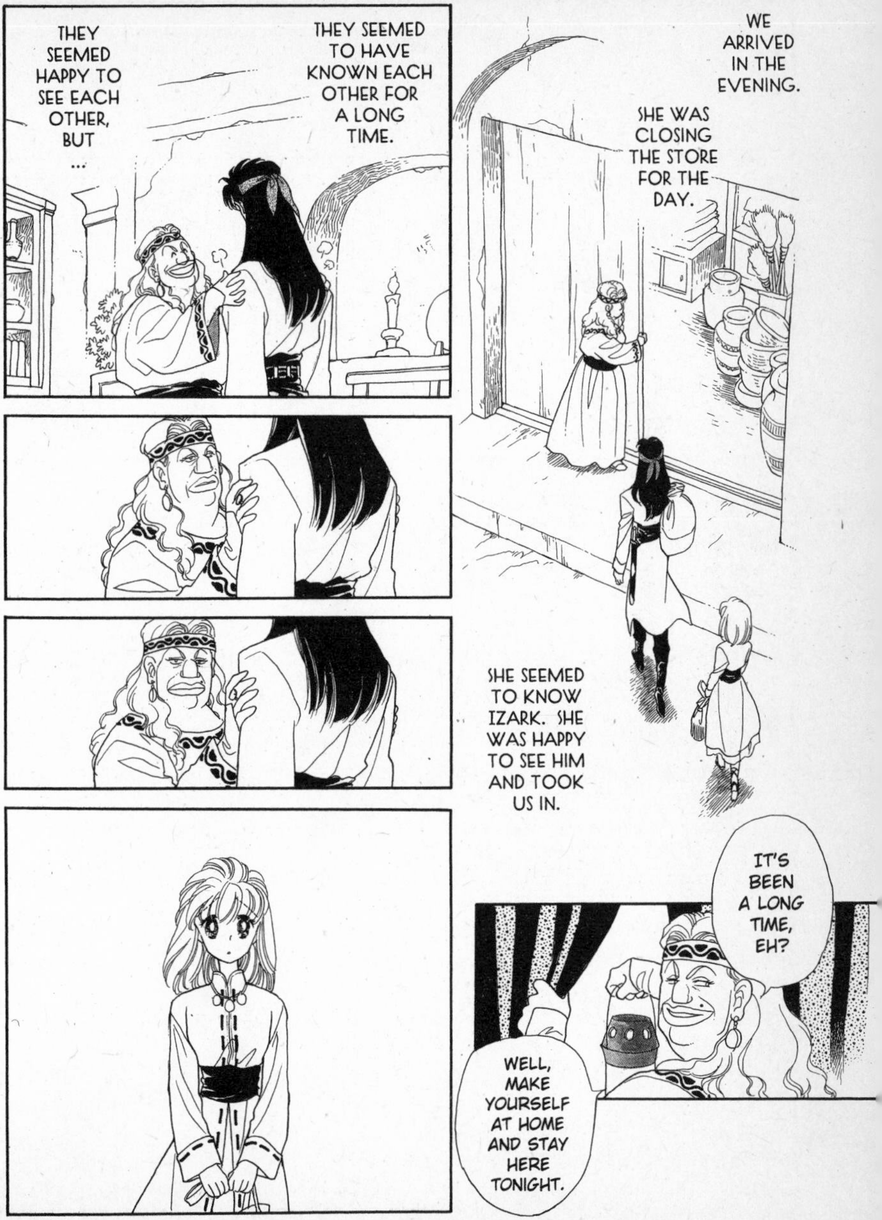
WE ARRIVED IN THE EVENING.
SHE WAS CLOSING THE STORE FOR THE DAY.
SHE SEEMED TO KNOW IZARK. SHE WAS HAPPY TO SEE HIM AND TOOK US IN.
THEY SEEMED TO HAVE KNOWN EACH OTHER FOR A LONG TIME.
THEY SEEMED HAPPY TO SEE EACH OTHER, BUT ...
IT'S BEEN A LONG TIME, EH?
WELL, MAKE YOURSELF AT HOME AND STAY HERE TONIGHT.

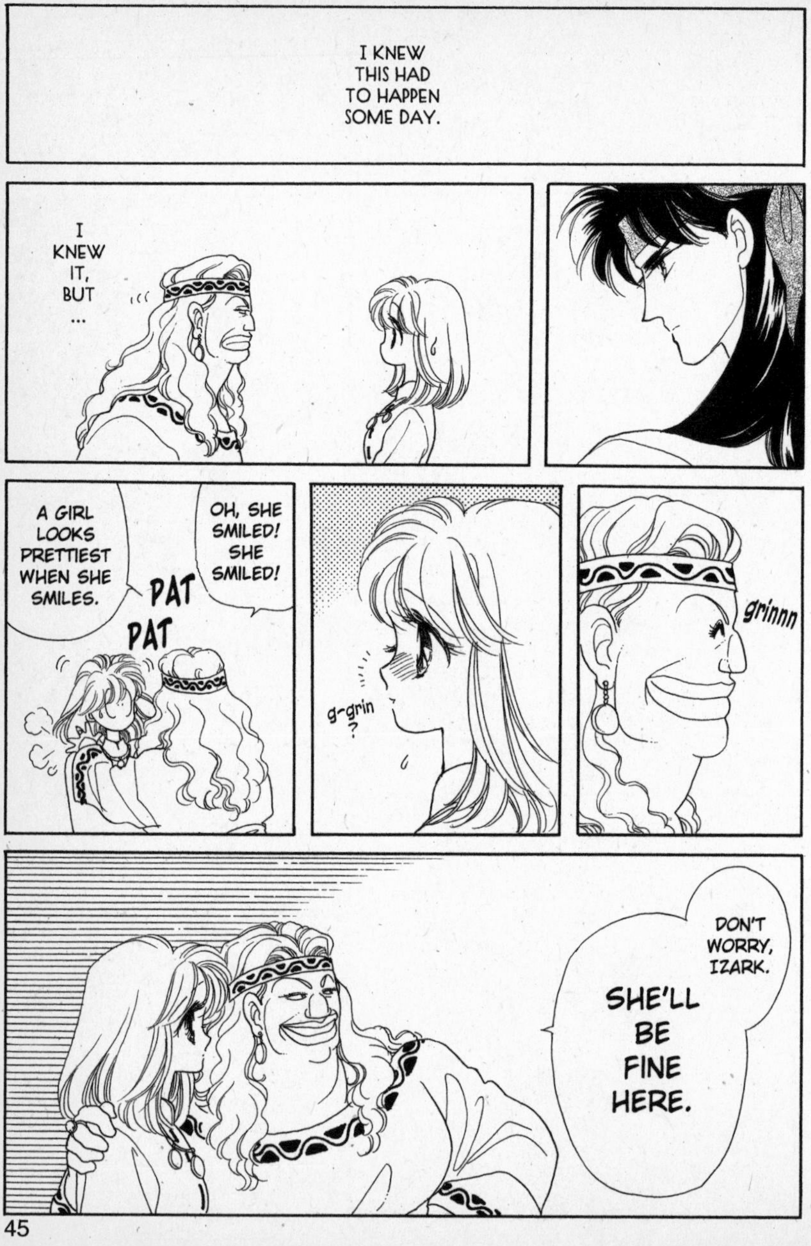

I KNEW THIS HAD TO HAPPEN SOME DAY.
I KNEW IT, BUT ...
grinnn
g-grin ?
OH, SHE SMILED! SHE SMILED!
A GIRL LOOKS PRETTIEST WHEN SHE SMILES.
PAT PAT
DON'T WORRY, IZARK.
SHE'LL BE FINE HERE.

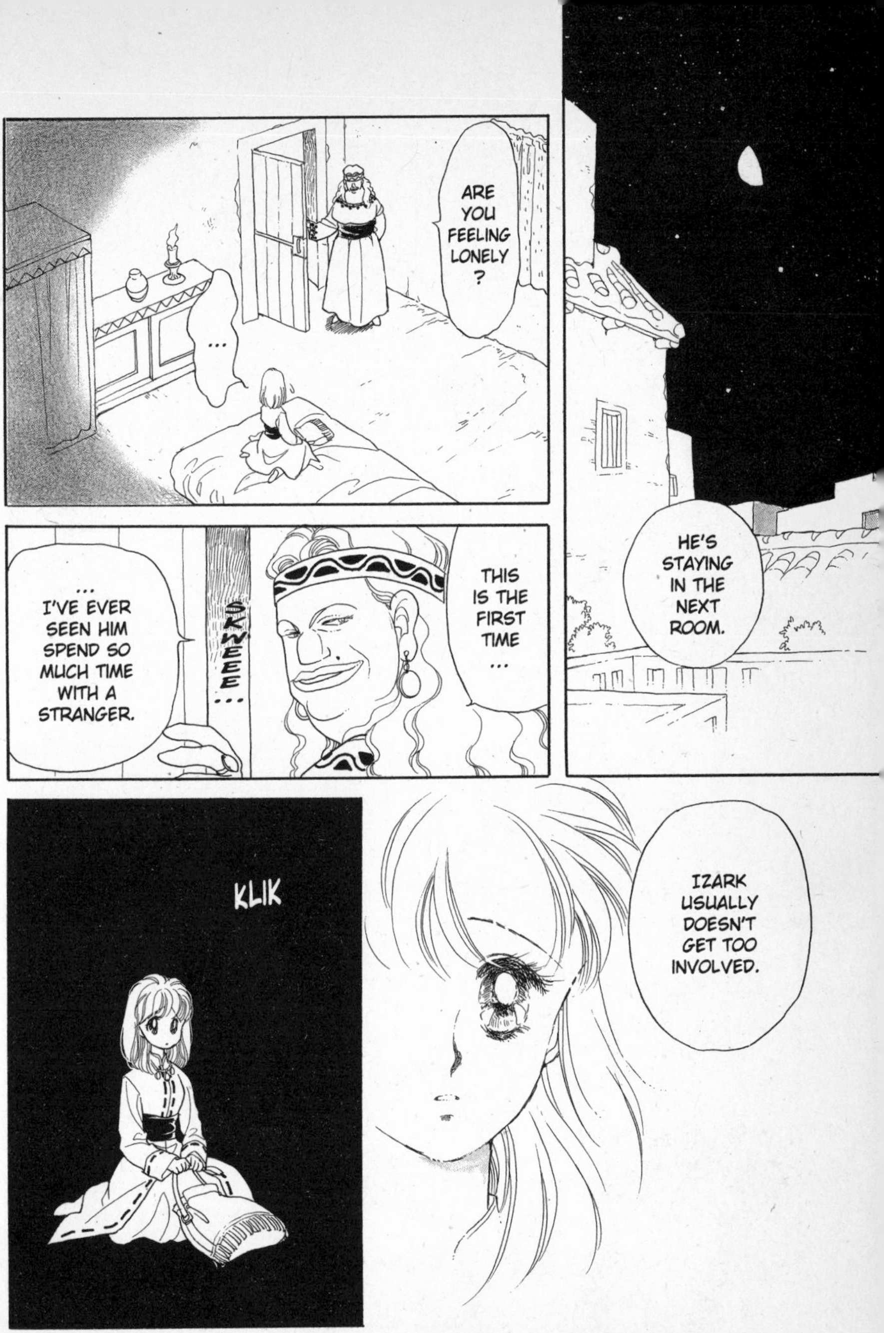
HE'S STAYING IN THE NEXT ROOM.
ARE YOU FEELING LONELY ?
...
THIS IS THE FIRST TIME ...
SKWEEE...
... I'VE EVER SEEN HIM SPEND SO MUCH TIME WITH A STRANGER.
IZARK USUALLY DOESN'T GET TOO INVOLVED.
KLIK

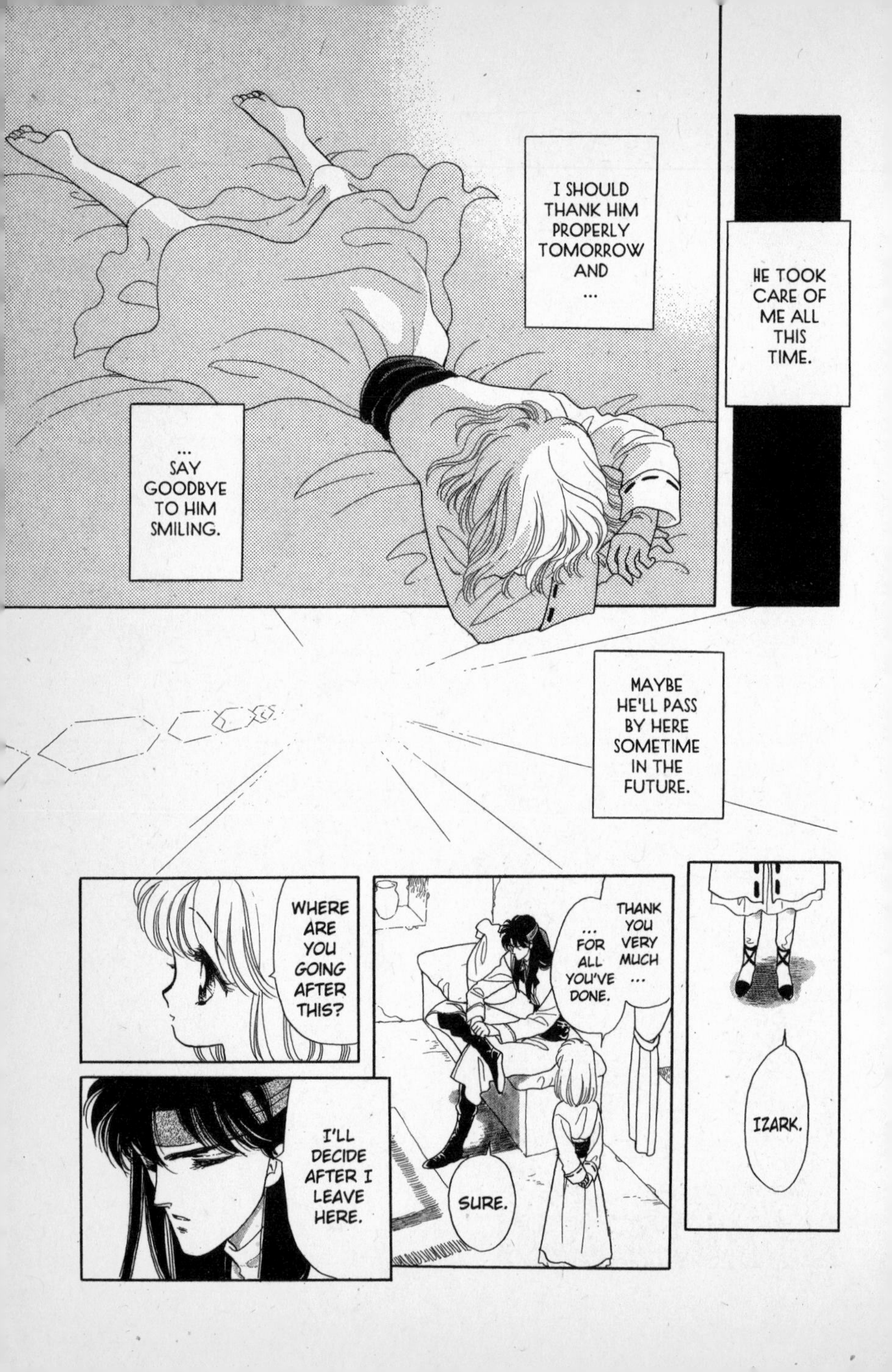
HE TOOK CARE OF ME ALL THIS TIME.
I SHOULD THANK HIM PROPERLY TOMORROW AND ...
... SAY GOODBYE TO HIM SMILING.
MAYBE HE'LL PASS BY HERE SOMETIME IN THE FUTURE.
IZARK.
THANK YOU VERY MUCH ...
... FOR ALL YOU'VE DONE.
SURE.
WHERE ARE YOU GOING AFTER THIS?
I'LL DECIDE AFTER I LEAVE HERE.

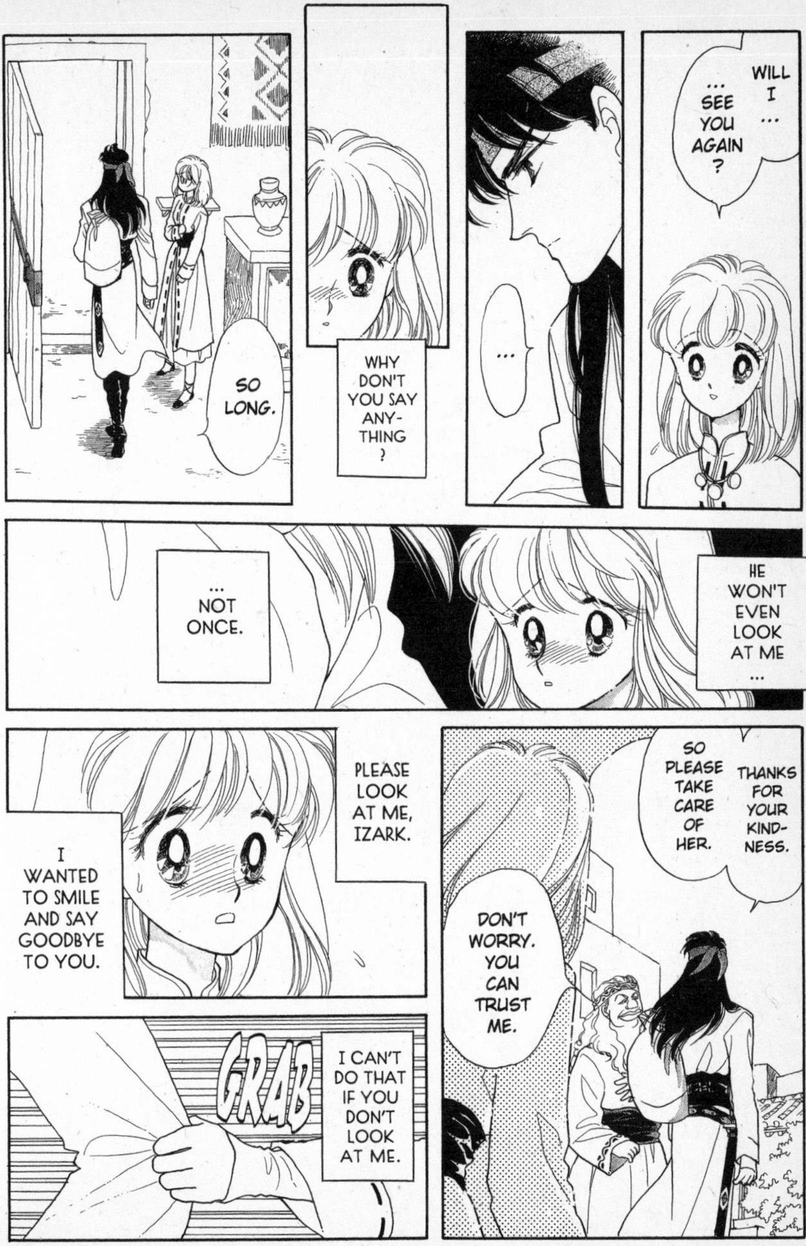
WILL I ... SEE YOU AGAIN ?
...
WHY DON'T YOU SAY ANY- THING ?
SO LONG.
HE WON'T EVEN LOOK AT ME ...
... NOT ONCE.
THANKS FOR YOUR KIND- NESS.
SO PLEASE TAKE CARE OF HER.
DON'T WORRY. YOU CAN TRUST ME.
PLEASE LOOK AT ME, IZARK.
I WANTED TO SMILE AND SAY GOODBYE TO YOU.
I CAN'T DO THAT IF YOU DON'T LOOK AT ME.
GRAB

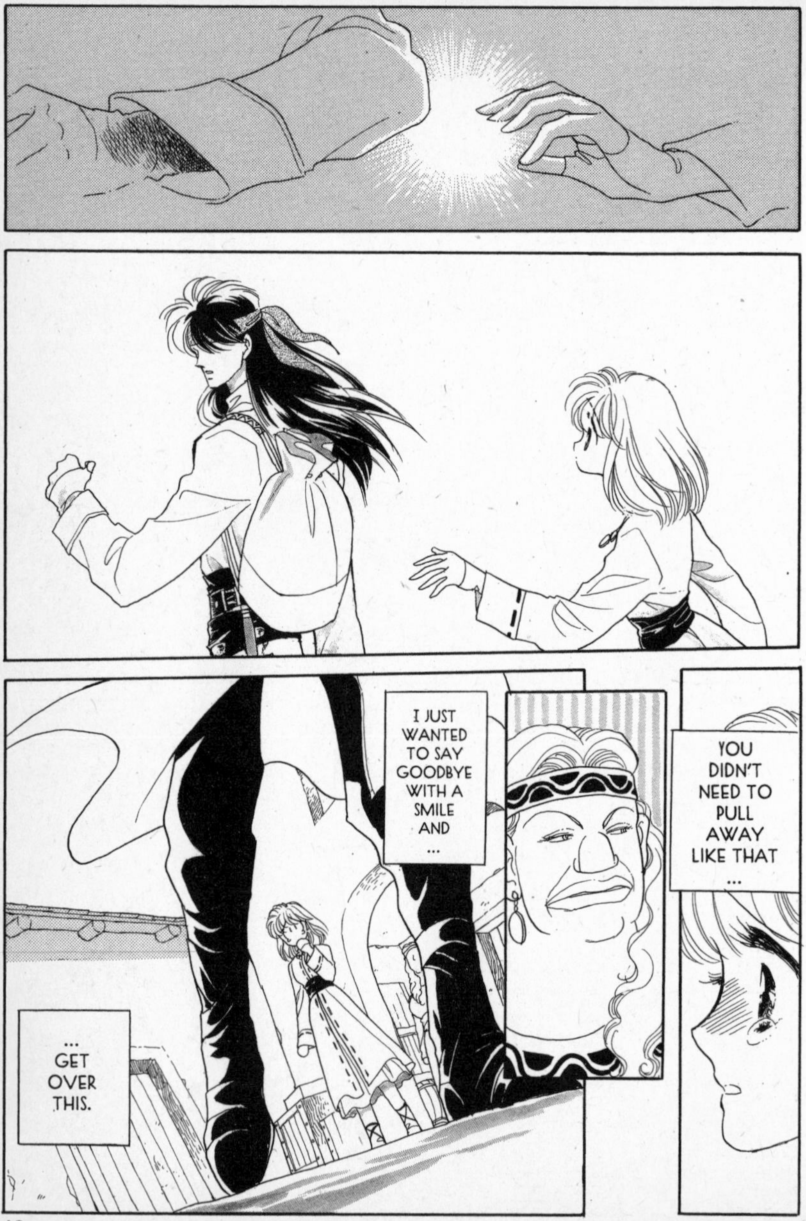
YOU DIDN'T NEED TO PULL AWAY LIKE THAT ...
I JUST WANTED TO SAY GOODBYE WITH A SMILE AND ...
... GET OVER THIS.

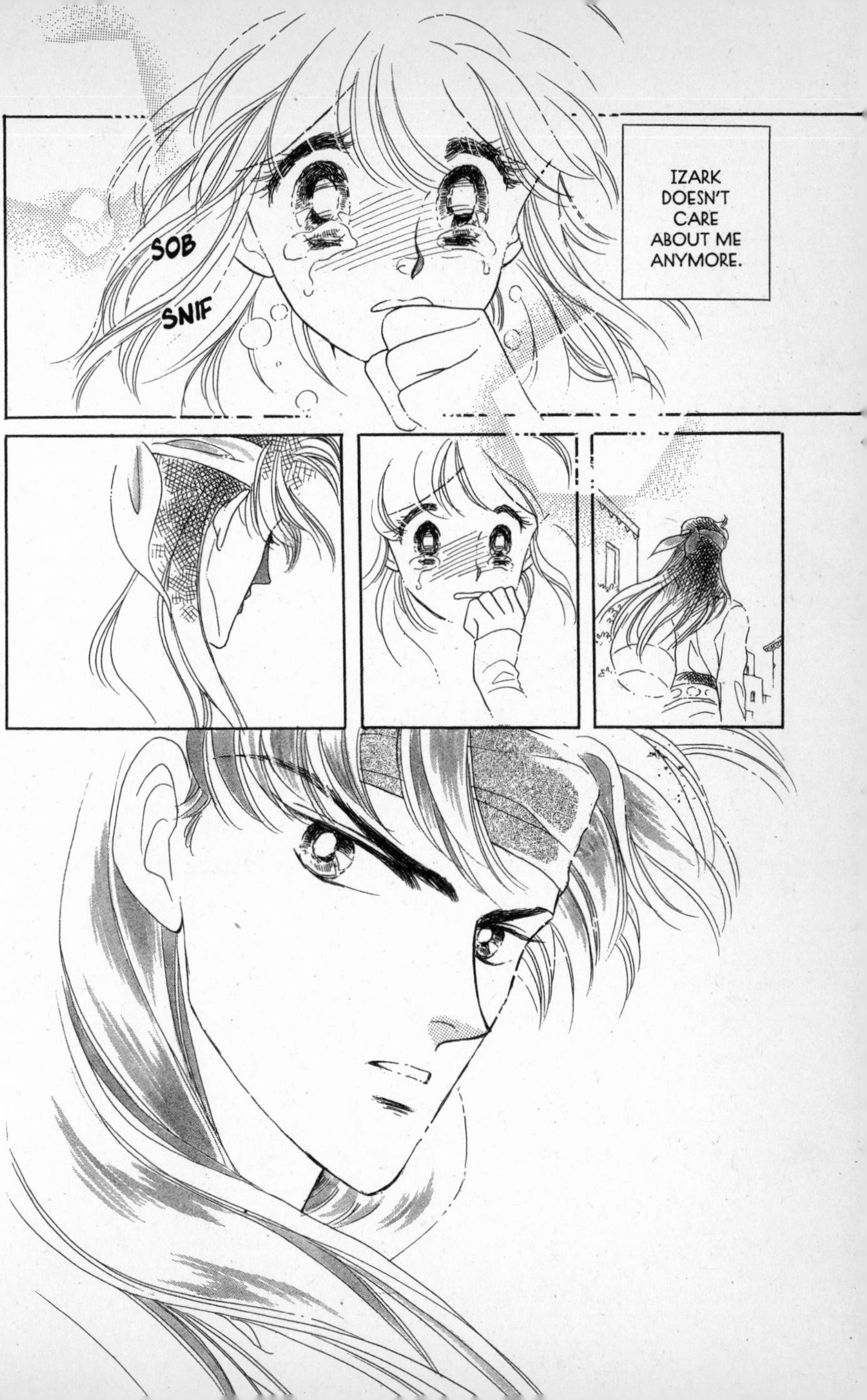
IZARK DOESN'T CARE ABOUT ME ANYMORE.
SOB
SNIF

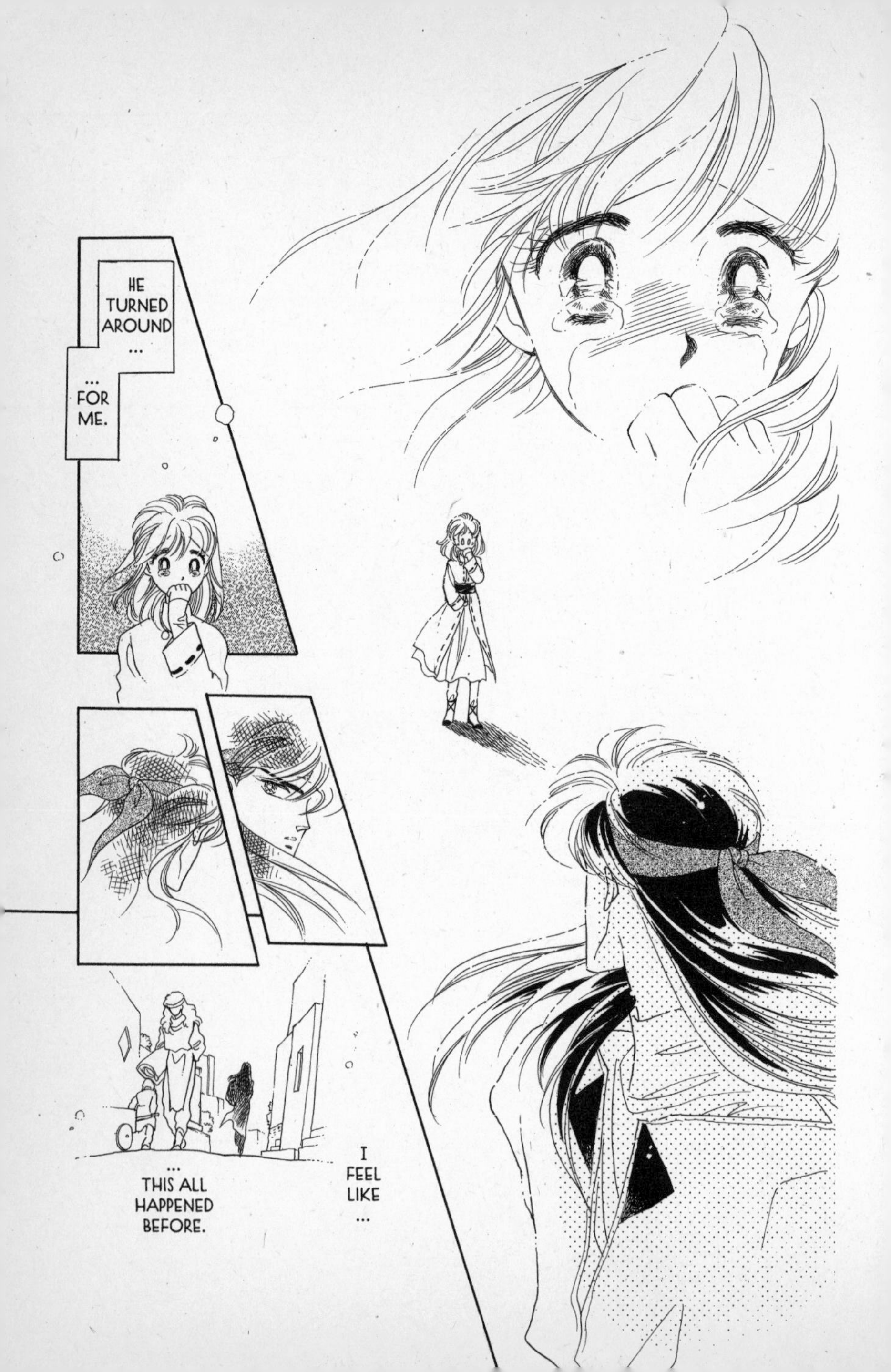
HE TURNED AROUND ...
... FOR ME.
I FEEL LIKE ...
... THIS ALL HAPPENED BEFORE.

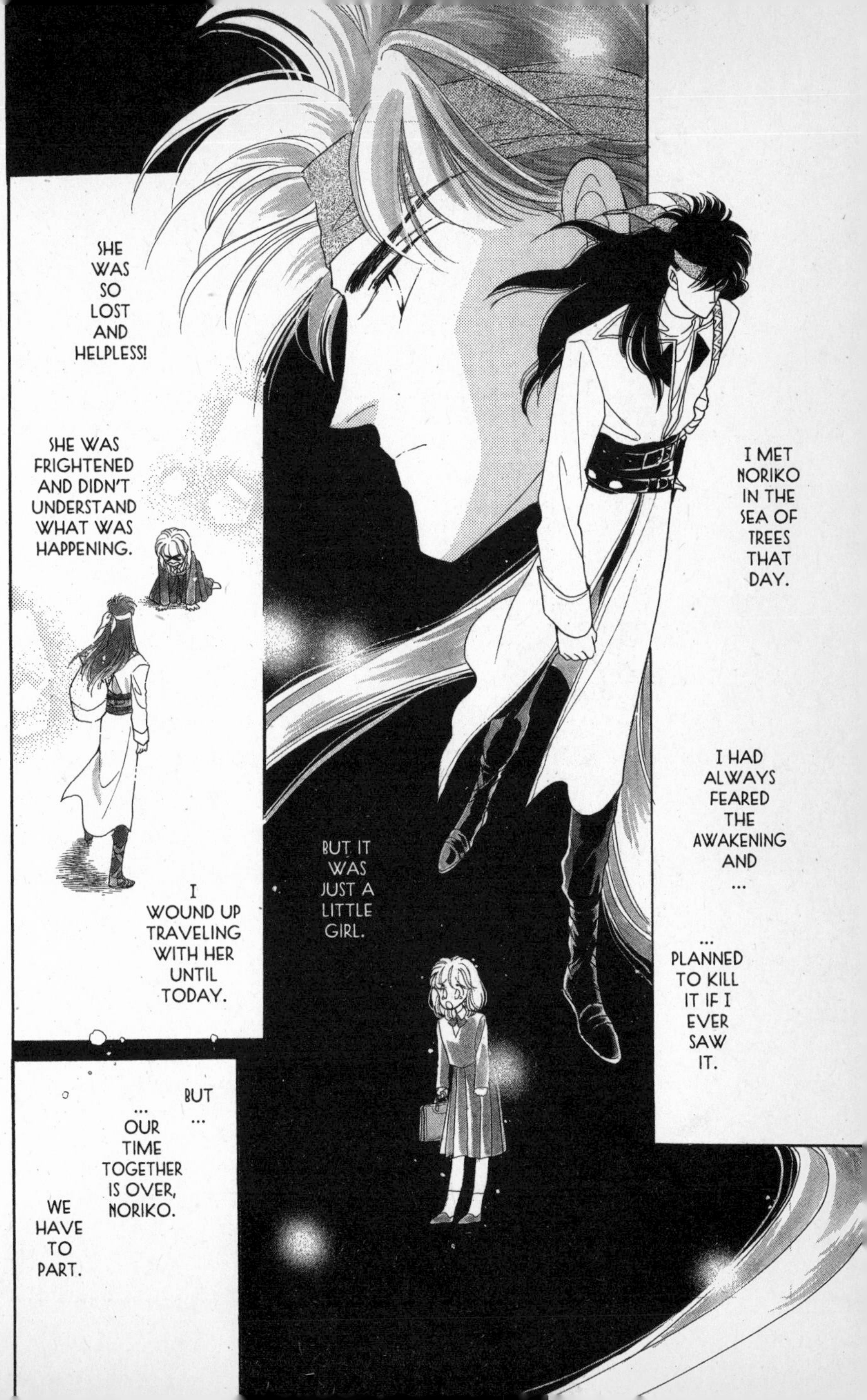
I MET NORIKO IN THE SEA OF TREES THAT DAY.
I HAD ALWAYS FEARED THE AWAKENING AND ...
... PLANNED TO KILL IT IF I EVER SAW IT.
BUT IT WAS JUST A LITTLE GIRL.
SHE WAS SO LOST AND HELPLESS!
SHE WAS FRIGHTENED AND DIDN'T UNDERSTAND WHAT WAS HAPPENING.
I WOUND UP TRAVELING WITH HER UNTIL TODAY.
BUT ...
... OUR TIME TOGETHER IS OVER, NORIKO.
WE HAVE TO PART.

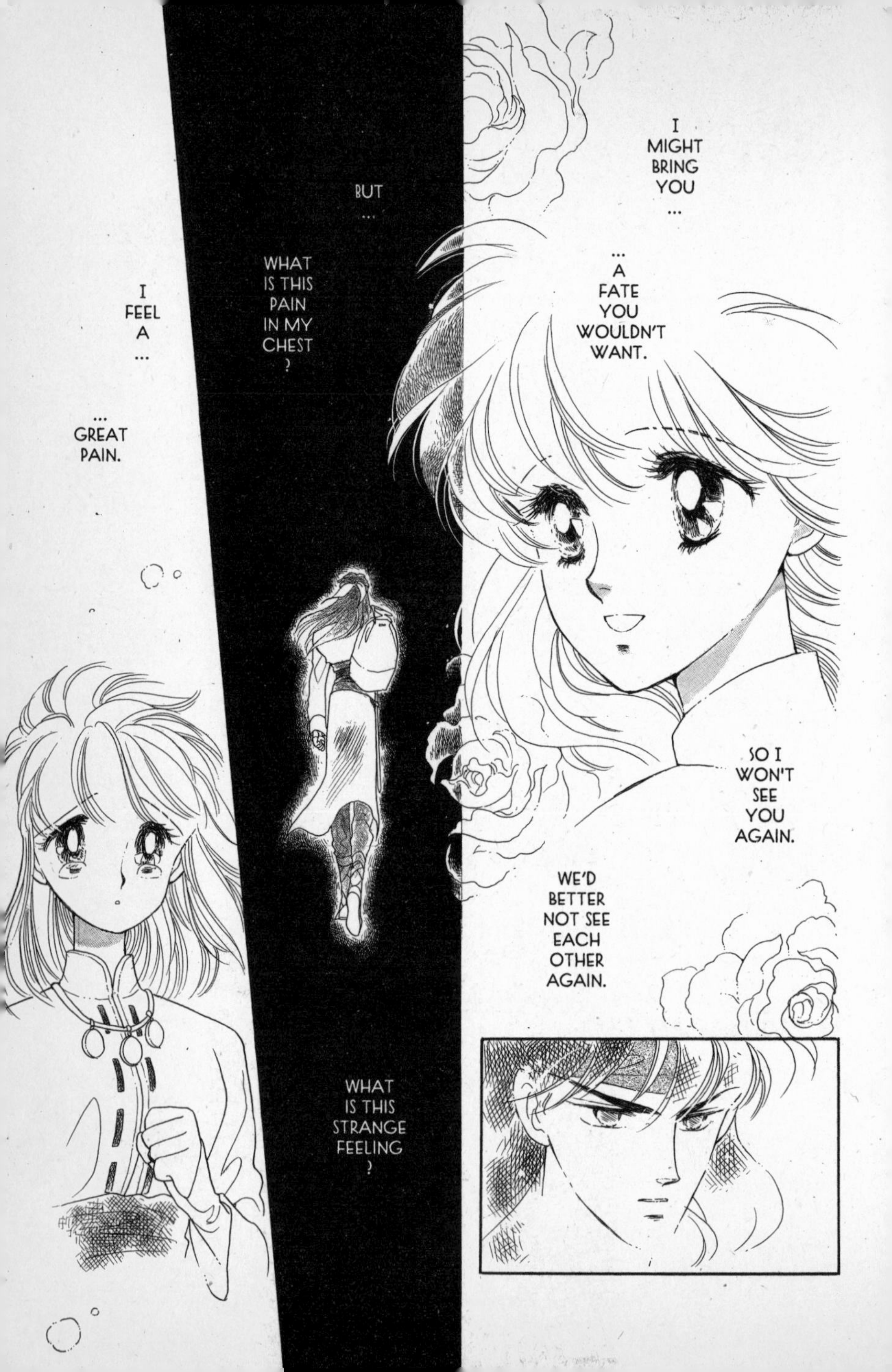
I MIGHT BRING YOU ...
... A FATE YOU WOULDN'T WANT.
SO I WON'T SEE YOU AGAIN.
WE'D BETTER NOT SEE EACH OTHER AGAIN.
BUT ...
WHAT IS THIS PAIN IN MY CHEST ?
WHAT IS THIS STRANGE FEELING ?
I FEEL A ...
... GREAT PAIN.

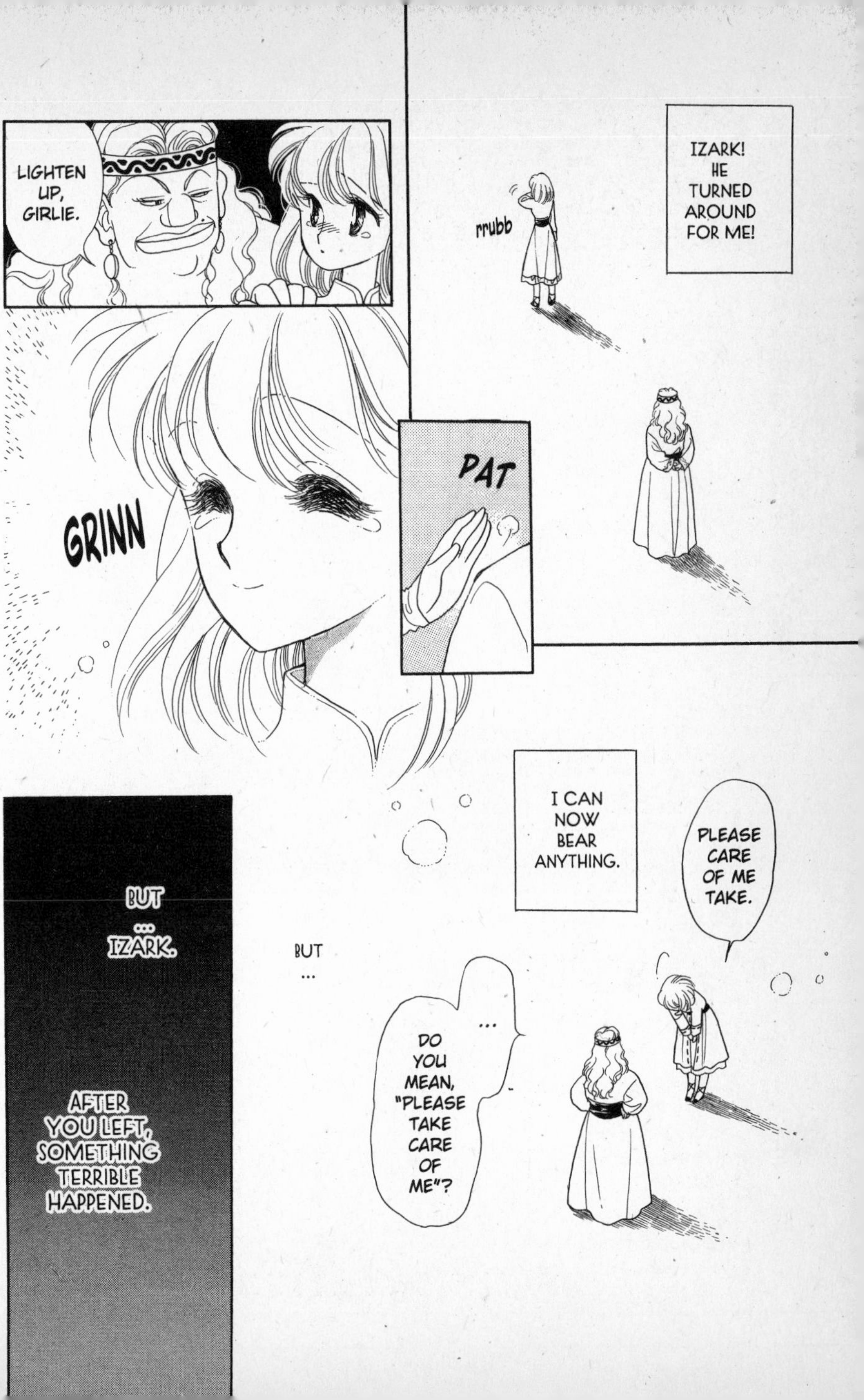
IZARK! HE TURNED AROUND FOR ME!
rrubb
LIGHTEN UP, GIRLIE.
PAT
GRINN
I CAN NOW BEAR ANYTHING.
PLEASE CARE OF ME TAKE.
...
DO YOU MEAN, "PLEASE TAKE CARE OF ME"?
BUT ...
BUT ... IZARK.
AFTER YOU LEFT, SOMETHING TERRIBLE HAPPENED.

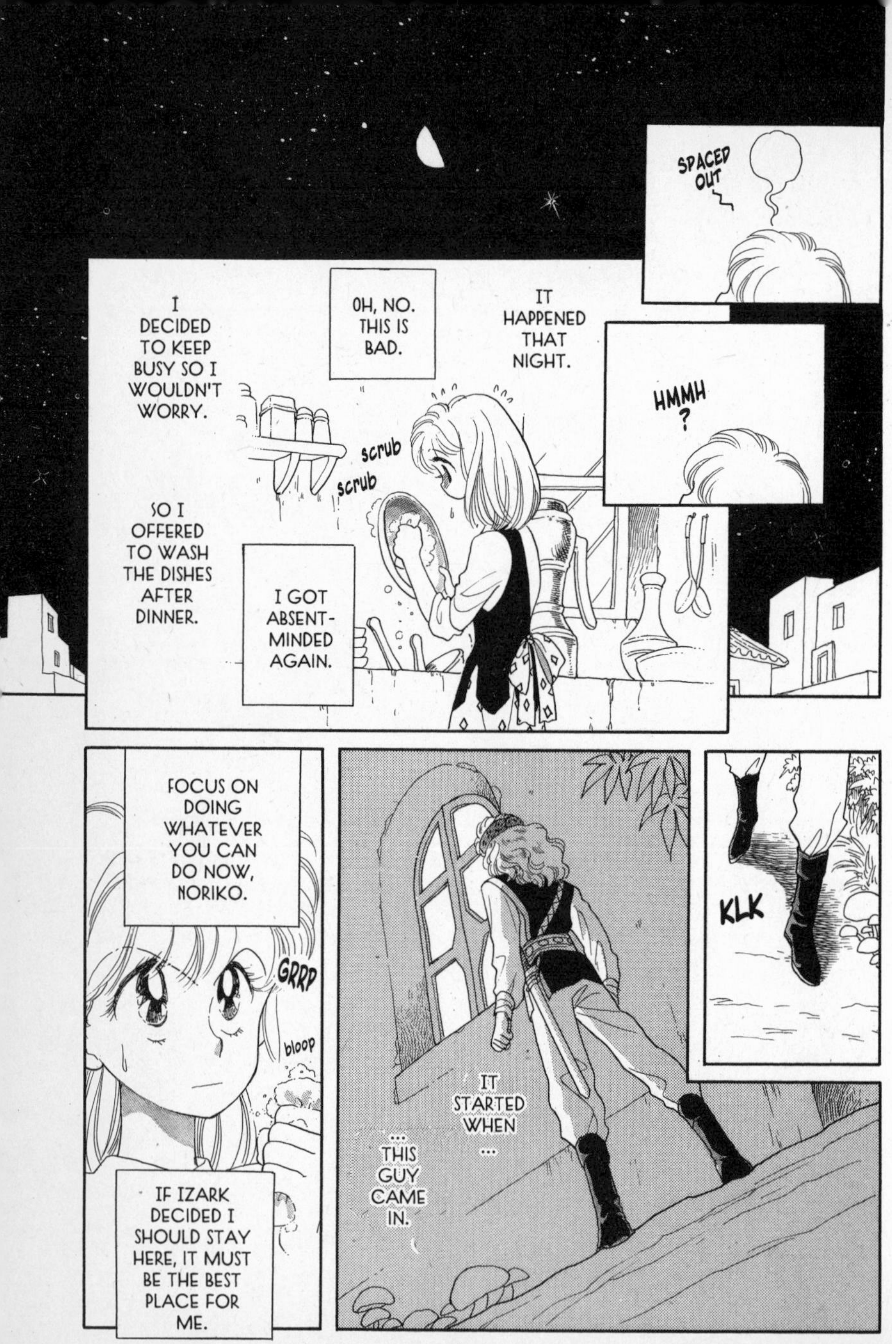
SPACED OUT
HMMH ?
IT HAPPENED THAT NIGHT.
OH, NO. THIS IS BAD.
I DECIDED TO KEEP BUSY SO I WOULDN'T WORRY.
scrub
scrub
SO I OFFERED TO WASH THE DISHES AFTER DINNER.
I GOT ABSENT-MINDED AGAIN.
KLK
IT STARTED WHEN ...
... THIS GUY CAME IN.
FOCUS ON DOING WHATEVER YOU CAN DO NOW, NORIKO.
GRRP
bloop
IF IZARK DECIDED I SHOULD STAY HERE, IT MUST BE THE BEST PLACE FOR ME.

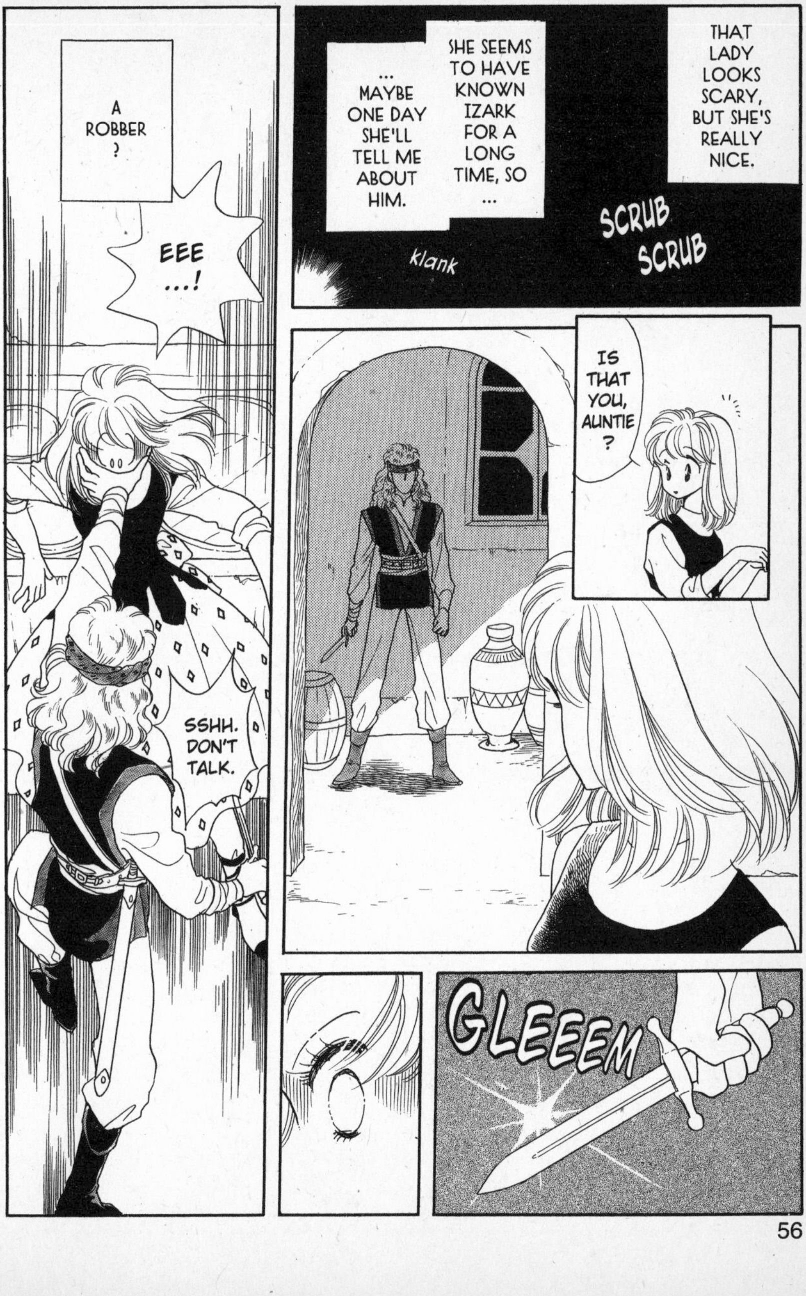
THAT LADY LOOKS SCARY, BUT SHE'S REALLY NICE.
SHE SEEMS TO HAVE KNOWN IZARK FOR A LONG TIME, SO ...
... MAYBE ONE DAY SHE'LL TELL ME ABOUT HIM.
SCRUB SCRUB
klank
IS THAT YOU, AUNTIE?
GLEEEM
A ROBBER?
EEE ...!
SSHH. DON'T TALK.

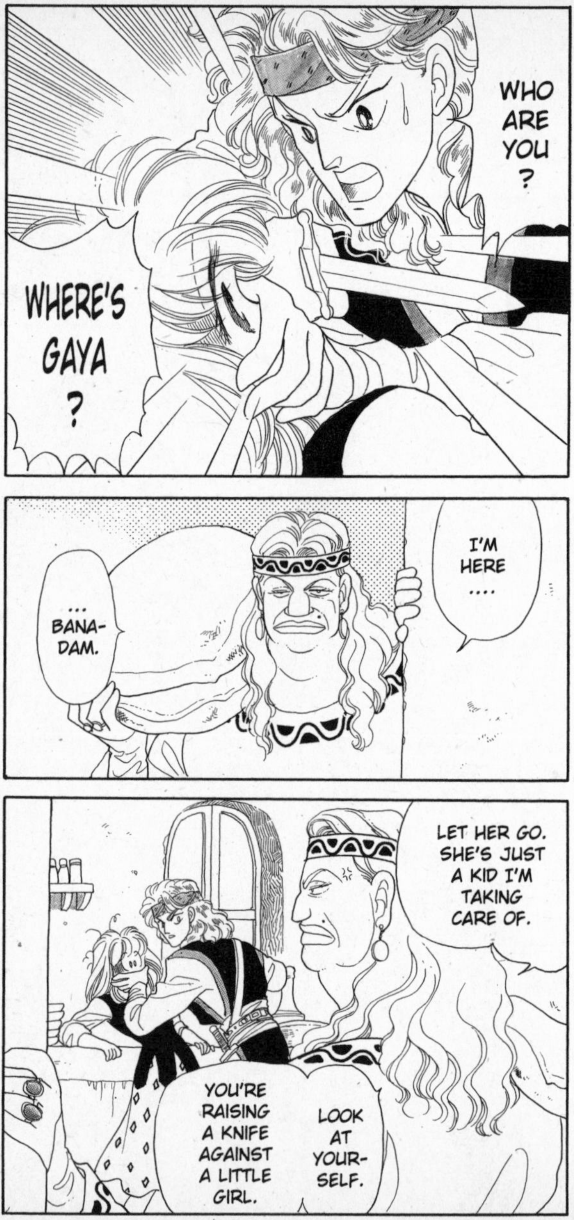
WHO ARE YOU?
WHERE'S GAYA?
I'M HERE ....
... BANA-DAM.
LET HER GO. SHE'S JUST A KID I'M TAKING CARE OF.
LOOK AT YOUR-SELF.
YOU'RE RAISING A KNIFE AGAINST A LITTLE GIRL.

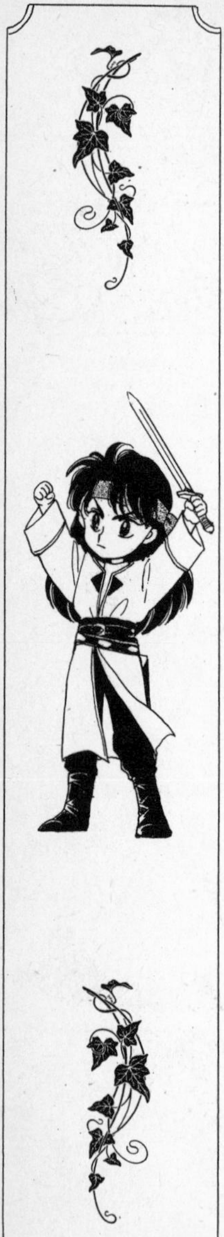

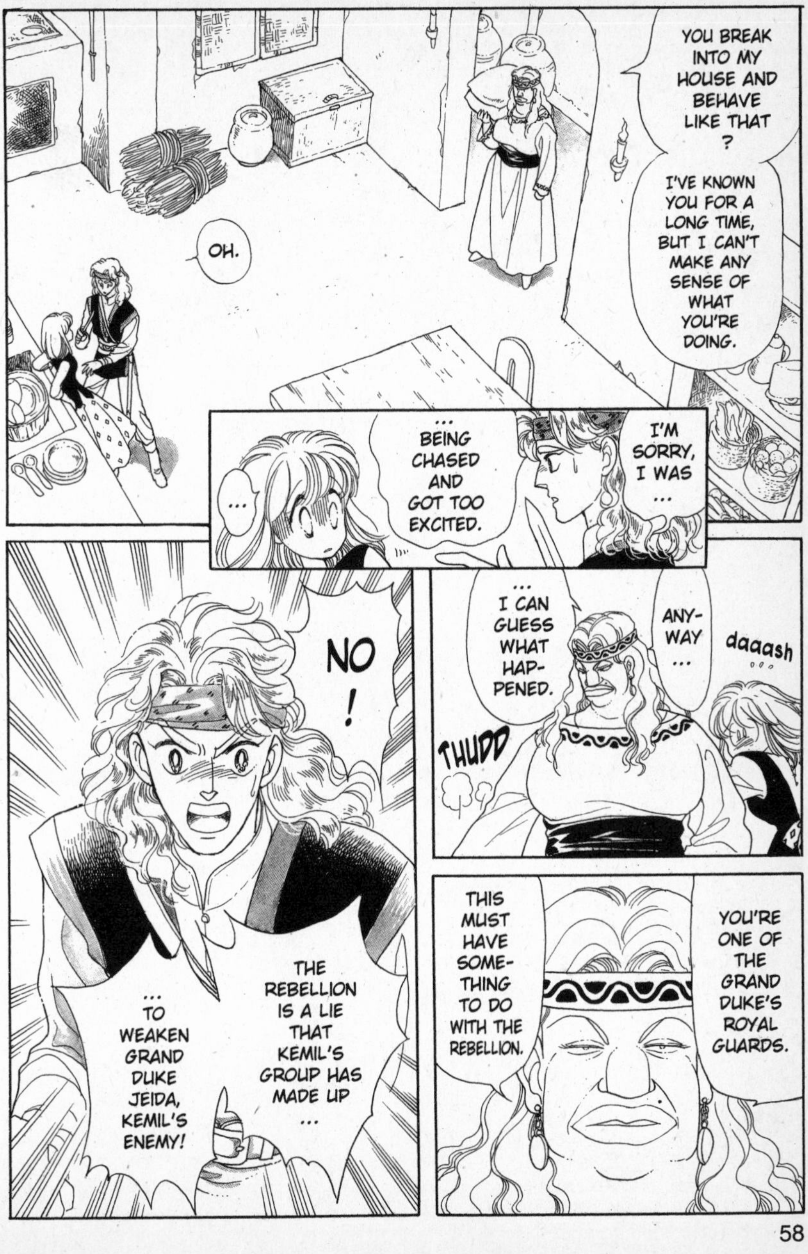
YOU BREAK INTO MY HOUSE AND BEHAVE LIKE THAT ?
I'VE KNOWN YOU FOR A LONG TIME, BUT I CAN'T MAKE ANY SENSE OF WHAT YOU'RE DOING.
OH.
I'M SORRY, I WAS ...
... BEING CHASED AND GOT TOO EXCITED.
...
ANY-WAY ...
... I CAN GUESS WHAT HAP-PENED.
daaash
THUDD
YOU'RE ONE OF THE GRAND DUKE'S ROYAL GUARDS.
THIS MUST HAVE SOME-THING TO DO WITH THE REBELLION.
NO !
THE REBELLION IS A LIE THAT KEMIL'S GROUP HAS MADE UP ...
... TO WEAKEN GRAND DUKE JEIDA, KEMIL'S ENEMY!

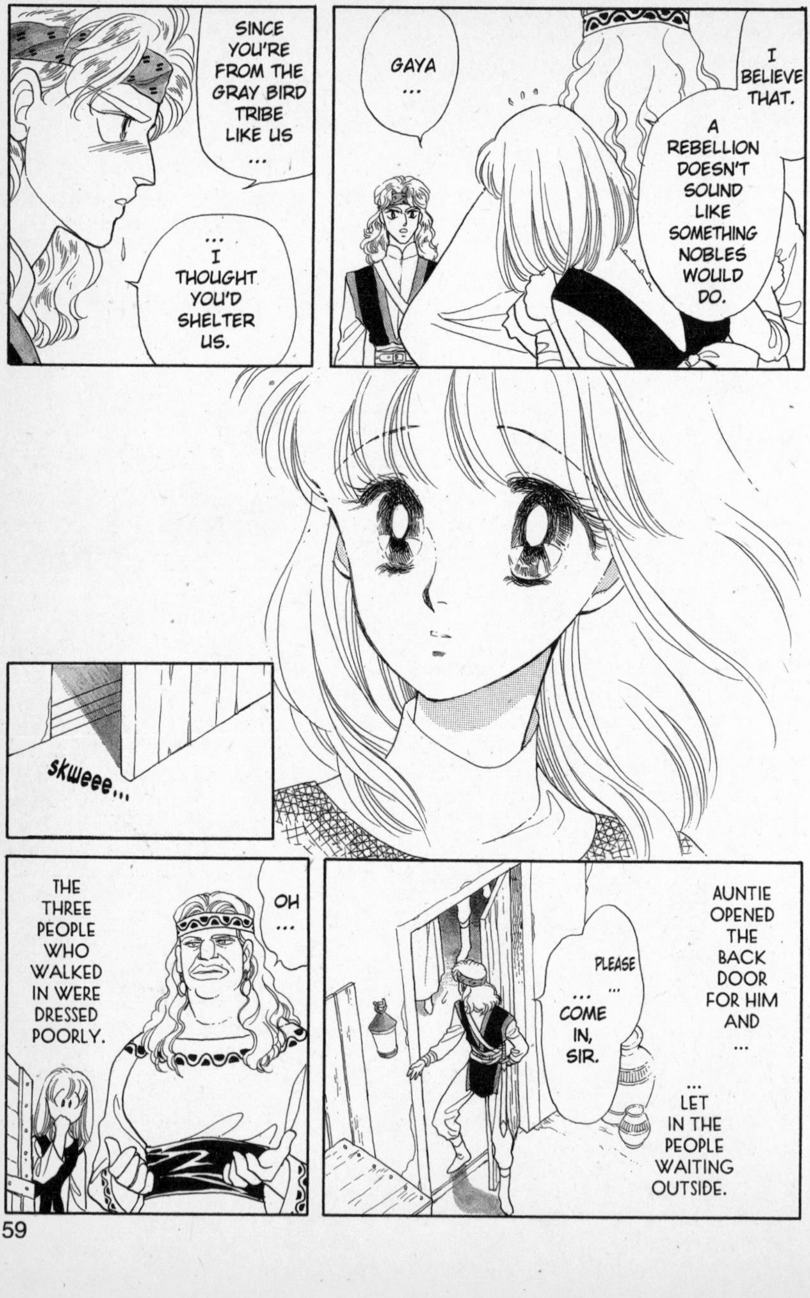
I BELIEVE THAT.
A REBELLION DOESN'T SOUND LIKE SOMETHING NOBLES WOULD DO.
GAYA ...
SINCE YOU'RE FROM THE GRAY BIRD TRIBE LIKE US ...
... I THOUGHT YOU'D SHELTER US.
skweee...
AUNTIE OPENED THE BACK DOOR FOR HIM AND ...
PLEASE ...
... COME IN, SIR.
... LET IN THE PEOPLE WAITING OUTSIDE.
OH ...
THE THREE PEOPLE WHO WALKED IN WERE DRESSED POORLY.

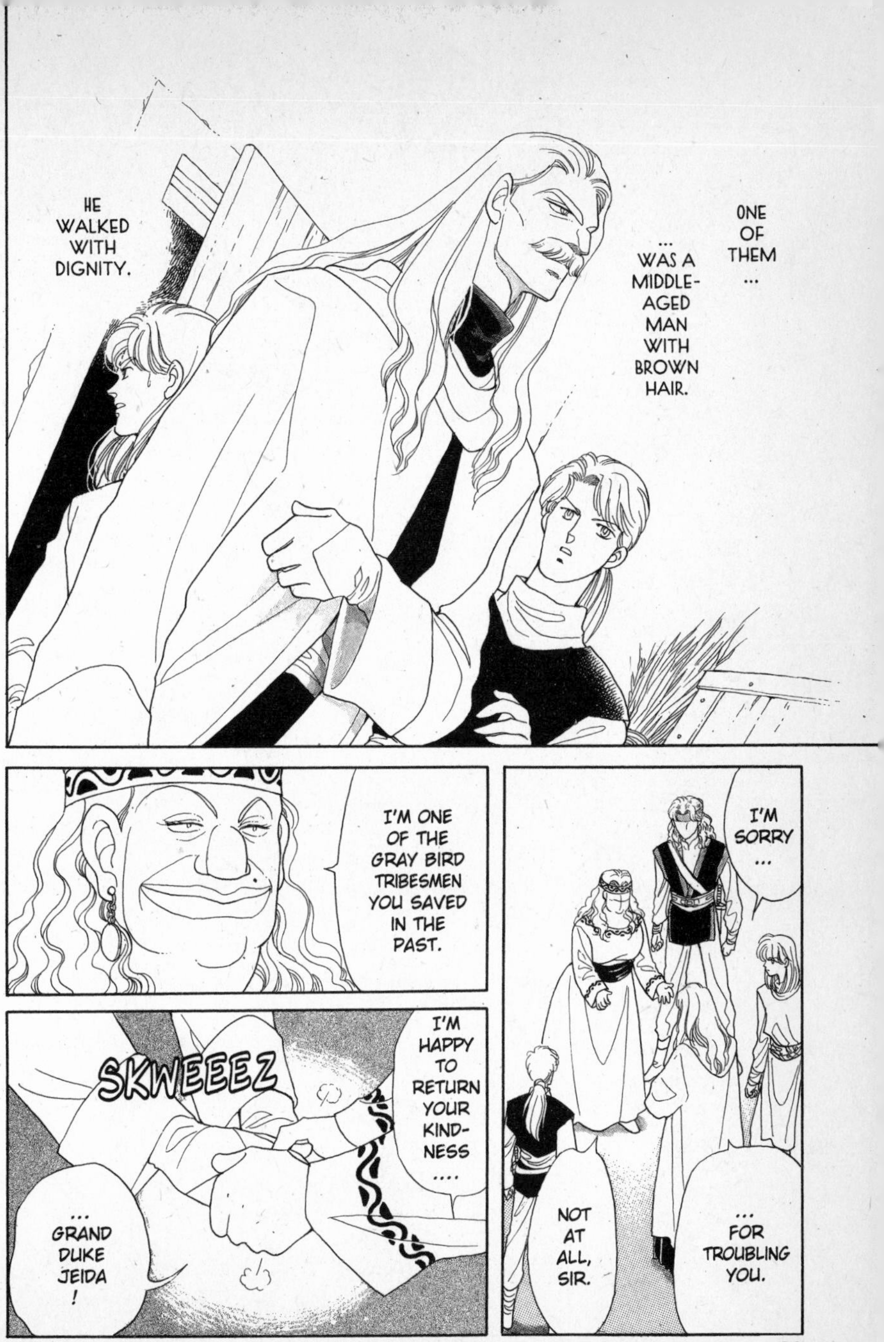
ONE OF THEM ...
... WAS A MIDDLE-AGED MAN WITH BROWN HAIR.
HE WALKED WITH DIGNITY.
I'M SORRY ...
... FOR TROUBLING YOU.
NOT AT ALL, SIR.
I'M ONE OF THE GRAY BIRD TRIBESMEN YOU SAVED IN THE PAST.
I'M HAPPY TO RETURN YOUR KINDNESS ....
SKWEEEZ
... GRAND DUKE JEIDA !

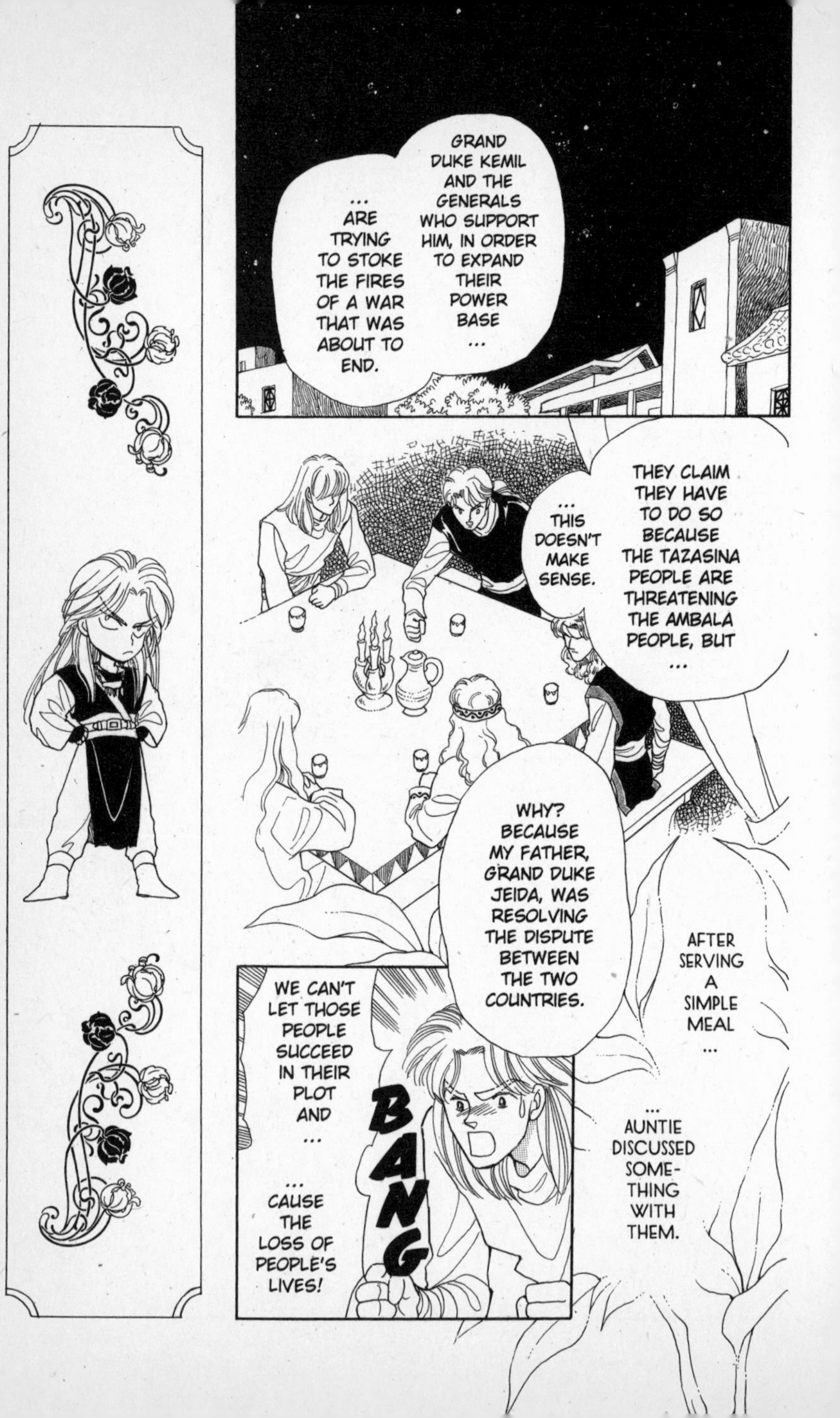
GRAND DUKE KEMIL AND THE GENERALS WHO SUPPORT HIM, IN ORDER TO EXPAND THEIR POWER BASE ...
... ARE TRYING TO STOKE THE FIRES OF A WAR THAT WAS ABOUT TO END.
THEY CLAIM THEY HAVE TO DO SO BECAUSE THE TAZASINA PEOPLE ARE THREATENING THE AMBALA PEOPLE, BUT ...
... THIS DOESN'T MAKE SENSE.
WHY? BECAUSE MY FATHER, GRAND DUKE JEIDA, WAS RESOLVING THE DISPUTE BETWEEN THE TWO COUNTRIES.
AFTER SERVING A SIMPLE MEAL ...
... AUNTIE DISCUSSED SOME-THING WITH THEM.
WE CAN'T LET THOSE PEOPLE SUCCEED IN THEIR PLOT AND ...
... CAUSE THE LOSS OF PEOPLE'S LIVES!
BANG

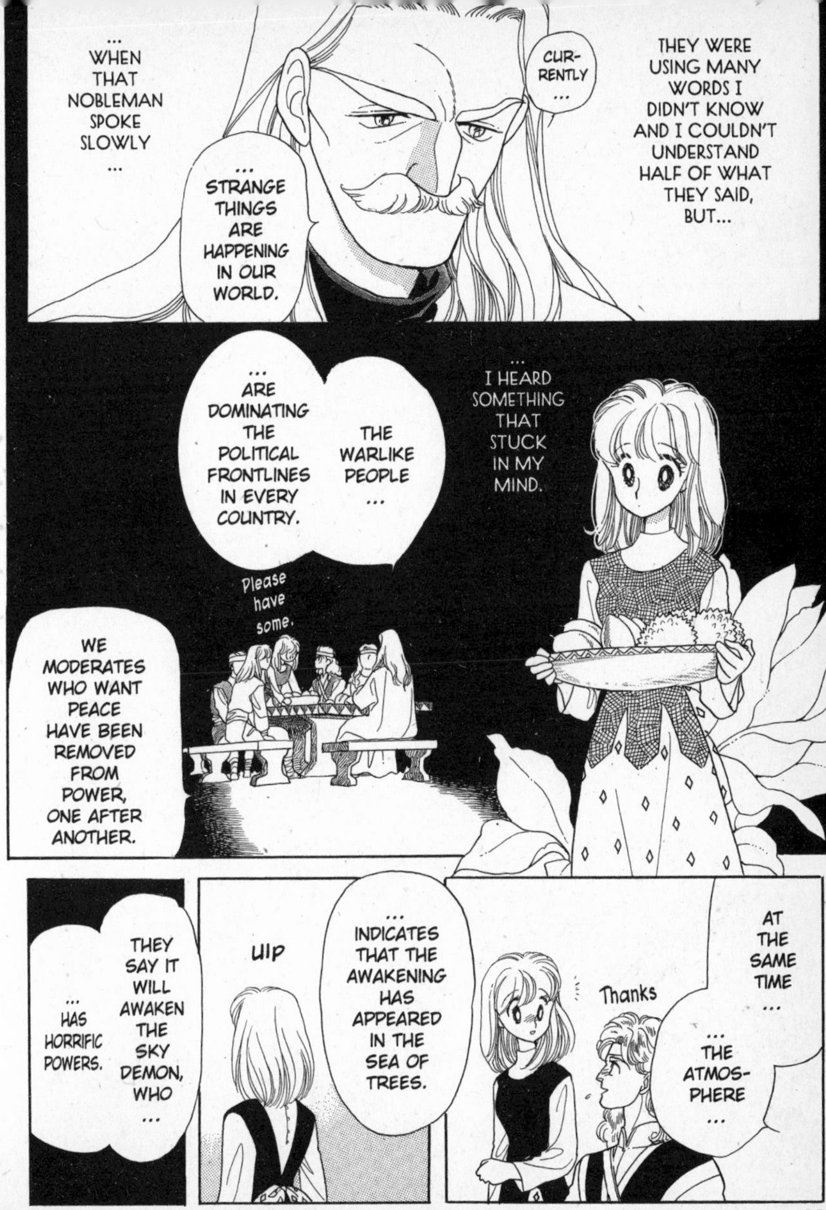
THEY WERE USING MANY WORDS I DIDN'T KNOW AND I COULDN'T UNDERSTAND HALF OF WHAT THEY SAID, BUT...
CUR-RENTLY ...
... WHEN THAT NOBLEMAN SPOKE SLOWLY ...
... STRANGE THINGS ARE HAPPENING IN OUR WORLD.
... I HEARD SOMETHING THAT STUCK IN MY MIND.
THE WARLIKE PEOPLE ...
... ARE DOMINATING THE POLITICAL FRONTLINES IN EVERY COUNTRY.
Please have some.
WE MODERATES WHO WANT PEACE HAVE BEEN REMOVED FROM POWER, ONE AFTER ANOTHER.
AT THE SAME TIME ...
... THE ATMOS-PHERE ...
Thanks
... INDICATES THAT THE AWAKENING HAS APPEARED IN THE SEA OF TREES.
Ulp
THEY SAY IT WILL AWAKEN THE SKY DEMON, WHO ...
... HAS HORRIFIC POWERS.

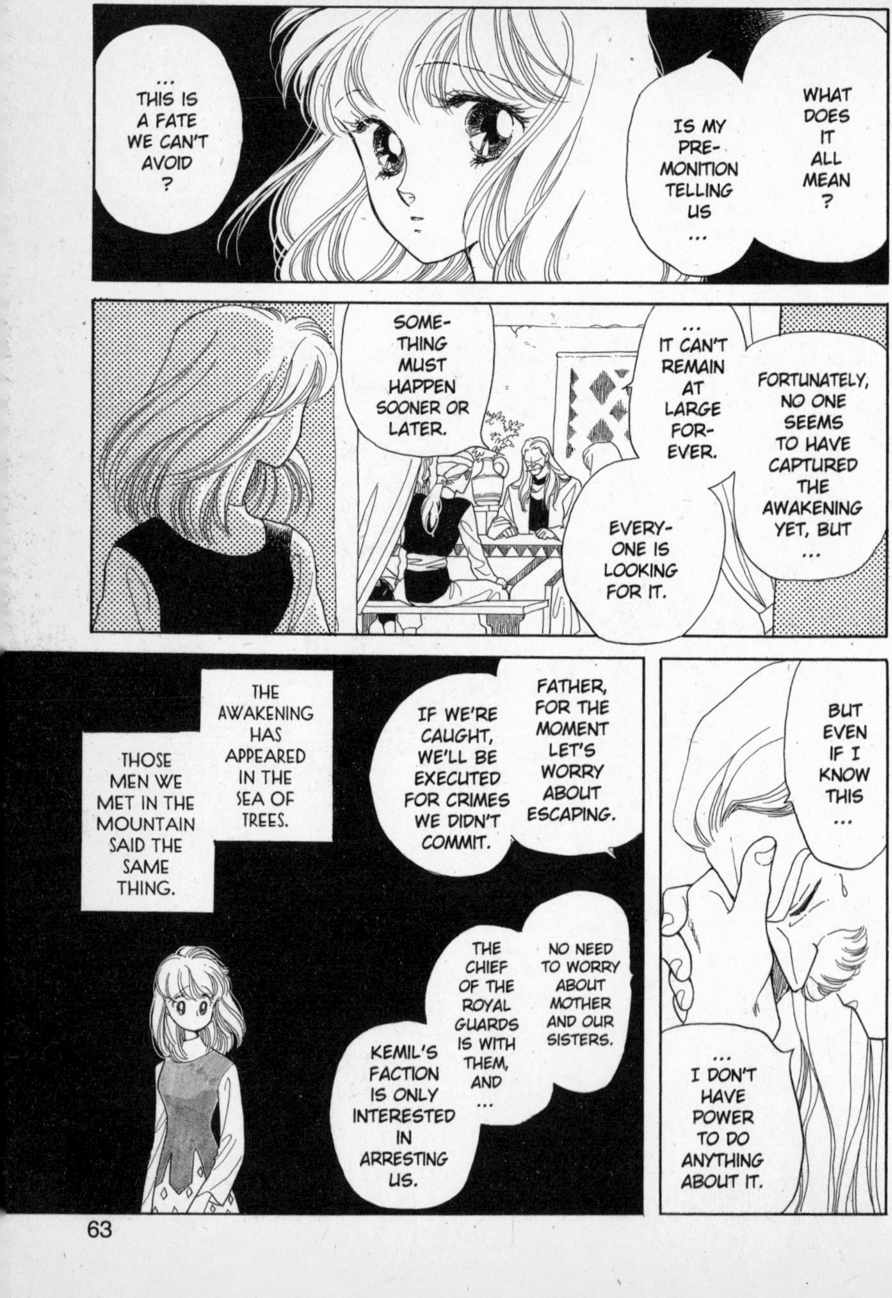
WHAT DOES IT ALL MEAN?
IS MY PRE-MONITION TELLING US ...
... THIS IS A FATE WE CAN'T AVOID?
FORTUNATELY, NO ONE SEEMS TO HAVE CAPTURED THE AWAKENING YET, BUT ...
... IT CAN'T REMAIN AT LARGE FOR-EVER.
EVERY-ONE IS LOOKING FOR IT.
SOME-THING MUST HAPPEN SOONER OR LATER.
BUT EVEN IF I KNOW THIS ...
... I DON'T HAVE POWER TO DO ANYTHING ABOUT IT.
FATHER, FOR THE MOMENT LET'S WORRY ABOUT ESCAPING.
IF WE'RE CAUGHT, WE'LL BE EXECUTED FOR CRIMES WE DIDN'T COMMIT.
THE AWAKENING HAS APPEARED IN THE SEA OF TREES.
THOSE MEN WE MET IN THE MOUNTAIN SAID THE SAME THING.
NO NEED TO WORRY ABOUT MOTHER AND OUR SISTERS.
THE CHIEF OF THE ROYAL GUARDS IS WITH THEM, AND ...
KEMIL'S FACTION IS ONLY INTERESTED IN ARRESTING US.

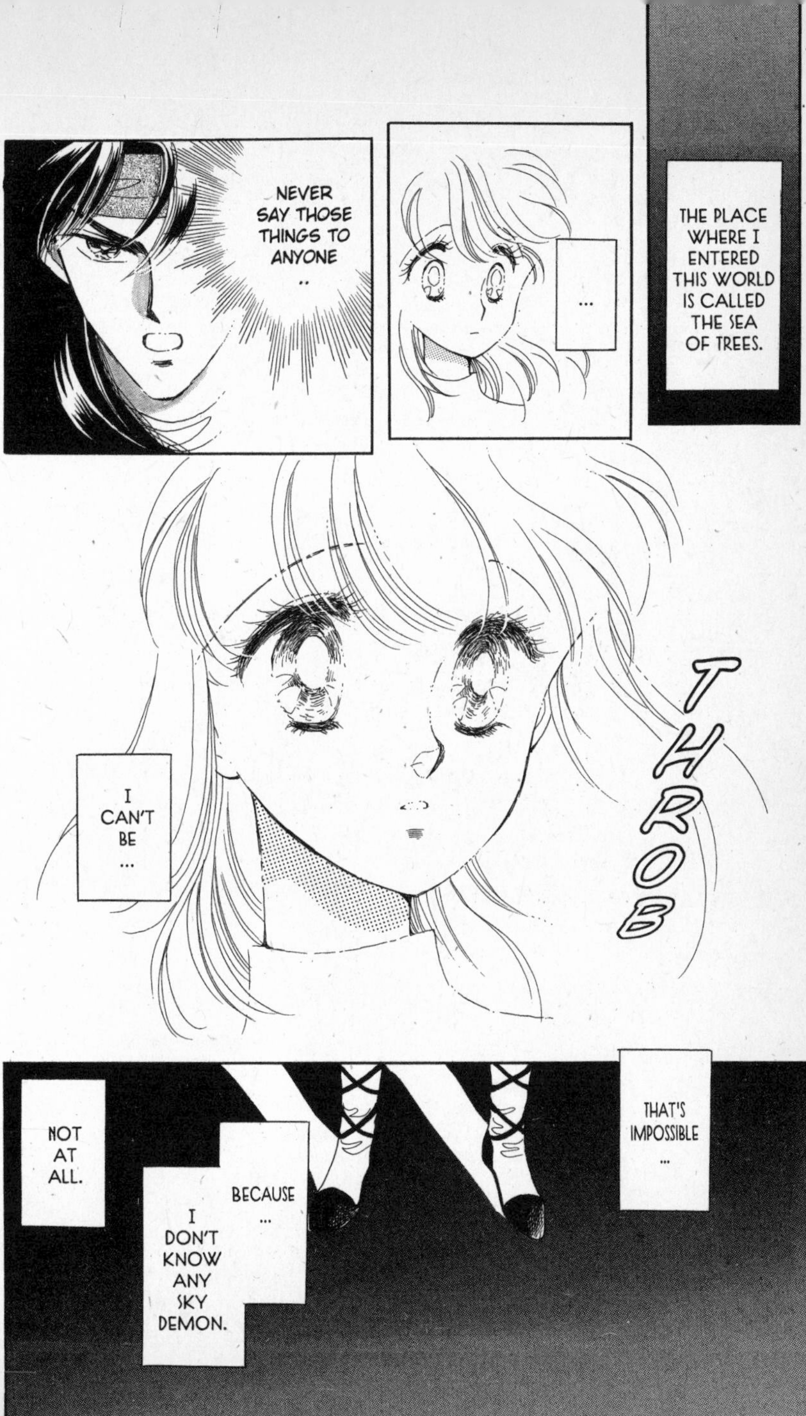
THE PLACE WHERE I ENTERED THIS WORLD IS CALLED THE SEA OF TREES.
...
NEVER SAY THOSE THINGS TO ANYONE ..
THROB
I CAN'T BE ...
THAT'S IMPOSSIBLE ...
BECAUSE ...
I DON'T KNOW ANY SKY DEMON.
NOT AT ALL.

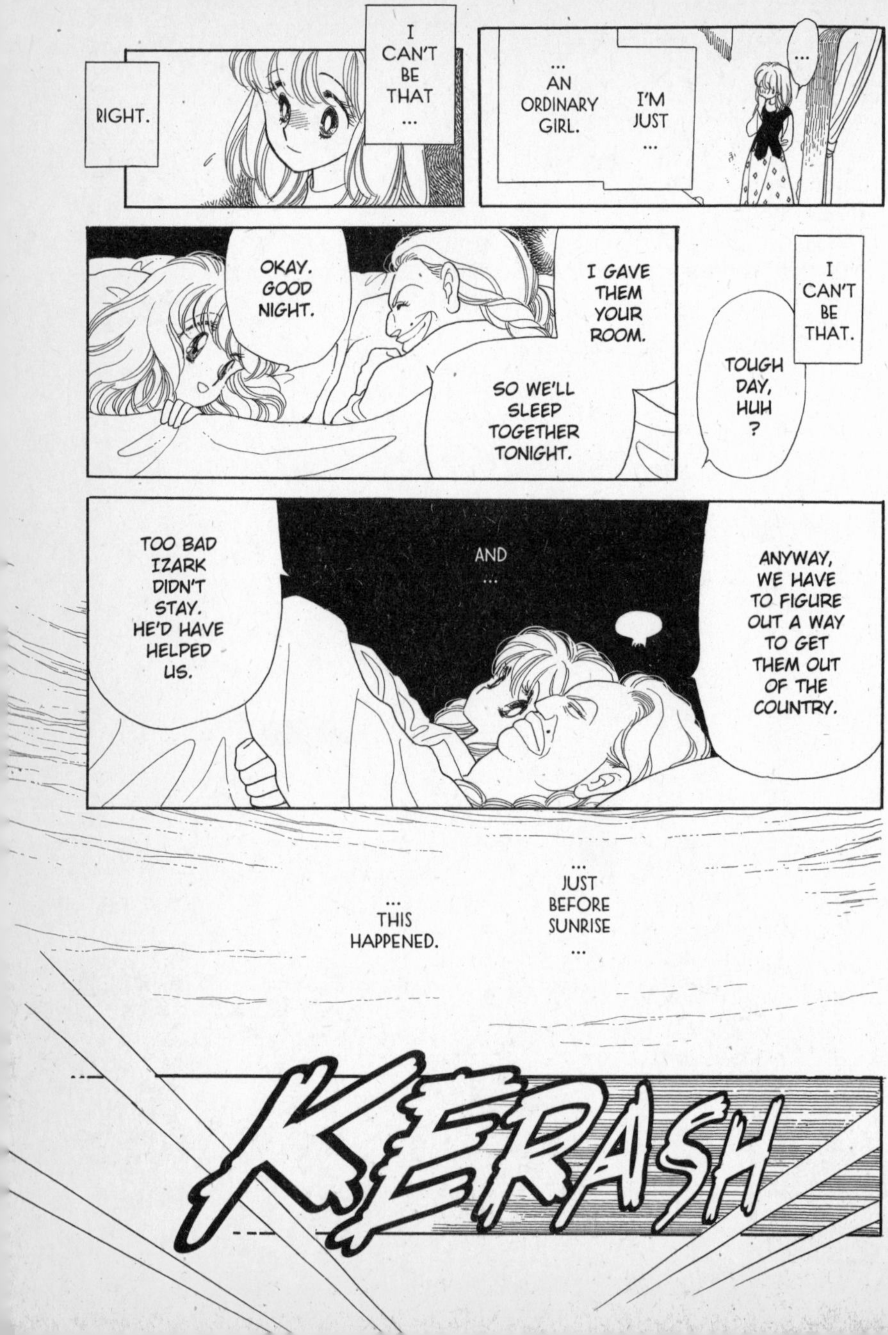
...
I'M JUST ...
... AN ORDINARY GIRL.
I CAN'T BE THAT ...
RIGHT.
I CAN'T BE THAT.
TOUGH DAY, HUH?
I GAVE THEM YOUR ROOM.
SO WE'LL SLEEP TOGETHER TONIGHT.
OKAY. GOOD NIGHT.
ANYWAY, WE HAVE TO FIGURE OUT A WAY TO GET THEM OUT OF THE COUNTRY.
AND ...
TOO BAD IZARK DIDN'T STAY. HE'D HAVE HELPED US.
... JUST BEFORE SUNRISE ...
... THIS HAPPENED.
KERASH

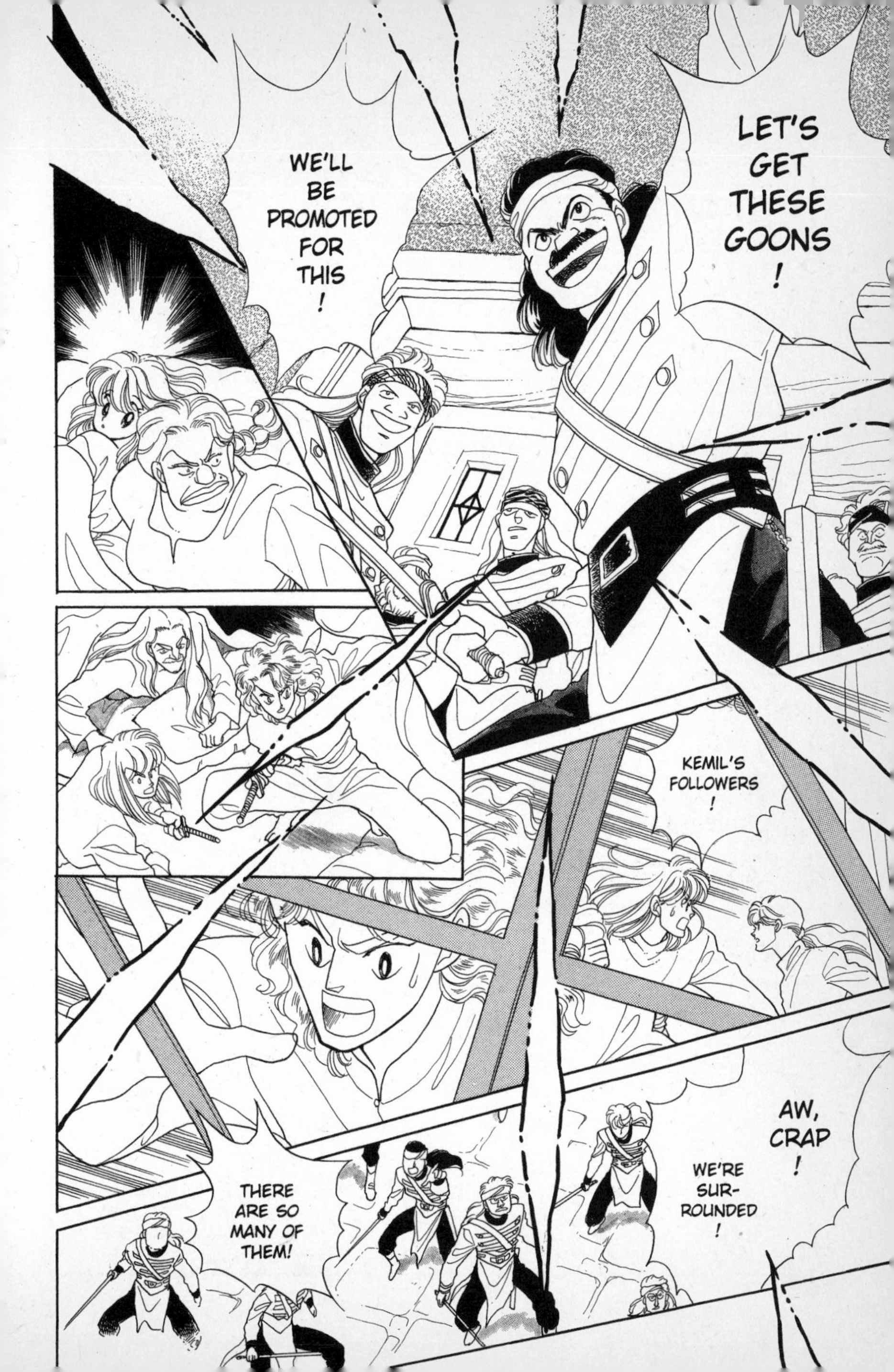
LET'S GET THESE GOONS!
WE'LL BE PROMOTED FOR THIS!
KEMIL'S FOLLOWERS!
AW, CRAP!
WE'RE SUR-ROUNDED!
THERE ARE SO MANY OF THEM!

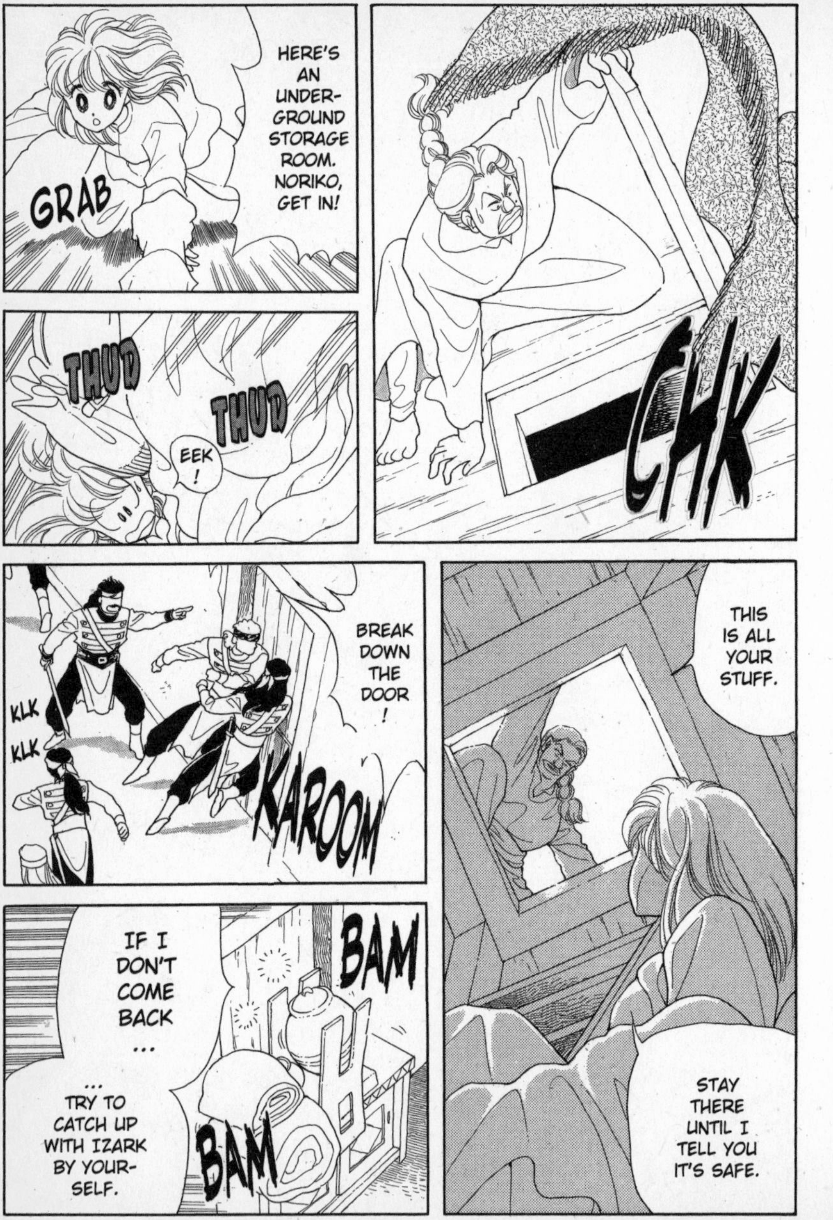
HERE'S AN UNDER-GROUND STORAGE ROOM. NORIKO, GET IN!
GRAB
THUD
THUD
EEK!
CHK
BREAK DOWN THE DOOR!
KLK
KLK
KAROOM
IF I DON'T COME BACK ...
... TRY TO CATCH UP WITH IZARK BY YOUR-SELF.
BAM
BAM
THIS IS ALL YOUR STUFF.
STAY THERE UNTIL I TELL YOU IT'S SAFE.

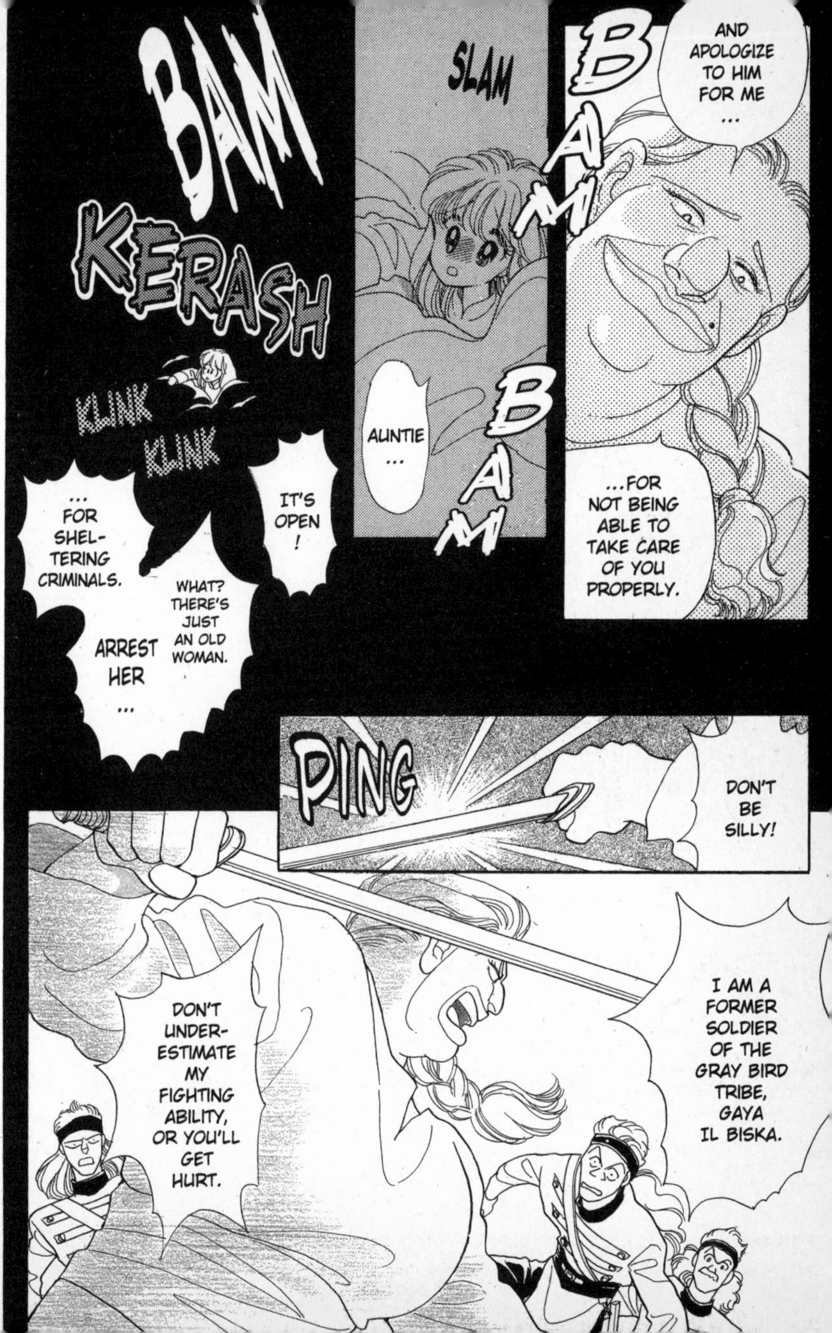
AND APOLOGIZE TO HIM FOR ME ...
BAM
...FOR NOT BEING ABLE TO TAKE CARE OF YOU PROPERLY.
SLAM
AUNTIE ...
BAM
BAM
KERASH
KLINK
KLINK
IT'S OPEN !
... FOR SHEL-TERING CRIMINALS.
WHAT? THERE'S JUST AN OLD WOMAN.
ARREST HER ...
PING
DON'T BE SILLY!
I AM A FORMER SOLDIER OF THE GRAY BIRD TRIBE, GAYA IL BISKA.
DON'T UNDER-ESTIMATE MY FIGHTING ABILITY, OR YOU'LL GET HURT.

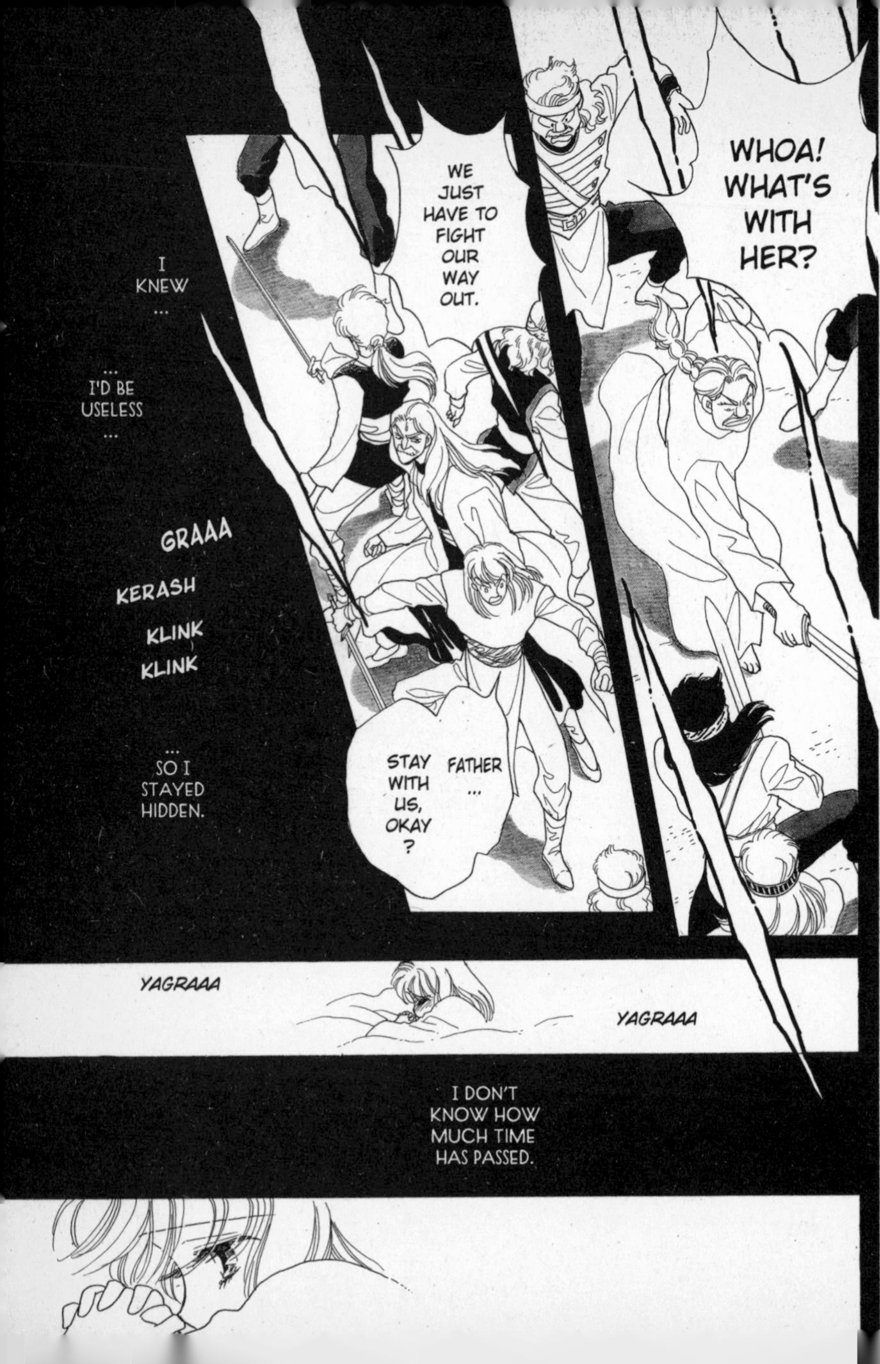
WHOA! WHAT'S WITH HER?
WE JUST HAVE TO FIGHT OUR WAY OUT.
FATHER...
STAY WITH US, OKAY?
I KNEW...
...I'D BE USELESS...
GRAAA
KERASH
KLINK
KLINK
...SO I STAYED HIDDEN.
YAGRAAA
YAGRAAA
I DON'T KNOW HOW MUCH TIME HAS PASSED.

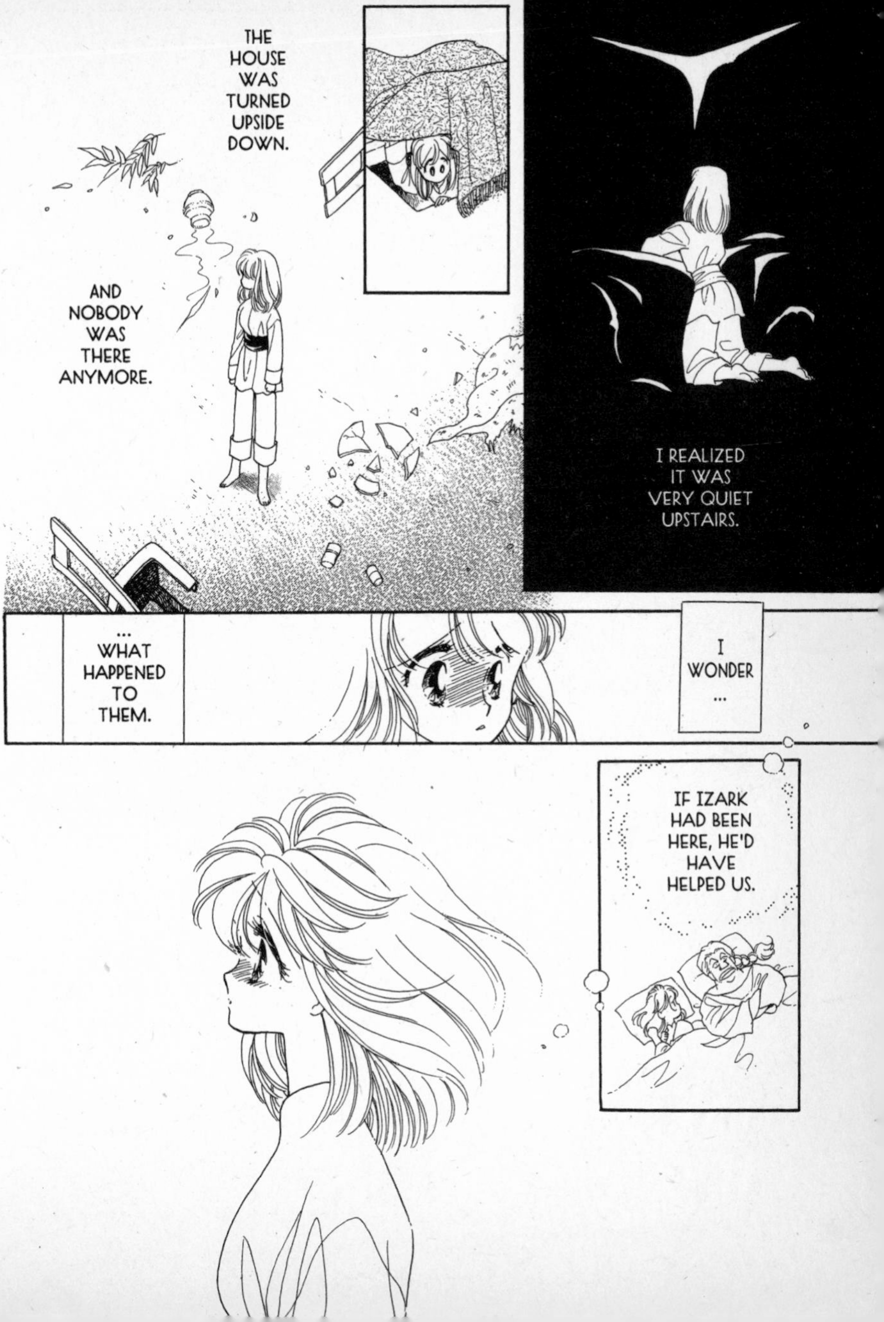
I REALIZED IT WAS VERY QUIET UPSTAIRS.
THE HOUSE WAS TURNED UPSIDE DOWN.
AND NOBODY WAS THERE ANYMORE.
I WONDER ...
... WHAT HAPPENED TO THEM.
IF IZARK HAD BEEN HERE, HE'D HAVE HELPED US.

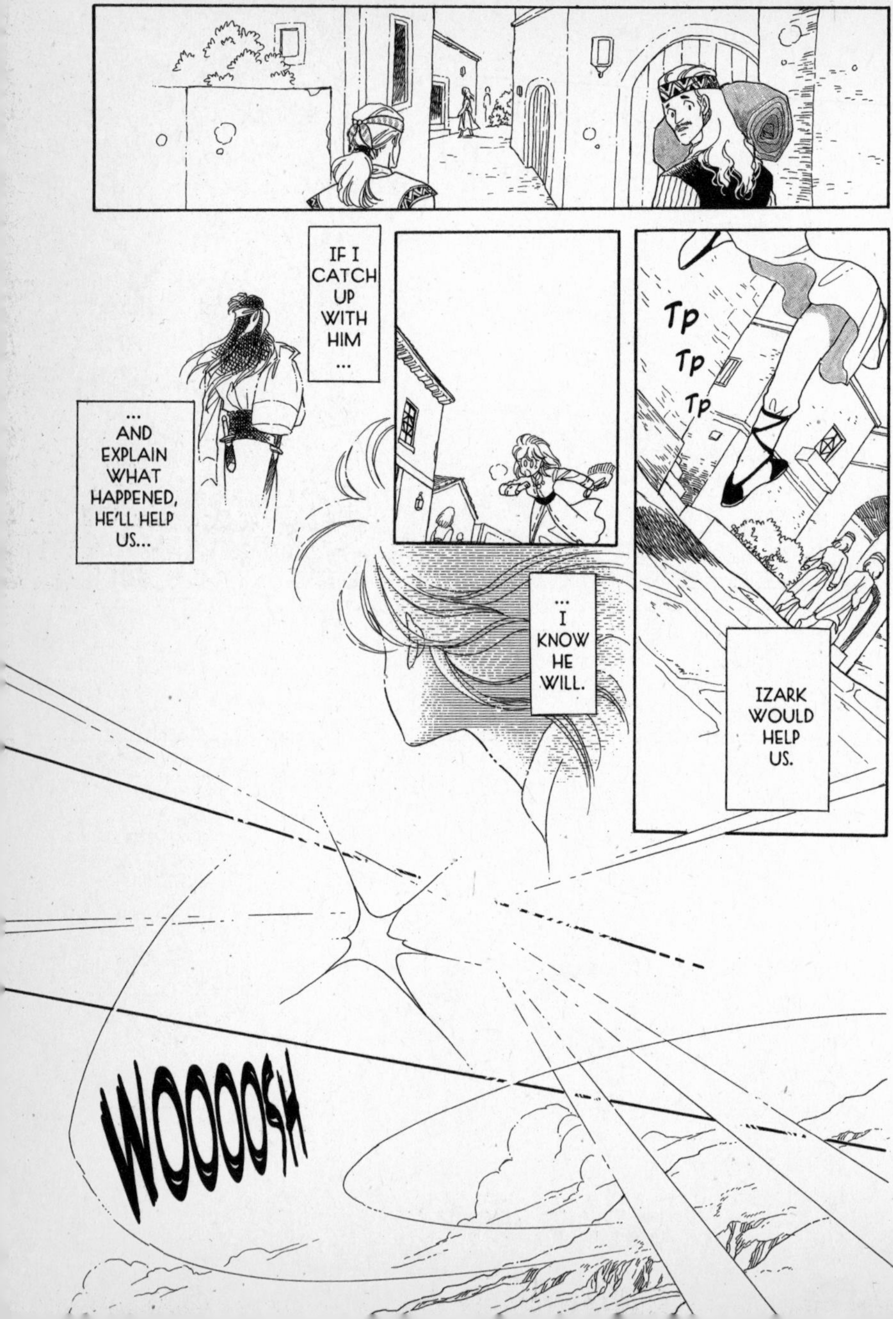
Tp
Tp
Tp
IZARK WOULD HELP US.
IF I CATCH UP WITH HIM ...
... AND EXPLAIN WHAT HAPPENED, HE'LL HELP US...
... I KNOW HE WILL.
WOOOSH

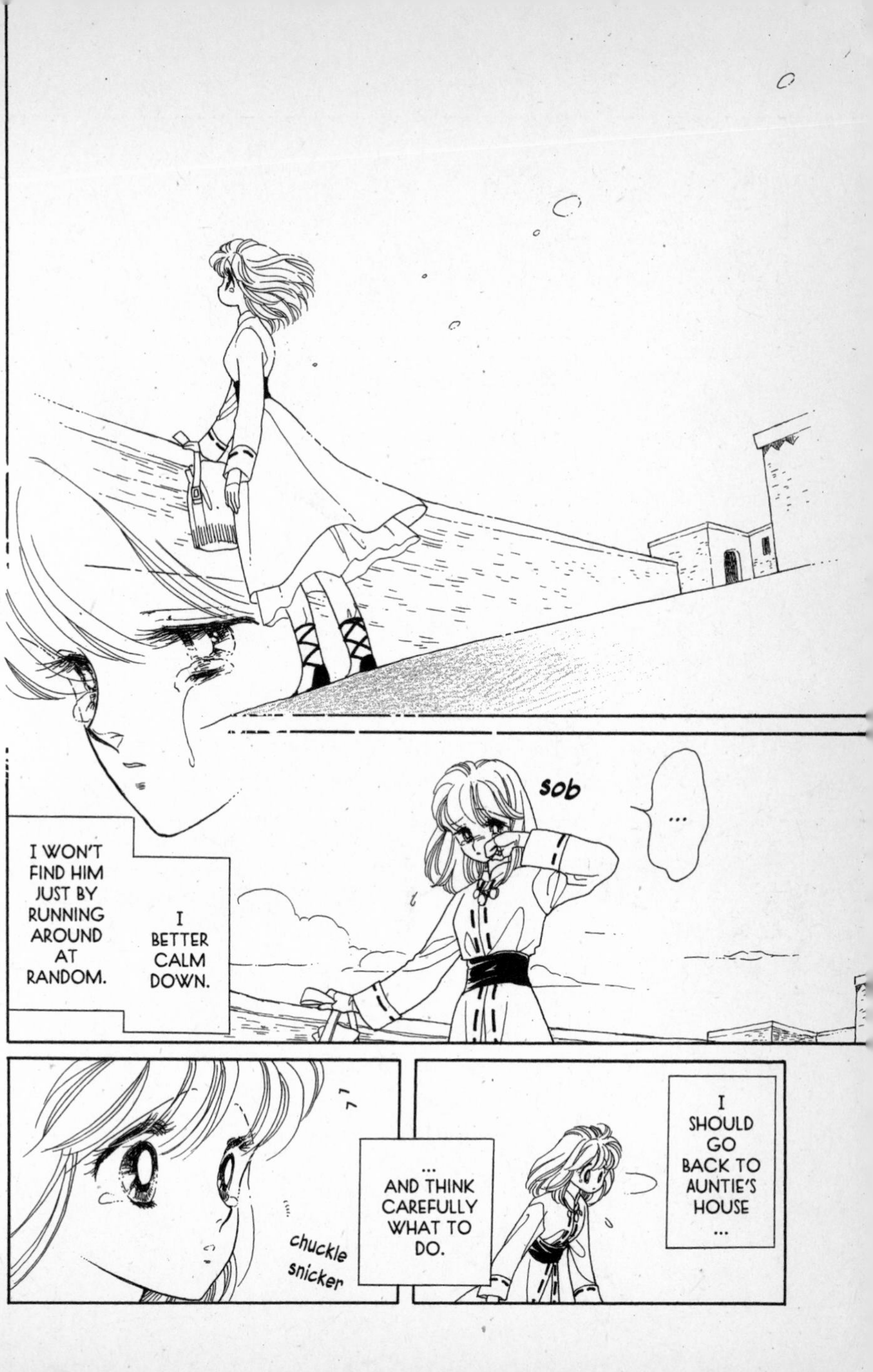

...
sob
I BETTER CALM DOWN.
I WON'T FIND HIM JUST BY RUNNING AROUND AT RANDOM.
I SHOULD GO BACK TO AUNTIE'S HOUSE ...
... AND THINK CAREFULLY WHAT TO DO.
chuckle snicker

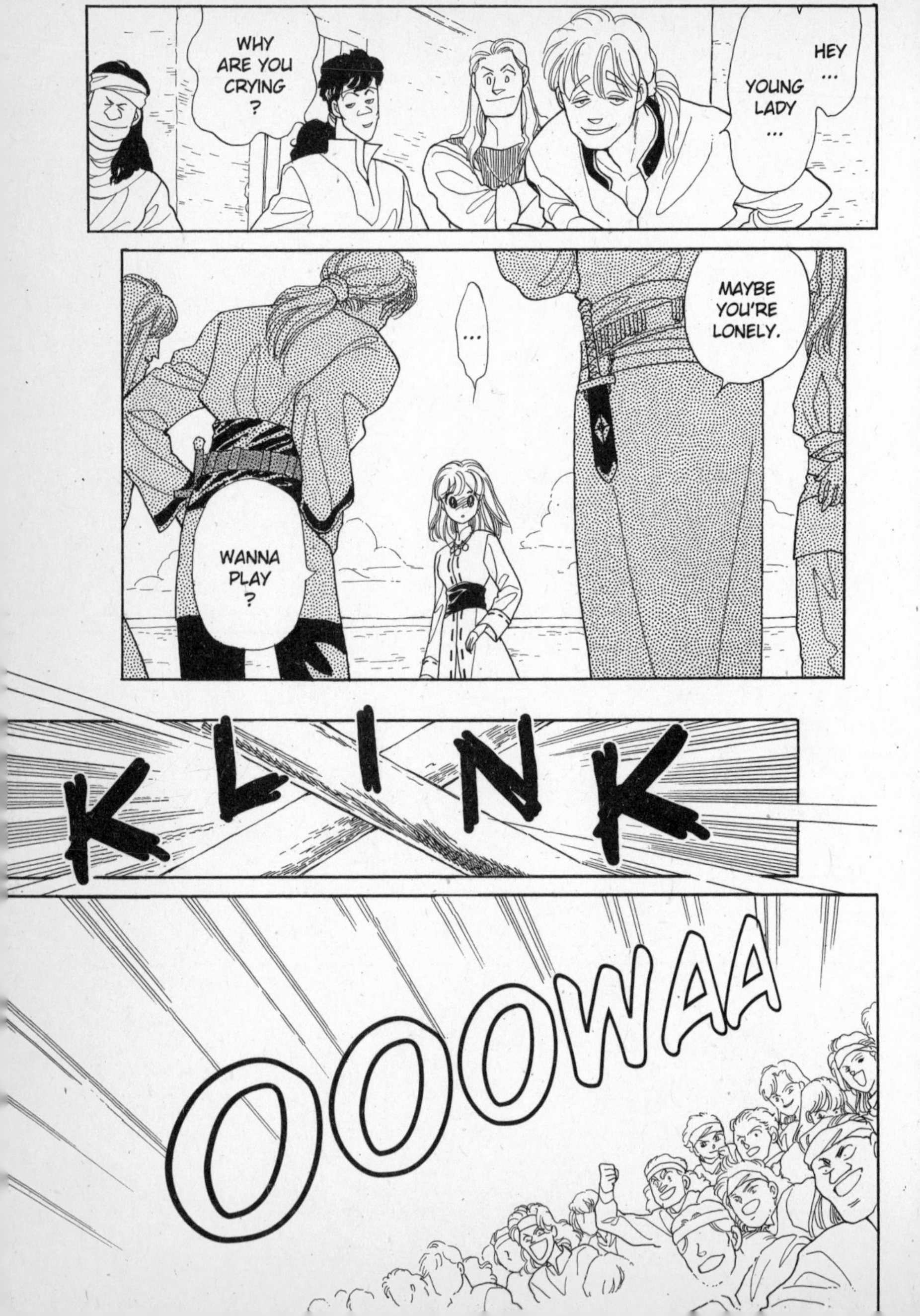
HEY ... YOUNG LADY ...
WHY ARE YOU CRYING ?
MAYBE YOU'RE LONELY.
...
WANNA PLAY ?
KLINK
OOOWAA

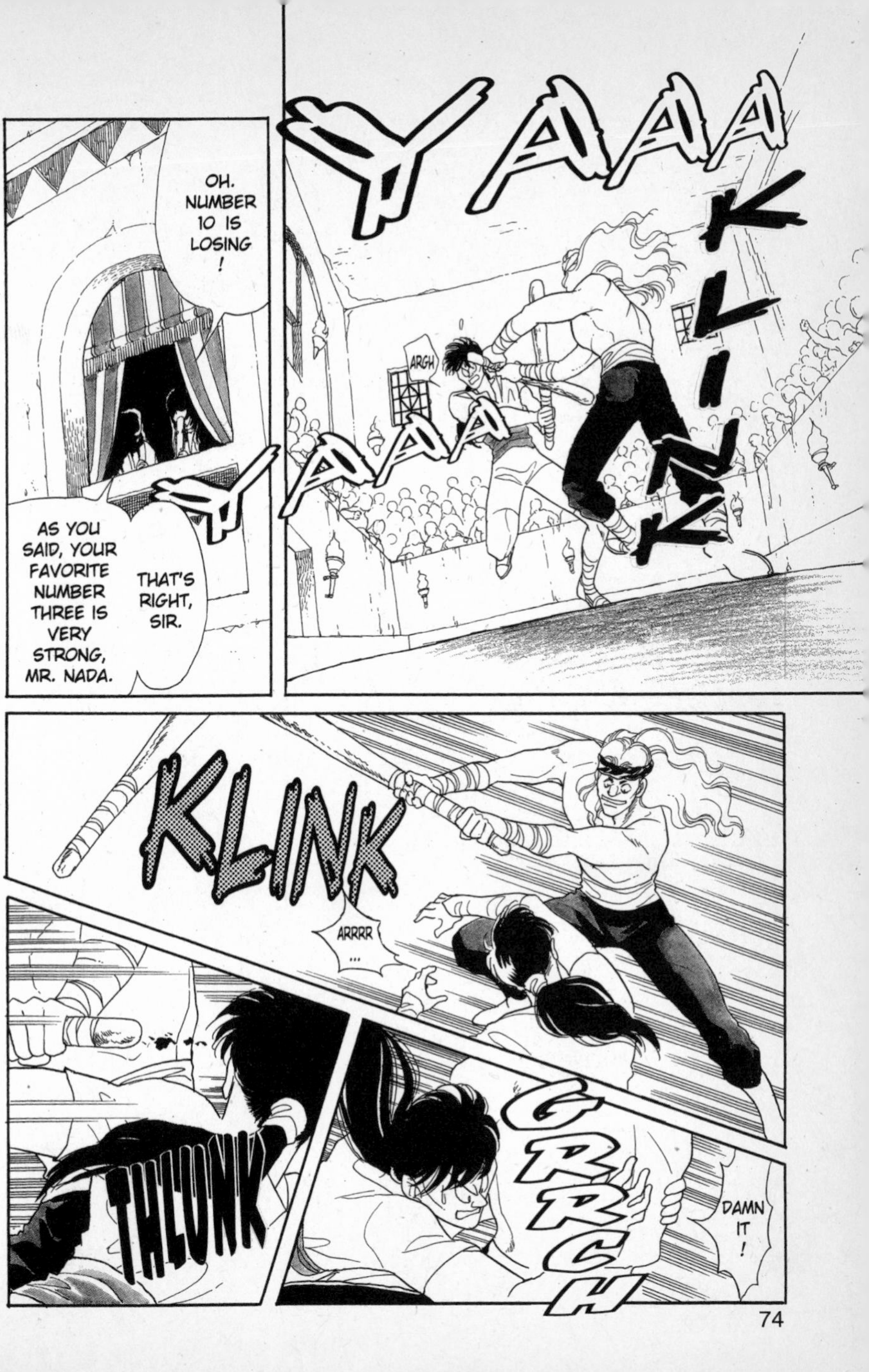
YAAAA
ARGH
YAAAA
KLINK
OH. NUMBER 10 IS LOSING!
AS YOU SAID, YOUR FAVORITE NUMBER THREE IS VERY STRONG, MR. NADA.
THAT'S RIGHT, SIR.
KLINK
ARRRR...
GRRCH
DAMN IT!
THLONK

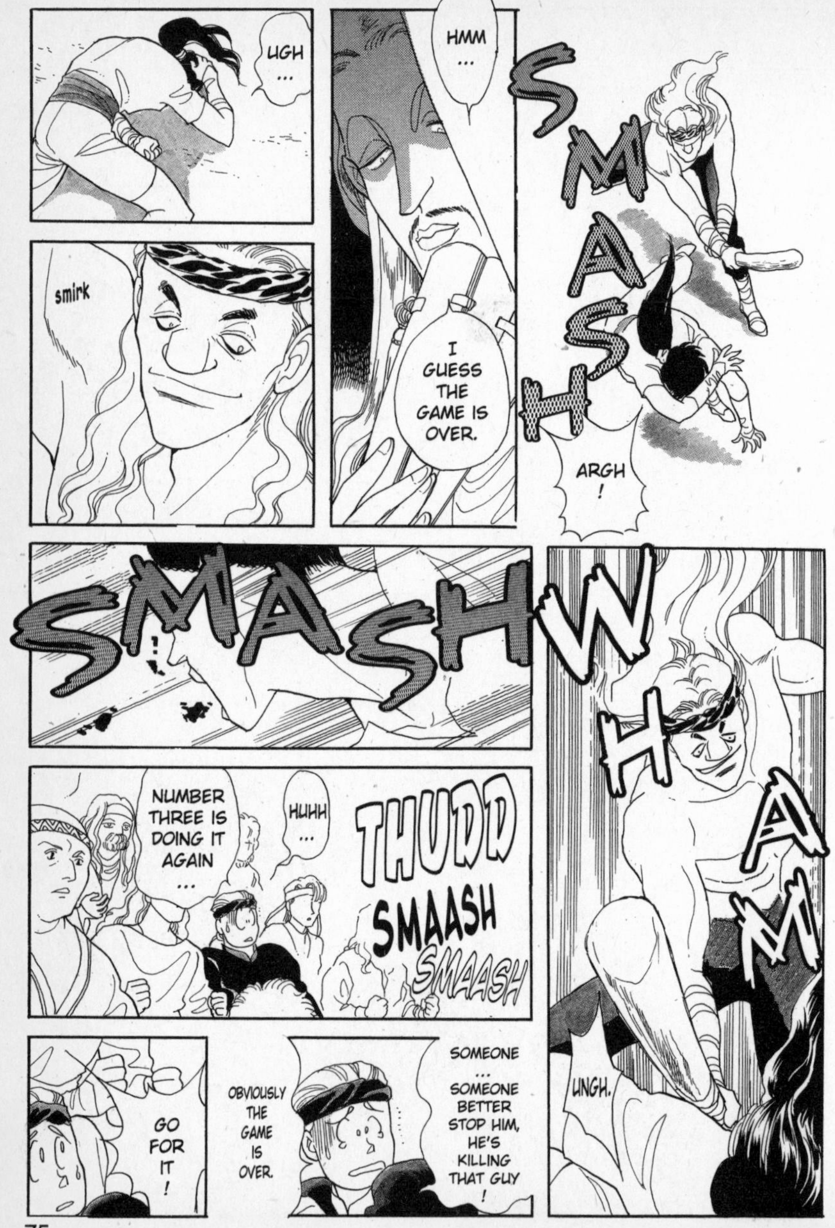
SMASH
ARGH!
HMM...
I GUESS THE GAME IS OVER.
UGH...
smirk
WHAM
UNGH.
SMASH
HUHH...
NUMBER THREE IS DOING IT AGAIN...
THUDD
SMAASH
SMAASH
SOMEONE... SOMEONE BETTER STOP HIM, HE'S KILLING THAT GUY!
OBVIOUSLY THE GAME IS OVER.
GO FOR IT!

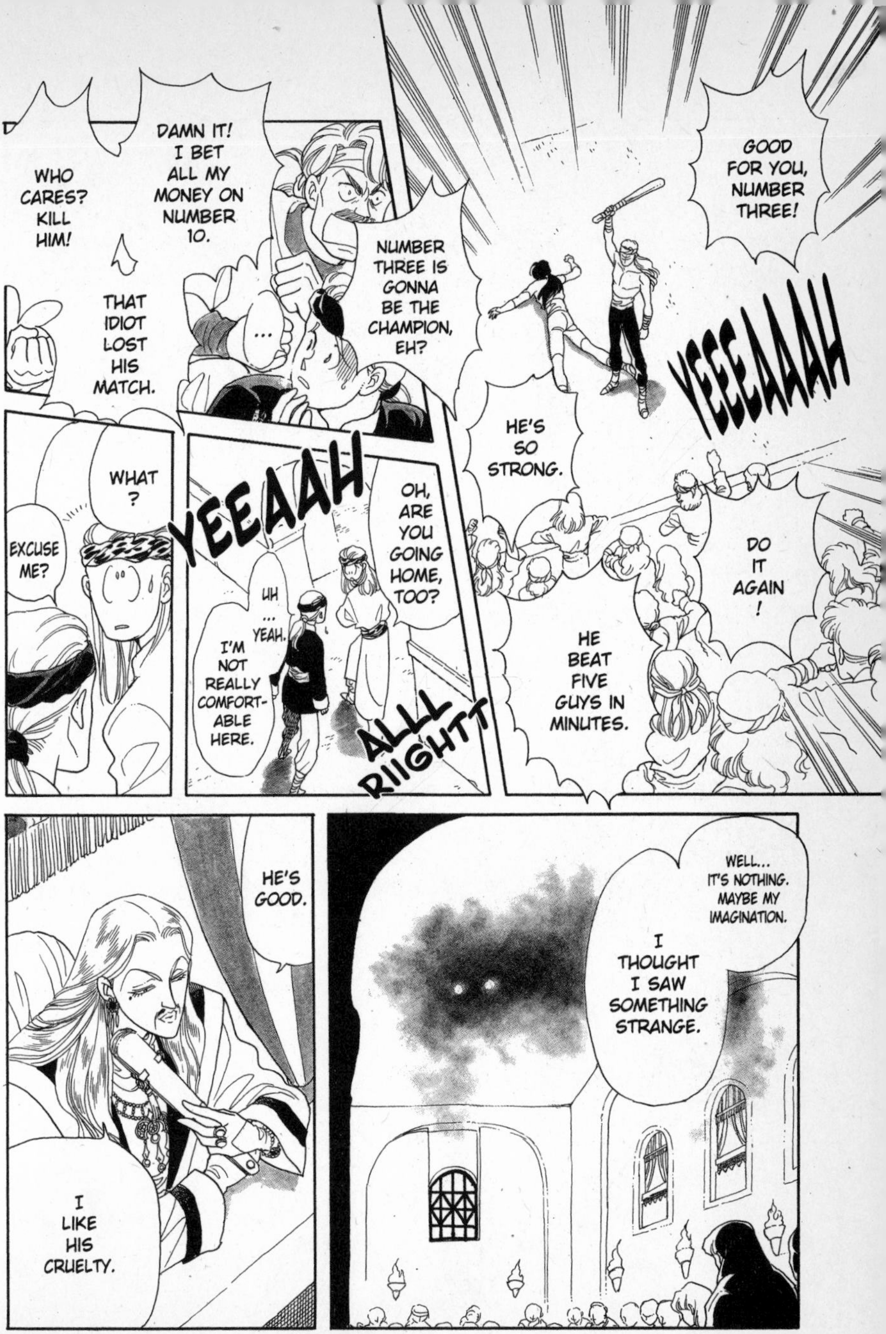
GOOD FOR YOU, NUMBER THREE!
YEEEAAAH
NUMBER THREE IS GONNA BE THE CHAMPION, EH?
HE'S SO STRONG.
DO IT AGAIN!
HE BEAT FIVE GUYS IN MINUTES.
DAMN IT! I BET ALL MY MONEY ON NUMBER 10.
WHO CARES? KILL HIM!
...
THAT IDIOT LOST HIS MATCH.
OH, ARE YOU GOING HOME, TOO?
YEEAAH
UH... YEAH.
I'M NOT REALLY COMFORT-ABLE HERE.
ALLL RIIGHTT
WHAT?
EXCUSE ME?
WELL... IT'S NOTHING. MAYBE MY IMAGINATION.
I THOUGHT I SAW SOMETHING STRANGE.
HE'S GOOD.
I LIKE HIS CRUELTY.

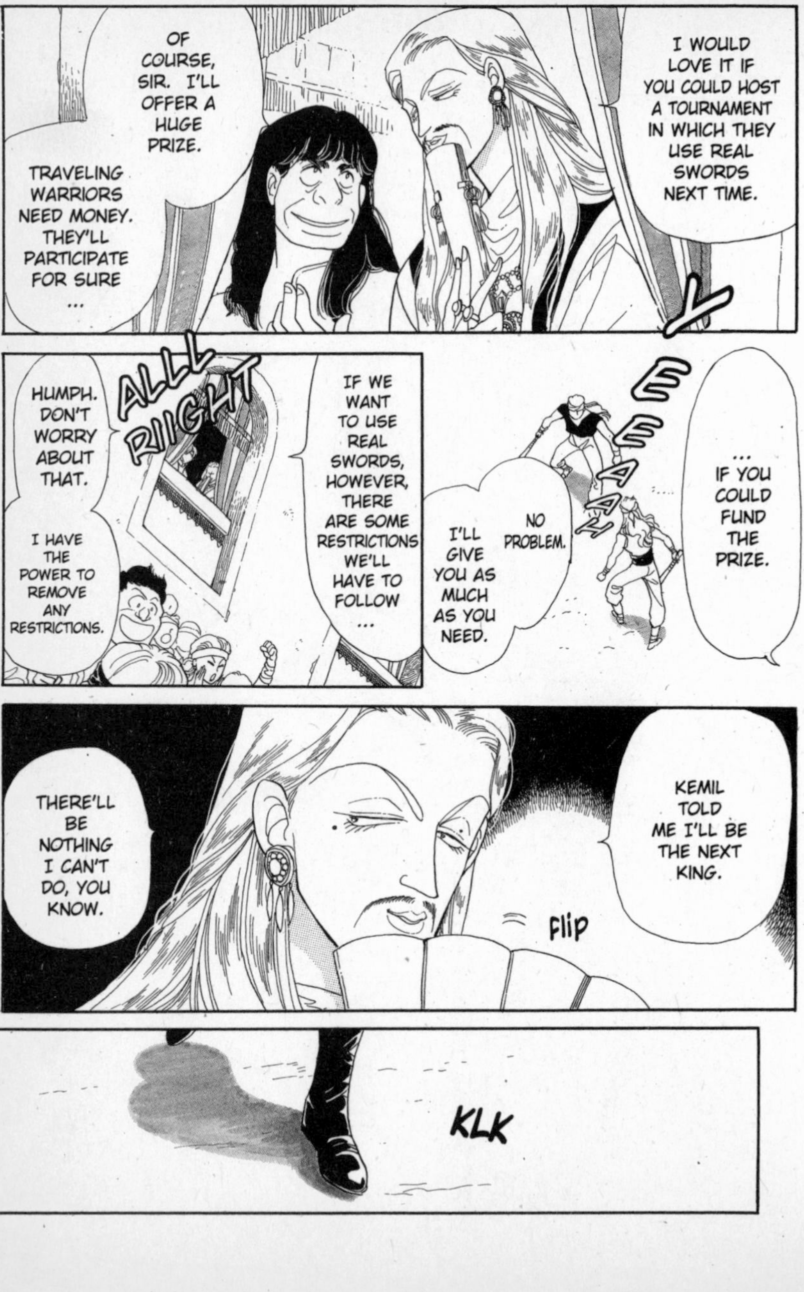
I WOULD LOVE IT IF YOU COULD HOST A TOURNAMENT IN WHICH THEY USE REAL SWORDS NEXT TIME.
OF COURSE, SIR. I'LL OFFER A HUGE PRIZE.
TRAVELING WARRIORS NEED MONEY. THEY'LL PARTICIPATE FOR SURE ...
YEEAAH
... IF YOU COULD FUND THE PRIZE.
NO PROBLEM.
I'LL GIVE YOU AS MUCH AS YOU NEED.
ALLL RIIGHT
IF WE WANT TO USE REAL SWORDS, HOWEVER, THERE ARE SOME RESTRICTIONS WE'LL HAVE TO FOLLOW ...
HUMPH. DON'T WORRY ABOUT THAT.
I HAVE THE POWER TO REMOVE ANY RESTRICTIONS.
KEMIL TOLD ME I'LL BE THE NEXT KING.
Flip
THERE'LL BE NOTHING I CAN'T DO, YOU KNOW.
KLK

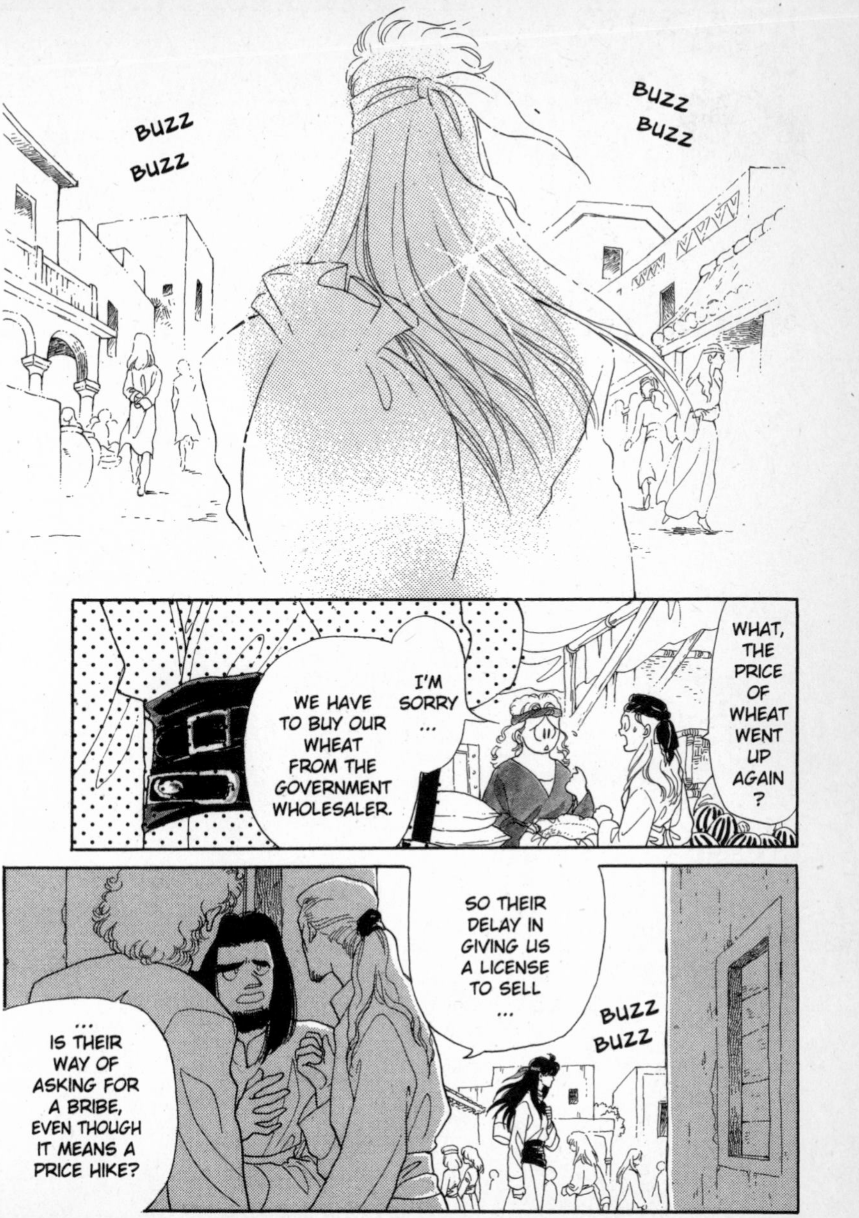
BUZZ BUZZ
BUZZ BUZZ
WHAT, THE PRICE OF WHEAT WENT UP AGAIN?
I'M SORRY...
WE HAVE TO BUY OUR WHEAT FROM THE GOVERNMENT WHOLESALER.
SO THEIR DELAY IN GIVING US A LICENSE TO SELL...
BUZZ BUZZ
...IS THEIR WAY OF ASKING FOR A BRIBE, EVEN THOUGH IT MEANS A PRICE HIKE?

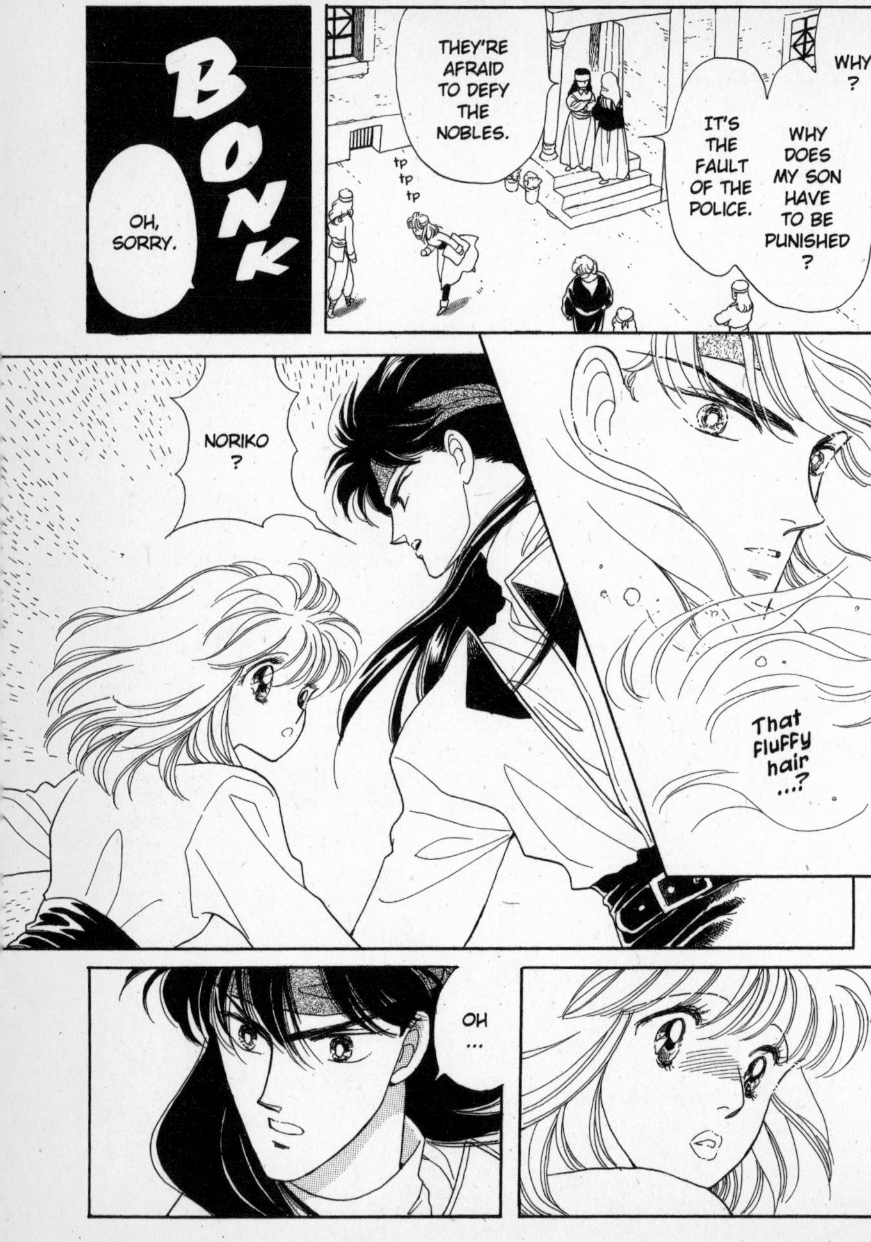
WHY?
WHY DOES MY SON HAVE TO BE PUNISHED?
IT'S THE FAULT OF THE POLICE.
THEY'RE AFRAID TO DEFY THE NOBLES.
tp tp tp
BONK
OH, SORRY.
That fluffy hair ...?
NORIKO?
OH ...

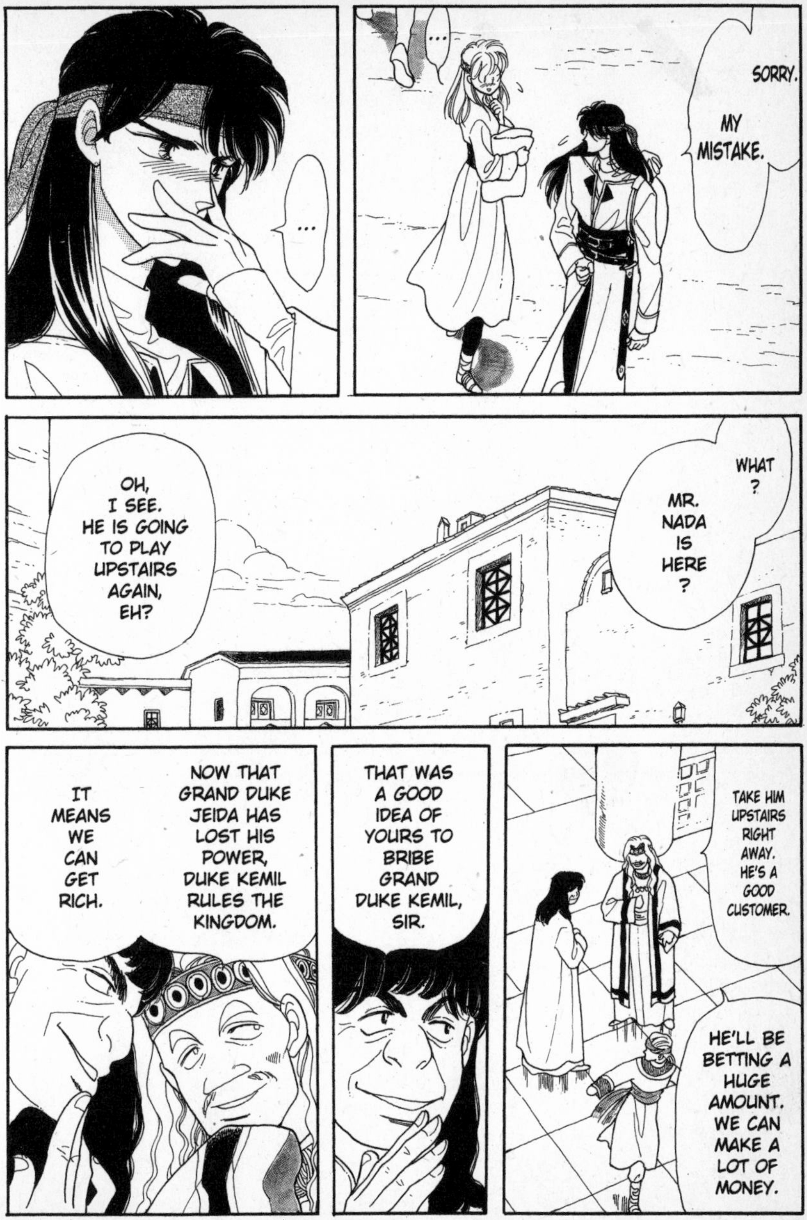
...
SORRY.
MY MISTAKE.
...
WHAT? MR. NADA IS HERE?
OH, I SEE. HE IS GOING TO PLAY UPSTAIRS AGAIN, EH?
TAKE HIM UPSTAIRS RIGHT AWAY. HE'S A GOOD CUSTOMER.
HE'LL BE BETTING A HUGE AMOUNT. WE CAN MAKE A LOT OF MONEY.
THAT WAS A GOOD IDEA OF YOURS TO BRIBE GRAND DUKE KEMIL, SIR.
NOW THAT GRAND DUKE JEIDA HAS LOST HIS POWER, DUKE KEMIL RULES THE KINGDOM.
IT MEANS WE CAN GET RICH.

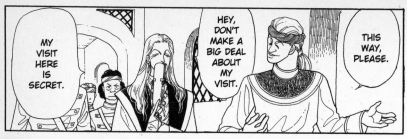

THIS WAY, PLEASE.
HEY, DON'T MAKE A BIG DEAL ABOUT MY VISIT.
MY VISIT HERE IS SECRET.
ANYWAY, OBSERVING THE COMMON PEOPLE IS ALWAYS INTERESTING.
I WISH I COULD DRINK THEIR ALCOHOL JUST ONCE.
THE FIRST FLOOR BAR IS FOR THE COMMON PEOPLE, SIR.
YOU WON'T FIND ANY LIQUOR THAT CAN SATISFY YOUR TASTE, MR. NADA.
HMM?

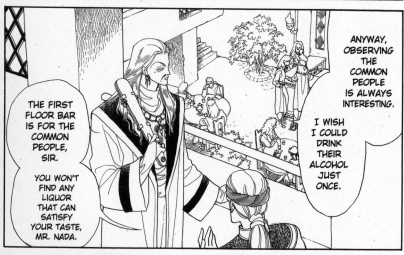

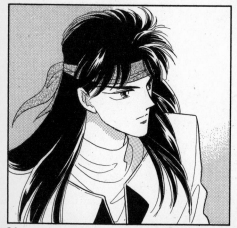

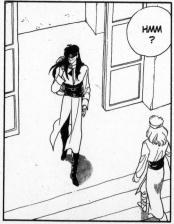

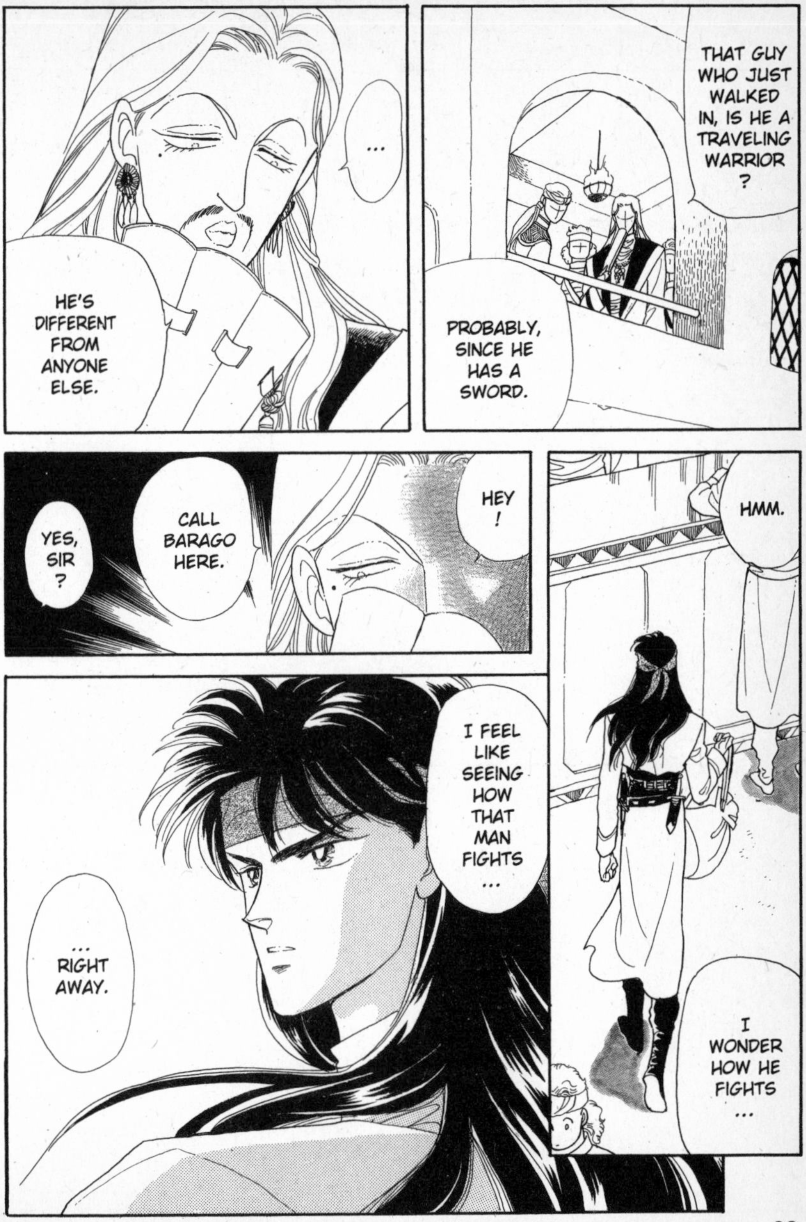
THAT GUY WHO JUST WALKED IN, IS HE A TRAVELING WARRIOR?
PROBABLY, SINCE HE HAS A SWORD.
...
HE'S DIFFERENT FROM ANYONE ELSE.
HMM.
I WONDER HOW HE FIGHTS...
HEY!
CALL BARAGO HERE.
YES, SIR?
I FEEL LIKE SEEING HOW THAT MAN FIGHTS...
...RIGHT AWAY.

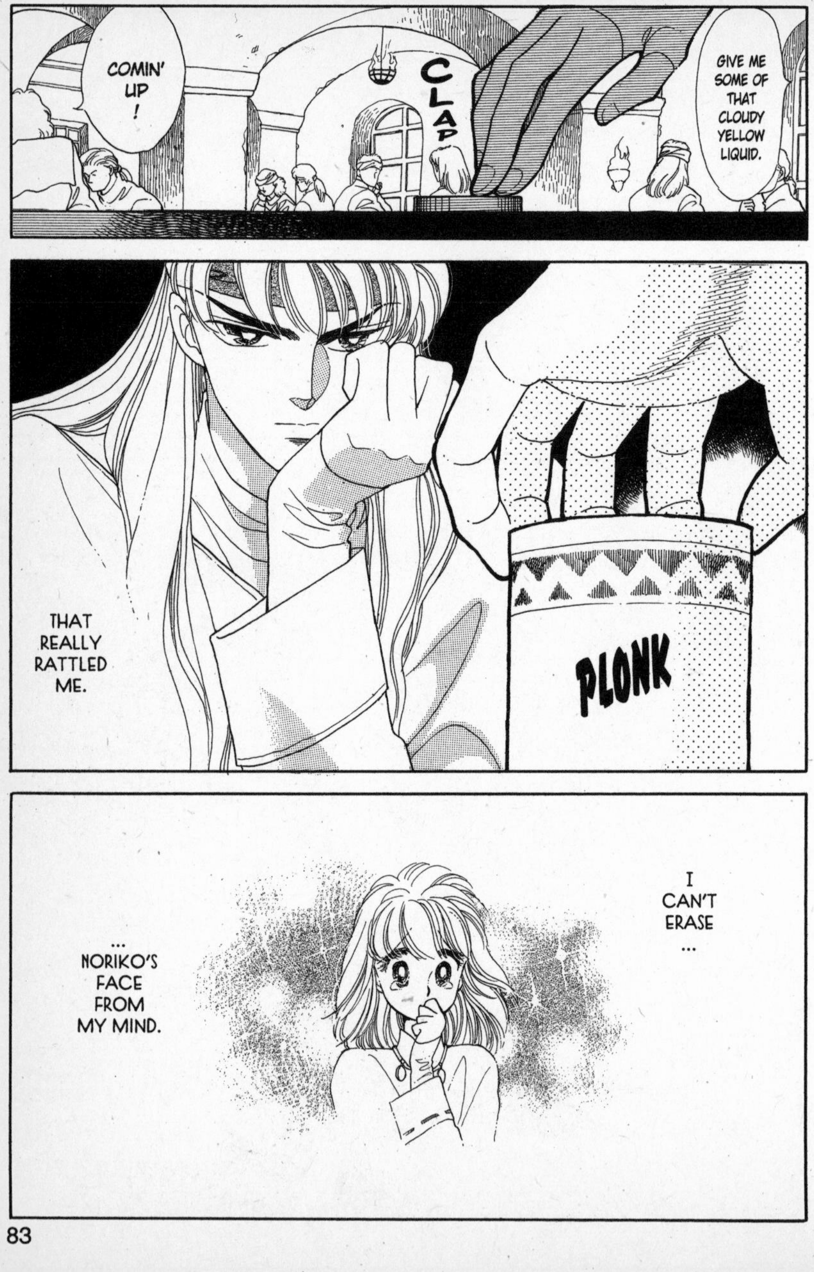
GIVE ME SOME OF THAT CLOUDY YELLOW LIQUID.
CLAP
COMIN' UP!
PLONK
THAT REALLY RATTLED ME.
I CAN'T ERASE ...
... NORIKO'S FACE FROM MY MIND.

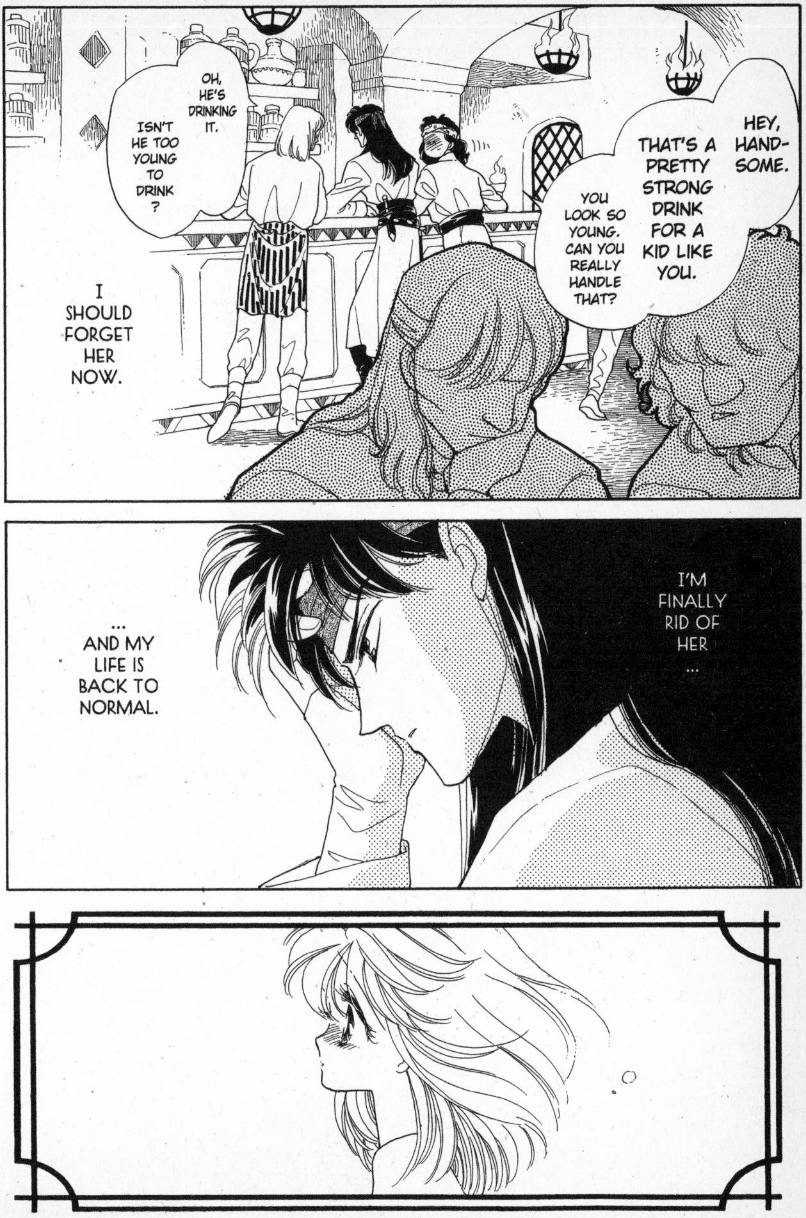
HEY, HANDSOME.
THAT'S A PRETTY STRONG DRINK FOR A KID LIKE YOU.
YOU LOOK SO YOUNG. CAN YOU REALLY HANDLE THAT?
OH, HE'S DRINKING IT.
ISN'T HE TOO YOUNG TO DRINK?
I SHOULD FORGET HER NOW.
I'M FINALLY RID OF HER ...
... AND MY LIFE IS BACK TO NORMAL.

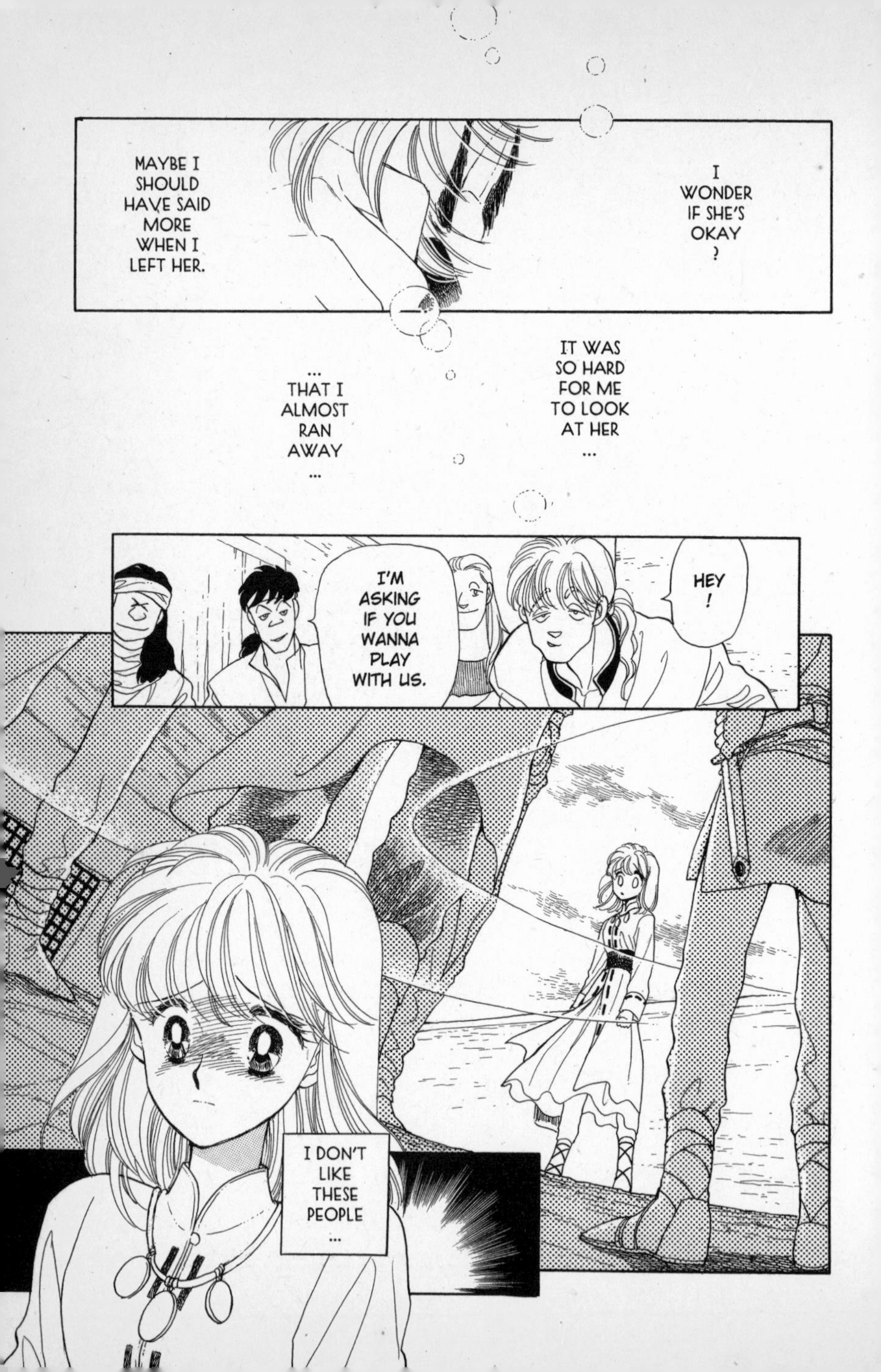
I WONDER IF SHE'S OKAY ?
MAYBE I SHOULD HAVE SAID MORE WHEN I LEFT HER.
IT WAS SO HARD FOR ME TO LOOK AT HER ...
... THAT I ALMOST RAN AWAY ...
HEY !
I'M ASKING IF YOU WANNA PLAY WITH US.
I DON'T LIKE THESE PEOPLE ...

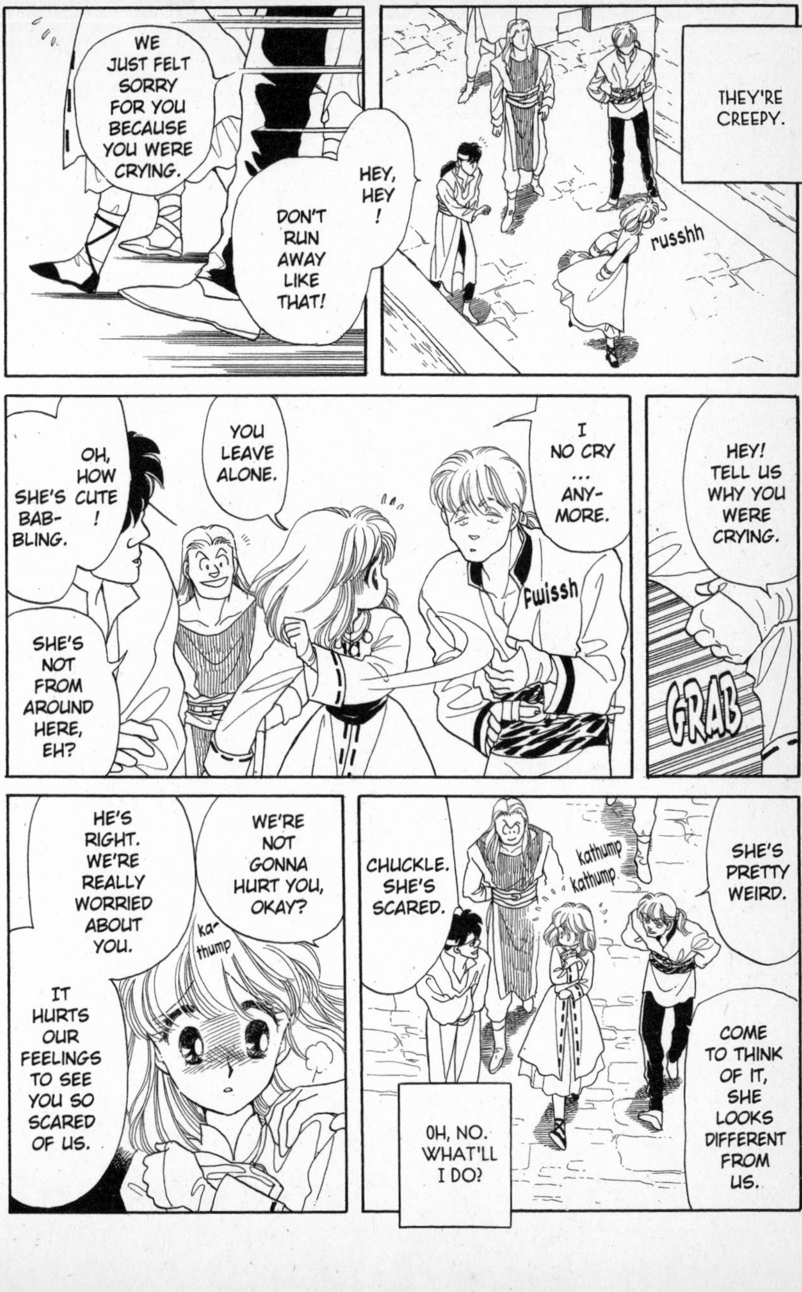
THEY'RE CREEPY.
russhh
HEY, HEY!
DON'T RUN AWAY LIKE THAT!
WE JUST FELT SORRY FOR YOU BECAUSE YOU WERE CRYING.
HEY! TELL US WHY YOU WERE CRYING.
GRAB
I NO CRY ... ANY-MORE.
Fwissh
YOU LEAVE ALONE.
OH, HOW CUTE!
SHE'S BAB-BLING.
SHE'S NOT FROM AROUND HERE, EH?
SHE'S PRETTY WEIRD.
kathump kathump
CHUCKLE. SHE'S SCARED.
COME TO THINK OF IT, SHE LOOKS DIFFERENT FROM US.
OH, NO. WHAT'LL I DO?
WE'RE NOT GONNA HURT YOU, OKAY?
HE'S RIGHT. WE'RE REALLY WORRIED ABOUT YOU.
ka-thump
IT HURTS OUR FEELINGS TO SEE YOU SO SCARED OF US.

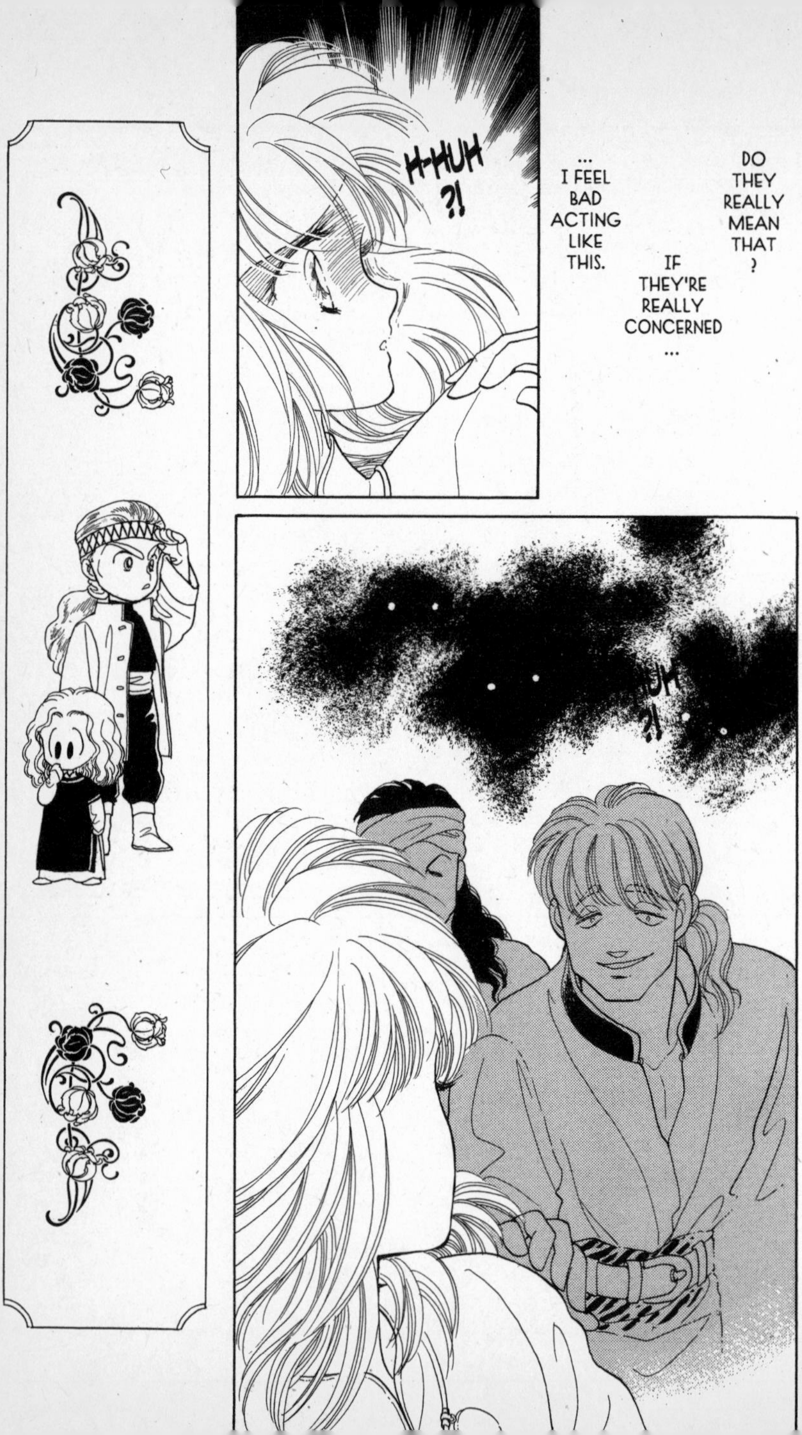
DO THEY REALLY MEAN THAT?
IF THEY'RE REALLY CONCERNED...
...I FEEL BAD ACTING LIKE THIS.
H-HUH ?!
HUH ?!

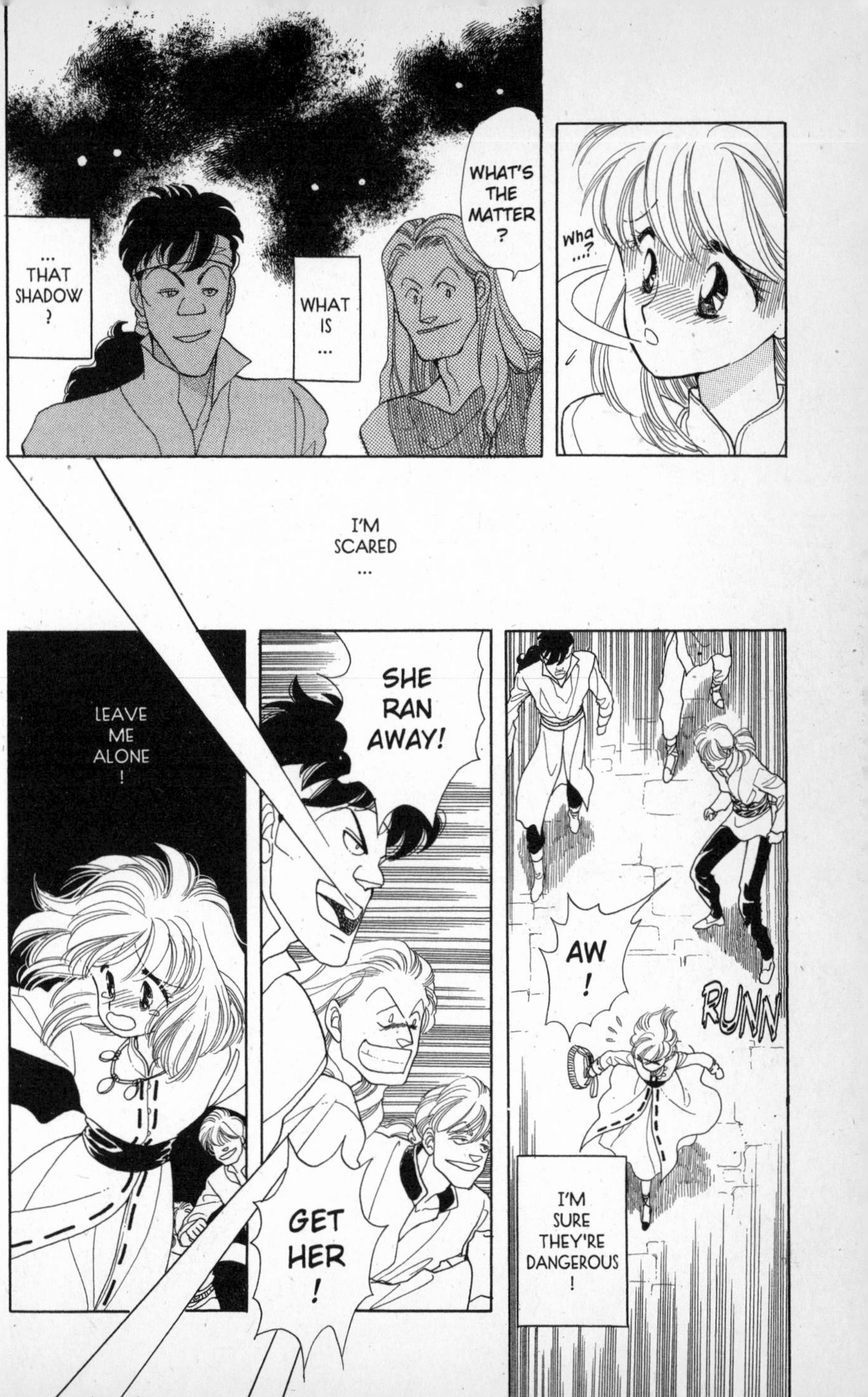
Wha ...?
WHAT'S THE MATTER?
WHAT IS ...
... THAT SHADOW?
I'M SCARED ...
AW!
RUNN
I'M SURE THEY'RE DANGEROUS!
SHE RAN AWAY!
GET HER!
LEAVE ME ALONE!

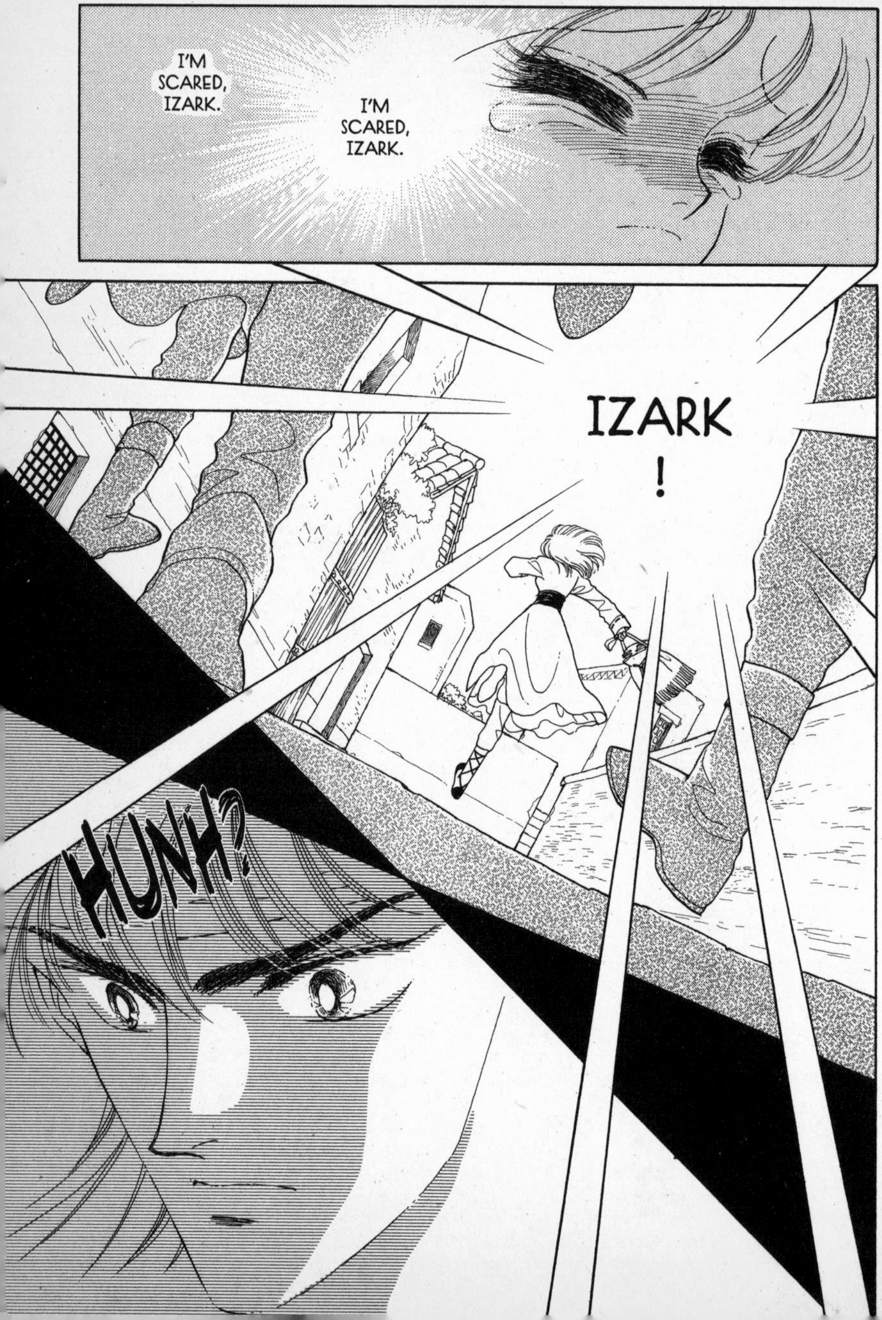

I'M SCARED, IZARK.
I'M SCARED, IZARK.
IZARK !
HUNH?

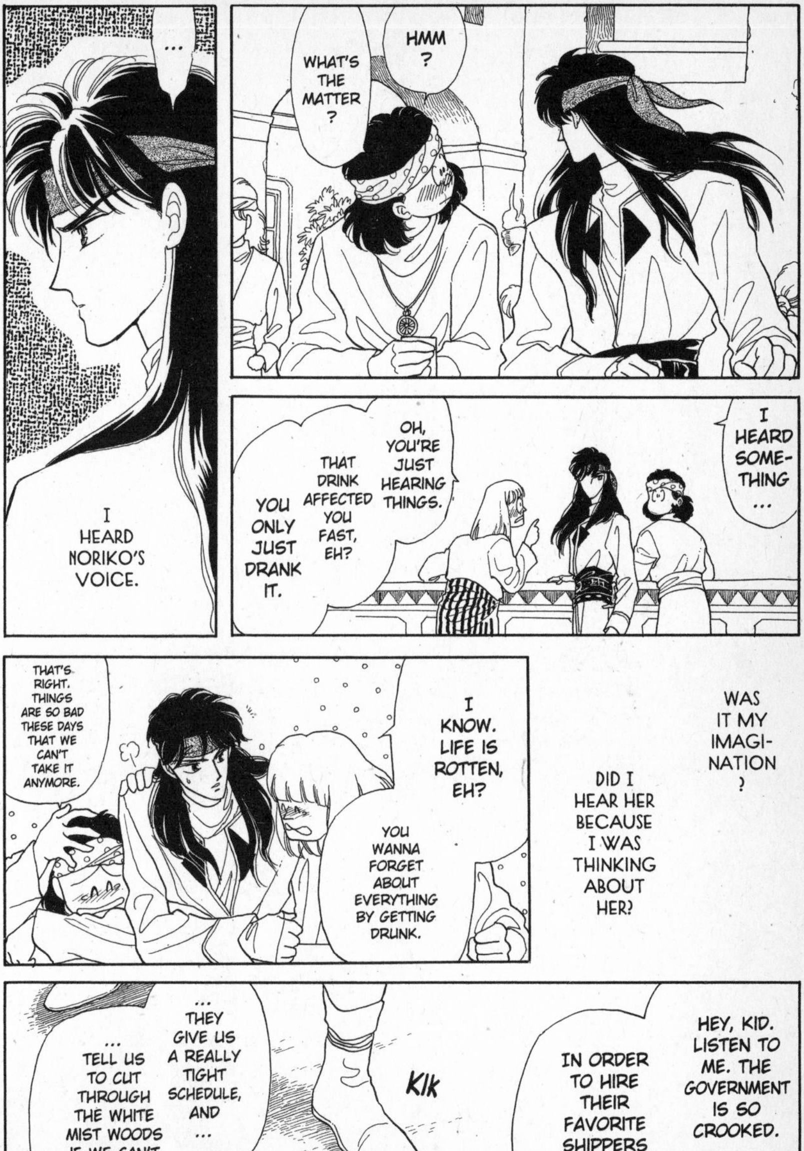
HMM ?
WHAT'S THE MATTER ?
I HEARD SOME-THING ...
OH, YOU'RE JUST HEARING THINGS.
THAT DRINK AFFECTED YOU FAST, EH?
YOU ONLY JUST DRANK IT.
...
I HEARD NORIKO'S VOICE.
WAS IT MY IMAGI-NATION ?
DID I HEAR HER BECAUSE I WAS THINKING ABOUT HER?
I KNOW. LIFE IS ROTTEN, EH?
YOU WANNA FORGET ABOUT EVERYTHING BY GETTING DRUNK.
THAT'S RIGHT. THINGS ARE SO BAD THESE DAYS THAT WE CAN'T TAKE IT ANYMORE.
HEY, KID. LISTEN TO ME. THE GOVERNMENT IS SO CROOKED.
IN ORDER TO HIRE THEIR FAVORITE SHIPPERS INSTEAD OF US...
KIK
... THEY GIVE US A REALLY TIGHT SCHEDULE, AND ...
... TELL US TO CUT THROUGH THE WHITE MIST WOODS IF WE CAN'T MAKE IT ON TIME.

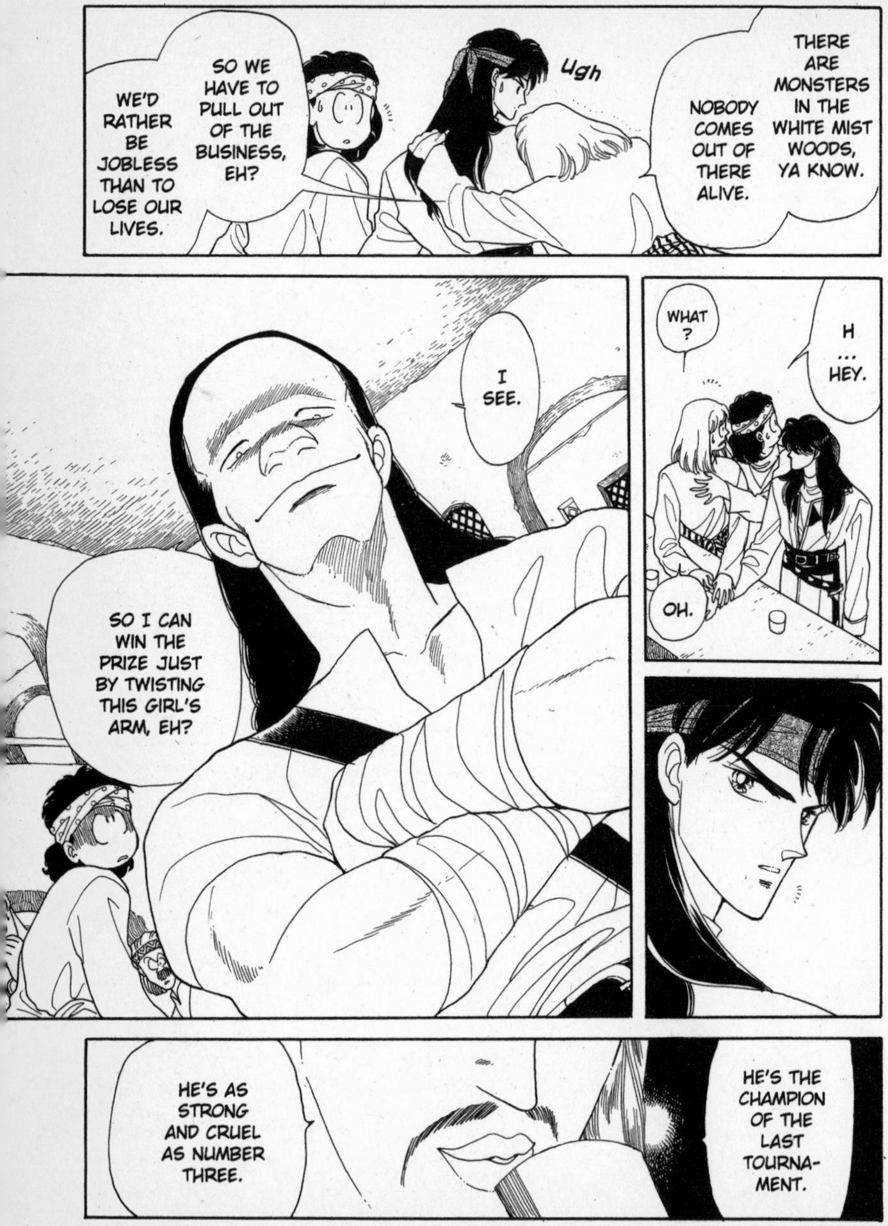
THERE ARE MONSTERS IN THE WHITE MIST WOODS, YA KNOW.
NOBODY COMES OUT OF THERE ALIVE.
Ugh
SO WE HAVE TO PULL OUT OF THE BUSINESS, EH?
WE'D RATHER BE JOBLESS THAN TO LOSE OUR LIVES.
H ... HEY.
WHAT?
OH.
I SEE.
SO I CAN WIN THE PRIZE JUST BY TWISTING THIS GIRL'S ARM, EH?
HE'S THE CHAMPION OF THE LAST TOURNAMENT.
HE'S AS STRONG AND CRUEL AS NUMBER THREE.

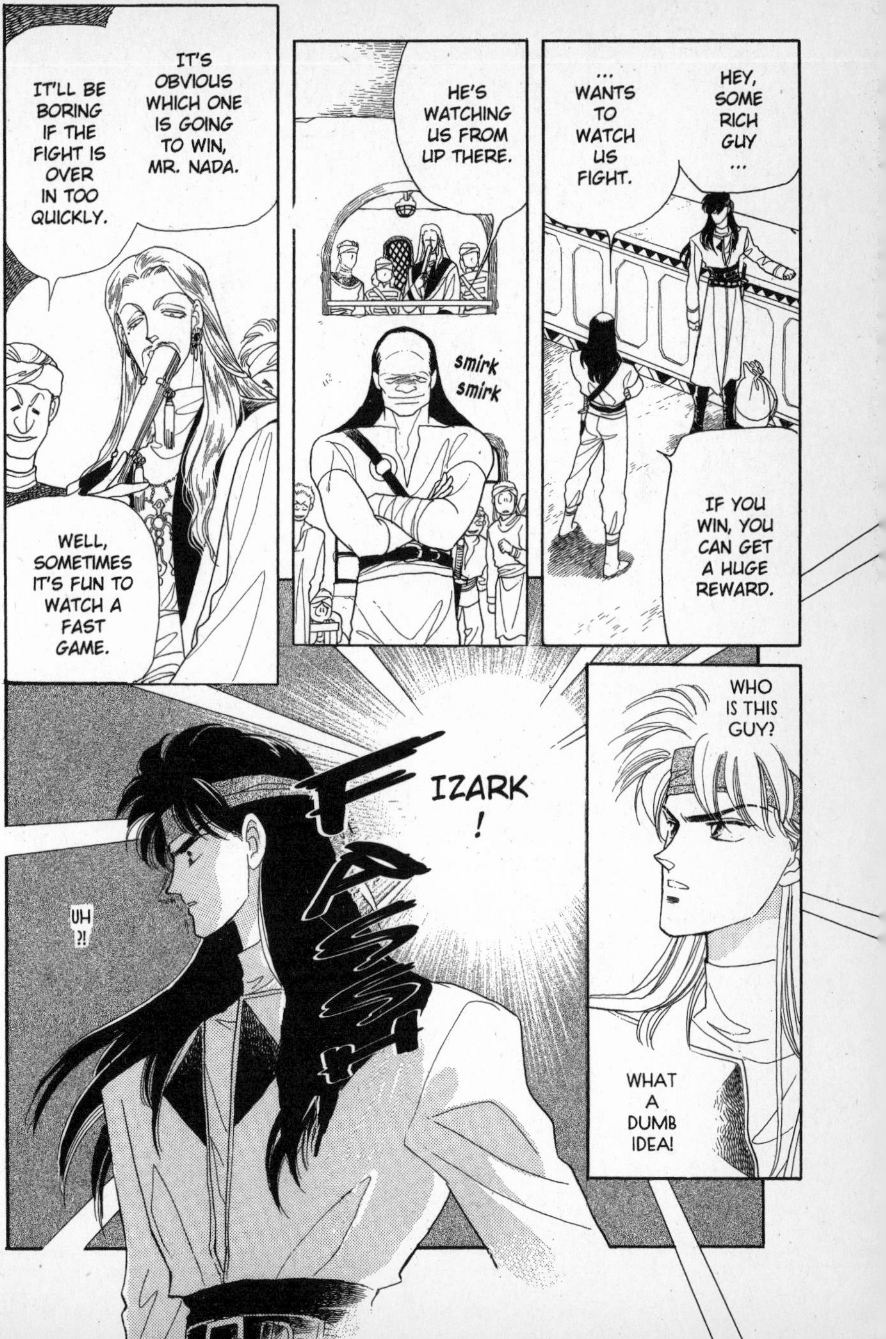
HEY, SOME RICH GUY ...
... WANTS TO WATCH US FIGHT.
IF YOU WIN, YOU CAN GET A HUGE REWARD.
HE'S WATCHING US FROM UP THERE.
smirk smirk
IT'S OBVIOUS WHICH ONE IS GOING TO WIN, MR. NADA.
IT'LL BE BORING IF THE FIGHT IS OVER IN TOO QUICKLY.
WELL, SOMETIMES IT'S FUN TO WATCH A FAST GAME.
WHO IS THIS GUY?
WHAT A DUMB IDEA!
IZARK !
UH ?!

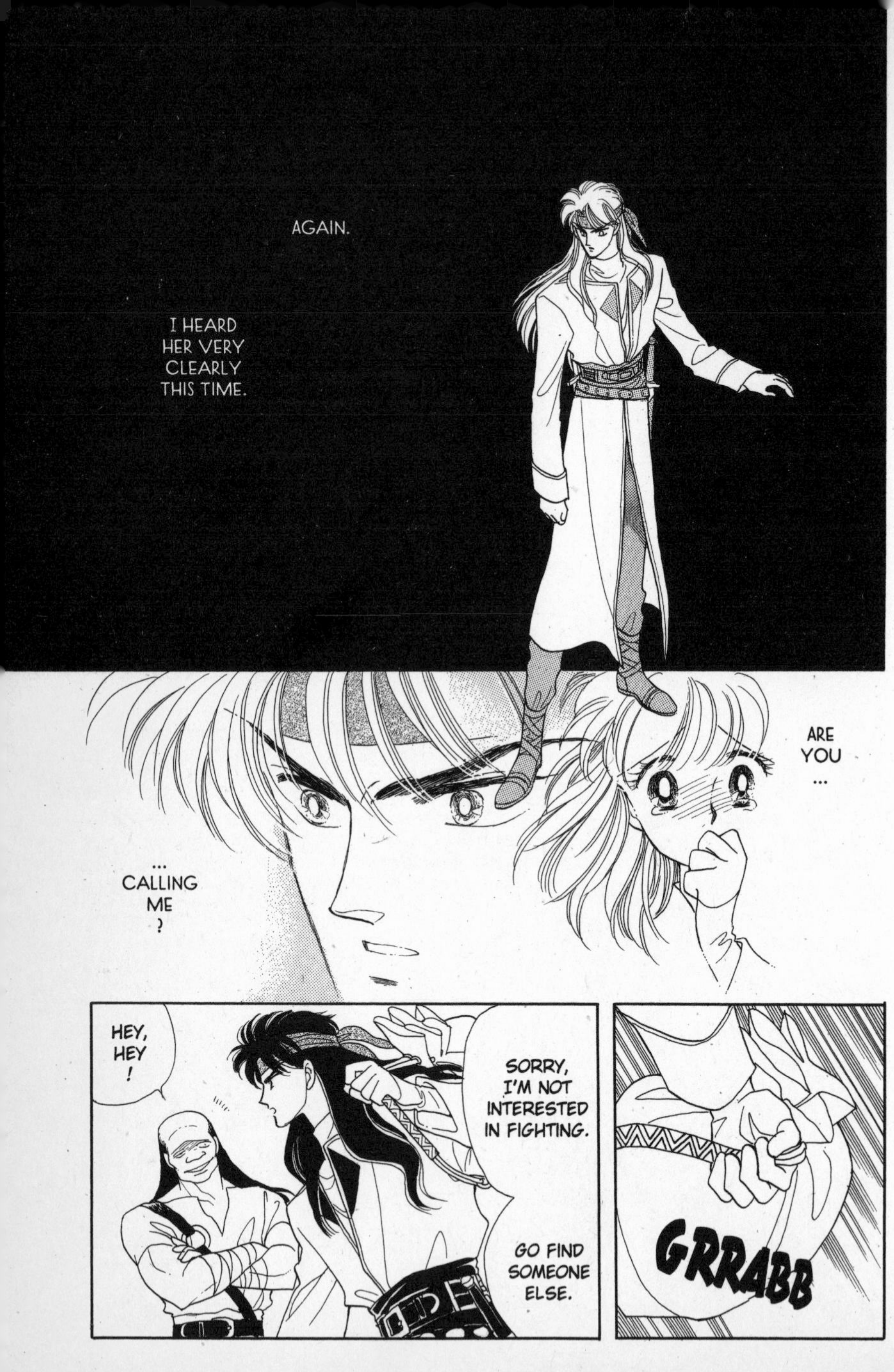
AGAIN.
I HEARD HER VERY CLEARLY THIS TIME.
ARE YOU ...
... CALLING ME ?
GRRABB
SORRY, I'M NOT INTERESTED IN FIGHTING.
HEY, HEY !
GO FIND SOMEONE ELSE.

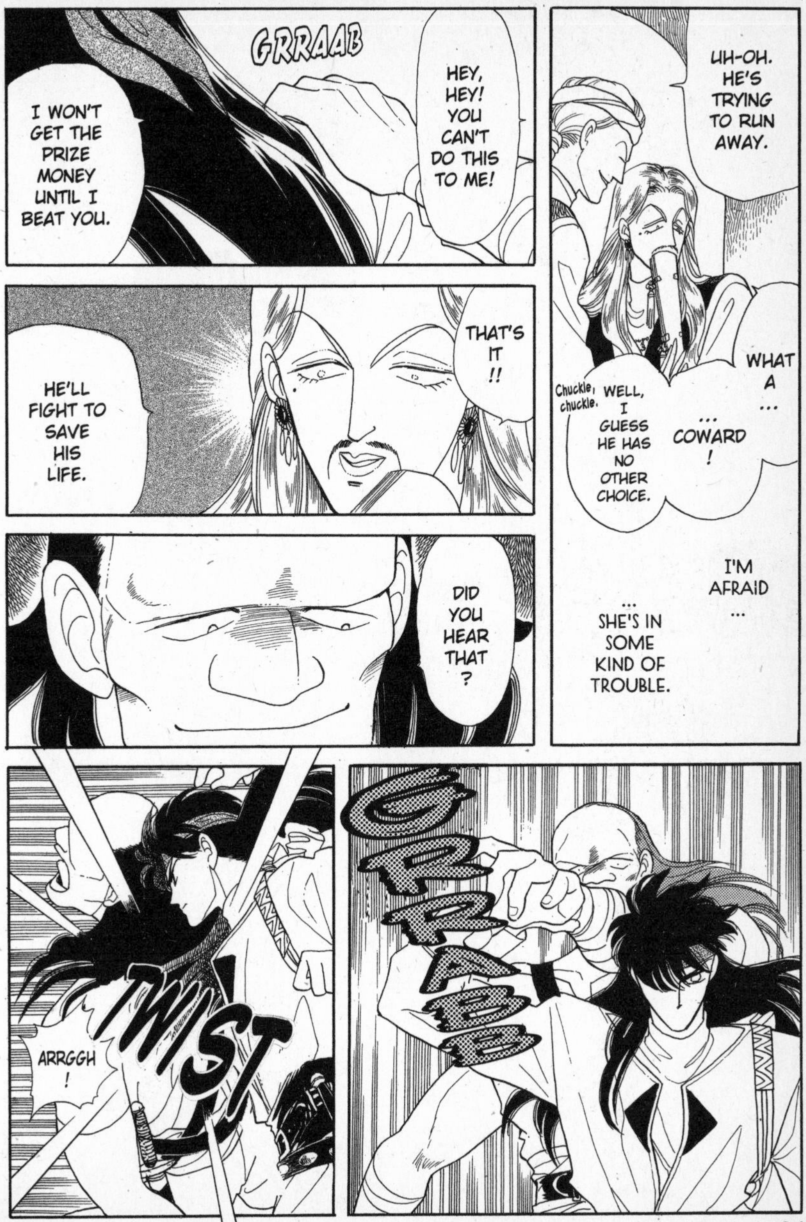
UH-OH. HE'S TRYING TO RUN AWAY.
WHAT A ... ... COWARD!
Chuckle, chuckle.
WELL, I GUESS HE HAS NO OTHER CHOICE.
I'M AFRAID ...
... SHE'S IN SOME KIND OF TROUBLE.
GRRAAB
HEY, HEY! YOU CAN'T DO THIS TO ME!
I WON'T GET THE PRIZE MONEY UNTIL I BEAT YOU.
THAT'S IT!!
HE'LL FIGHT TO SAVE HIS LIFE.
DID YOU HEAR THAT?
GRRABB
TWIST
ARRGGH!

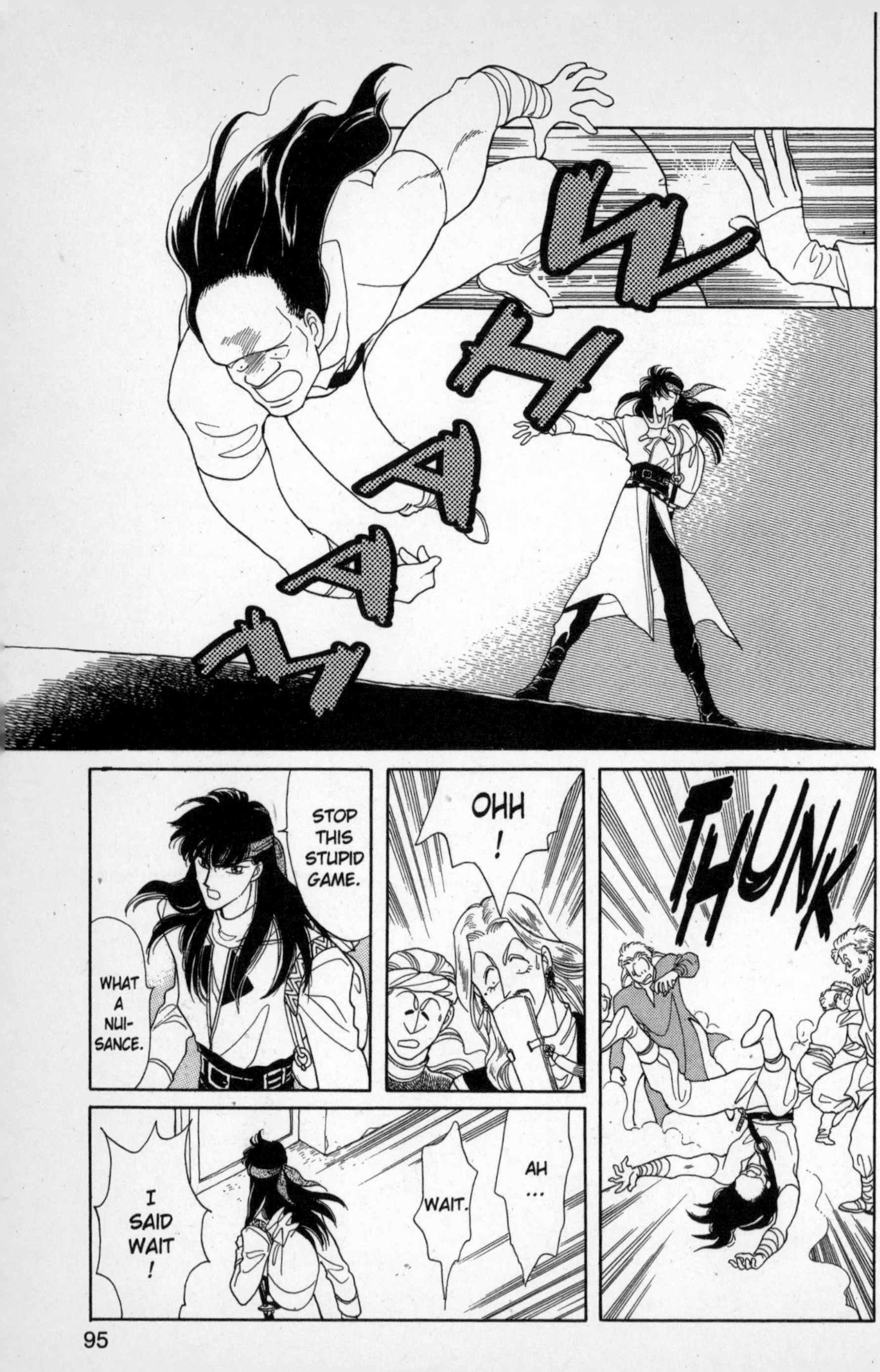
WHAAM
THUNK
OHH!
STOP THIS STUPID GAME.
WHAT A NUI-SANCE.
AH ...
WAIT.
I SAID WAIT!

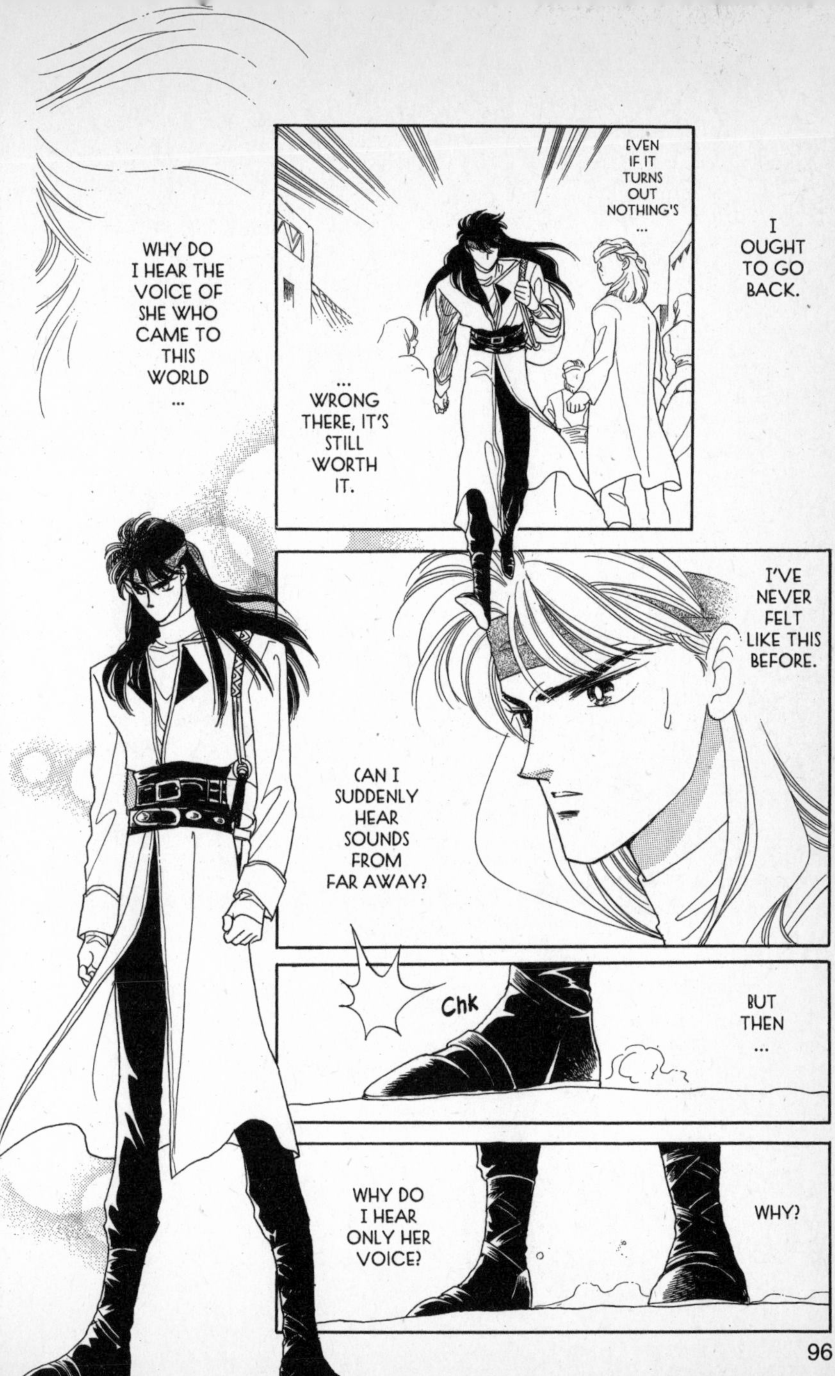
I OUGHT TO GO BACK.
EVEN IF IT TURNS OUT NOTHING'S ...
... WRONG THERE, IT'S STILL WORTH IT.
I'VE NEVER FELT LIKE THIS BEFORE.
CAN I SUDDENLY HEAR SOUNDS FROM FAR AWAY?
BUT THEN ...
Chk
WHY?
WHY DO I HEAR ONLY HER VOICE?
WHY DO I HEAR THE VOICE OF SHE WHO CAME TO THIS WORLD ...

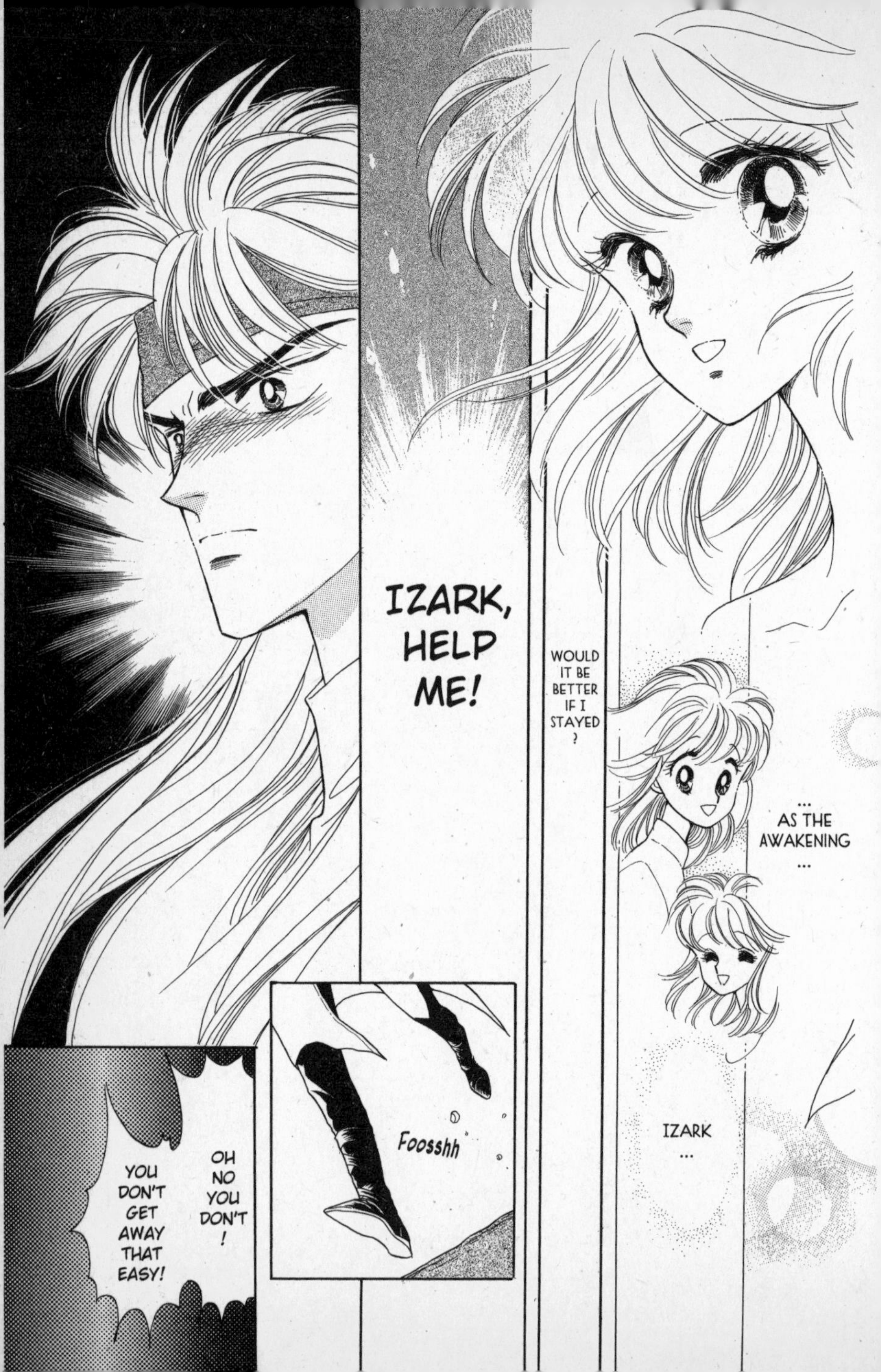
WOULD IT BE BETTER IF I STAYED?
... AS THE AWAKENING ...
IZARK ...
IZARK, HELP ME!
Foosshh
OH NO YOU DON'T!
YOU DON'T GET AWAY THAT EASY!

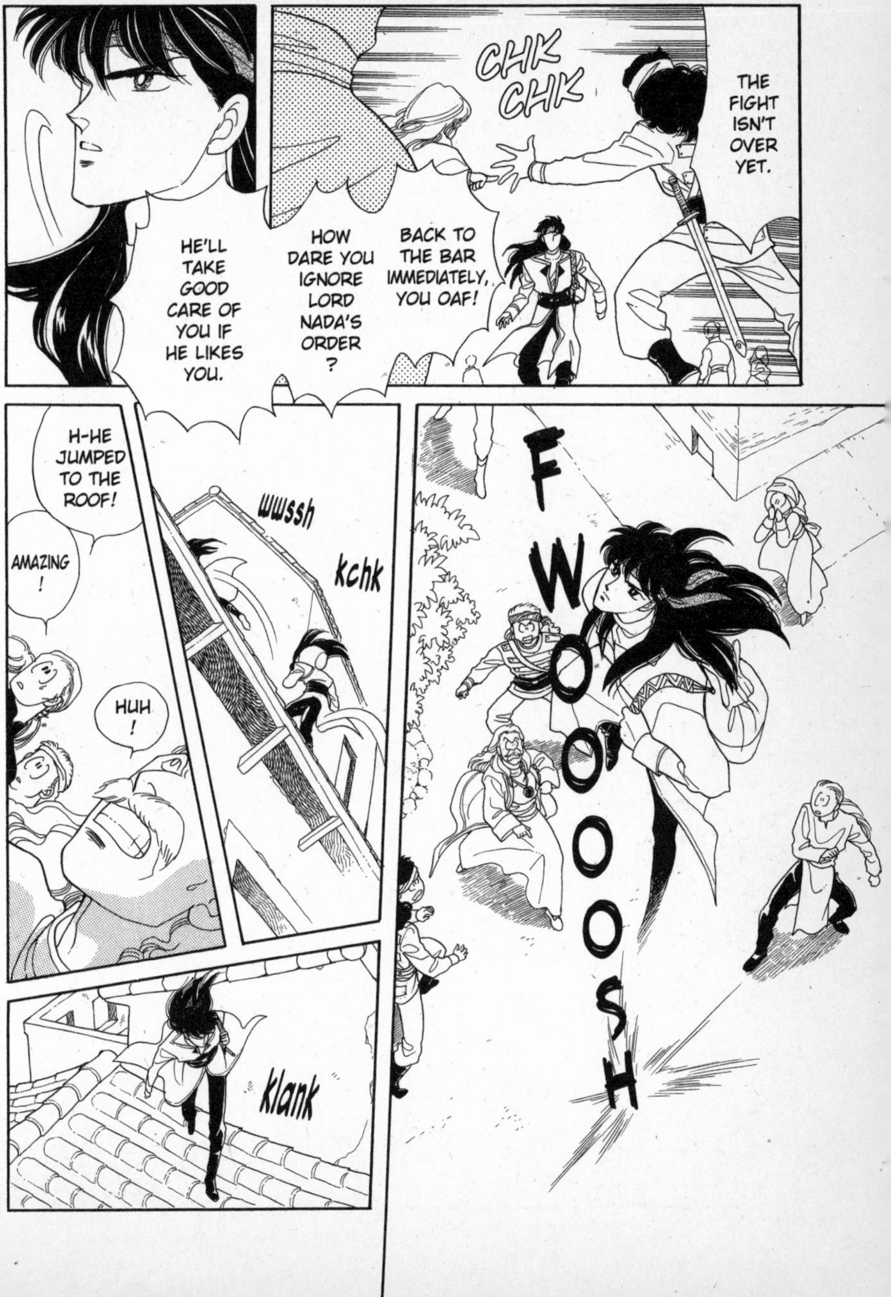
THE FIGHT ISN'T OVER YET.
CHK CHK
BACK TO THE BAR IMMEDIATELY, YOU OAF!
HOW DARE YOU IGNORE LORD NADA'S ORDER?
HE'LL TAKE GOOD CARE OF YOU IF HE LIKES YOU.
FWOOOOOSH
wwssh
kchk
H-HE JUMPED TO THE ROOF!
AMAZING!
HUH!
klank

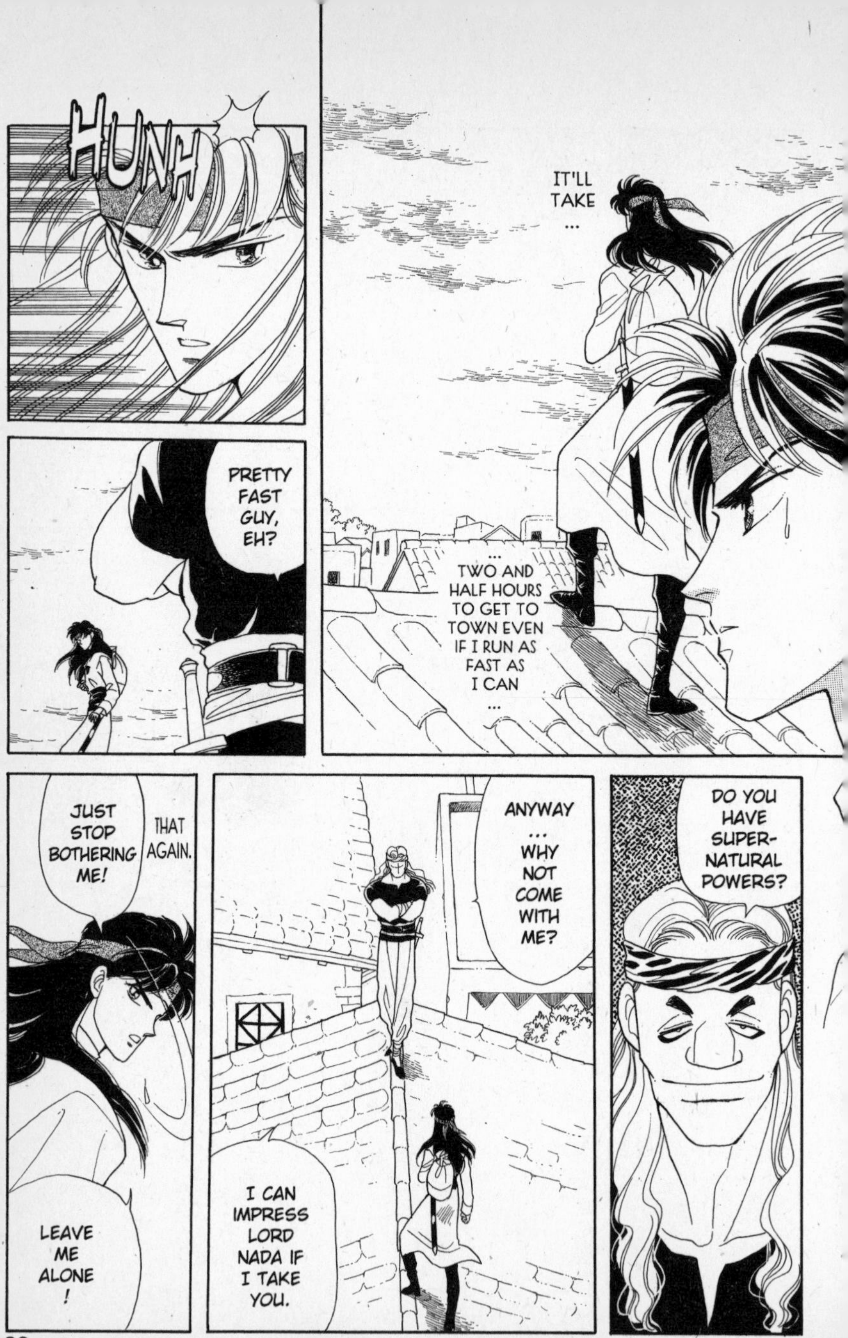
IT'LL TAKE ...
... TWO AND HALF HOURS TO GET TO TOWN EVEN IF I RUN AS FAST AS I CAN ...
HUNH
PRETTY FAST GUY, EH?
DO YOU HAVE SUPER-NATURAL POWERS?
ANYWAY ... WHY NOT COME WITH ME?
I CAN IMPRESS LORD NADA IF I TAKE YOU.
THAT AGAIN.
JUST STOP BOTHERING ME!
LEAVE ME ALONE !

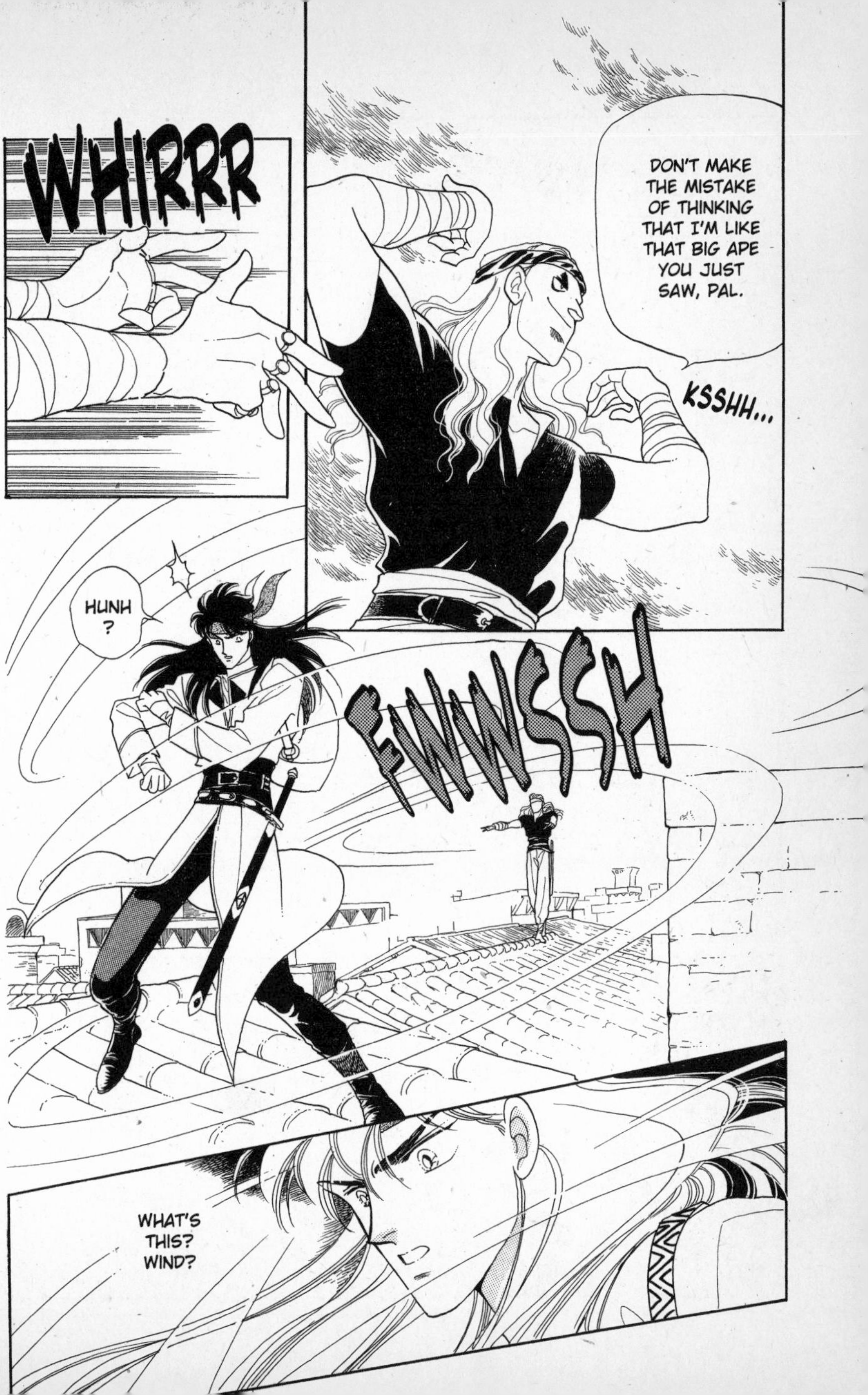
DON'T MAKE THE MISTAKE OF THINKING THAT I'M LIKE THAT BIG APE YOU JUST SAW, PAL.
KSSHH...
WHIRRR
FWWSSH
HUNH ?
WHAT'S THIS? WIND?

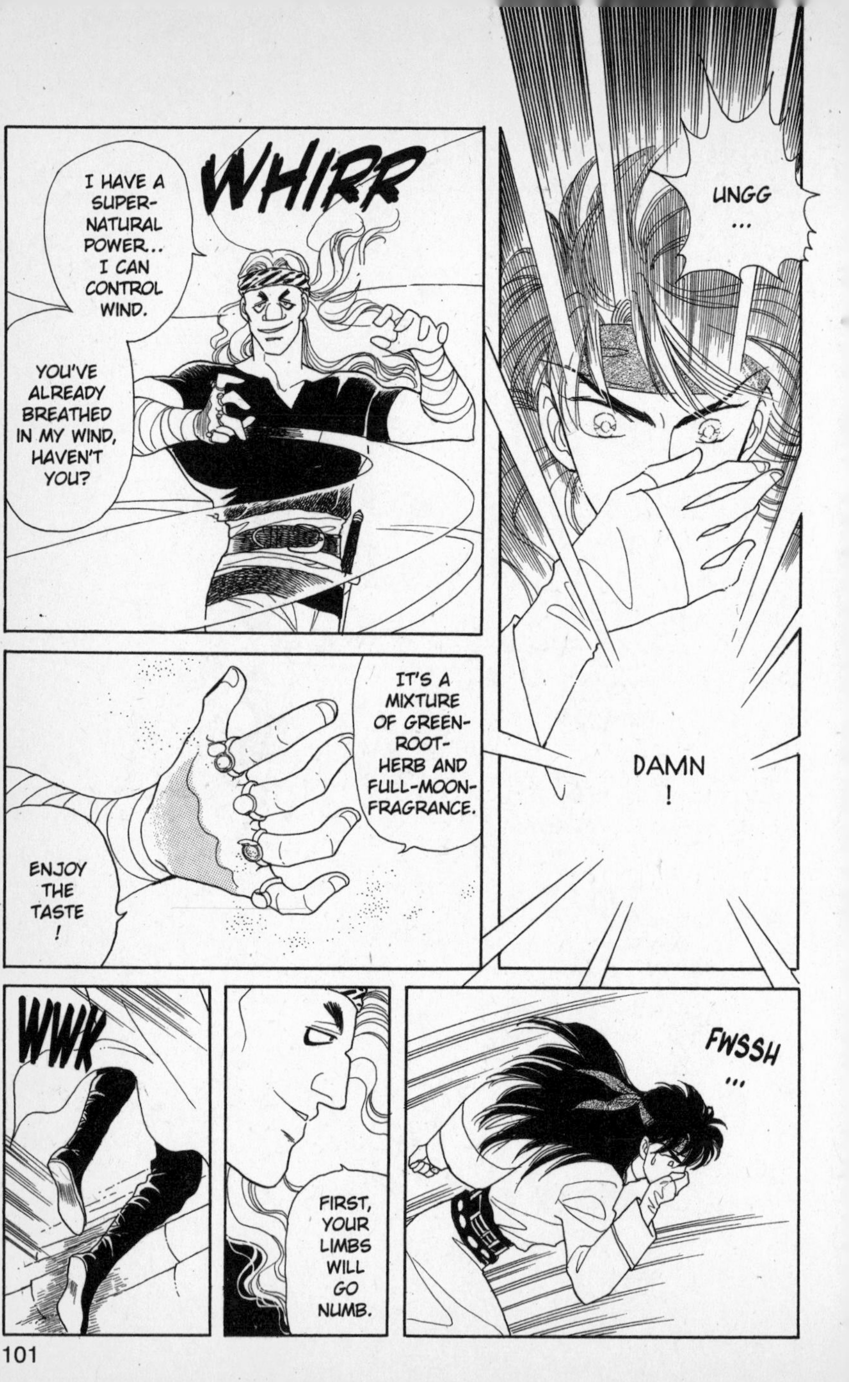
UNGG ...
DAMN !
WHIRR
I HAVE A SUPER-NATURAL POWER... I CAN CONTROL WIND.
YOU'VE ALREADY BREATHED IN MY WIND, HAVEN'T YOU?
IT'S A MIXTURE OF GREEN-ROOT-HERB AND FULL-MOON-FRAGRANCE.
ENJOY THE TASTE !
FWSSH ...
FIRST, YOUR LIMBS WILL GO NUMB.
WWK

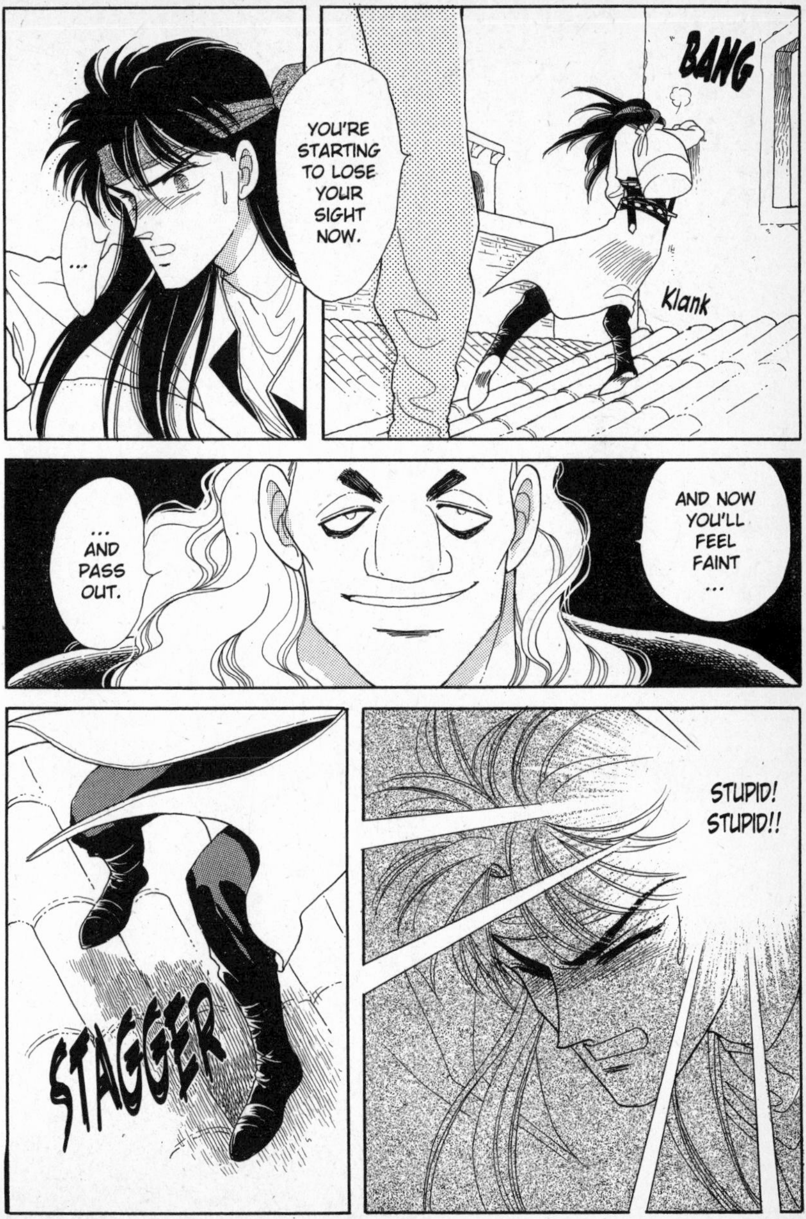
BANG
Klank
YOU'RE STARTING TO LOSE YOUR SIGHT NOW.
...
AND NOW YOU'LL FEEL FAINT ...
... AND PASS OUT.
STUPID! STUPID!!
STAGGER

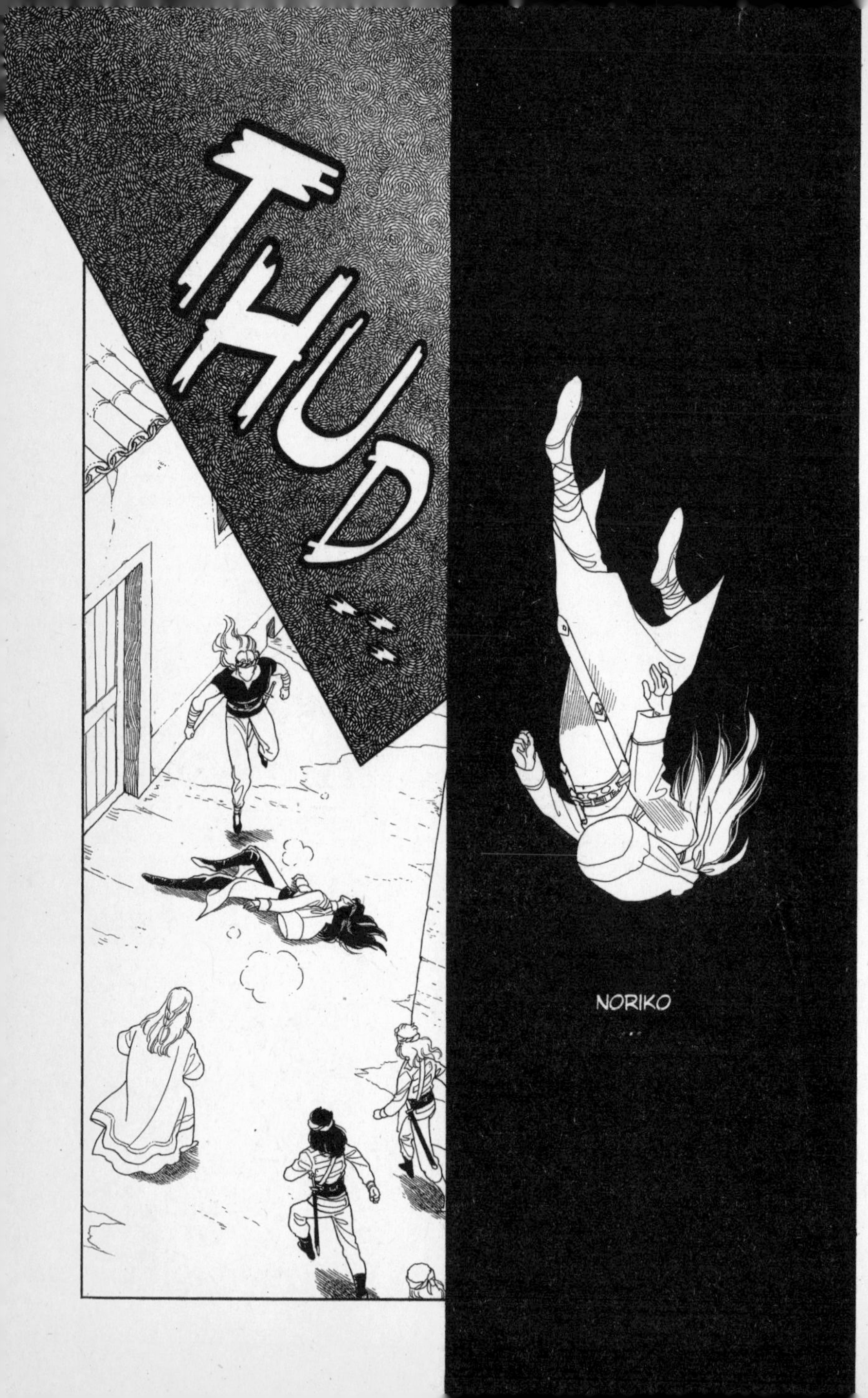
NORIKO
...
THUD

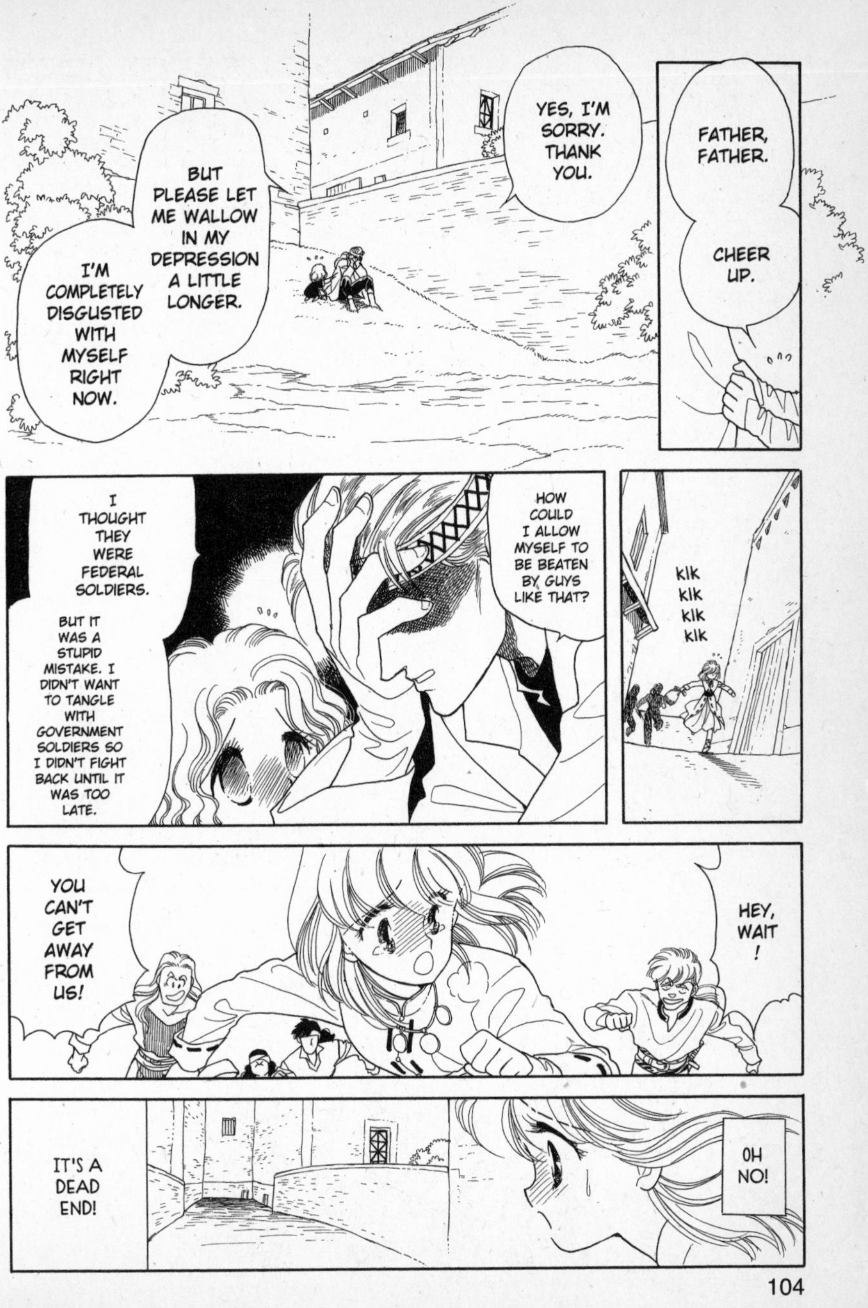
FATHER, FATHER.
CHEER UP.
YES, I'M SORRY. THANK YOU.
BUT PLEASE LET ME WALLOW IN MY DEPRESSION A LITTLE LONGER.
I'M COMPLETELY DISGUSTED WITH MYSELF RIGHT NOW.
KIK KIK KIK KIK
HOW COULD I ALLOW MYSELF TO BE BEATEN BY GUYS LIKE THAT?
I THOUGHT THEY WERE FEDERAL SOLDIERS.
BUT IT WAS A STUPID MISTAKE. I DIDN'T WANT TO TANGLE WITH GOVERNMENT SOLDIERS SO I DIDN'T FIGHT BACK UNTIL IT WAS TOO LATE.
HEY, WAIT!
YOU CAN'T GET AWAY FROM US!
OH NO!
IT'S A DEAD END!

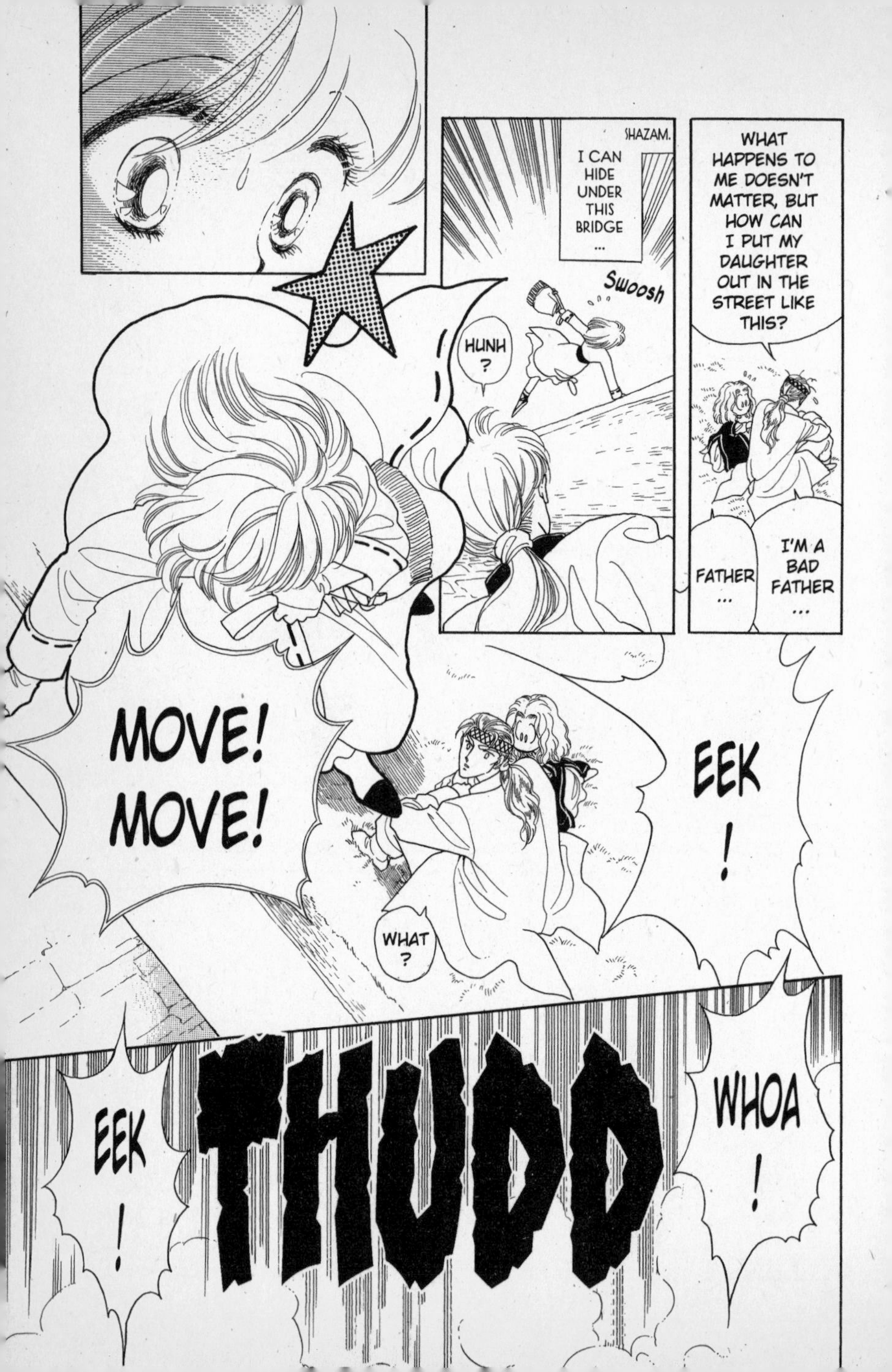
WHAT HAPPENS TO ME DOESN'T MATTER, BUT HOW CAN I PUT MY DAUGHTER OUT IN THE STREET LIKE THIS?
I'M A BAD FATHER ...
FATHER ...
SHAZAM.
I CAN HIDE UNDER THIS BRIDGE ...
Swoosh
HUNH ?
EEK !
MOVE! MOVE!
WHAT ?
WHOA !
THUDD
EEK !

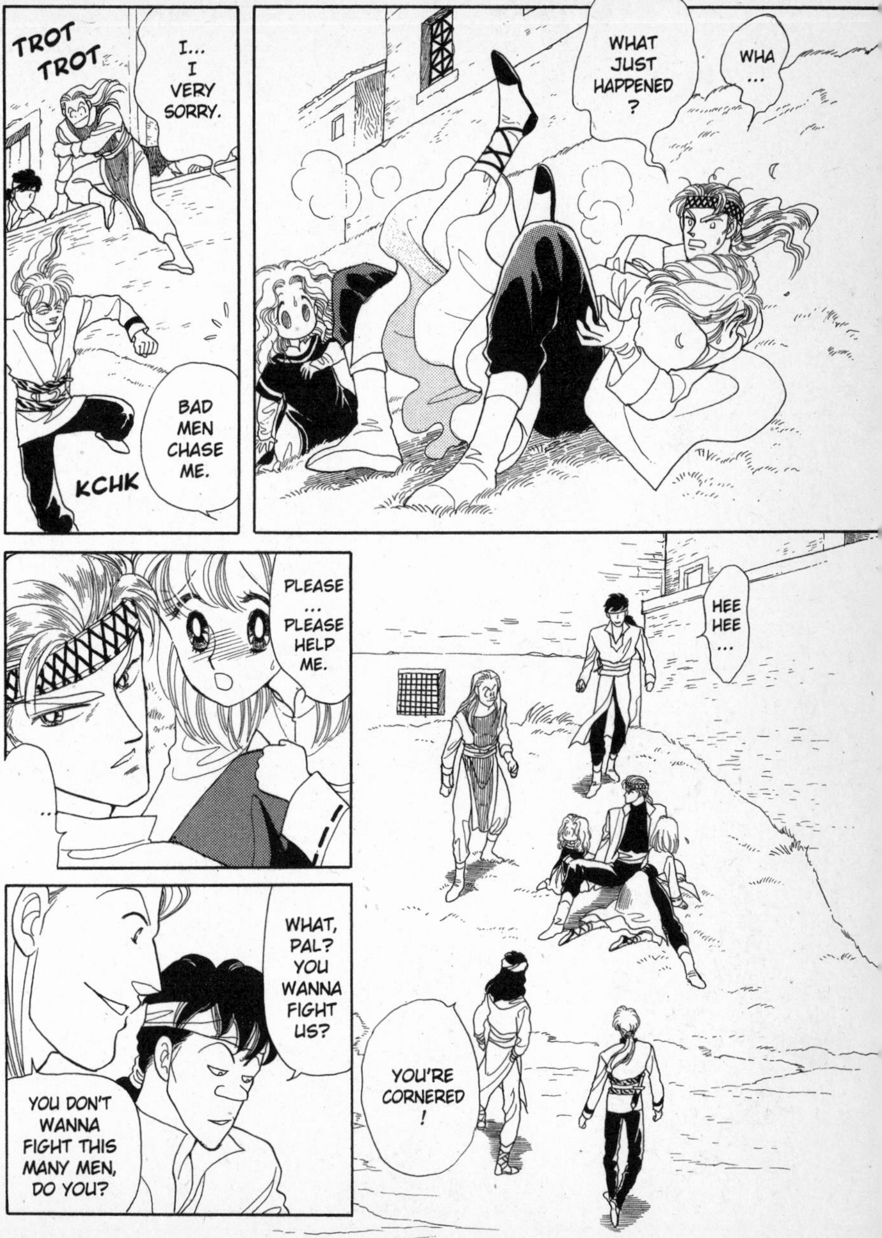
WHA ...
WHAT JUST HAPPENED ?
I... I VERY SORRY.
TROT TROT
BAD MEN CHASE ME.
KCHK
HEE HEE ...
YOU'RE CORNERED !
PLEASE ... PLEASE HELP ME.
...
WHAT, PAL? YOU WANNA FIGHT US?
YOU DON'T WANNA FIGHT THIS MANY MEN, DO YOU?

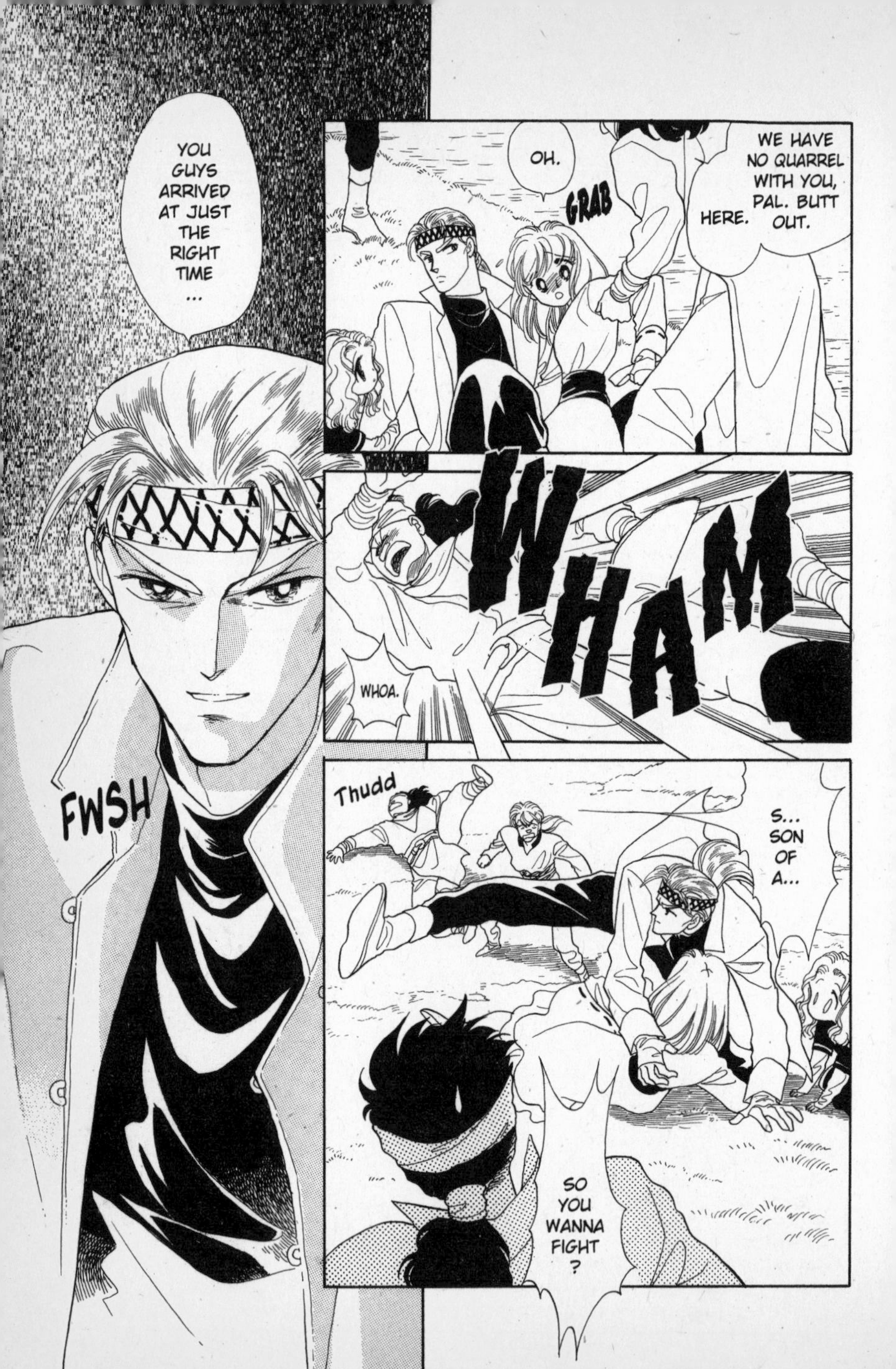
WE HAVE NO QUARREL WITH YOU, PAL. BUTT OUT.
HERE.
GRAB
OH.
WHAM
WHOA.
S... SON OF A...
Thudd
SO YOU WANNA FIGHT?
YOU GUYS ARRIVED AT JUST THE RIGHT TIME ...
FWSH

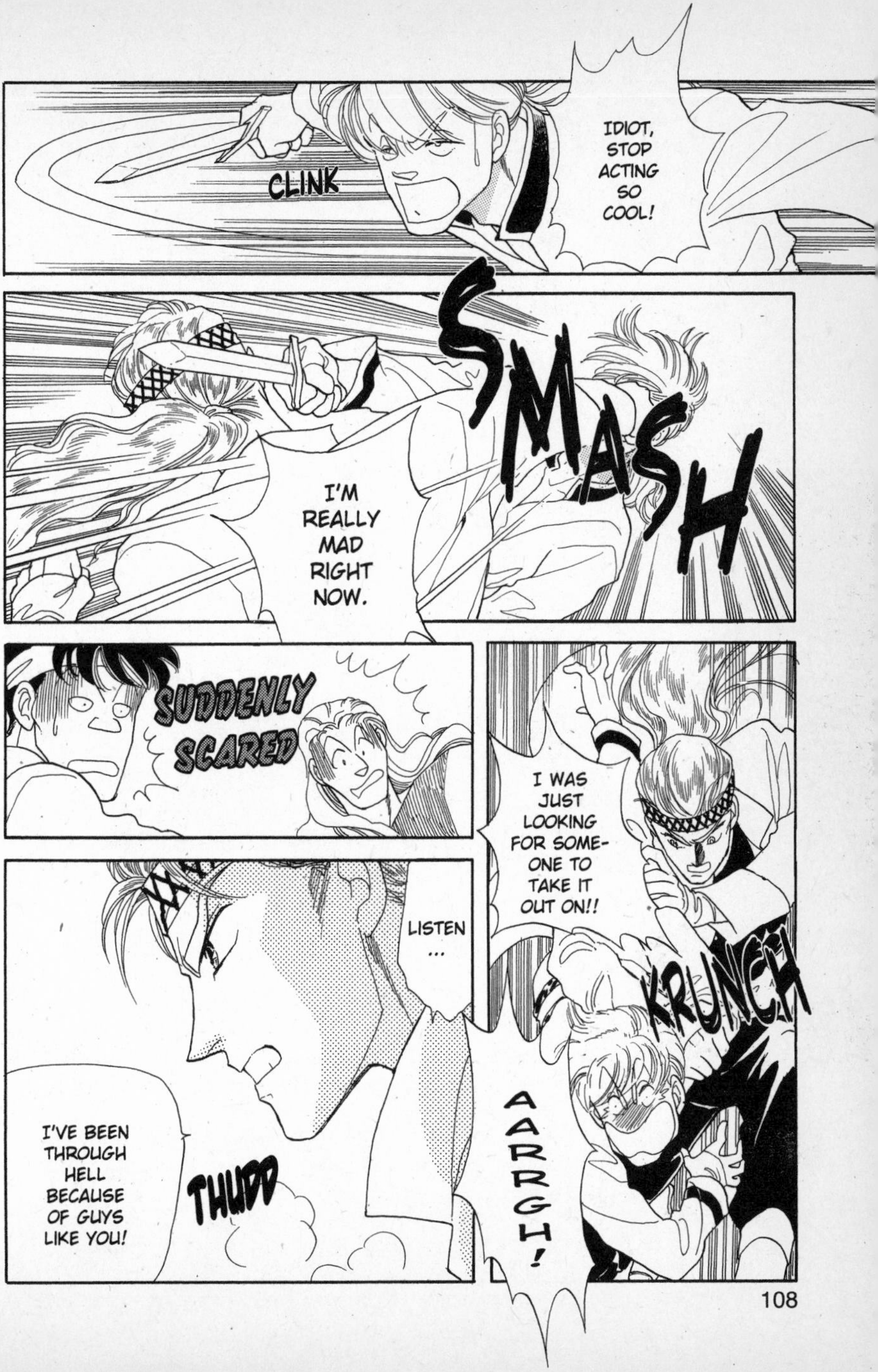

IDIOT, STOP ACTING SO COOL!
CLINK
SMASH
I'M REALLY MAD RIGHT NOW.
I WAS JUST LOOKING FOR SOME-ONE TO TAKE IT OUT ON!!
KRUNCH
AARRGH!
SUDDENLY SCARED
LISTEN ...
THUDD
I'VE BEEN THROUGH HELL BECAUSE OF GUYS LIKE YOU!

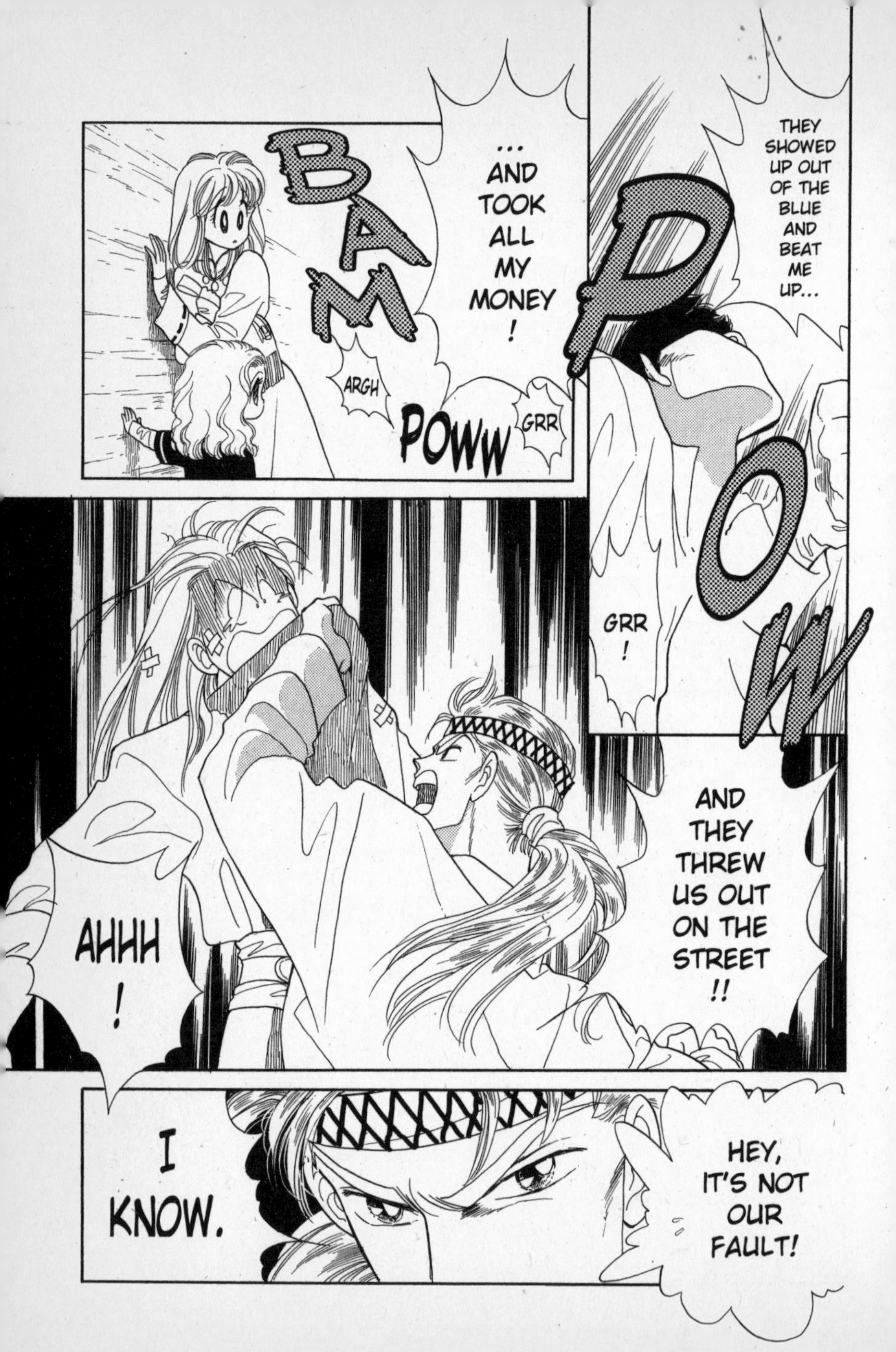
THEY SHOWED UP OUT OF THE BLUE AND BEAT ME UP...
POW
GRR!
...AND TOOK ALL MY MONEY!
BAM
ARGH
POWW
GRR
AND THEY THREW US OUT ON THE STREET!!
AHHH!
HEY, IT'S NOT OUR FAULT!
I KNOW.

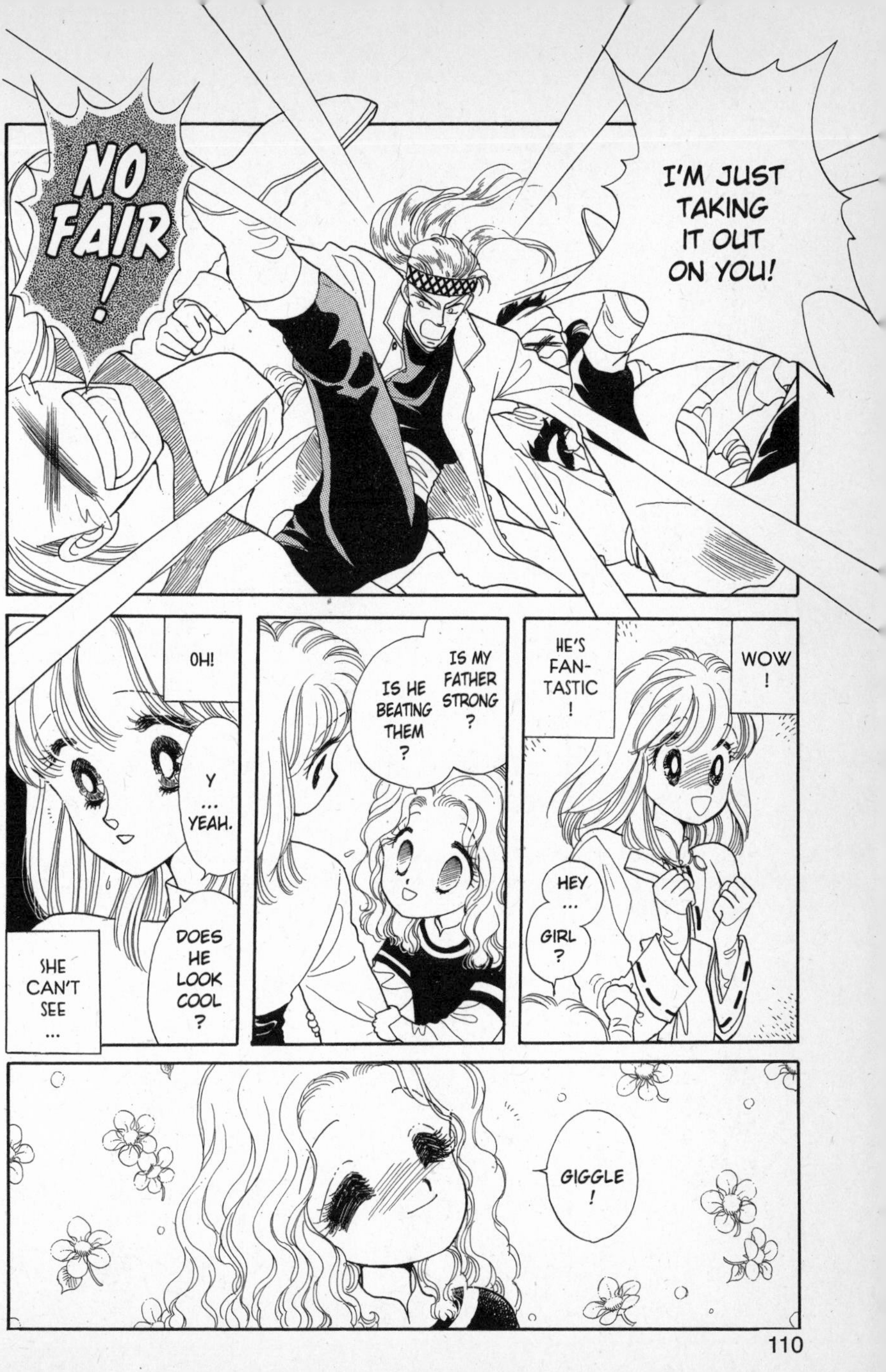
I'M JUST TAKING IT OUT ON YOU!
NO FAIR!
WOW!
HE'S FAN-TASTIC!
HEY... GIRL?
IS MY FATHER STRONG?
IS HE BEATING THEM?
OH!
Y... YEAH.
DOES HE LOOK COOL?
SHE CAN'T SEE...
GIGGLE!

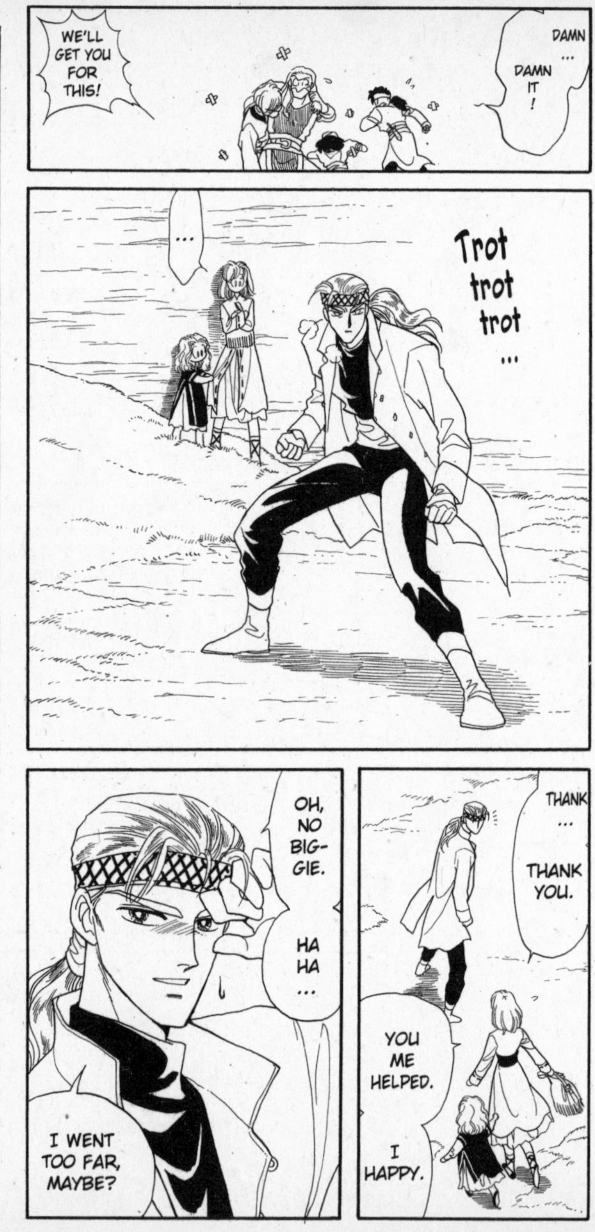
DAMN ... DAMN IT!
WE'LL GET YOU FOR THIS!
Trot trot trot ...
...
THANK ... THANK YOU.
YOU ME HELPED.
I HAPPY.
OH, NO BIG-GIE.
HA HA ...
I WENT TOO FAR, MAYBE?

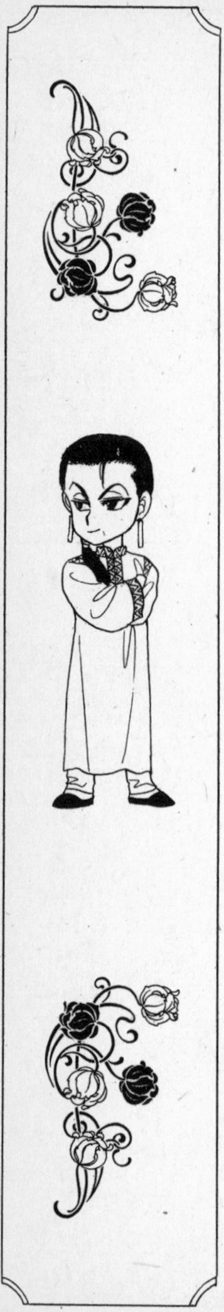

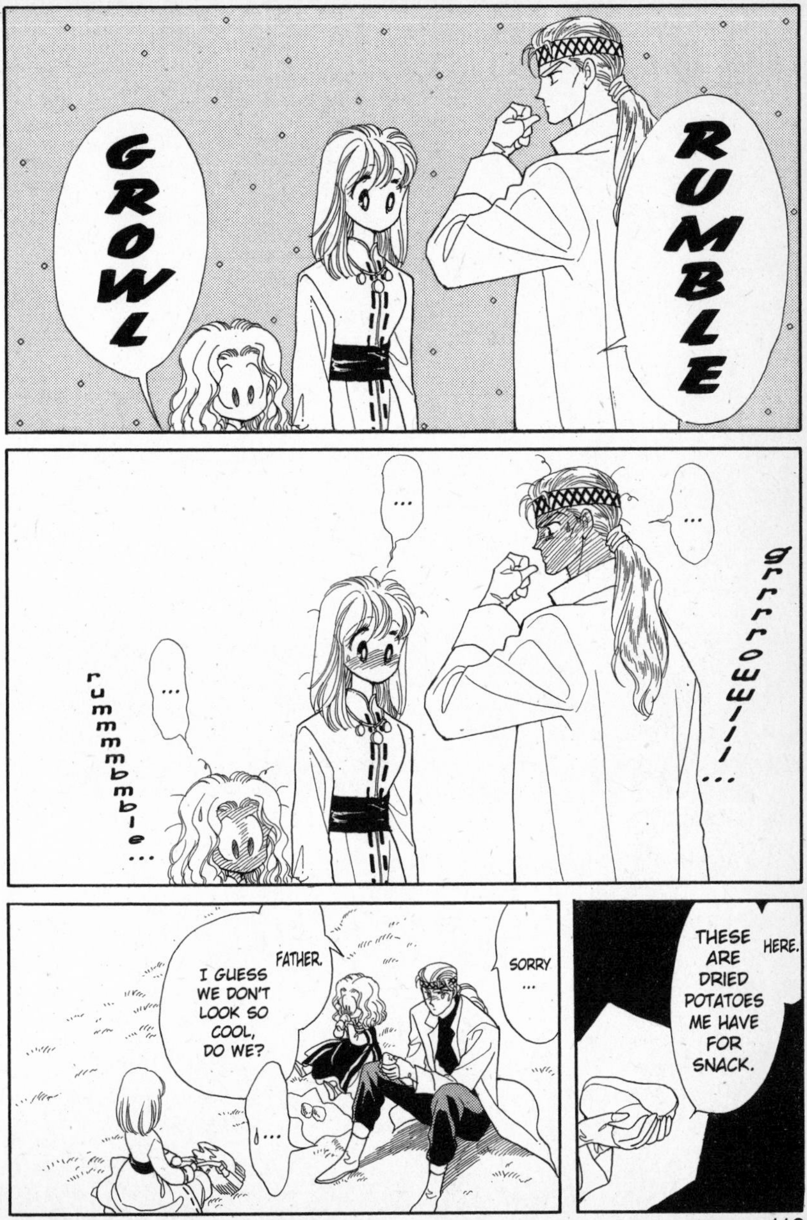

RUMBLE
GROWL
...
grrrrowwlll...
...
...
rummmmbble...
HERE.
THESE ARE DRIED POTATOES ME HAVE FOR SNACK.
SORRY ...
FATHER.
I GUESS WE DON'T LOOK SO COOL, DO WE?
...

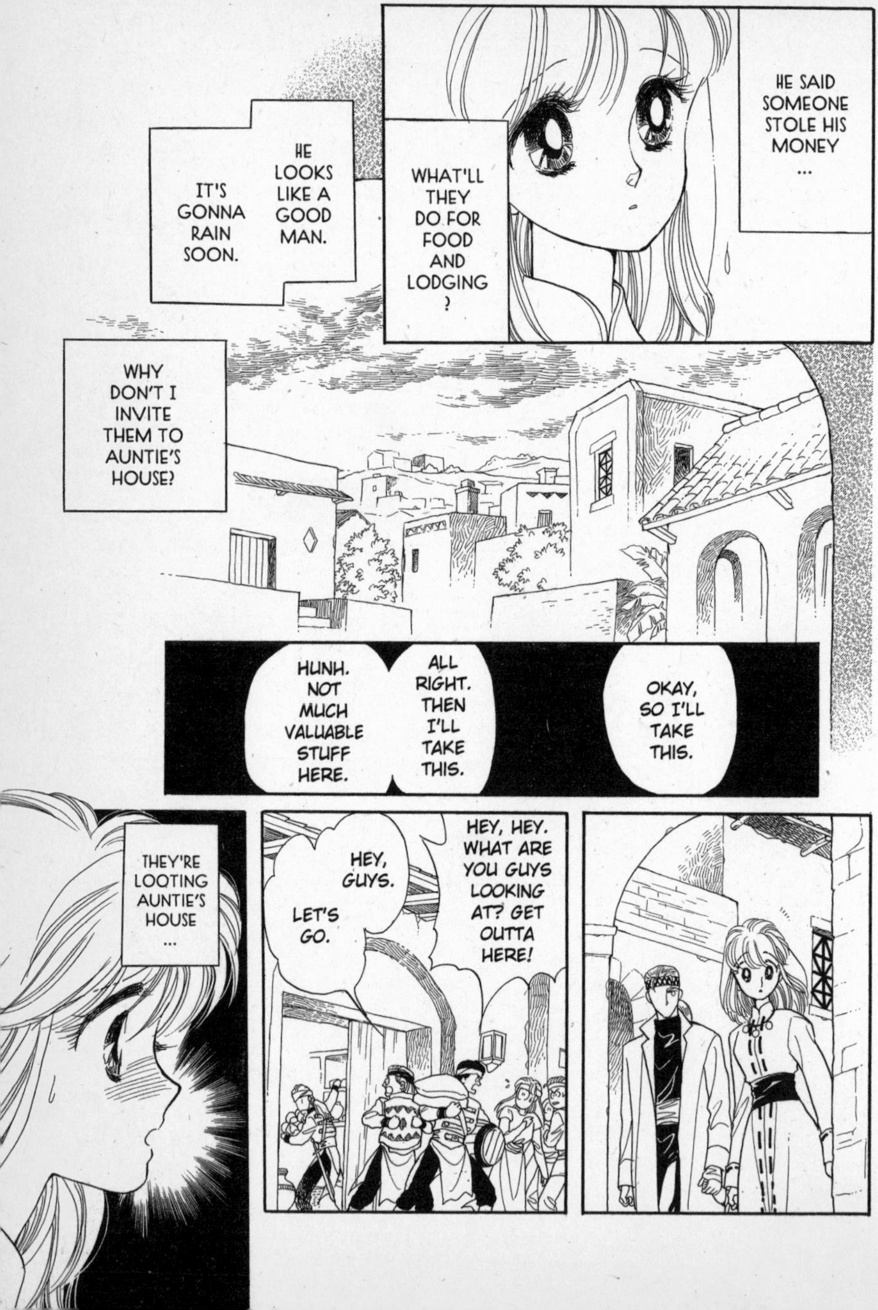
HE SAID SOMEONE STOLE HIS MONEY ...
WHAT'LL THEY DO FOR FOOD AND LODGING?
HE LOOKS LIKE A GOOD MAN.
IT'S GONNA RAIN SOON.
WHY DON'T I INVITE THEM TO AUNTIE'S HOUSE?
OKAY, SO I'LL TAKE THIS.
ALL RIGHT. THEN I'LL TAKE THIS.
HUNH. NOT MUCH VALUABLE STUFF HERE.
HEY, HEY. WHAT ARE YOU GUYS LOOKING AT? GET OUTTA HERE!
HEY, GUYS.
LET'S GO.
THEY'RE LOOTING AUNTIE'S HOUSE ...

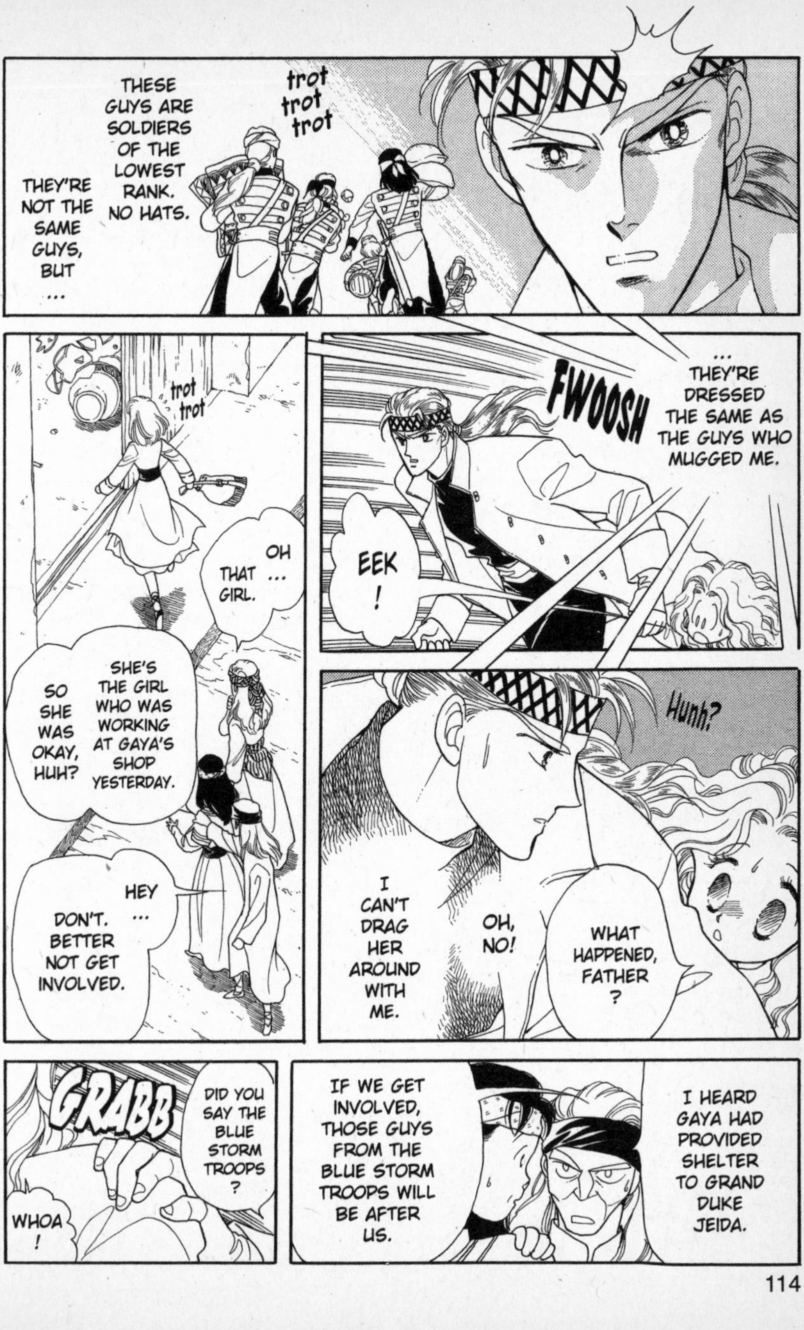
trot trot trot
THESE GUYS ARE SOLDIERS OF THE LOWEST RANK. NO HATS.
THEY'RE NOT THE SAME GUYS, BUT ...
... THEY'RE DRESSED THE SAME AS THE GUYS WHO MUGGED ME.
FWOOSH
EEK !
Hunh?
WHAT HAPPENED, FATHER ?
OH, NO!
I CAN'T DRAG HER AROUND WITH ME.
trot trot
OH ... THAT GIRL.
SHE'S THE GIRL WHO WAS WORKING AT GAYA'S SHOP YESTERDAY.
SO SHE WAS OKAY, HUH?
HEY ...
DON'T. BETTER NOT GET INVOLVED.
I HEARD GAYA HAD PROVIDED SHELTER TO GRAND DUKE JEIDA.
IF WE GET INVOLVED, THOSE GUYS FROM THE BLUE STORM TROOPS WILL BE AFTER US.
DID YOU SAY THE BLUE STORM TROOPS ?
GRABB
WHOA !

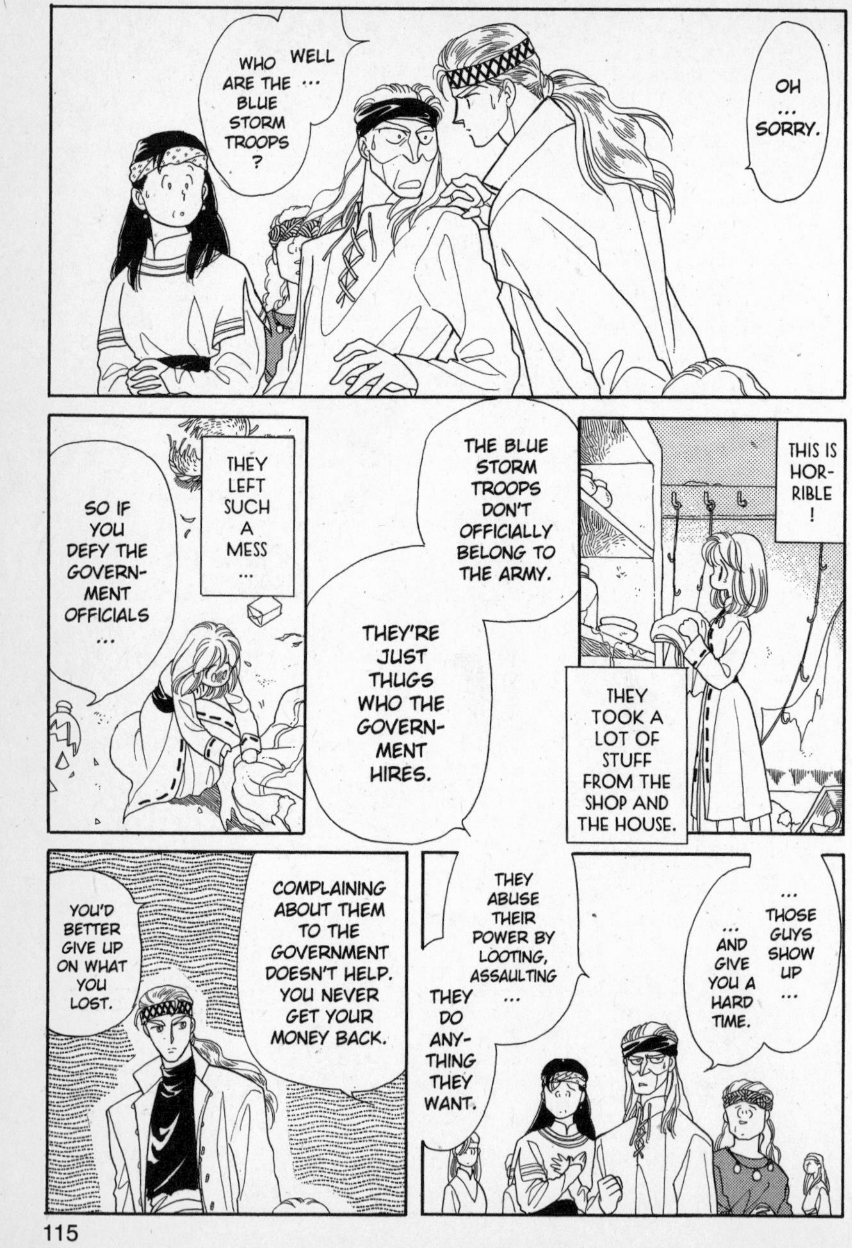
OH ... SORRY.
WELL ... WHO ARE THE BLUE STORM TROOPS ?
THIS IS HORRIBLE !
THEY TOOK A LOT OF STUFF FROM THE SHOP AND THE HOUSE.
THE BLUE STORM TROOPS DON'T OFFICIALLY BELONG TO THE ARMY.
THEY'RE JUST THUGS WHO THE GOVERNMENT HIRES.
THEY LEFT SUCH A MESS ...
SO IF YOU DEFY THE GOVERNMENT OFFICIALS ...
... THOSE GUYS SHOW UP ...
... AND GIVE YOU A HARD TIME.
THEY ABUSE THEIR POWER BY LOOTING, ASSAULTING ...
THEY DO ANYTHING THEY WANT.
COMPLAINING ABOUT THEM TO THE GOVERNMENT DOESN'T HELP. YOU NEVER GET YOUR MONEY BACK.
YOU'D BETTER GIVE UP ON WHAT YOU LOST.

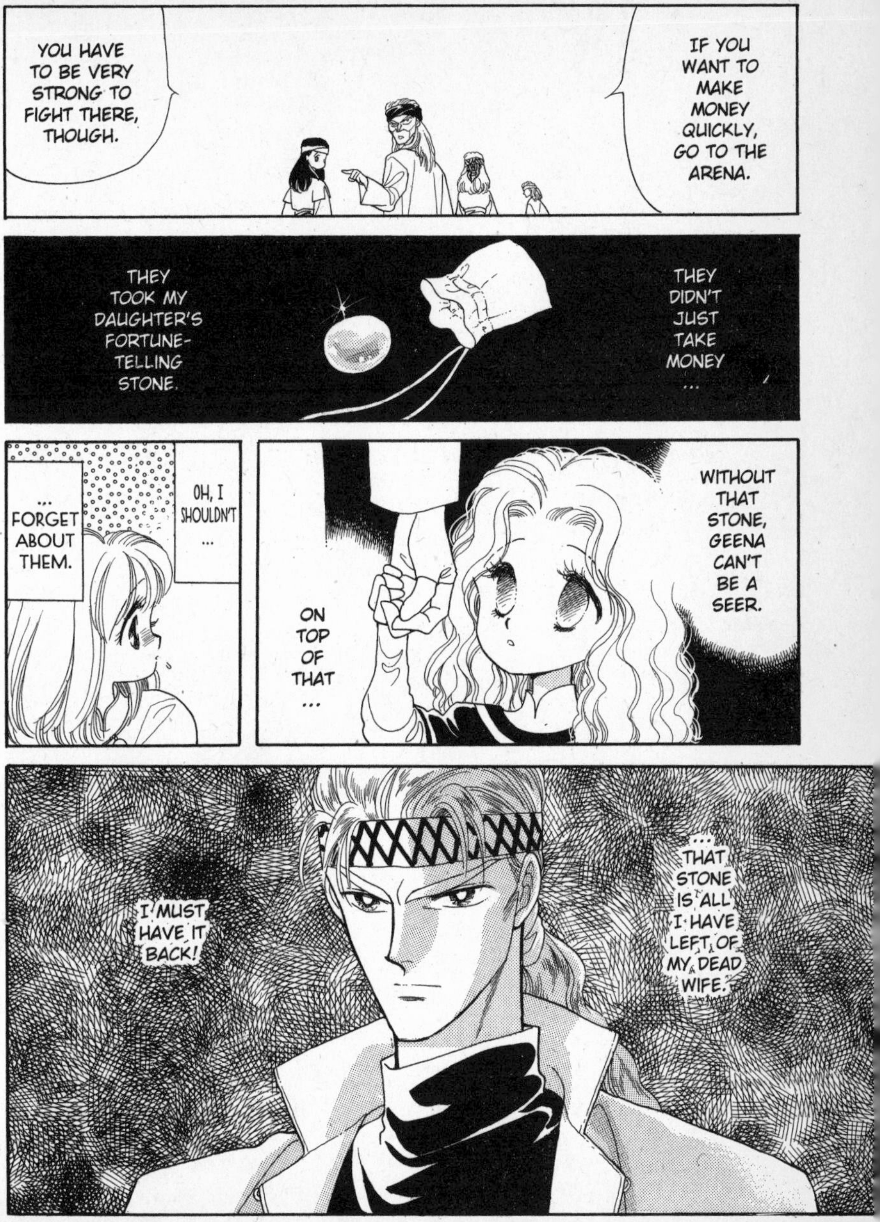
IF YOU WANT TO MAKE MONEY QUICKLY, GO TO THE ARENA.
YOU HAVE TO BE VERY STRONG TO FIGHT THERE, THOUGH.
THEY DIDN'T JUST TAKE MONEY ...
THEY TOOK MY DAUGHTER'S FORTUNE-TELLING STONE.
WITHOUT THAT STONE, GEENA CAN'T BE A SEER.
ON TOP OF THAT ...
OH, I SHOULDN'T ...
... FORGET ABOUT THEM.
... THAT STONE IS ALL I HAVE LEFT OF MY DEAD WIFE.
I MUST HAVE IT BACK!

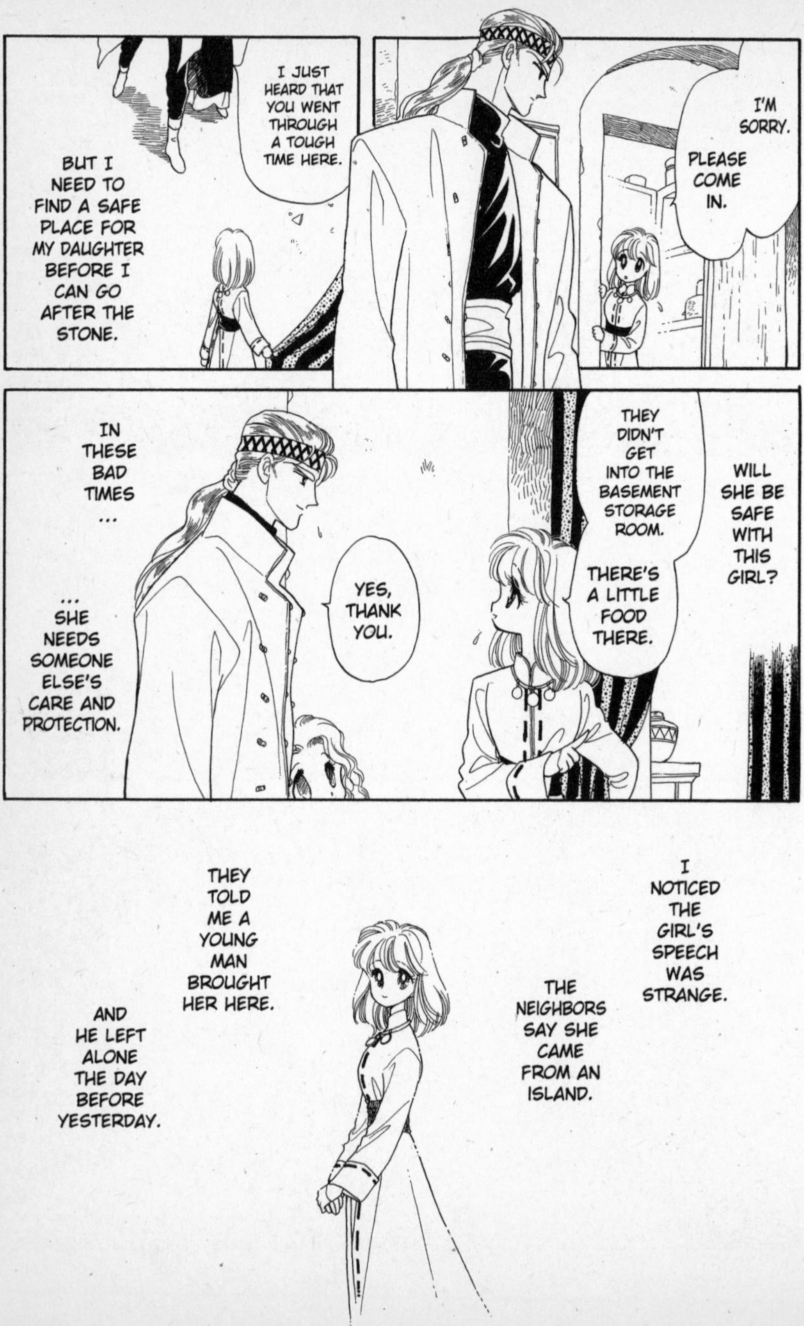
I'M SORRY.
PLEASE COME IN.
I JUST HEARD THAT YOU WENT THROUGH A TOUGH TIME HERE.
BUT I NEED TO FIND A SAFE PLACE FOR MY DAUGHTER BEFORE I CAN GO AFTER THE STONE.
WILL SHE BE SAFE WITH THIS GIRL?
THEY DIDN'T GET INTO THE BASEMENT STORAGE ROOM.
THERE'S A LITTLE FOOD THERE.
YES, THANK YOU.
IN THESE BAD TIMES...
...SHE NEEDS SOMEONE ELSE'S CARE AND PROTECTION.
I NOTICED THE GIRL'S SPEECH WAS STRANGE.
THE NEIGHBORS SAY SHE CAME FROM AN ISLAND.
THEY TOLD ME A YOUNG MAN BROUGHT HER HERE.
AND HE LEFT ALONE THE DAY BEFORE YESTERDAY.

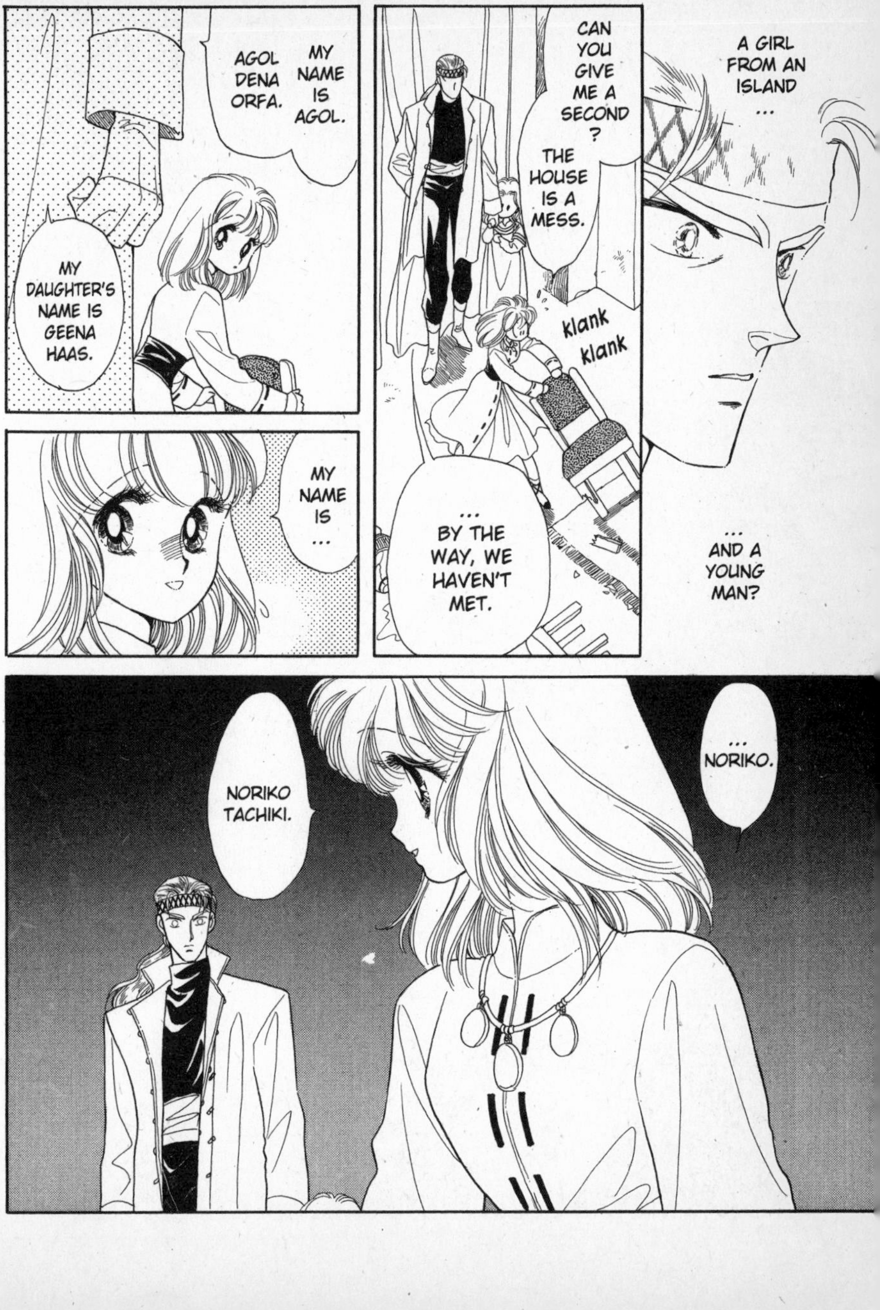
A GIRL FROM AN ISLAND ...
... AND A YOUNG MAN?
CAN YOU GIVE ME A SECOND?
THE HOUSE IS A MESS.
klank klank
... BY THE WAY, WE HAVEN'T MET.
MY NAME IS AGOL.
AGOL DENA ORFA.
MY DAUGHTER'S NAME IS GEENA HAAS.
MY NAME IS ...
... NORIKO.
NORIKO TACHIKI.

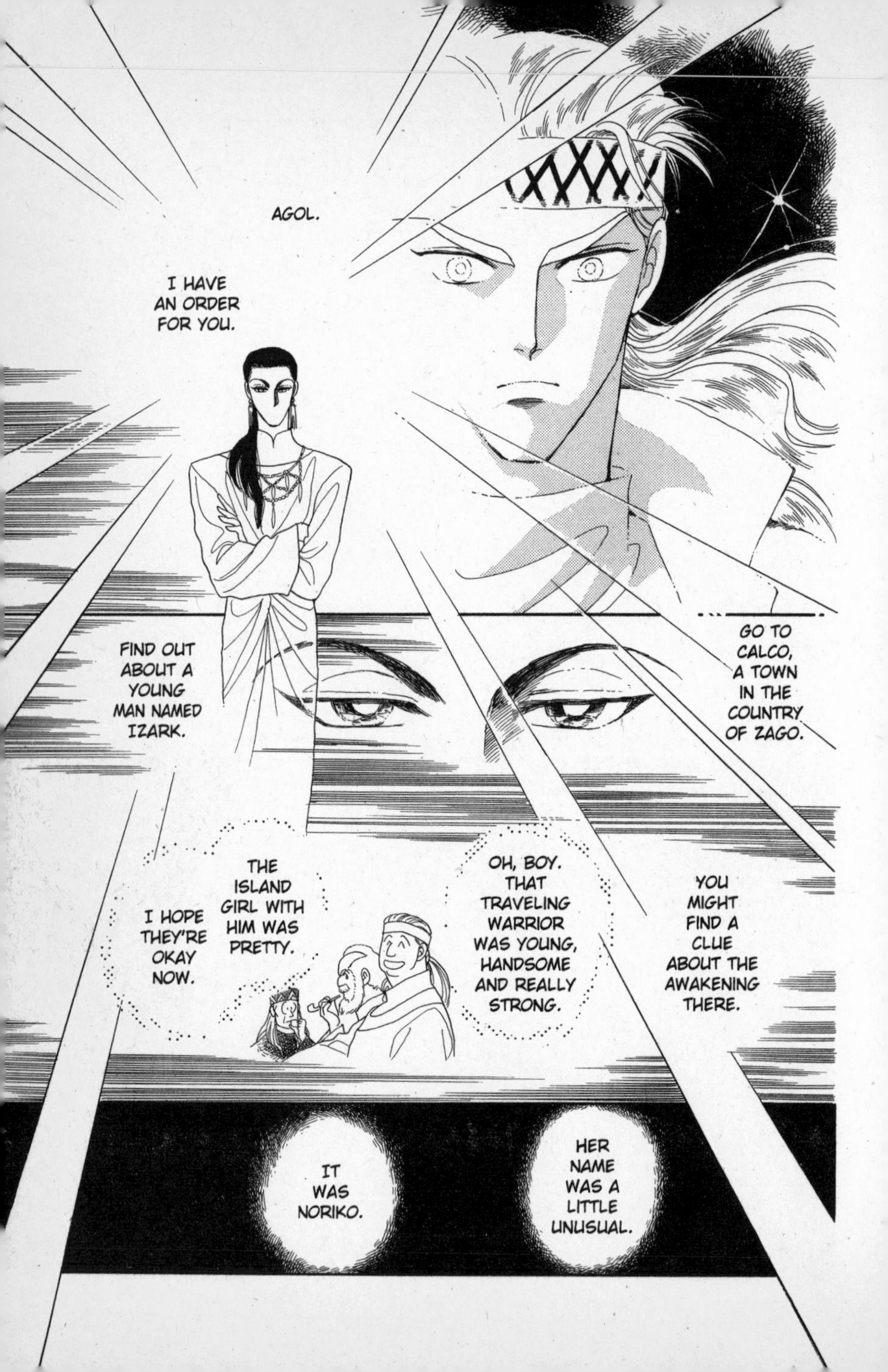
AGOL.
I HAVE AN ORDER FOR YOU.
GO TO CALCO, A TOWN IN THE COUNTRY OF ZAGO.
FIND OUT ABOUT A YOUNG MAN NAMED IZARK.
YOU MIGHT FIND A CLUE ABOUT THE AWAKENING THERE.
OH, BOY. THAT TRAVELING WARRIOR WAS YOUNG, HANDSOME AND REALLY STRONG.
THE ISLAND GIRL WITH HIM WAS PRETTY.
I HOPE THEY'RE OKAY NOW.
HER NAME WAS A LITTLE UNUSUAL.
IT WAS NORIKO.

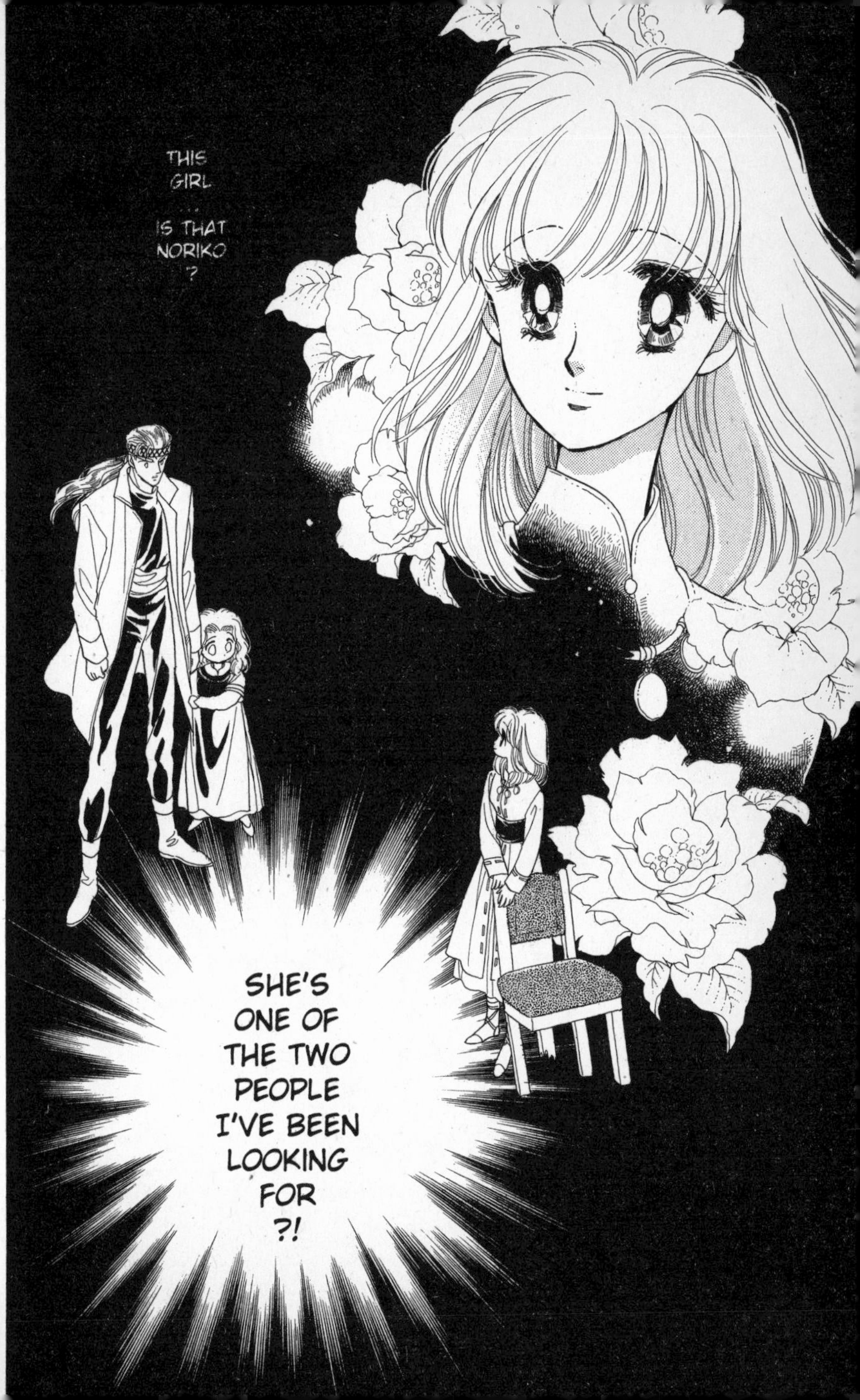
THIS GIRL ... IS THAT NORIKO ?
SHE'S ONE OF THE TWO PEOPLE I'VE BEEN LOOKING FOR ?!

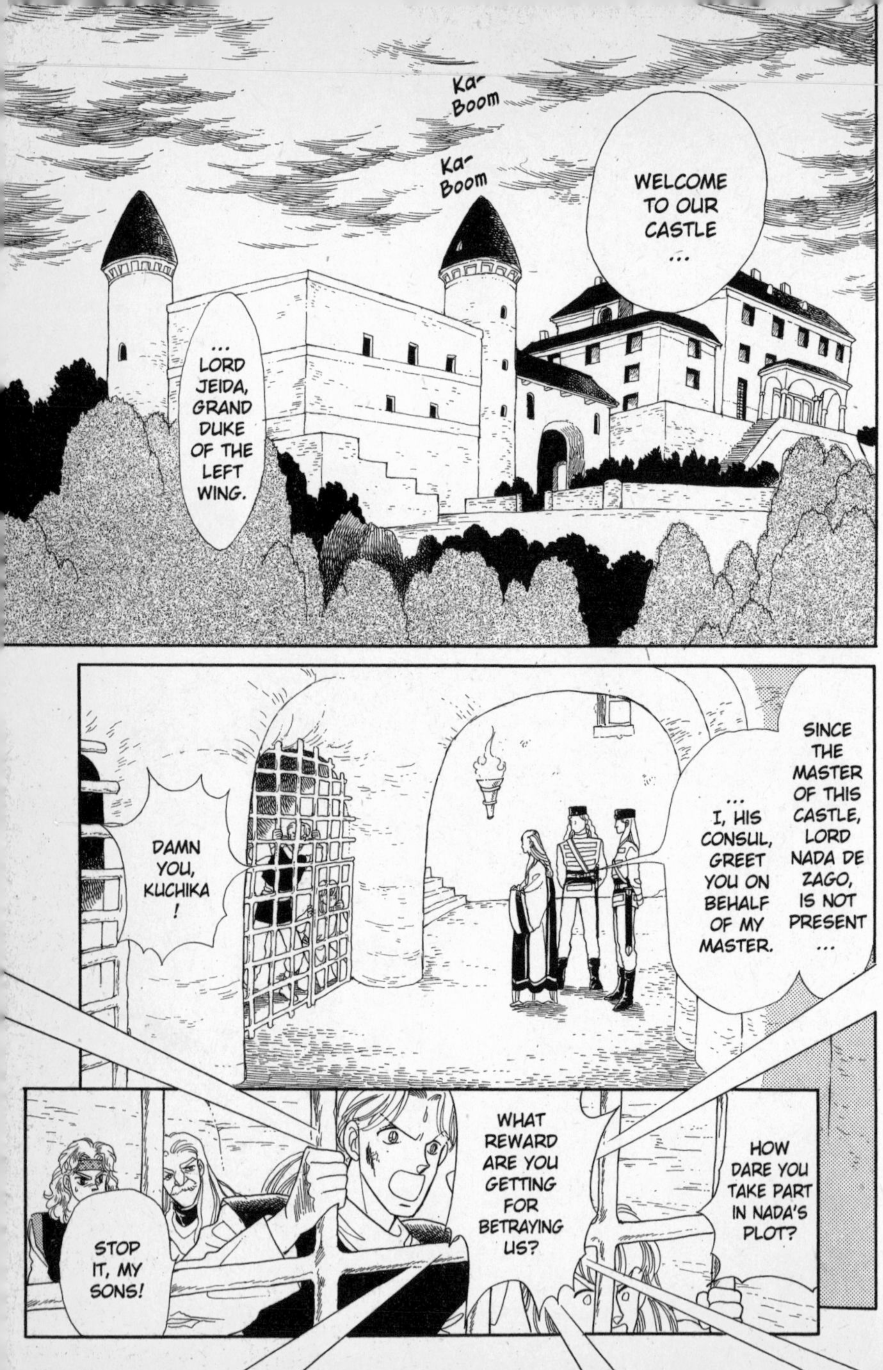
WELCOME TO OUR CASTLE ...
Ka-Boom
Ka-Boom
... LORD JEIDA, GRAND DUKE OF THE LEFT WING.
SINCE THE MASTER OF THIS CASTLE, LORD NADA DE ZAGO, IS NOT PRESENT ...
... I, HIS CONSUL, GREET YOU ON BEHALF OF MY MASTER.
DAMN YOU, KUCHIKA!
HOW DARE YOU TAKE PART IN NADA'S PLOT?
WHAT REWARD ARE YOU GETTING FOR BETRAYING US?
STOP IT, MY SONS!

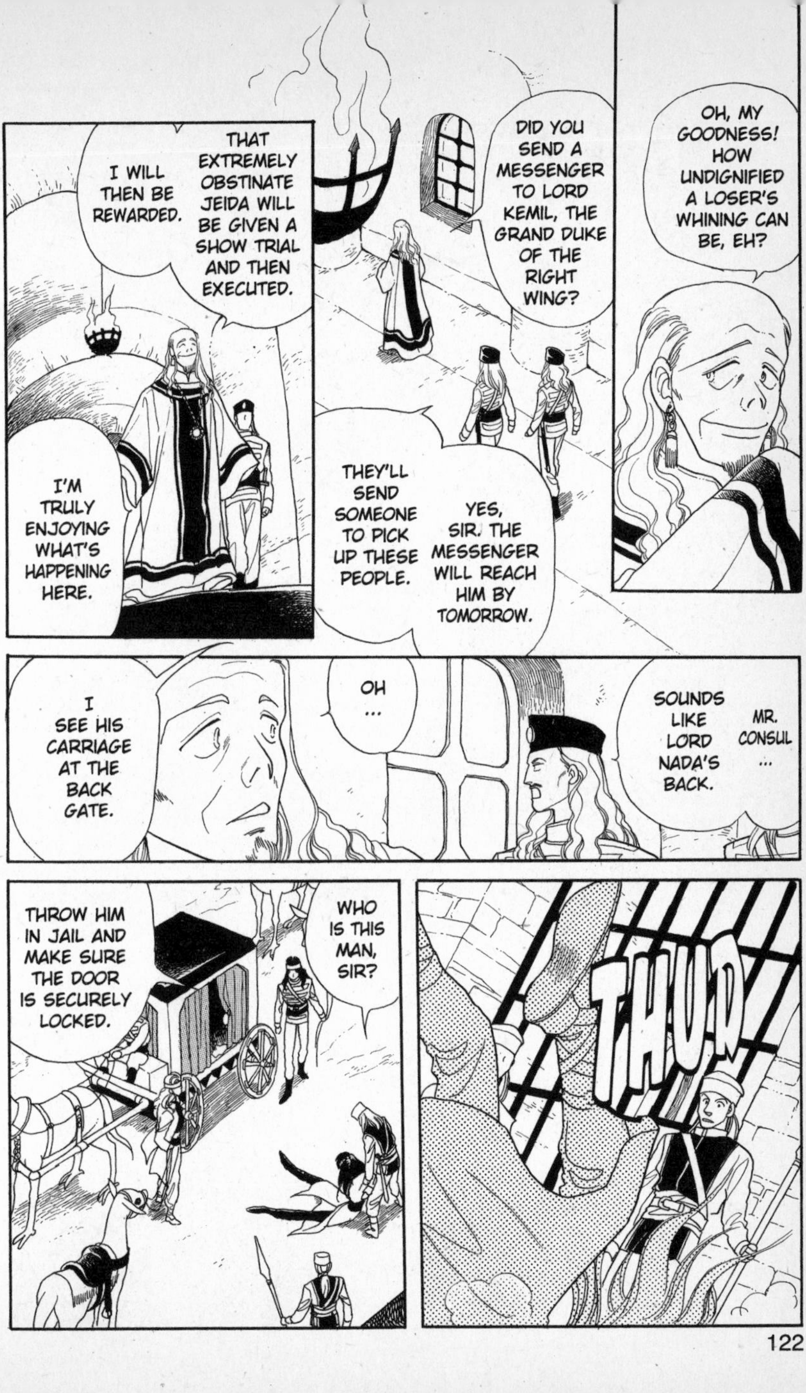
OH, MY GOODNESS! HOW UNDIGNIFIED A LOSER'S WHINING CAN BE, EH?
DID YOU SEND A MESSENGER TO LORD KEMIL, THE GRAND DUKE OF THE RIGHT WING?
YES, SIR. THE MESSENGER WILL REACH HIM BY TOMORROW.
THEY'LL SEND SOMEONE TO PICK UP THESE PEOPLE.
THAT EXTREMELY OBSTINATE JEIDA WILL BE GIVEN A SHOW TRIAL AND THEN EXECUTED.
I WILL THEN BE REWARDED.
I'M TRULY ENJOYING WHAT'S HAPPENING HERE.
MR. CONSUL ...
SOUNDS LIKE LORD NADA'S BACK.
OH ...
I SEE HIS CARRIAGE AT THE BACK GATE.
THUD
WHO IS THIS MAN, SIR?
THROW HIM IN JAIL AND MAKE SURE THE DOOR IS SECURELY LOCKED.

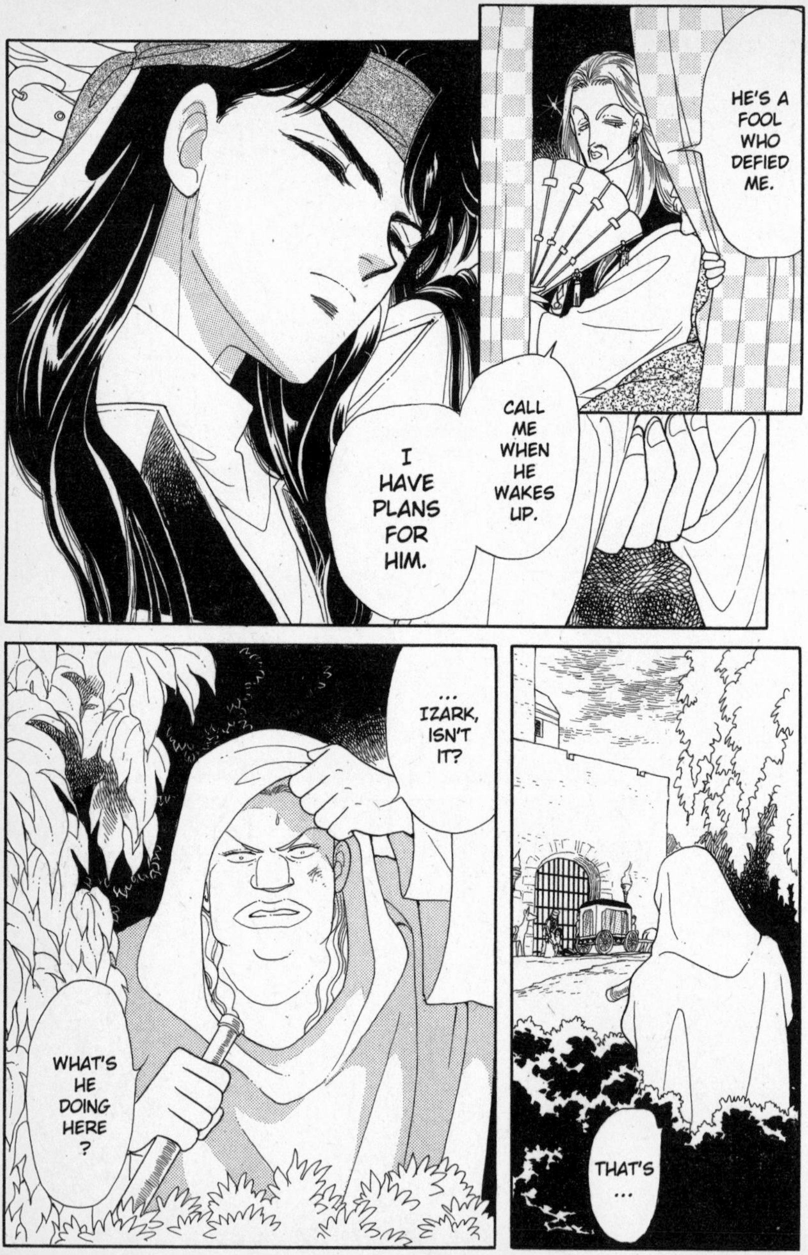
HE'S A FOOL WHO DEFIED ME.
CALL ME WHEN HE WAKES UP.
I HAVE PLANS FOR HIM.
THAT'S ...
... IZARK, ISN'T IT?
WHAT'S HE DOING HERE ?

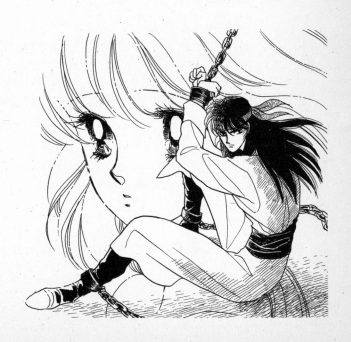

★ ★ ★ **What follows after this** ★ ★ ★

"See You Tomorrow!" -
the third episode of
"Girls Have a Lot of
Room in Their Hearts."

You can find the
first and second
episodes in the Comic,
"Girls Have a lot of
Room in Their Hearts."

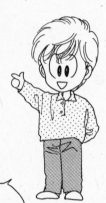

This is one of my
favorite series.
Enjoy the following
episode!

The eight pages that follow the
episode are called "The Author's Pages"
and they first appeared in "LA LA DX."

Readers' responses are
included here, too!

★ ★ ★ ★ ★ ★ ★ ★ ★ ★ ★ ★ ★

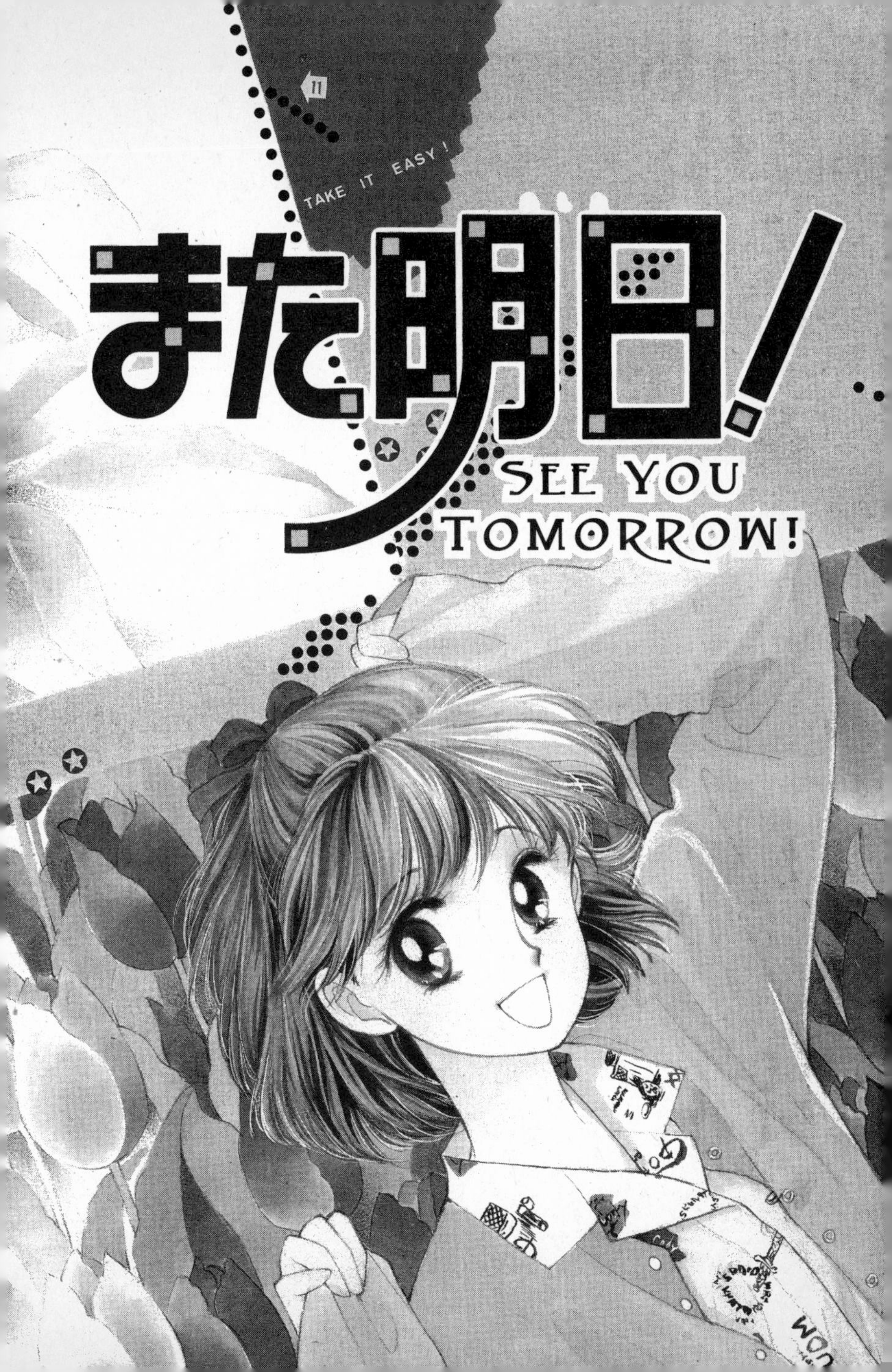
11
TAKE IT EASY!
また明日!
SEE YOU TOMORROW!

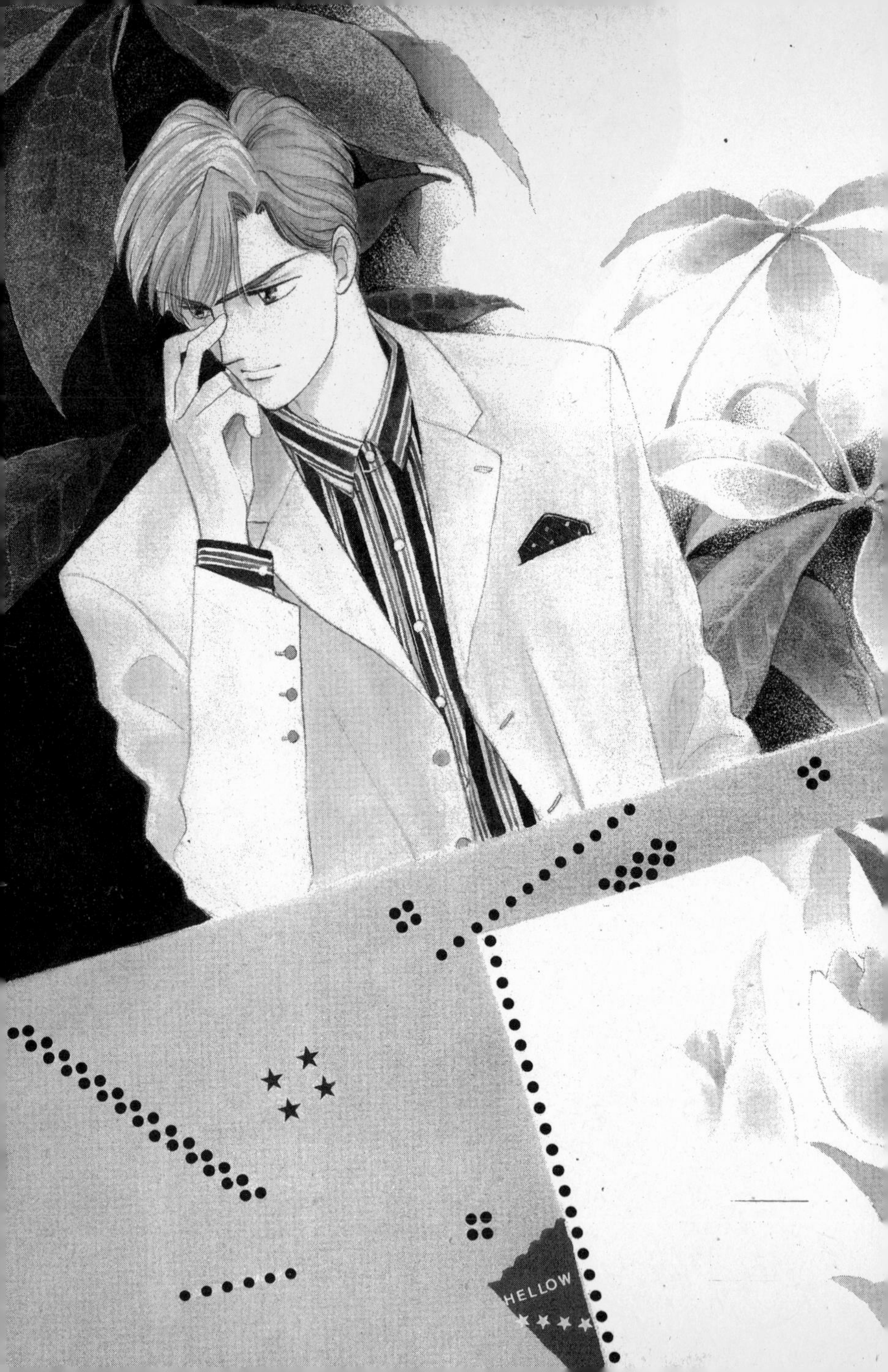
HELLOW

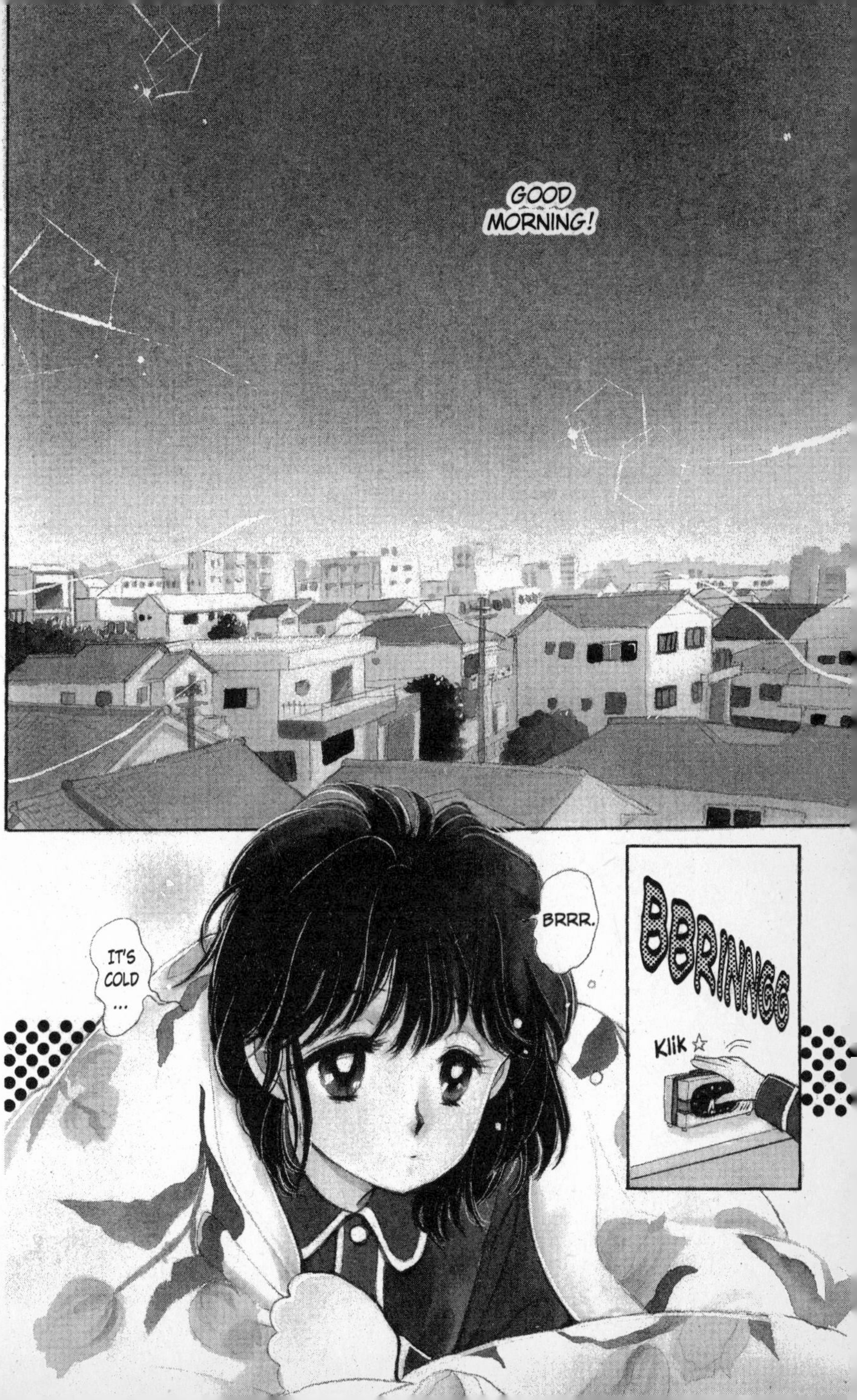
GOOD MORNING!
BBRINNGG
Klik ☆
BRRR.
IT'S COLD ...

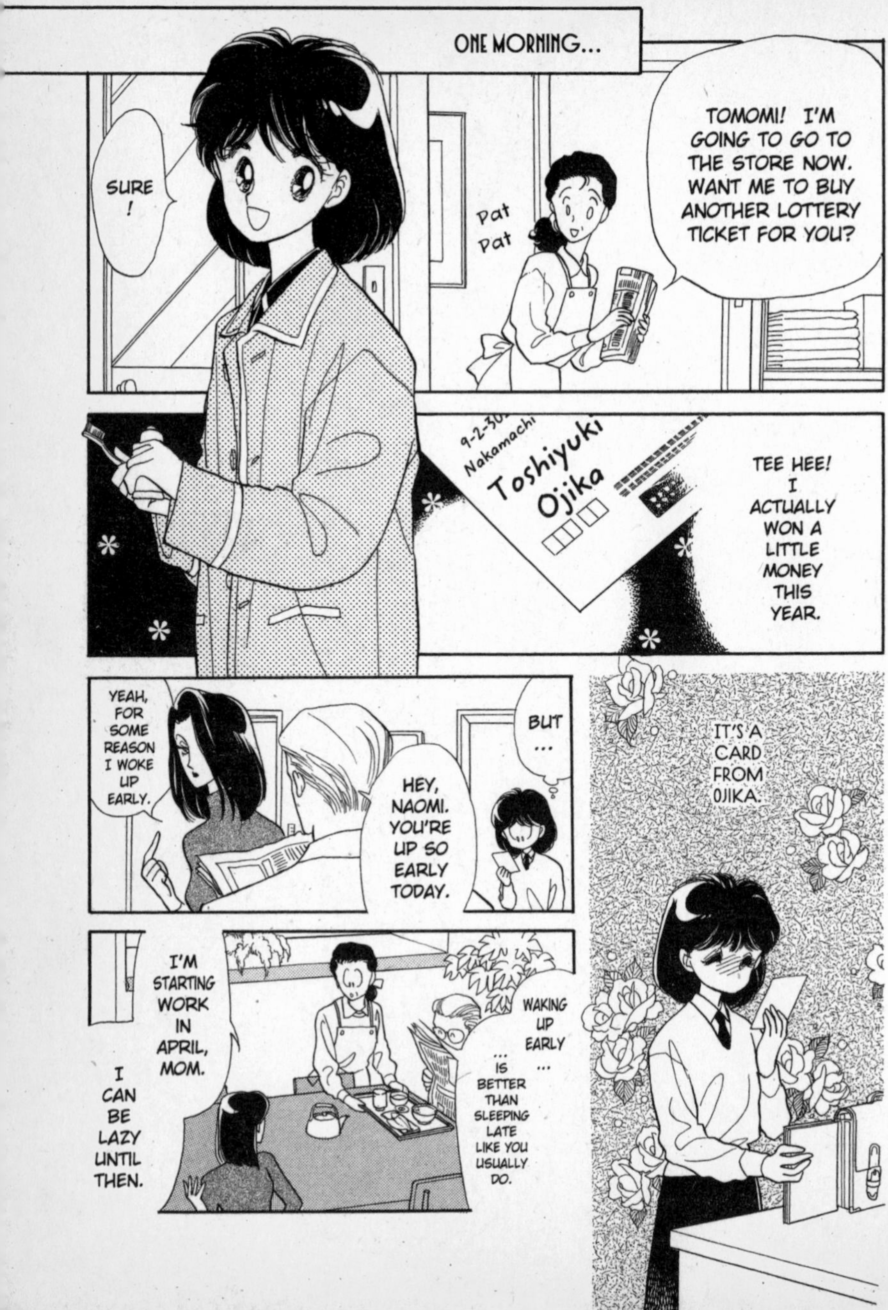
ONE MORNING...
TOMOMI! I'M GOING TO GO TO THE STORE NOW. WANT ME TO BUY ANOTHER LOTTERY TICKET FOR YOU?
Pat Pat
SURE!
TEE HEE! I ACTUALLY WON A LITTLE MONEY THIS YEAR.
9-2-30
Nakamachi
Toshiyuki Ojika
IT'S A CARD FROM OJIKA.
BUT ...
HEY, NAOMI. YOU'RE UP SO EARLY TODAY.
YEAH, FOR SOME REASON I WOKE UP EARLY.
WAKING UP EARLY ...
... IS BETTER THAN SLEEPING LATE LIKE YOU USUALLY DO.
I'M STARTING WORK IN APRIL, MOM.
I CAN BE LAZY UNTIL THEN.

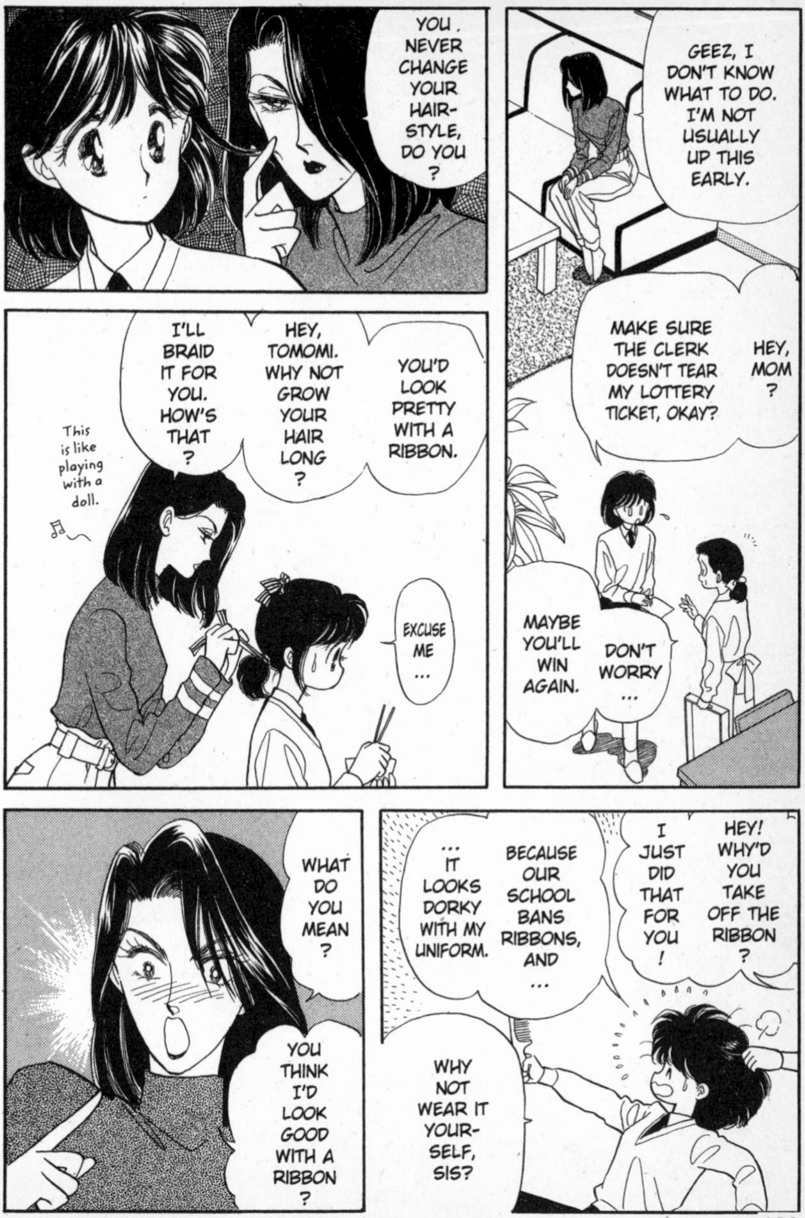
GEEZ, I DON'T KNOW WHAT TO DO. I'M NOT USUALLY UP THIS EARLY.
HEY, MOM?
MAKE SURE THE CLERK DOESN'T TEAR MY LOTTERY TICKET, OKAY?
DON'T WORRY...
MAYBE YOU'LL WIN AGAIN.
YOU. NEVER CHANGE YOUR HAIR-STYLE, DO YOU?
YOU'D LOOK PRETTY WITH A RIBBON.
HEY, TOMOMI. WHY NOT GROW YOUR HAIR LONG?
I'LL BRAID IT FOR YOU. HOW'S THAT?
This is like playing with a doll.
EXCUSE ME...
HEY! WHY'D YOU TAKE OFF THE RIBBON?
I JUST DID THAT FOR YOU!
BECAUSE OUR SCHOOL BANS RIBBONS, AND...
... IT LOOKS DORKY WITH MY UNIFORM.
WHY NOT WEAR IT YOUR-SELF, SIS?
WHAT DO YOU MEAN?
YOU THINK I'D LOOK GOOD WITH A RIBBON?

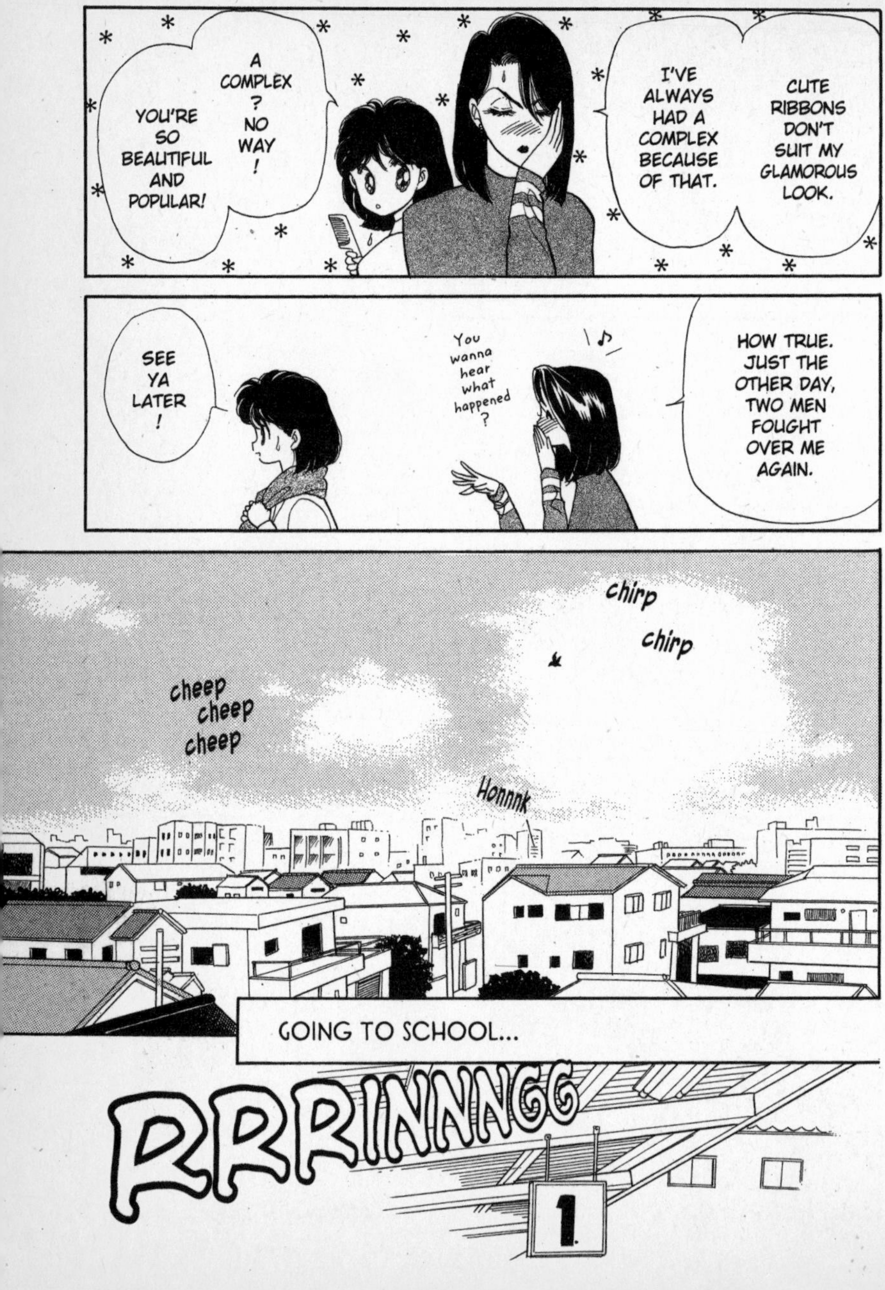
CUTE RIBBONS DON'T SUIT MY GLAMOROUS LOOK.
I'VE ALWAYS HAD A COMPLEX BECAUSE OF THAT.
A COMPLEX? NO WAY!
YOU'RE SO BEAUTIFUL AND POPULAR!
HOW TRUE. JUST THE OTHER DAY, TWO MEN FOUGHT OVER ME AGAIN.
♪
You wanna hear what happened?
SEE YA LATER!
chirp
chirp
cheep cheep cheep
Honnnk
GOING TO SCHOOL...
RRRINNNGG
1

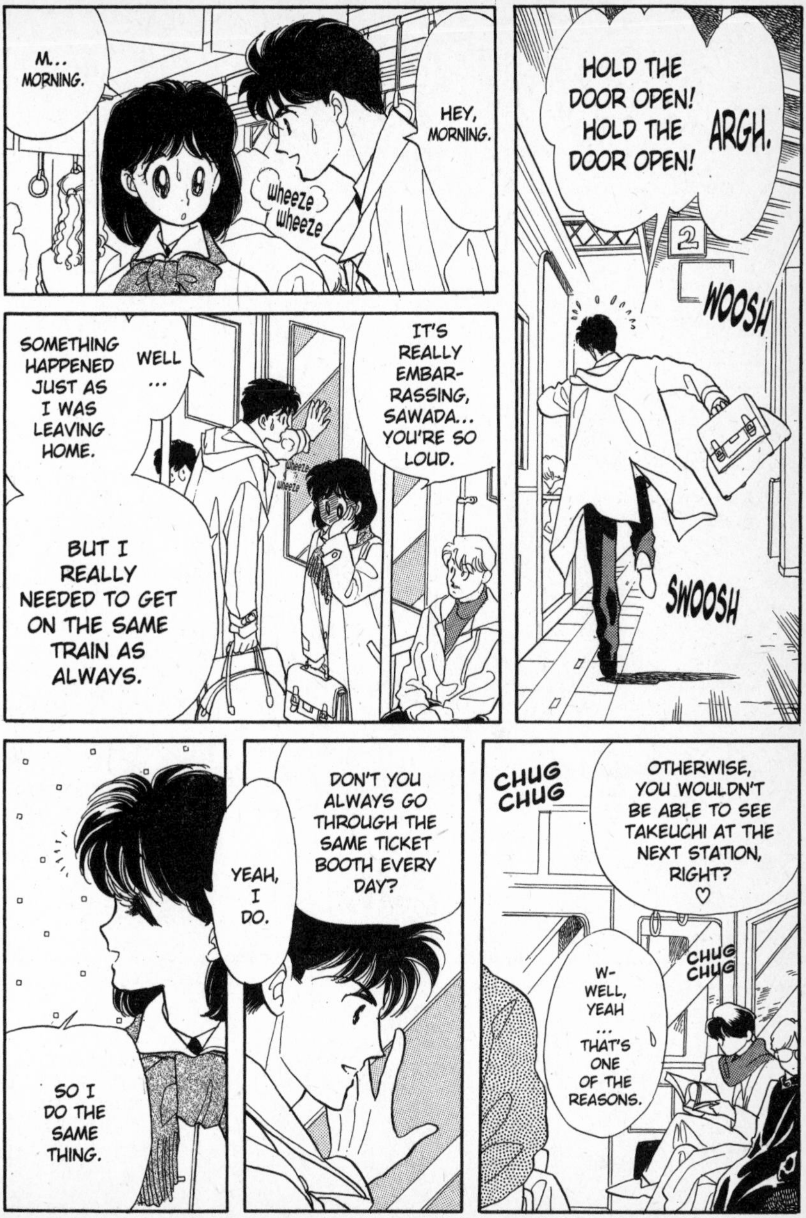
HOLD THE DOOR OPEN! HOLD THE DOOR OPEN!
ARGH.
2
WOOSH
SWOOSH
HEY, MORNING.
wheeze wheeze
M... MORNING.
IT'S REALLY EMBARRASSING, SAWADA... YOU'RE SO LOUD.
wheeze wheeze
WELL ...
SOMETHING HAPPENED JUST AS I WAS LEAVING HOME.
BUT I REALLY NEEDED TO GET ON THE SAME TRAIN AS ALWAYS.
OTHERWISE, YOU WOULDN'T BE ABLE TO SEE TAKEUCHI AT THE NEXT STATION, RIGHT? ♡
CHUG CHUG
CHUG CHUG
W-WELL, YEAH ... THAT'S ONE OF THE REASONS.
DON'T YOU ALWAYS GO THROUGH THE SAME TICKET BOOTH EVERY DAY?
YEAH, I DO.
SO I DO THE SAME THING.

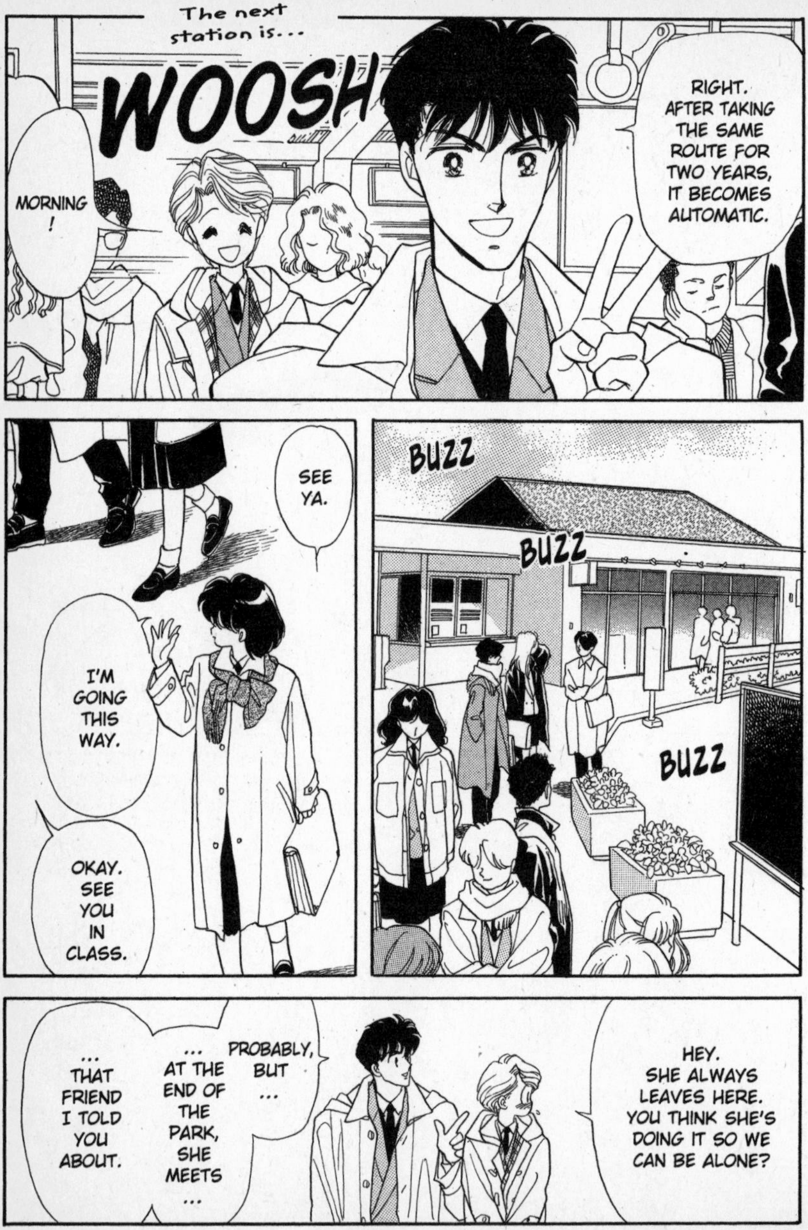
The next station is...
WOOSH
RIGHT. AFTER TAKING THE SAME ROUTE FOR TWO YEARS, IT BECOMES AUTOMATIC.
MORNING!
BUZZ
BUZZ
BUZZ
SEE YA.
I'M GOING THIS WAY.
OKAY. SEE YOU IN CLASS.
HEY. SHE ALWAYS LEAVES HERE. YOU THINK SHE'S DOING IT SO WE CAN BE ALONE?
PROBABLY, BUT ...
... AT THE END OF THE PARK, SHE MEETS ...
... THAT FRIEND I TOLD YOU ABOUT.

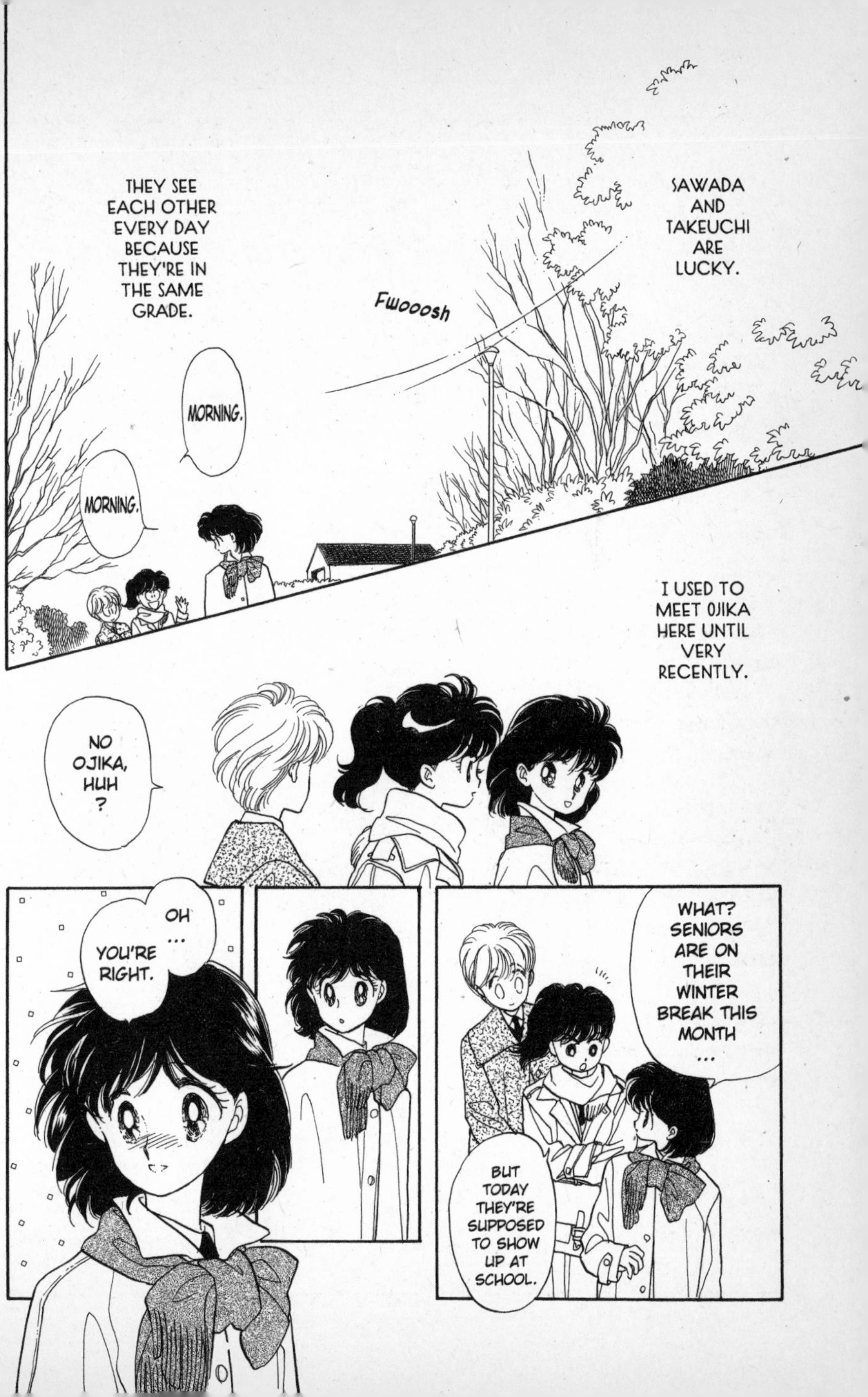
SAWADA AND TAKEUCHI ARE LUCKY.
THEY SEE EACH OTHER EVERY DAY BECAUSE THEY'RE IN THE SAME GRADE.
Fwooosh
MORNING.
MORNING.
I USED TO MEET OJIKA HERE UNTIL VERY RECENTLY.
NO OJIKA, HUH?
WHAT? SENIORS ARE ON THEIR WINTER BREAK THIS MONTH ...
BUT TODAY THEY'RE SUPPOSED TO SHOW UP AT SCHOOL.
OH ... YOU'RE RIGHT.

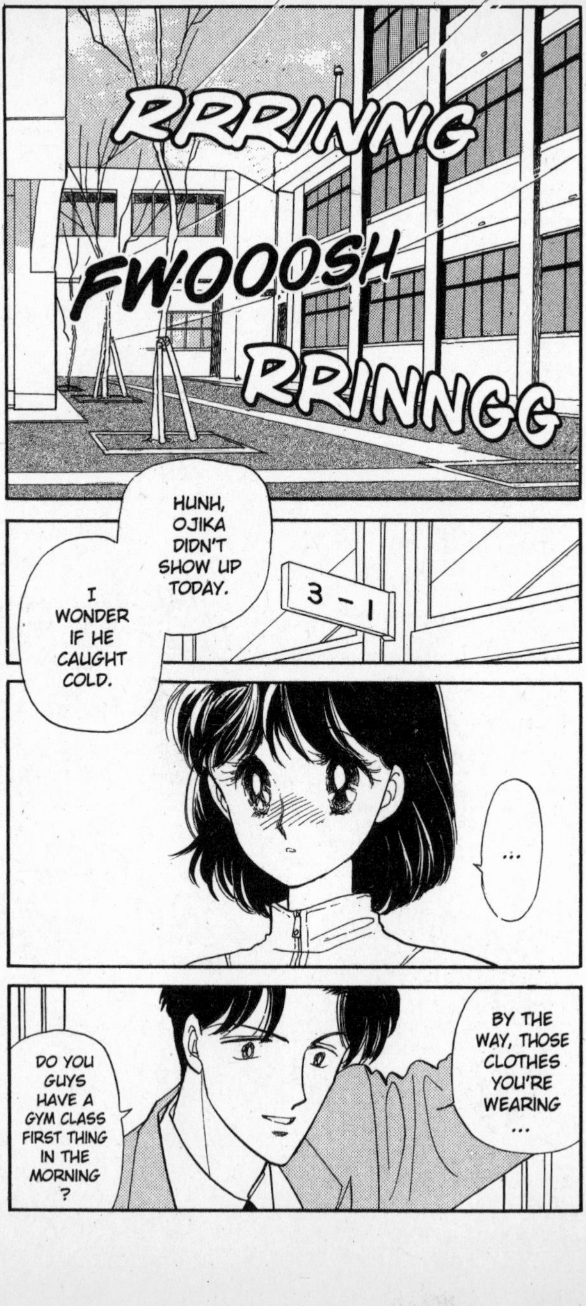
RRRINNG
FWOOOSH
RRINNGG
3 - 1
HUNH, OJIKA DIDN'T SHOW UP TODAY.
I WONDER IF HE CAUGHT COLD.
...
BY THE WAY, THOSE CLOTHES YOU'RE WEARING ...
DO YOU GUYS HAVE A GYM CLASS FIRST THING IN THE MORNING?

After writing that I didn't know the lyrics to "Box Lunch's Song" in the second episode of this series, I got tons of letters from readers, answering my question. Thanks everyone!

Here's what they wrote:

The song was not called "Box Lunch's Song." It was "Lunch Box's Song."

Also, it was not sung on the kids' TV show "Hirake Ponkiki." It's from "Together with Mom."

But maybe it was sung on both programs?

I'm not sure!

Anyhow, now I know the dance!

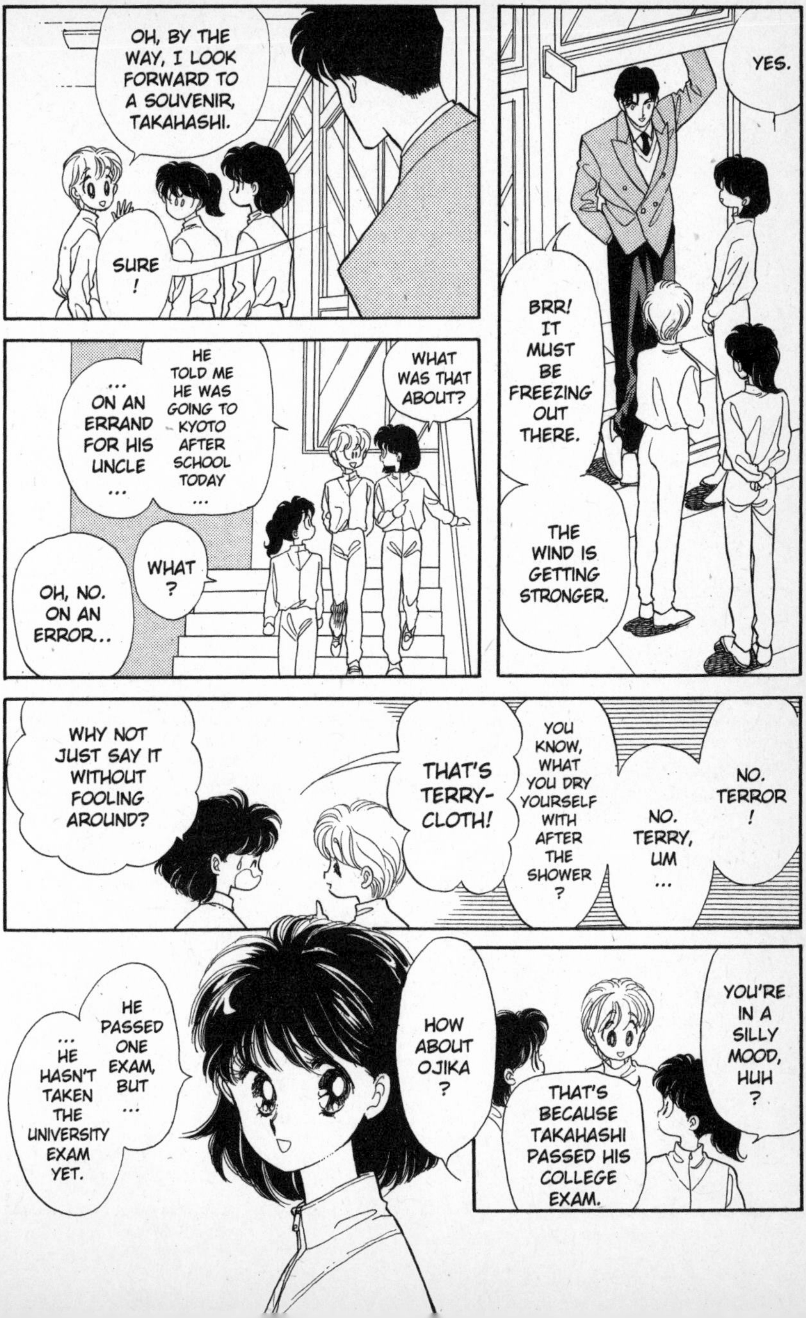
YES.
BRR! IT MUST BE FREEZING OUT THERE.
THE WIND IS GETTING STRONGER.
OH, BY THE WAY, I LOOK FORWARD TO A SOUVENIR, TAKAHASHI.
SURE!
WHAT WAS THAT ABOUT?
HE TOLD ME HE WAS GOING TO KYOTO AFTER SCHOOL TODAY...
...ON AN ERRAND FOR HIS UNCLE...
WHAT?
OH, NO. ON AN ERROR...
NO. TERROR!
NO. TERRY, UM...
YOU KNOW, WHAT YOU DRY YOURSELF WITH AFTER THE SHOWER?
THAT'S TERRY-CLOTH!
WHY NOT JUST SAY IT WITHOUT FOOLING AROUND?
YOU'RE IN A SILLY MOOD, HUH?
THAT'S BECAUSE TAKAHASHI PASSED HIS COLLEGE EXAM.
HOW ABOUT OJIKA?
HE PASSED ONE EXAM, BUT...
...HE HASN'T TAKEN THE UNIVERSITY EXAM YET.

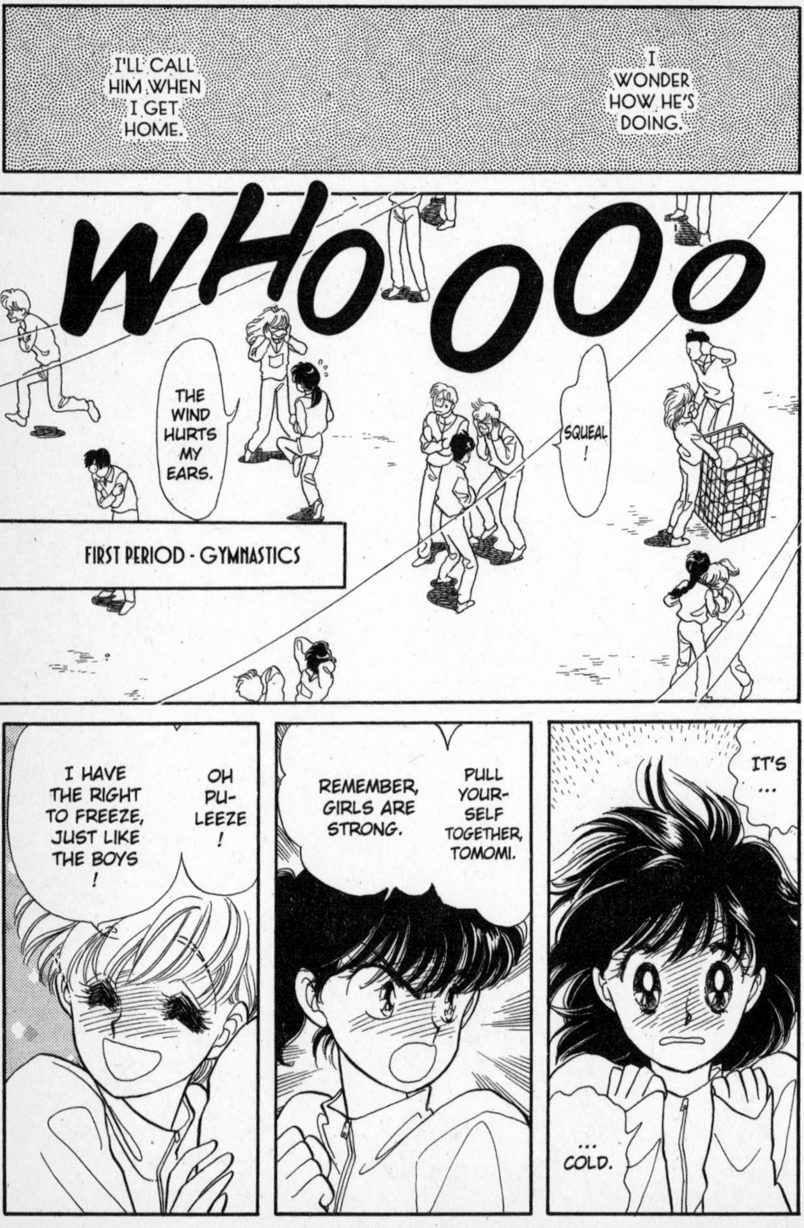
I WONDER HOW HE'S DOING.
I'LL CALL HIM WHEN I GET HOME.
WHOOOOO
SQUEAL!
THE WIND HURTS MY EARS.
FIRST PERIOD - GYMNASTICS
IT'S...
...COLD.
PULL YOURSELF TOGETHER, TOMOMI.
REMEMBER, GIRLS ARE STRONG.
OH PULEEZE!
I HAVE THE RIGHT TO FREEZE, JUST LIKE THE BOYS!

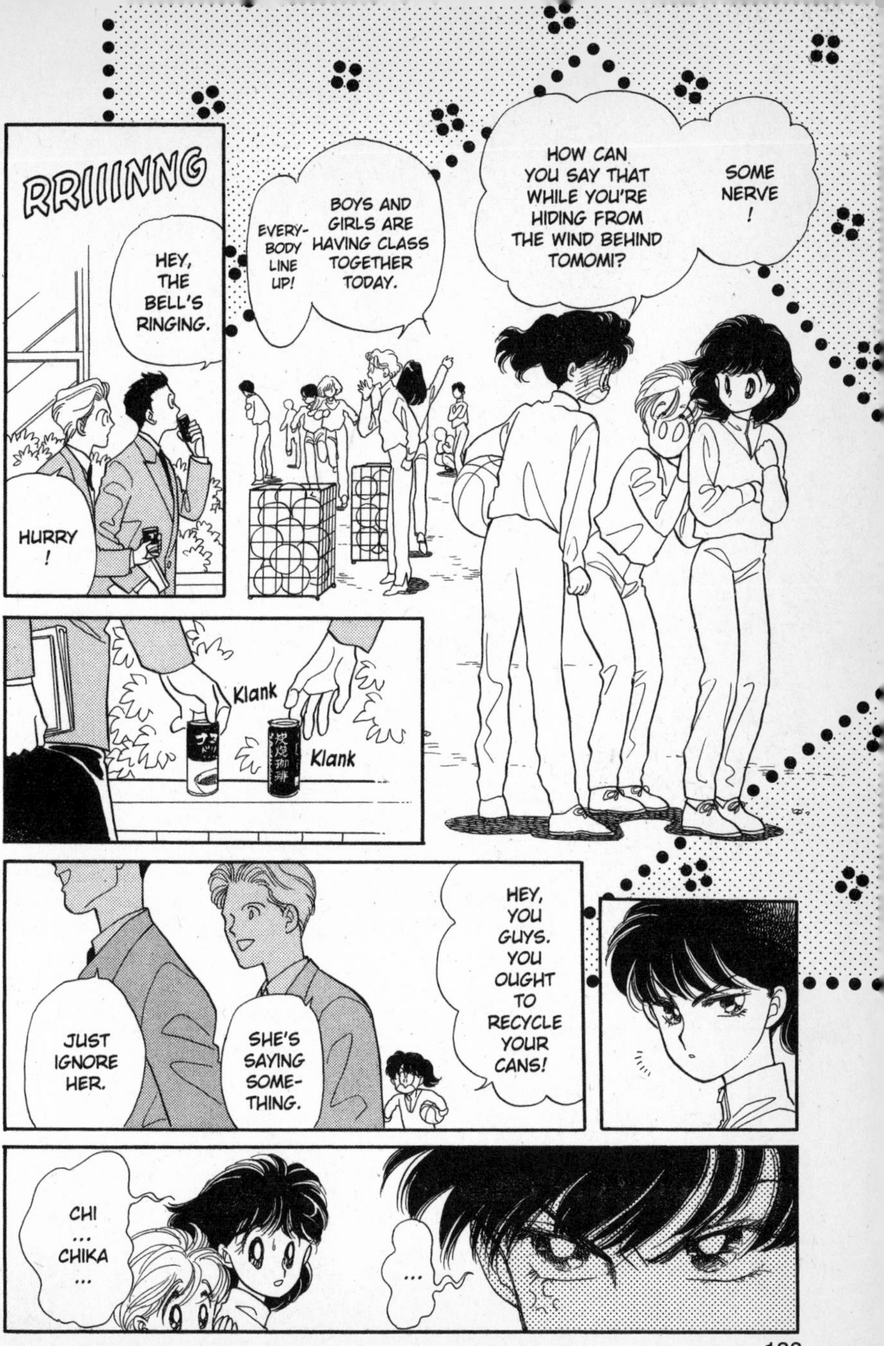
SOME NERVE!
HOW CAN YOU SAY THAT WHILE YOU'RE HIDING FROM THE WIND BEHIND TOMOMI?
BOYS AND GIRLS ARE HAVING CLASS TOGETHER TODAY.
EVERY-BODY LINE UP!
RRIIINNG
HEY, THE BELL'S RINGING.
HURRY!
Klank
Klank
HEY, YOU GUYS. YOU OUGHT TO RECYCLE YOUR CANS!
SHE'S SAYING SOME-THING.
JUST IGNORE HER.
...
CHI ... CHIKA ...

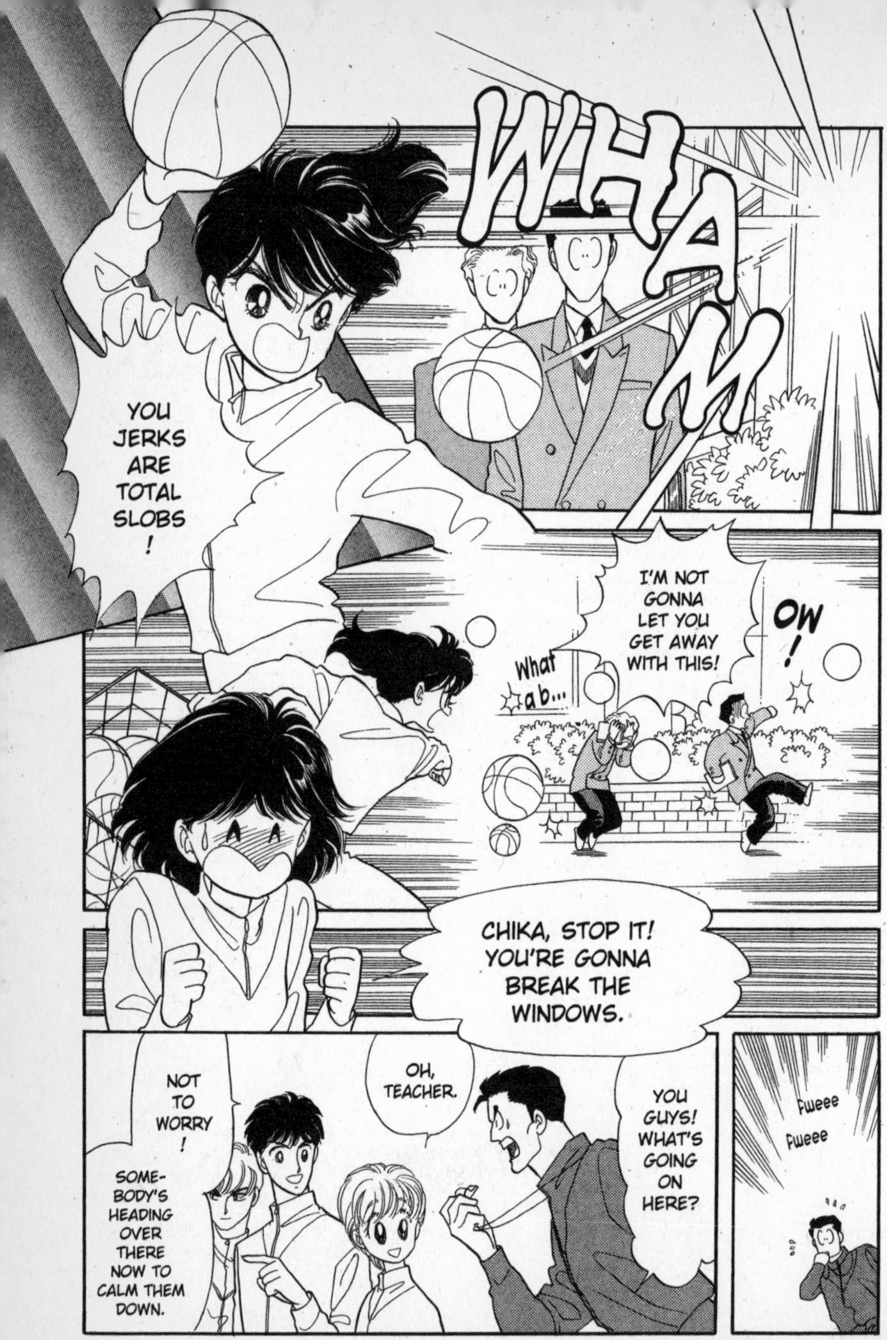
WHAM
YOU JERKS ARE TOTAL SLOBS!
OW!
I'M NOT GONNA LET YOU GET AWAY WITH THIS!
What a b...
CHIKA, STOP IT! YOU'RE GONNA BREAK THE WINDOWS.
Fweee
Fweee
YOU GUYS! WHAT'S GOING ON HERE?
OH, TEACHER.
NOT TO WORRY!
SOME-BODY'S HEADING OVER THERE NOW TO CALM THEM DOWN.

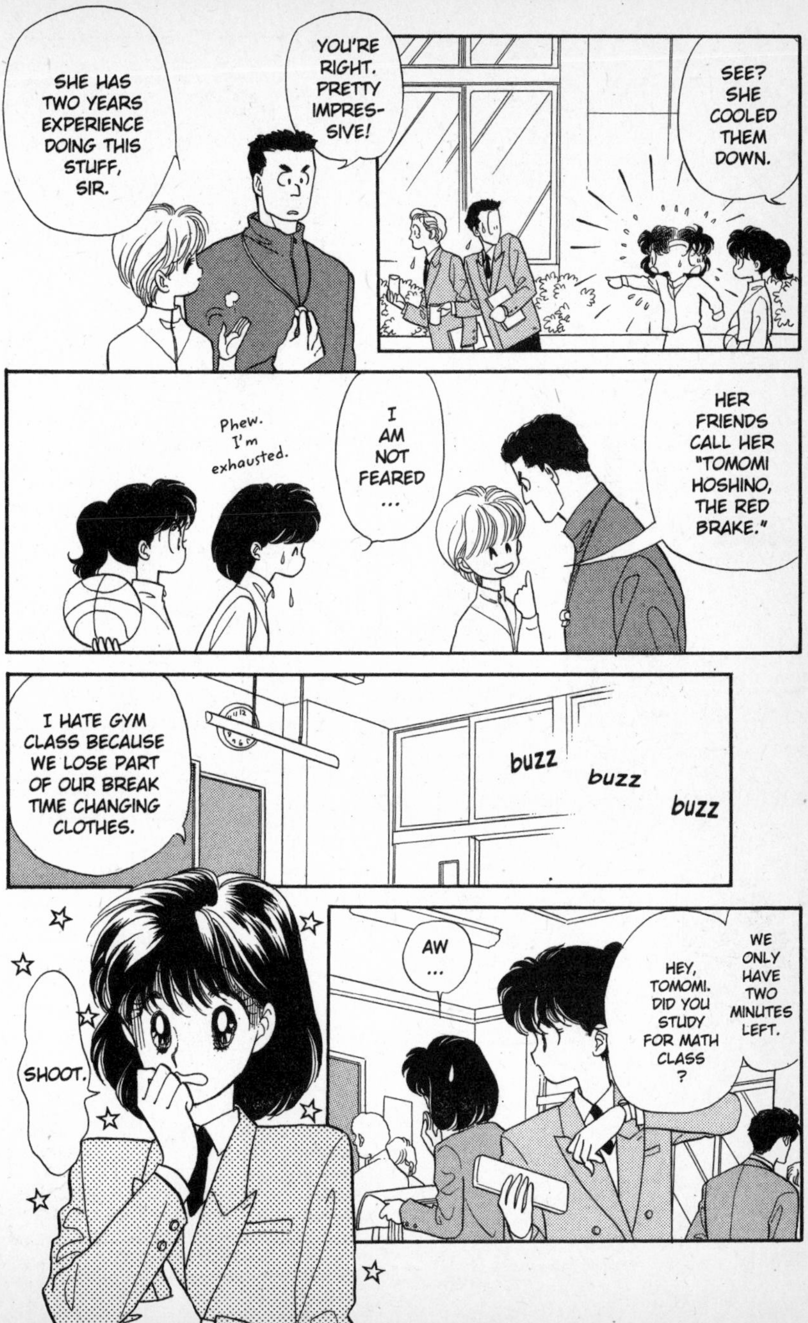
SEE? SHE COOLED THEM DOWN.
YOU'RE RIGHT. PRETTY IMPRES-SIVE!
SHE HAS TWO YEARS EXPERIENCE DOING THIS STUFF, SIR.
HER FRIENDS CALL HER "TOMOMI HOSHINO, THE RED BRAKE."
I AM NOT FEARED ...
Phew. I'm exhausted.
buzz
buzz
buzz
I HATE GYM CLASS BECAUSE WE LOSE PART OF OUR BREAK TIME CHANGING CLOTHES.
WE ONLY HAVE TWO MINUTES LEFT.
HEY, TOMOMI. DID YOU STUDY FOR MATH CLASS ?
AW ...
SHOOT.

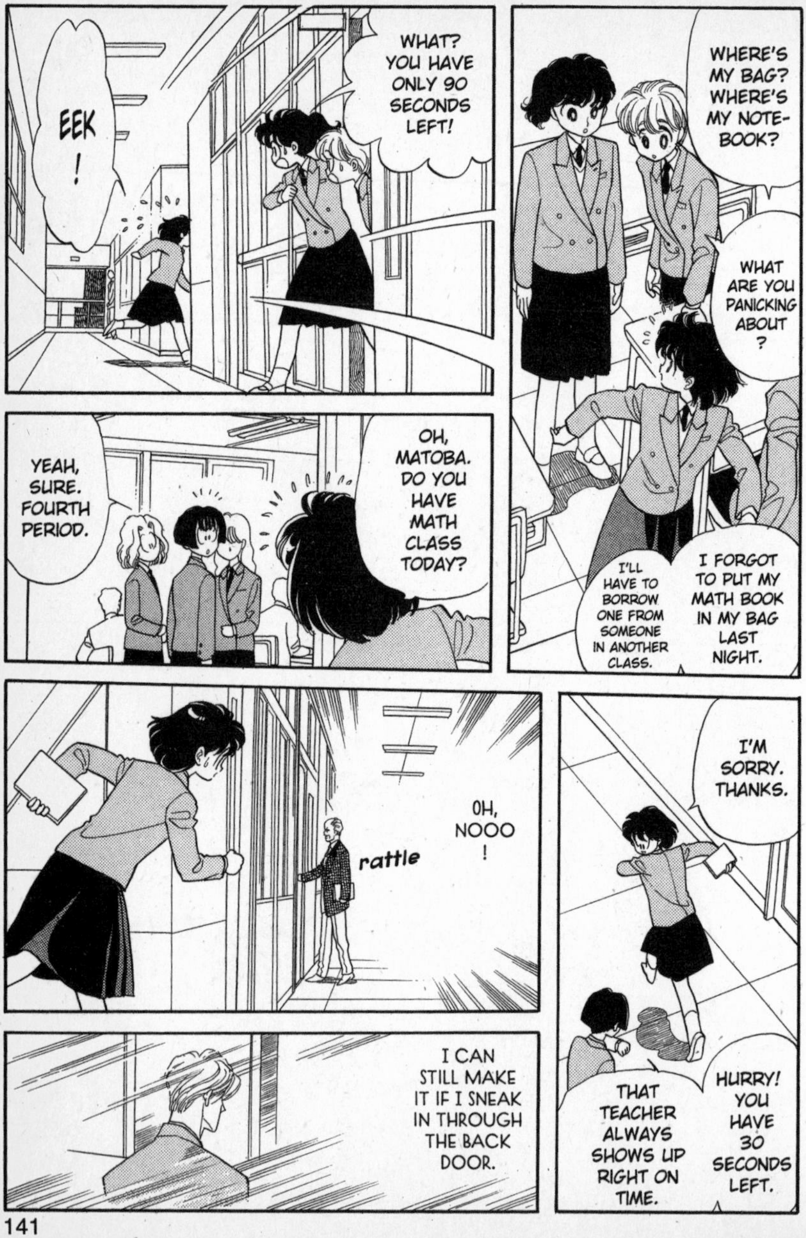
WHERE'S MY BAG? WHERE'S MY NOTE-BOOK?
WHAT ARE YOU PANICKING ABOUT?
I FORGOT TO PUT MY MATH BOOK IN MY BAG LAST NIGHT.
I'LL HAVE TO BORROW ONE FROM SOMEONE IN ANOTHER CLASS.
WHAT? YOU HAVE ONLY 90 SECONDS LEFT!
EEK!
OH, MATOBA. DO YOU HAVE MATH CLASS TODAY?
YEAH, SURE. FOURTH PERIOD.
I'M SORRY. THANKS.
HURRY! YOU HAVE 30 SECONDS LEFT.
THAT TEACHER ALWAYS SHOWS UP RIGHT ON TIME.
OH, NOOO!
rattle
I CAN STILL MAKE IT IF I SNEAK IN THROUGH THE BACK DOOR.

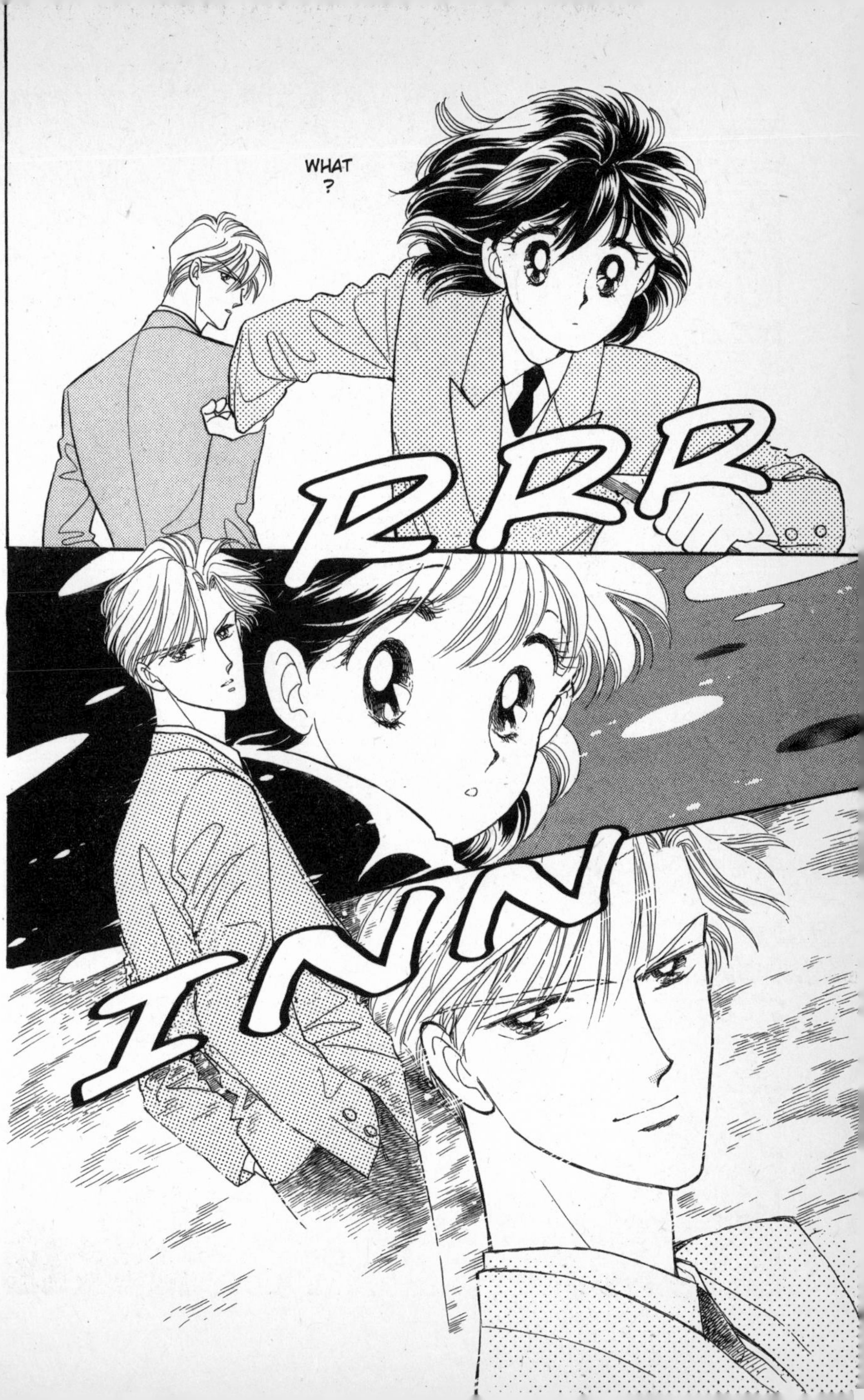
WHAT
?
RRR

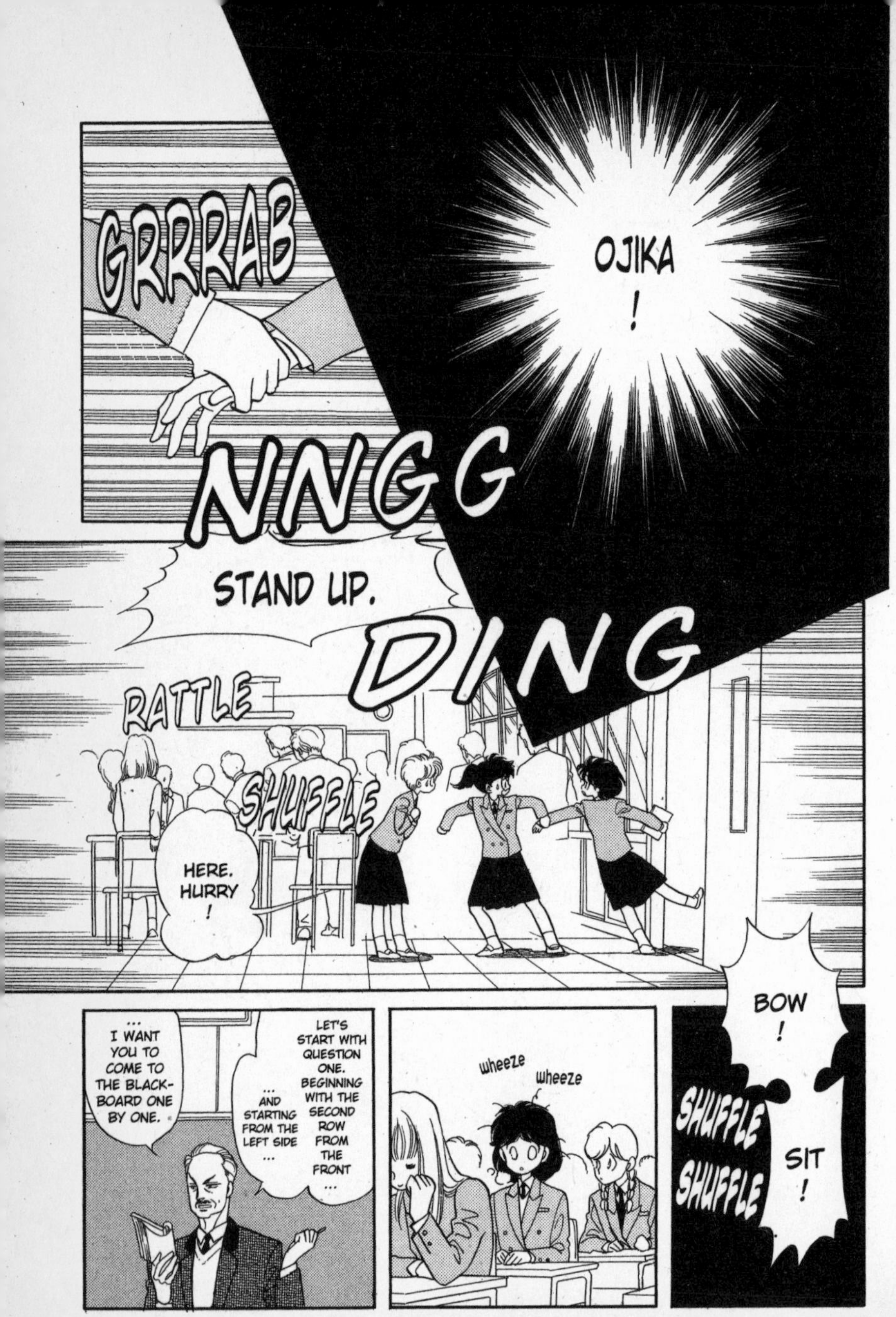
OJIKA !
GRRRAB
NNGG
DING
STAND UP.
RATTLE
SHUFFLE
HERE. HURRY !
BOW !
SHUFFLE SHUFFLE
SIT !
wheeze
wheeze
LET'S START WITH QUESTION ONE. BEGINNING WITH THE SECOND ROW FROM THE FRONT ...
... AND STARTING FROM THE LEFT SIDE ...
... I WANT YOU TO COME TO THE BLACK-BOARD ONE BY ONE.

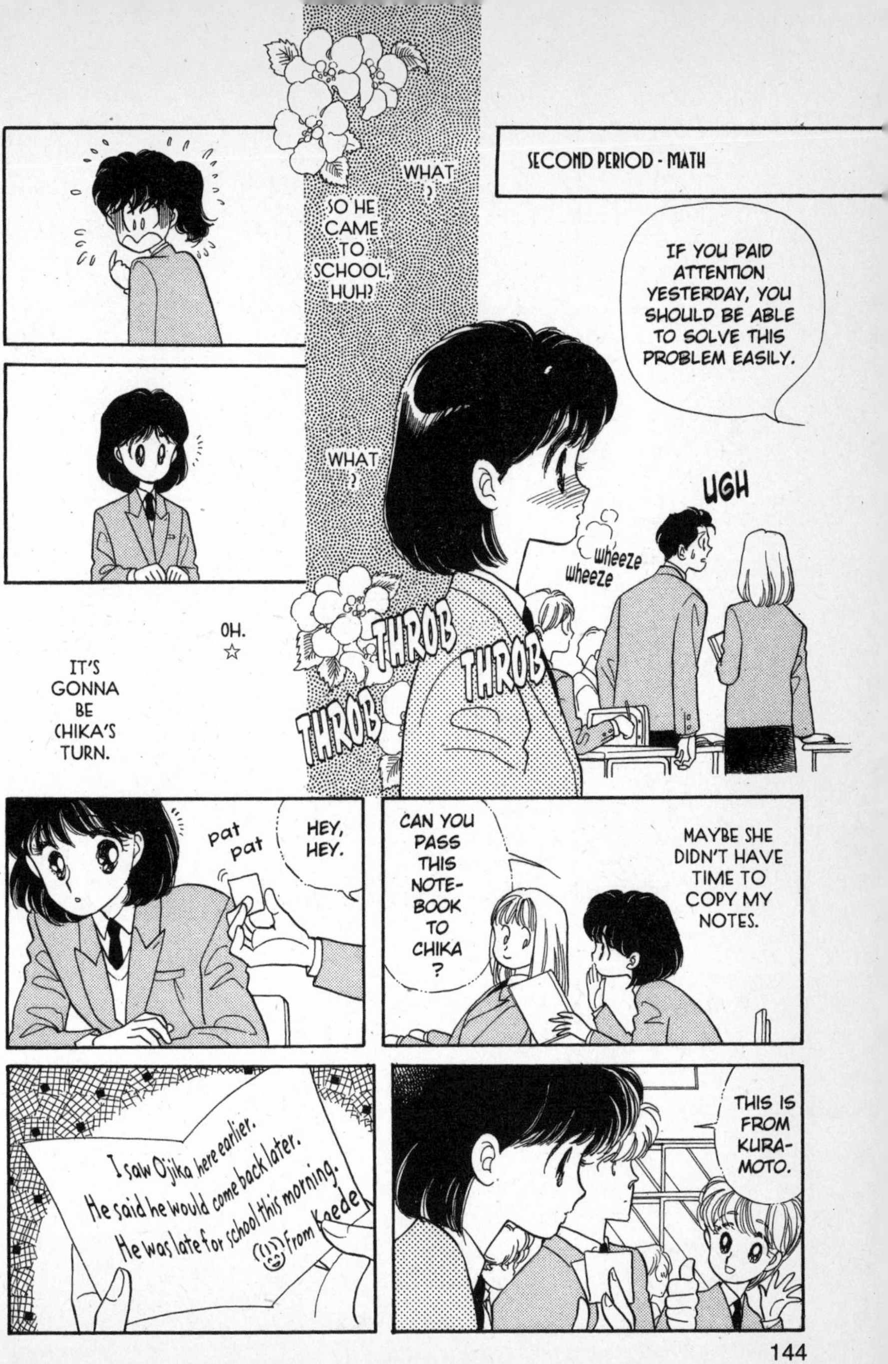
SECOND PERIOD - MATH
IF YOU PAID ATTENTION YESTERDAY, YOU SHOULD BE ABLE TO SOLVE THIS PROBLEM EASILY.
UGH
wheeze wheeze
THROB THROB THROB
WHAT?
SO HE CAME TO SCHOOL, HUH?
WHAT?
OH. ☆
IT'S GONNA BE CHIKA'S TURN.
MAYBE SHE DIDN'T HAVE TIME TO COPY MY NOTES.
CAN YOU PASS THIS NOTE-BOOK TO CHIKA?
HEY, HEY.
pat pat
THIS IS FROM KURA-MOTO.
I saw Ojika here earlier.
He said he would come back later.
He was late for school this morning.
From Kaede

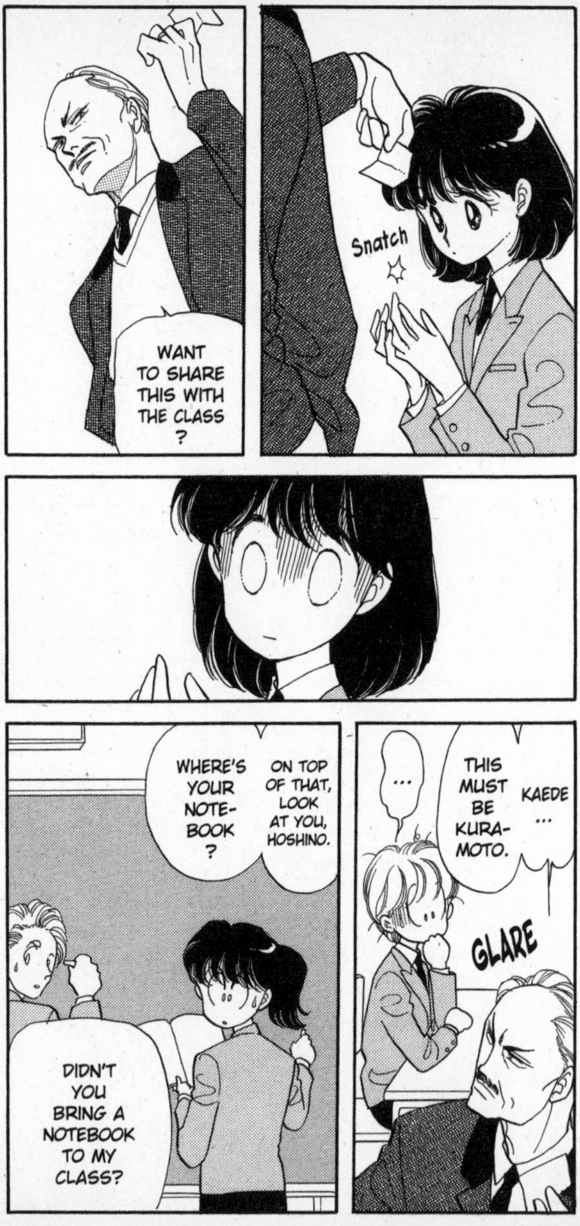
Snatch
WANT TO SHARE THIS WITH THE CLASS?
KAEDE ...
THIS MUST BE KURA-MOTO.
...
GLARE
ON TOP OF THAT, LOOK AT YOU, HOSHINO.
WHERE'S YOUR NOTE-BOOK?
DIDN'T YOU BRING A NOTEBOOK TO MY CLASS?

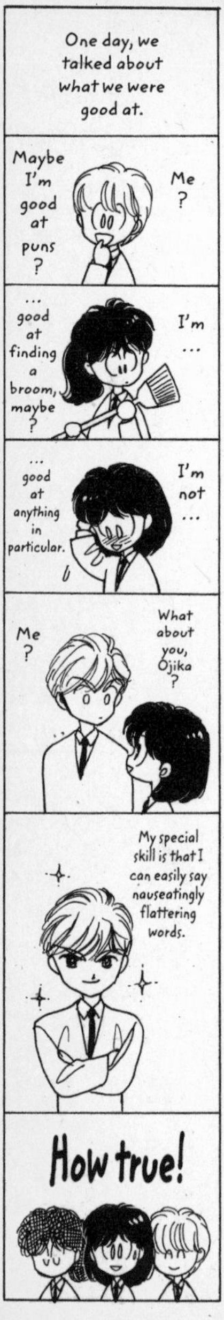
One day, we talked about what we were good at.
Me?
Maybe I'm good at puns?
I'm ...
... good at finding a broom, maybe?
I'm not ...
... good at anything in particular.
What about you, Ojika?
Me?
My special skill is that I can easily say nauseatingly flattering words.
How true!

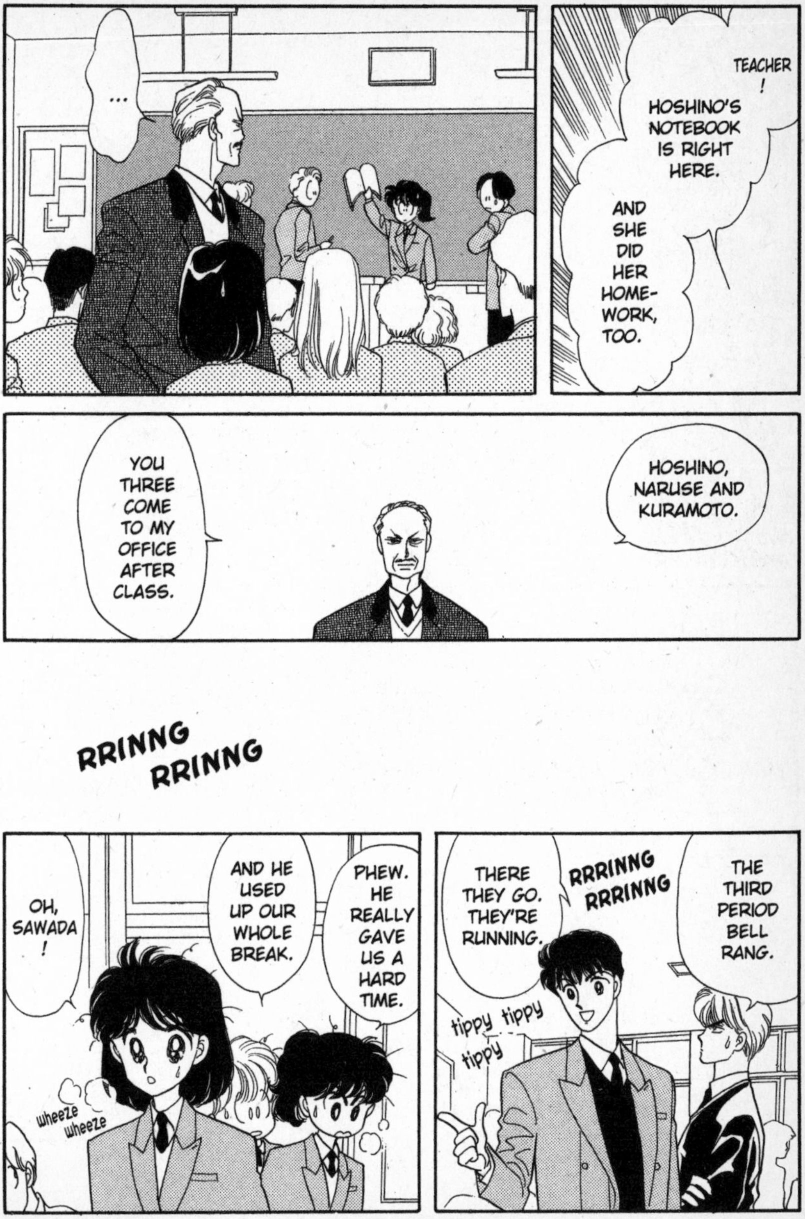
TEACHER !
HOSHINO'S NOTEBOOK IS RIGHT HERE.
AND SHE DID HER HOME-WORK, TOO.
...
HOSHINO, NARUSE AND KURAMOTO.
YOU THREE COME TO MY OFFICE AFTER CLASS.
RRINNG RRINNG
THE THIRD PERIOD BELL RANG.
RRRINNG RRRINNG
THERE THEY GO. THEY'RE RUNNING.
tippy tippy tippy
PHEW. HE REALLY GAVE US A HARD TIME.
AND HE USED UP OUR WHOLE BREAK.
OH, SAWADA !
wheeze wheeze

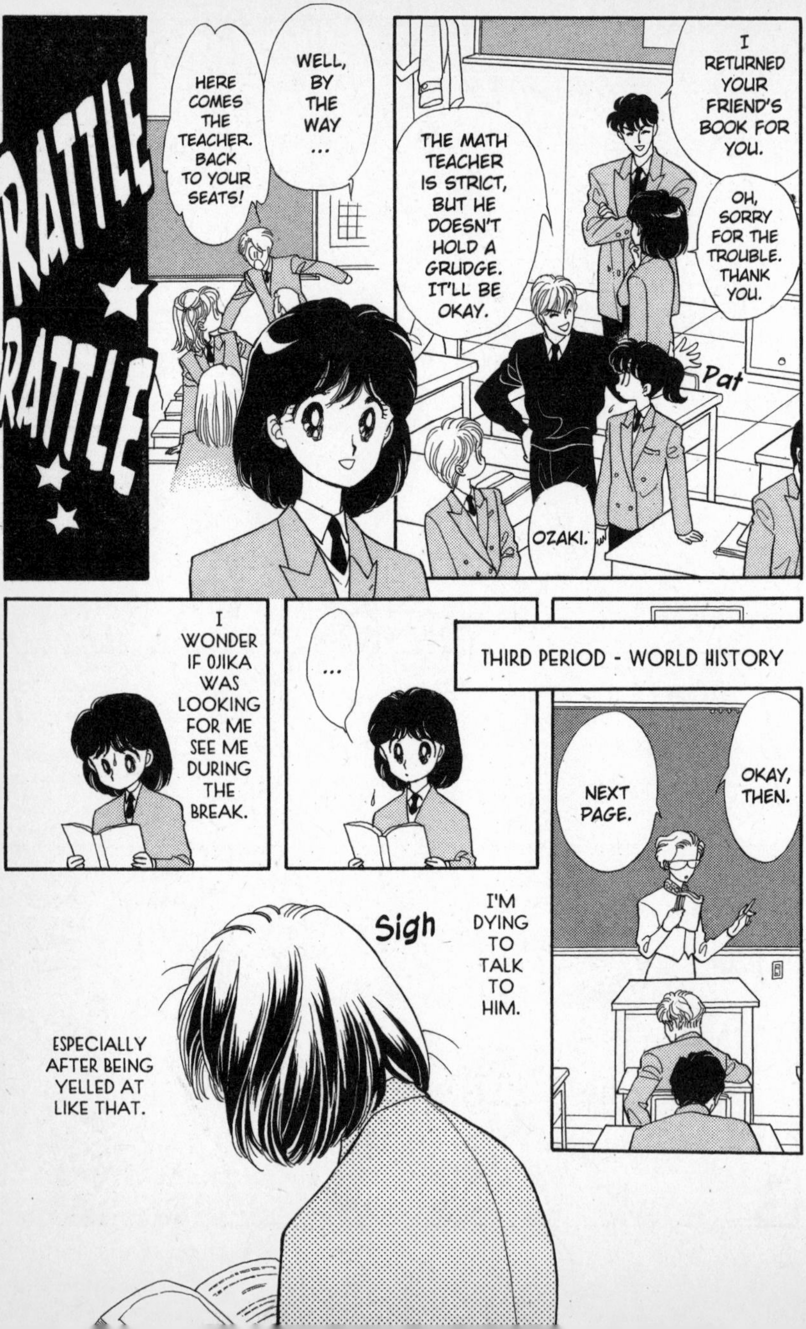
I RETURNED YOUR FRIEND'S BOOK FOR YOU.
OH, SORRY FOR THE TROUBLE. THANK YOU.
Pat
THE MATH TEACHER IS STRICT, BUT HE DOESN'T HOLD A GRUDGE. IT'LL BE OKAY.
OZAKI.
WELL, BY THE WAY ...
HERE COMES THE TEACHER. BACK TO YOUR SEATS!
RATTLE RATTLE
THIRD PERIOD - WORLD HISTORY
OKAY, THEN.
NEXT PAGE.
...
I WONDER IF OJIKA WAS LOOKING FOR ME SEE ME DURING THE BREAK.
I'M DYING TO TALK TO HIM.
Sigh
ESPECIALLY AFTER BEING YELLED AT LIKE THAT.

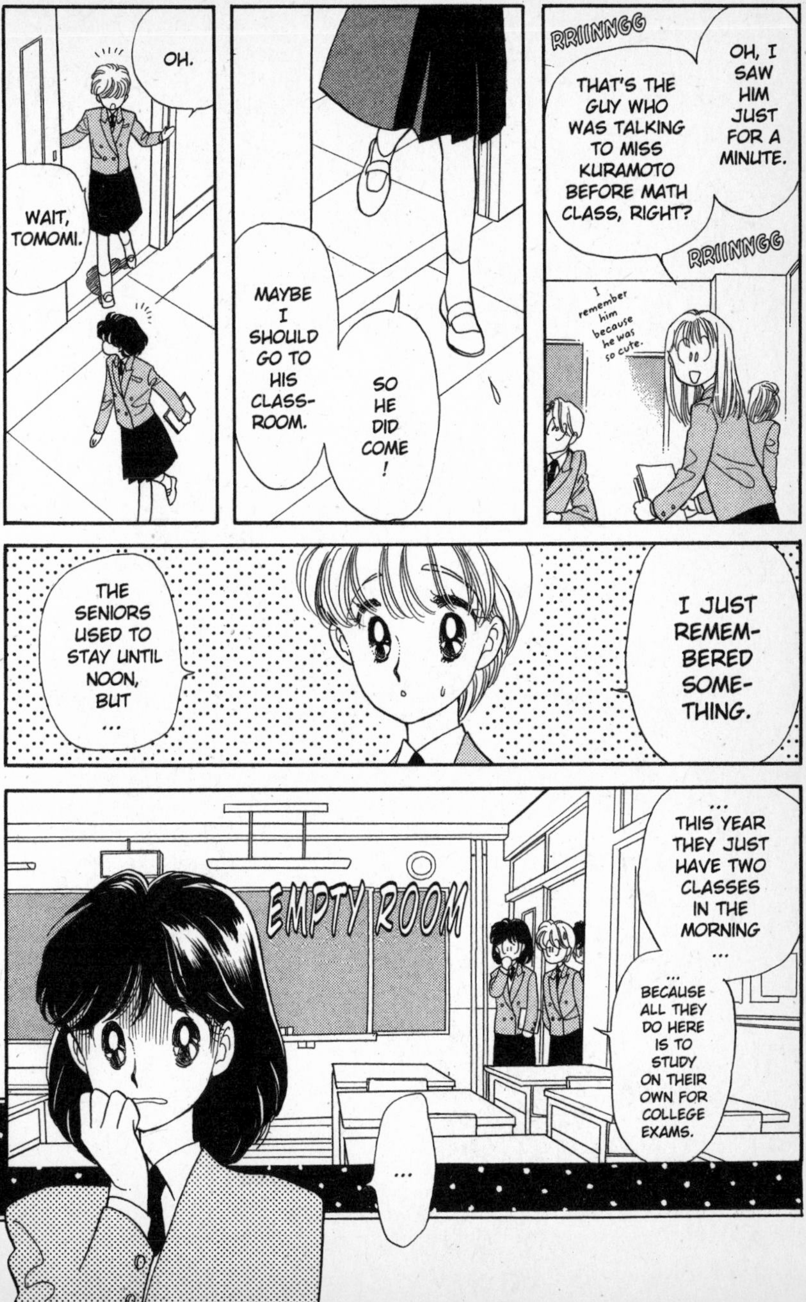
RRIINNGG
OH, I SAW HIM JUST FOR A MINUTE.
THAT'S THE GUY WHO WAS TALKING TO MISS KURAMOTO BEFORE MATH CLASS, RIGHT?
RRIINNGG
I remember him because he was so cute.
SO HE DID COME!
MAYBE I SHOULD GO TO HIS CLASSROOM.
OH.
WAIT, TOMOMI.
I JUST REMEM-BERED SOME-THING.
THE SENIORS USED TO STAY UNTIL NOON, BUT ...
... THIS YEAR THEY JUST HAVE TWO CLASSES IN THE MORNING ...
... BECAUSE ALL THEY DO HERE IS TO STUDY ON THEIR OWN FOR COLLEGE EXAMS.
EMPTY ROOM
...

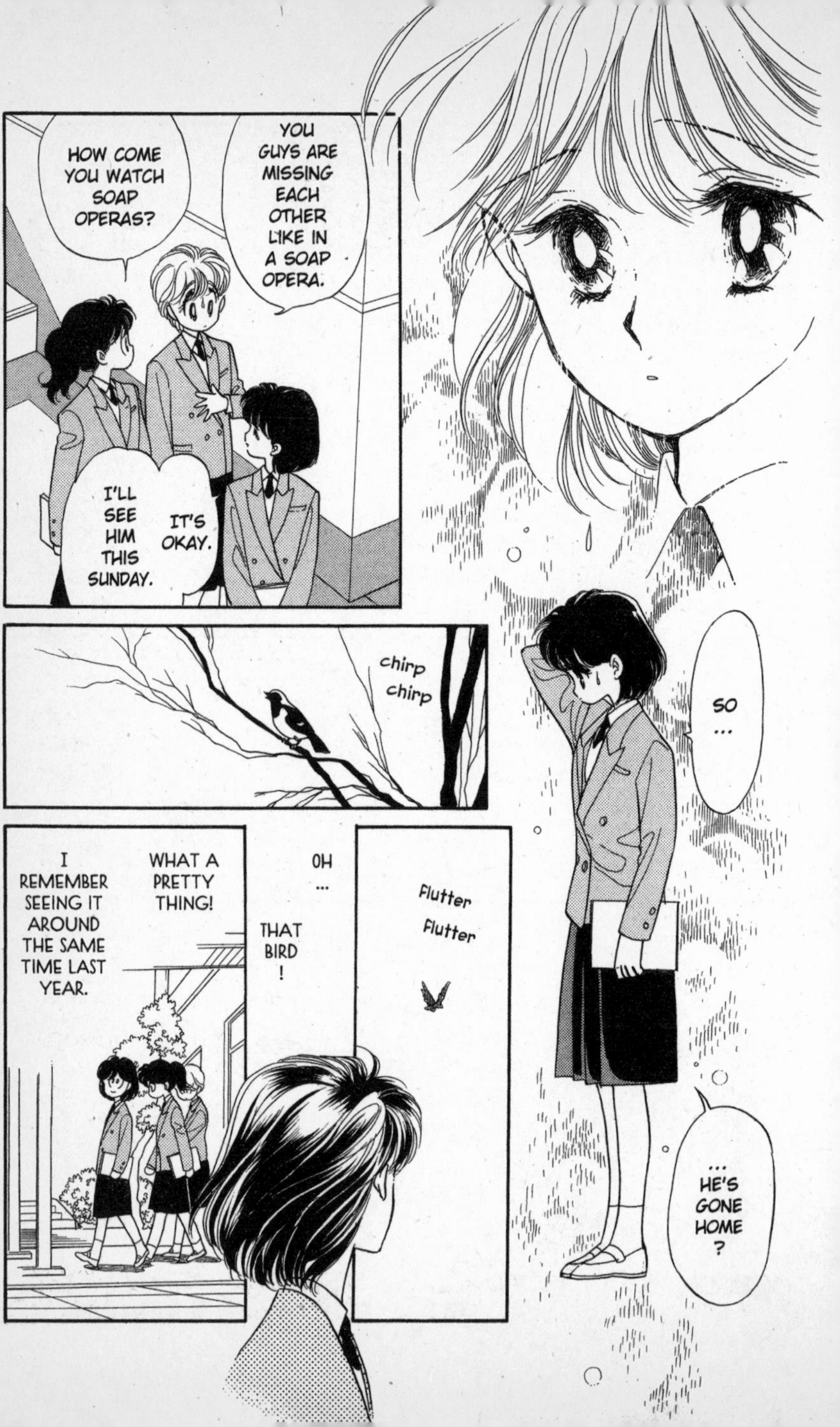
SO ...
... HE'S GONE HOME ?
YOU GUYS ARE MISSING EACH OTHER LIKE IN A SOAP OPERA.
HOW COME YOU WATCH SOAP OPERAS?
IT'S OKAY.
I'LL SEE HIM THIS SUNDAY.
chirp chirp
Flutter Flutter
OH ... THAT BIRD !
WHAT A PRETTY THING!
I REMEMBER SEEING IT AROUND THE SAME TIME LAST YEAR.

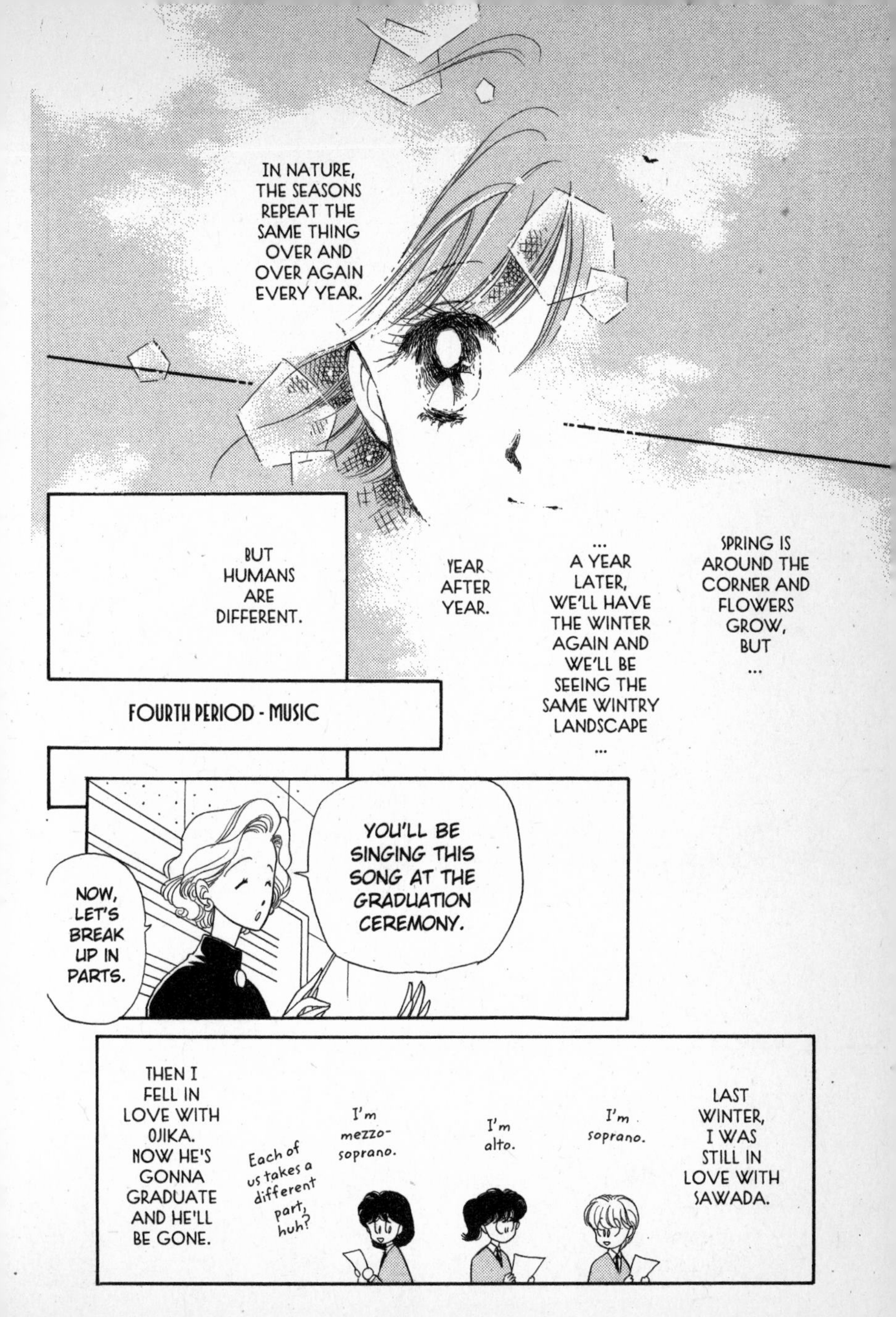
IN NATURE, THE SEASONS REPEAT THE SAME THING OVER AND OVER AGAIN EVERY YEAR.
SPRING IS AROUND THE CORNER AND FLOWERS GROW, BUT ...
... A YEAR LATER, WE'LL HAVE THE WINTER AGAIN AND WE'LL BE SEEING THE SAME WINTRY LANDSCAPE ...
YEAR AFTER YEAR.
BUT HUMANS ARE DIFFERENT.
FOURTH PERIOD - MUSIC
YOU'LL BE SINGING THIS SONG AT THE GRADUATION CEREMONY.
NOW, LET'S BREAK UP IN PARTS.
LAST WINTER, I WAS STILL IN LOVE WITH SAWADA.
I'm soprano.
I'm alto.
I'm mezzo-soprano.
Each of us takes a different part, huh?
THEN I FELL IN LOVE WITH OJIKA. NOW HE'S GONNA GRADUATE AND HE'LL BE GONE.

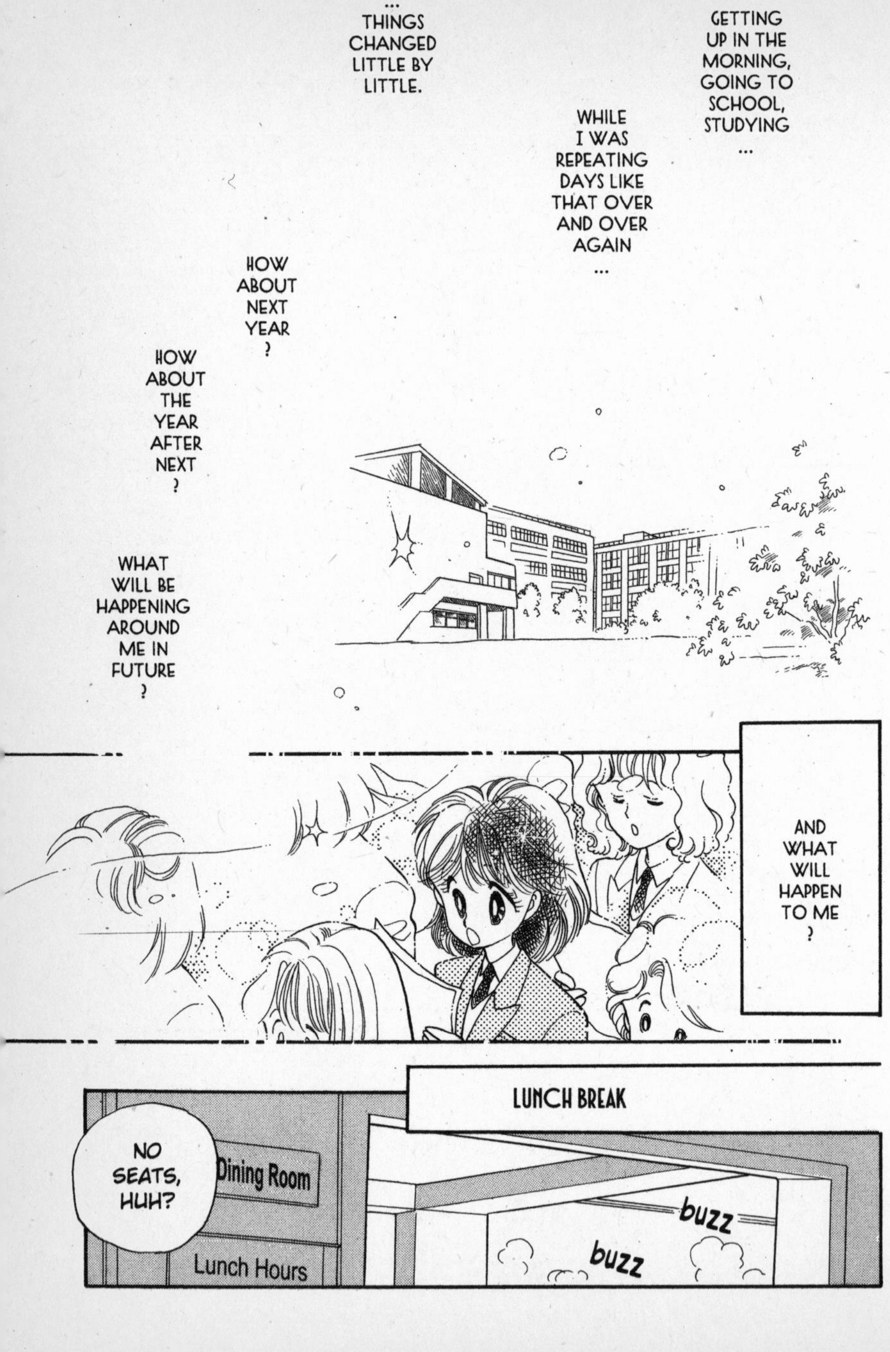
GETTING UP IN THE MORNING, GOING TO SCHOOL, STUDYING ...
WHILE I WAS REPEATING DAYS LIKE THAT OVER AND OVER AGAIN ...
... THINGS CHANGED LITTLE BY LITTLE.
HOW ABOUT NEXT YEAR ?
HOW ABOUT THE YEAR AFTER NEXT ?
WHAT WILL BE HAPPENING AROUND ME IN FUTURE ?
AND WHAT WILL HAPPEN TO ME ?
LUNCH BREAK
buzz
buzz
Dining Room
Lunch Hours
NO SEATS, HUH?

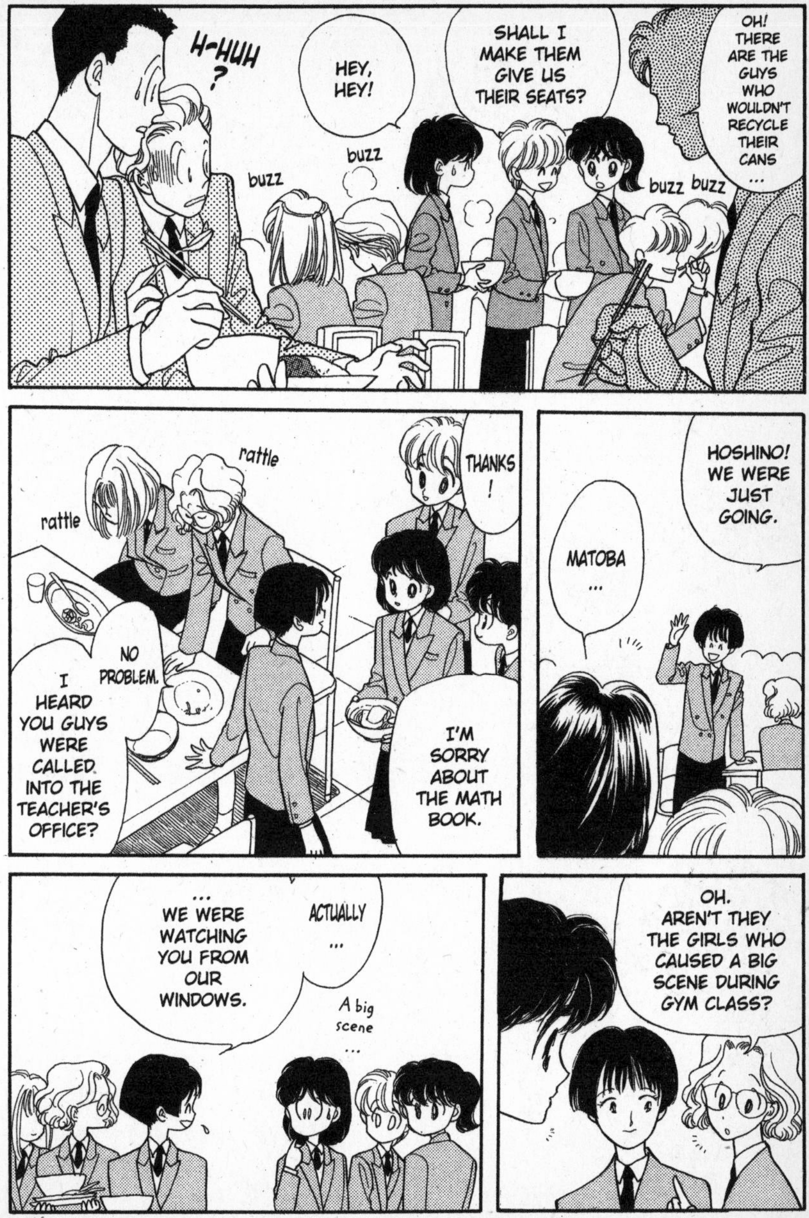

OH! THERE ARE THE GUYS WHO WOULDN'T RECYCLE THEIR CANS ...
buzz buzz
SHALL I MAKE THEM GIVE US THEIR SEATS?
HEY, HEY!
buzz
H-HUH ?
buzz
HOSHINO! WE WERE JUST GOING.
MATOBA ...
THANKS !
rattle
rattle
I'M SORRY ABOUT THE MATH BOOK.
NO PROBLEM.
I HEARD YOU GUYS WERE CALLED INTO THE TEACHER'S OFFICE?
OH. AREN'T THEY THE GIRLS WHO CAUSED A BIG SCENE DURING GYM CLASS?
ACTUALLY ...
... WE WERE WATCHING YOU FROM OUR WINDOWS.
A big scene ...

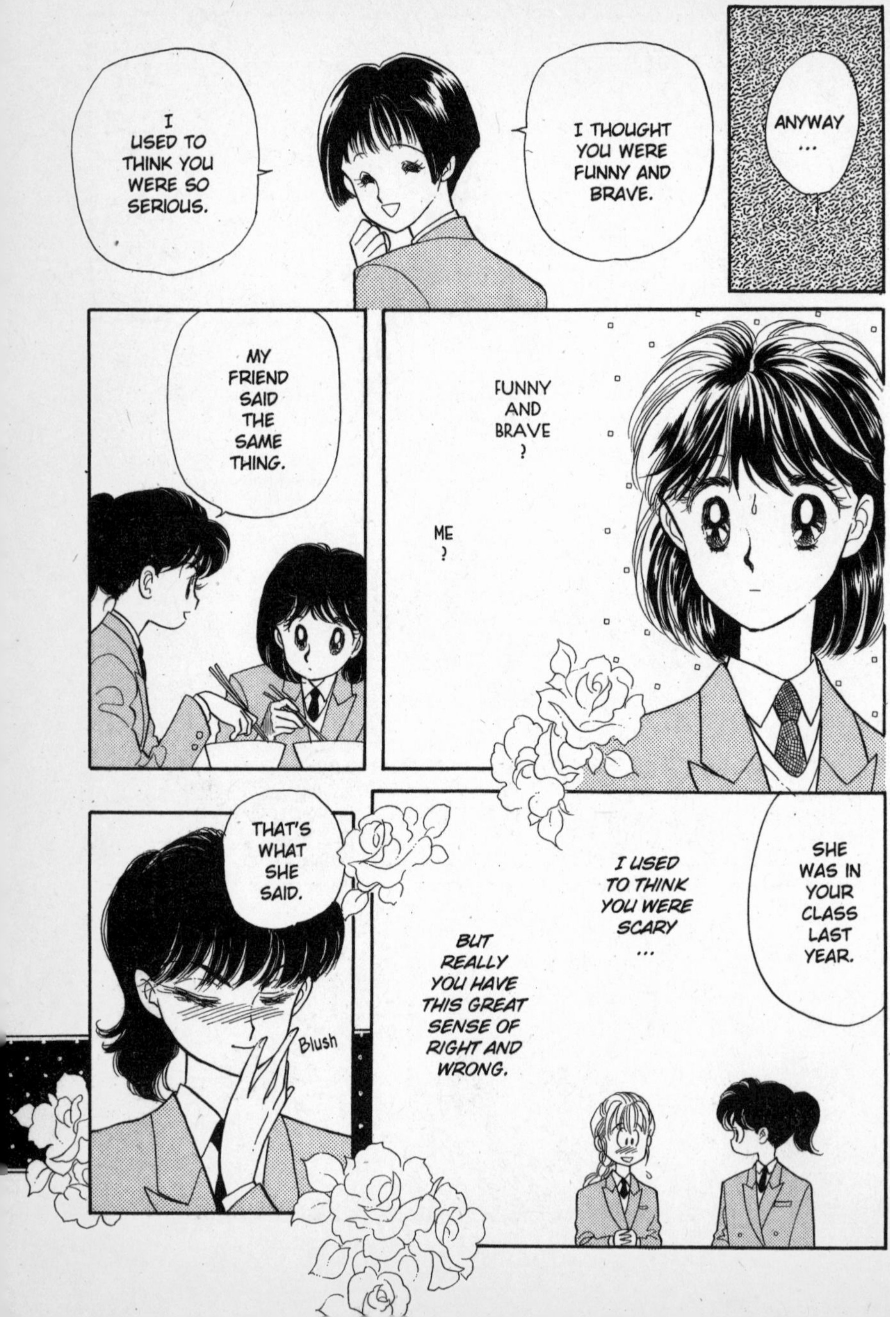
ANYWAY ...
I THOUGHT YOU WERE FUNNY AND BRAVE.
I USED TO THINK YOU WERE SO SERIOUS.
FUNNY AND BRAVE ?
ME ?
MY FRIEND SAID THE SAME THING.
SHE WAS IN YOUR CLASS LAST YEAR.
I USED TO THINK YOU WERE SCARY ...
BUT REALLY YOU HAVE THIS GREAT SENSE OF RIGHT AND WRONG.
THAT'S WHAT SHE SAID.
Blush

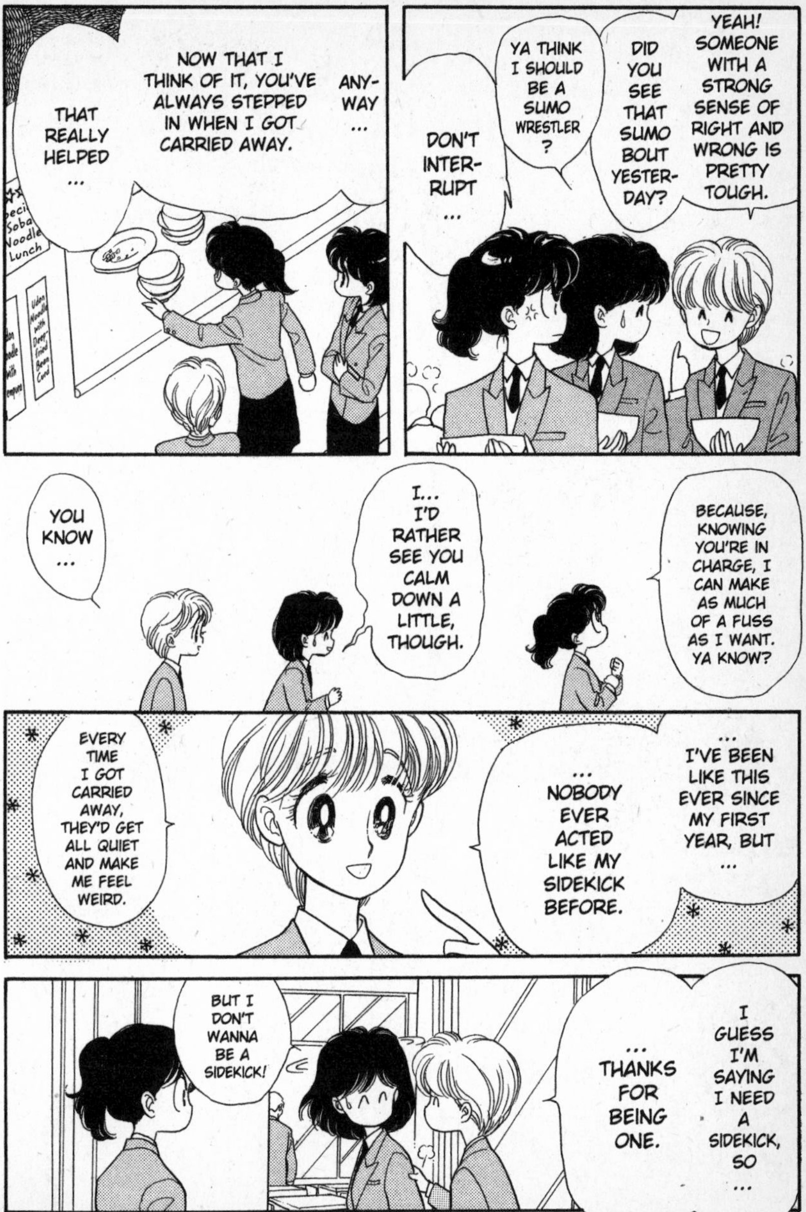
YEAH! SOMEONE WITH A STRONG SENSE OF RIGHT AND WRONG IS PRETTY TOUGH.
DID YOU SEE THAT SUMO BOUT YESTER-DAY?
YA THINK I SHOULD BE A SUMO WRESTLER ?
DON'T INTER-RUPT ...
ANY-WAY ...
NOW THAT I THINK OF IT, YOU'VE ALWAYS STEPPED IN WHEN I GOT CARRIED AWAY.
THAT REALLY HELPED ...
Udon Noodle with Deep-fried Bean Curd
BECAUSE, KNOWING YOU'RE IN CHARGE, I CAN MAKE AS MUCH OF A FUSS AS I WANT. YA KNOW?
I... I'D RATHER SEE YOU CALM DOWN A LITTLE, THOUGH.
YOU KNOW ...
... I'VE BEEN LIKE THIS EVER SINCE MY FIRST YEAR, BUT ...
... NOBODY EVER ACTED LIKE MY SIDEKICK BEFORE.
EVERY TIME I GOT CARRIED AWAY, THEY'D GET ALL QUIET AND MAKE ME FEEL WEIRD.
I GUESS I'M SAYING I NEED A SIDEKICK, SO ...
... THANKS FOR BEING ONE.
BUT I DON'T WANNA BE A SIDEKICK!

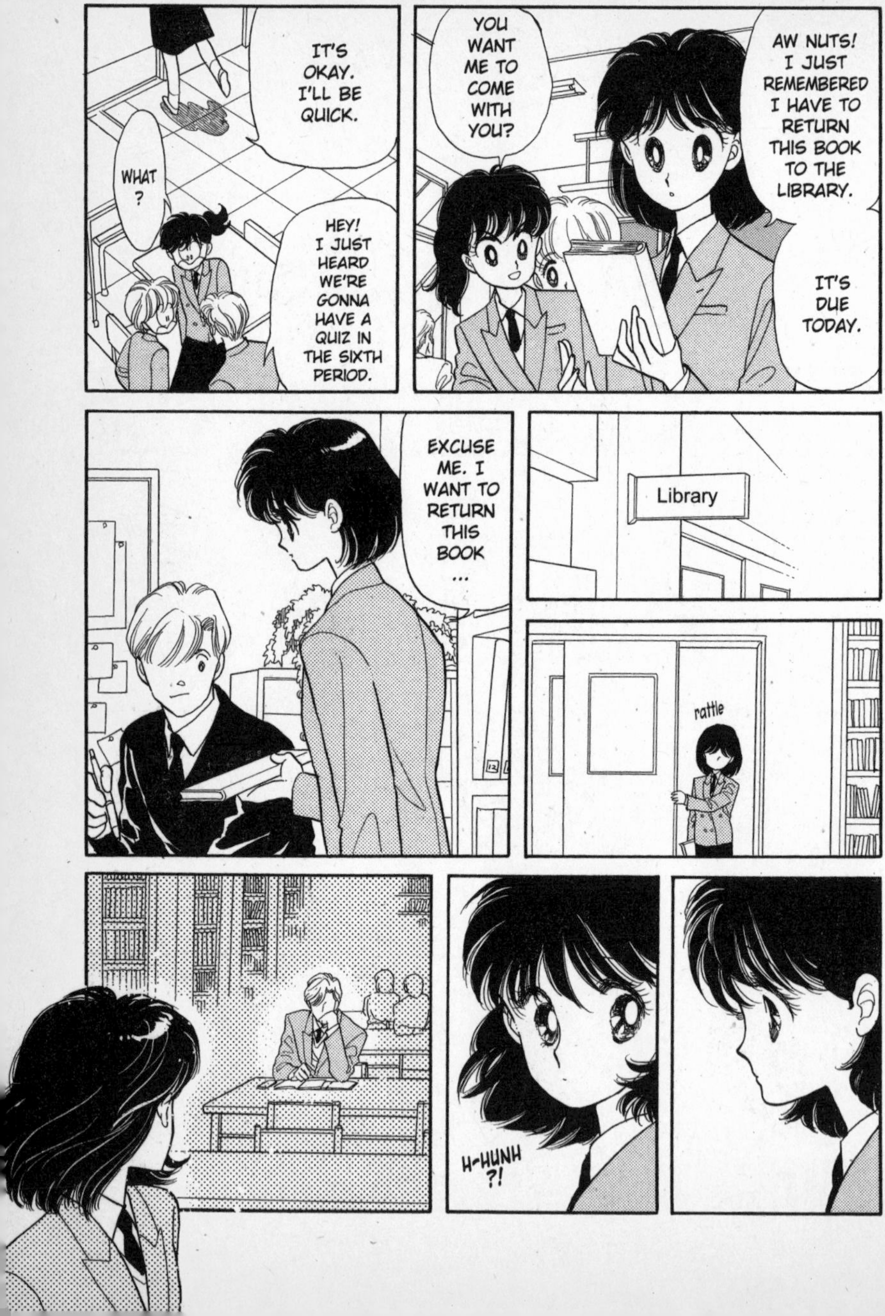
AW NUTS! I JUST REMEMBERED I HAVE TO RETURN THIS BOOK TO THE LIBRARY.
IT'S DUE TODAY.
YOU WANT ME TO COME WITH YOU?
IT'S OKAY. I'LL BE QUICK.
WHAT?
HEY! I JUST HEARD WE'RE GONNA HAVE A QUIZ IN THE SIXTH PERIOD.
Library
rattle
EXCUSE ME. I WANT TO RETURN THIS BOOK ...
H-HUNH ?!

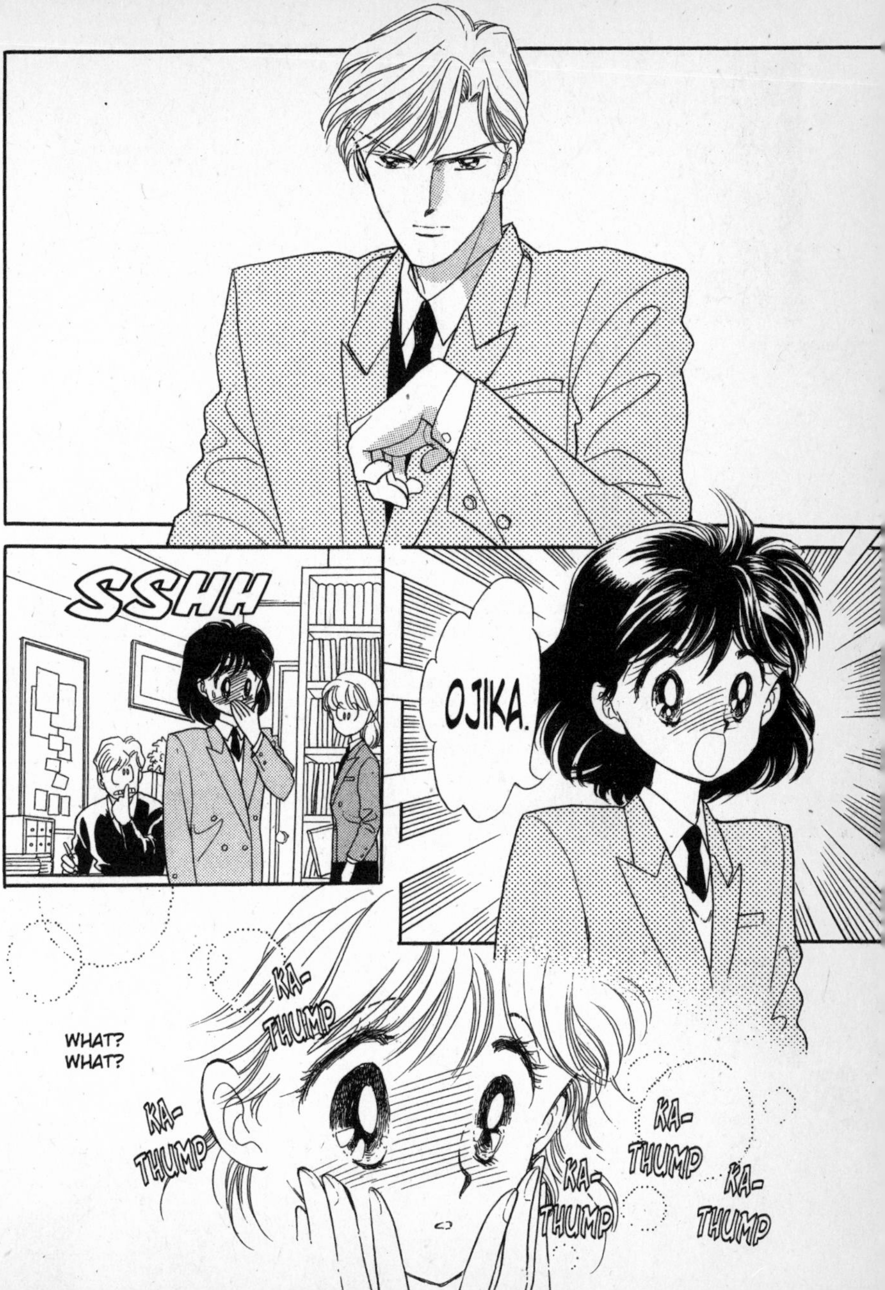
OJIKA.
SSHH
KA-THUMP
KA-THUMP
KA-THUMP
KA-THUMP
KA-THUMP
WHAT? WHAT?

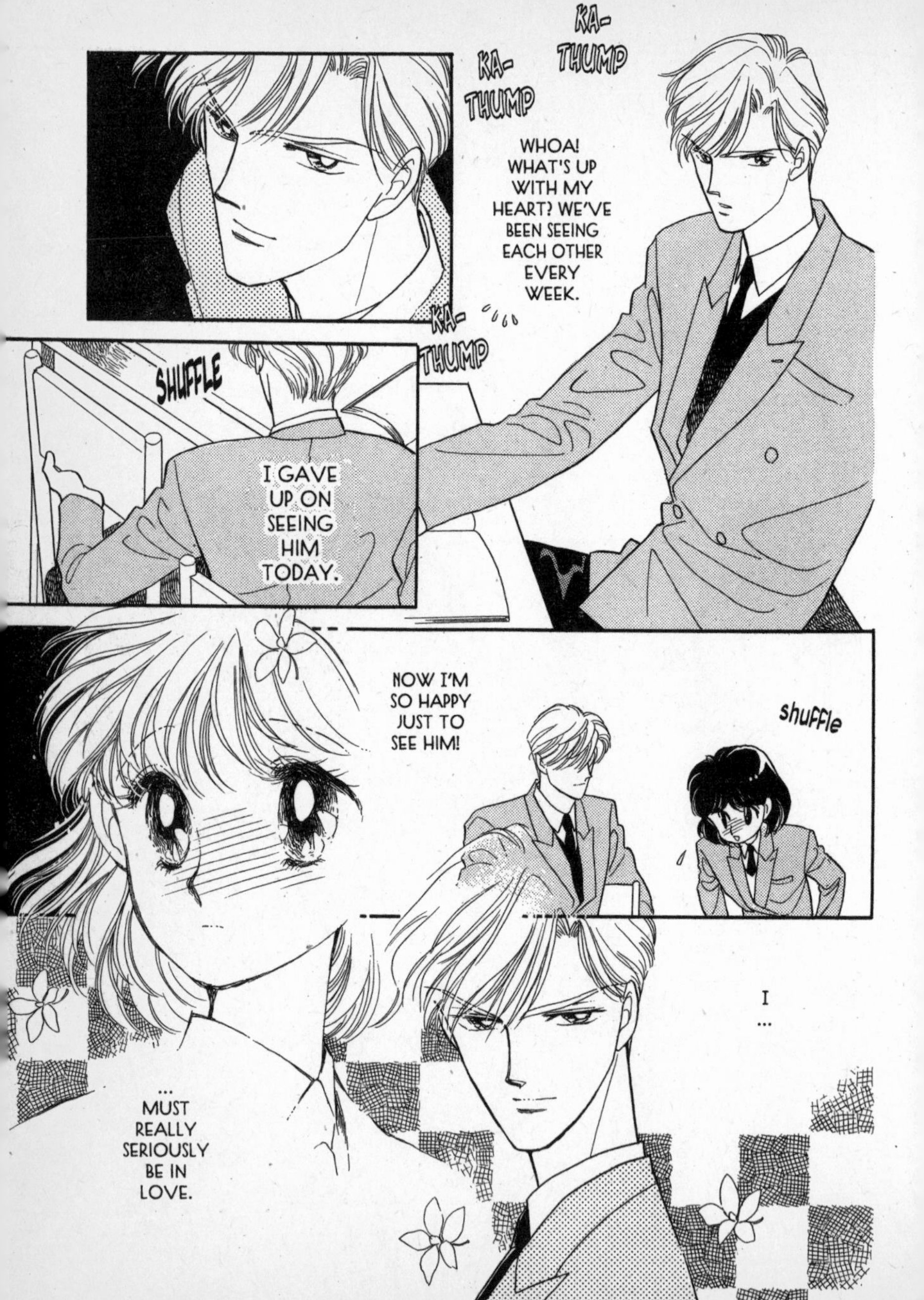
KA-THUMP
KA-THUMP
WHOA! WHAT'S UP WITH MY HEART? WE'VE BEEN SEEING EACH OTHER EVERY WEEK.
KA-THUMP
SHUFFLE
I GAVE UP ON SEEING HIM TODAY.
shuffle
NOW I'M SO HAPPY JUST TO SEE HIM!
I ...
... MUST REALLY SERIOUSLY BE IN LOVE.

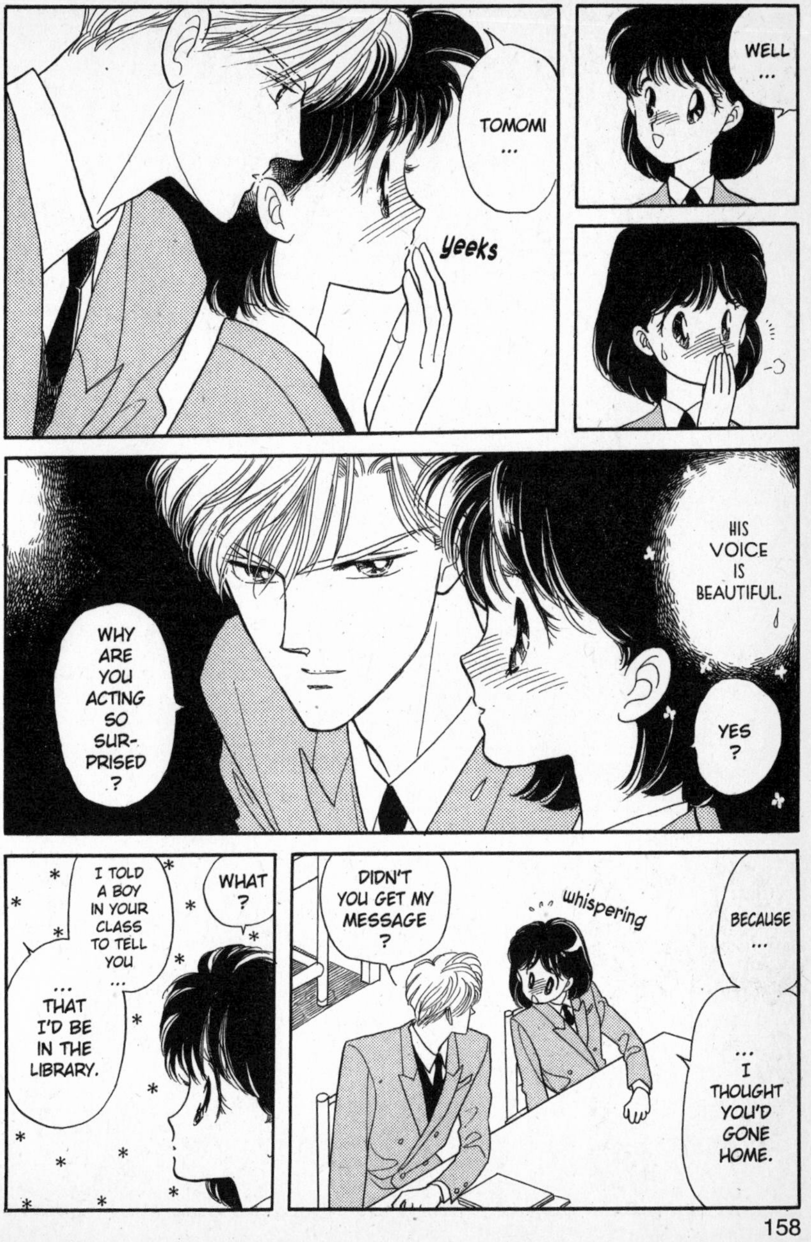
WELL ...
TOMOMI ...
yeeks
HIS VOICE IS BEAUTIFUL.
YES ?
WHY ARE YOU ACTING SO SUR-PRISED ?
BECAUSE ...
... I THOUGHT YOU'D GONE HOME.
whispering
DIDN'T YOU GET MY MESSAGE ?
WHAT ?
I TOLD A BOY IN YOUR CLASS TO TELL YOU ...
... THAT I'D BE IN THE LIBRARY.

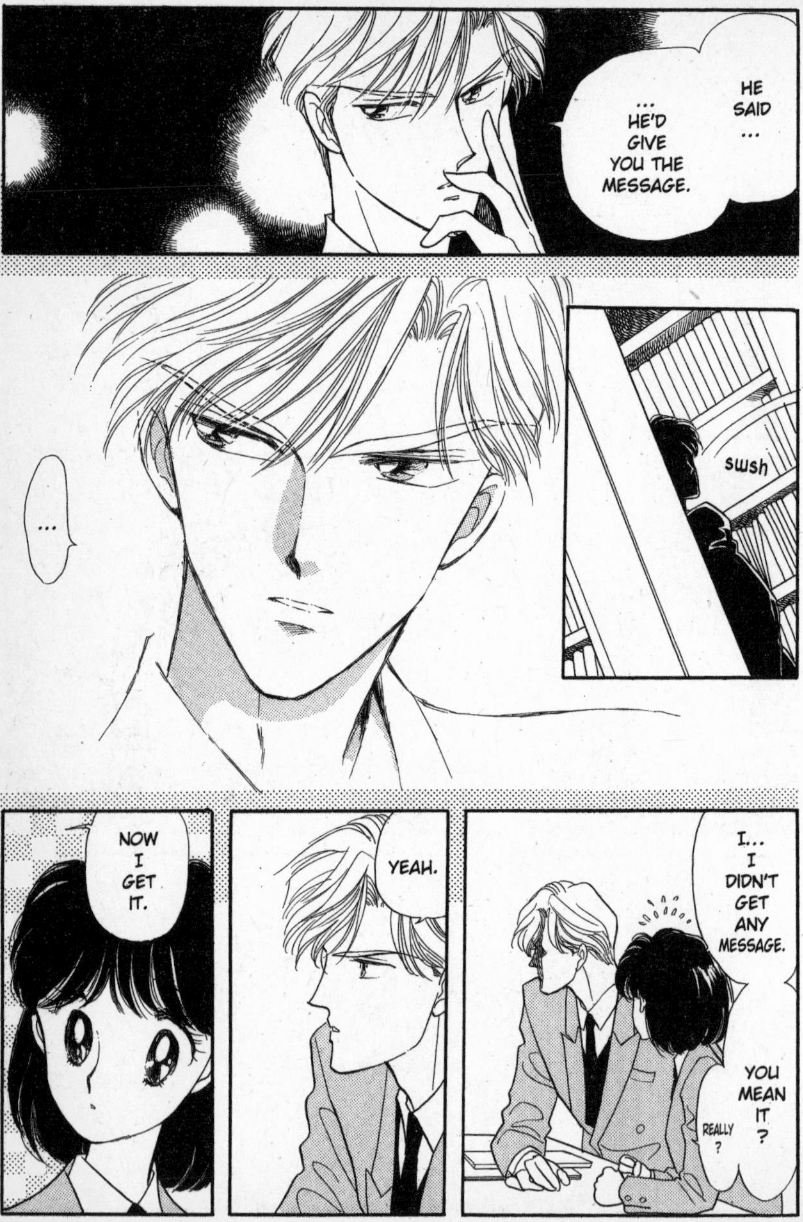
HE SAID ...
... HE'D GIVE YOU THE MESSAGE.
swsh
...
I... I DIDN'T GET ANY MESSAGE.
YOU MEAN IT?
REALLY?
YEAH.
NOW I GET IT.

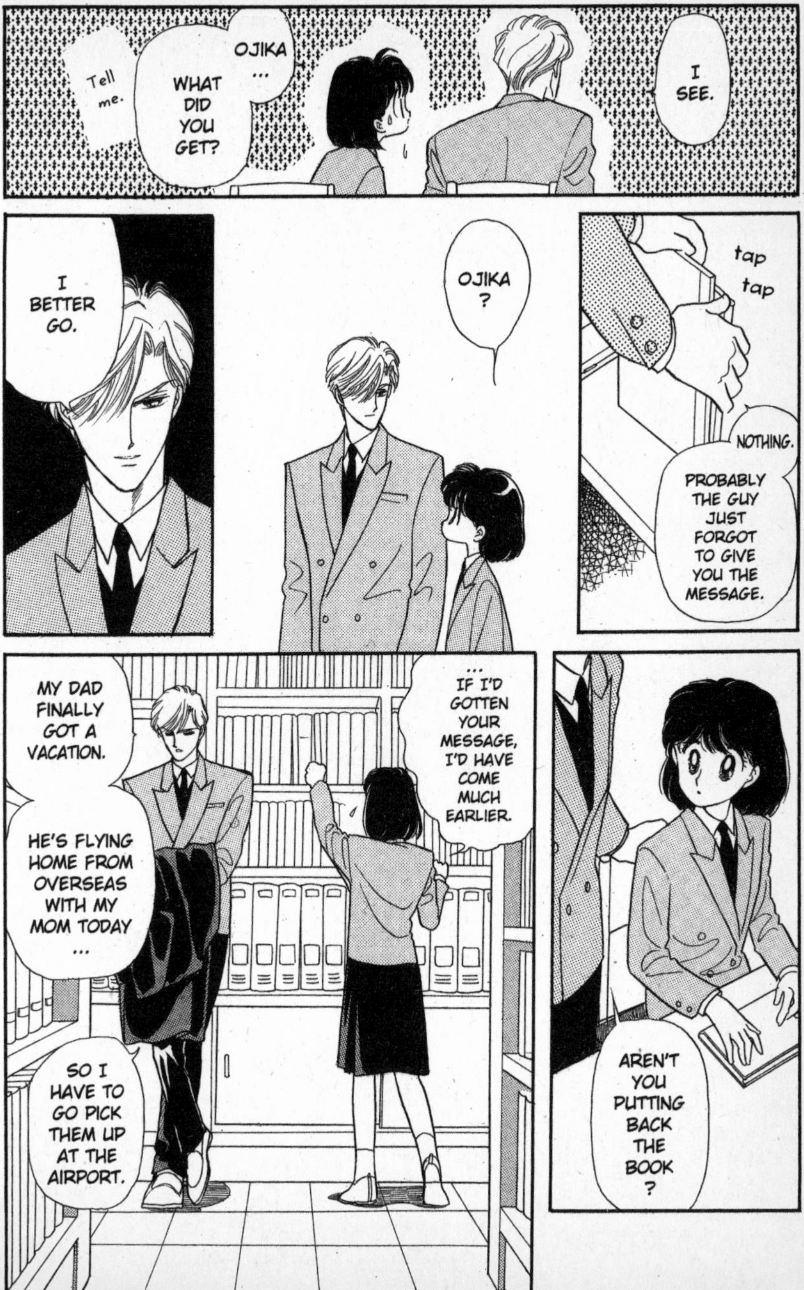
I SEE.
OJIKA ...
WHAT DID YOU GET?
Tell me.
tap tap
NOTHING.
PROBABLY THE GUY JUST FORGOT TO GIVE YOU THE MESSAGE.
OJIKA ?
I BETTER GO.
AREN'T YOU PUTTING BACK THE BOOK ?
... IF I'D GOTTEN YOUR MESSAGE, I'D HAVE COME MUCH EARLIER.
MY DAD FINALLY GOT A VACATION.
HE'S FLYING HOME FROM OVERSEAS WITH MY MOM TODAY ...
SO I HAVE TO GO PICK THEM UP AT THE AIRPORT.

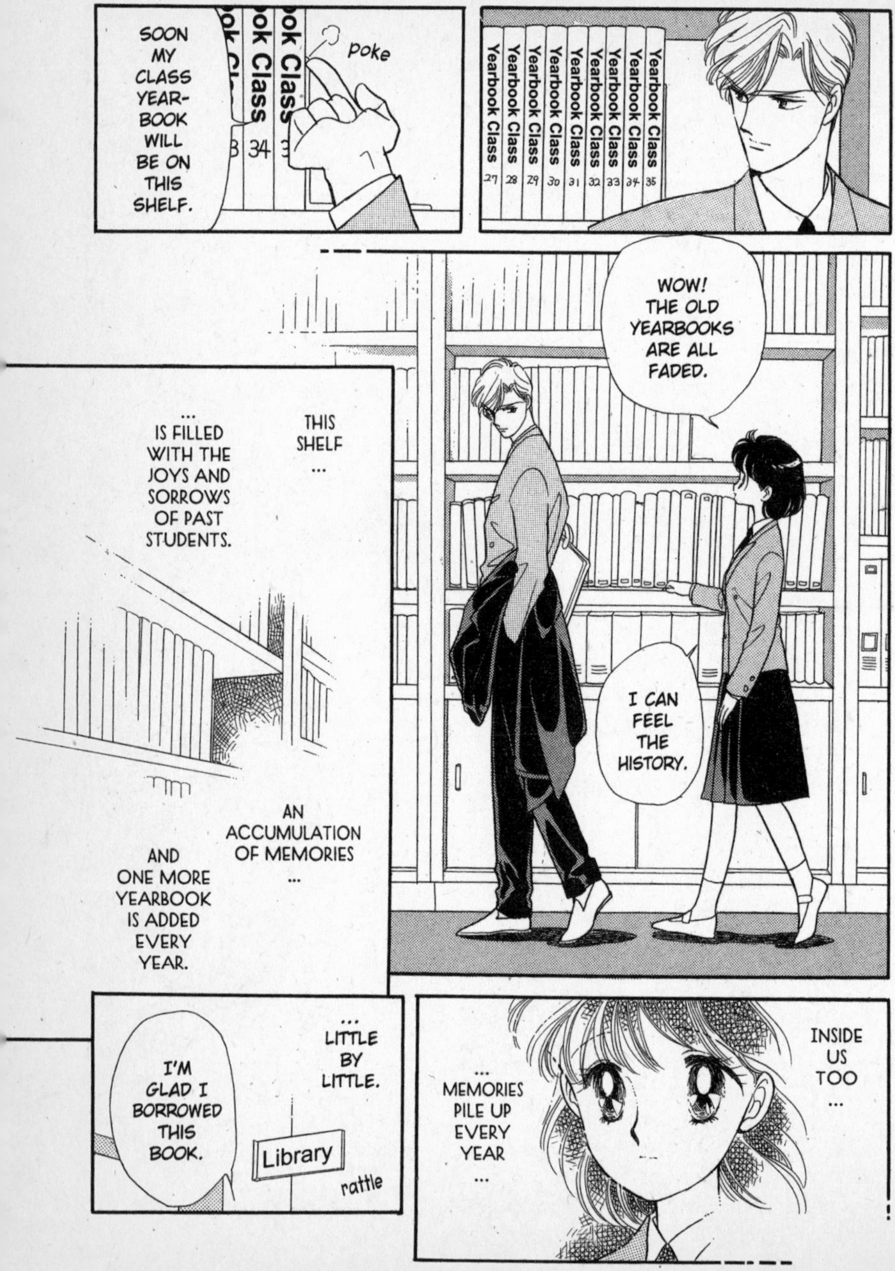

Yearbook Class 27
Yearbook Class 28
Yearbook Class 29
Yearbook Class 30
Yearbook Class 31
Yearbook Class 32
Yearbook Class 33
Yearbook Class 34
Yearbook Class 35
SOON MY CLASS YEAR-BOOK WILL BE ON THIS SHELF.
poke
WOW! THE OLD YEARBOOKS ARE ALL FADED.
I CAN FEEL THE HISTORY.
THIS SHELF ...
... IS FILLED WITH THE JOYS AND SORROWS OF PAST STUDENTS.
AN ACCUMULATION OF MEMORIES ...
AND ONE MORE YEARBOOK IS ADDED EVERY YEAR.
INSIDE US TOO ...
... MEMORIES PILE UP EVERY YEAR ...
... LITTLE BY LITTLE.
I'M GLAD I BORROWED THIS BOOK.
Library
rattle

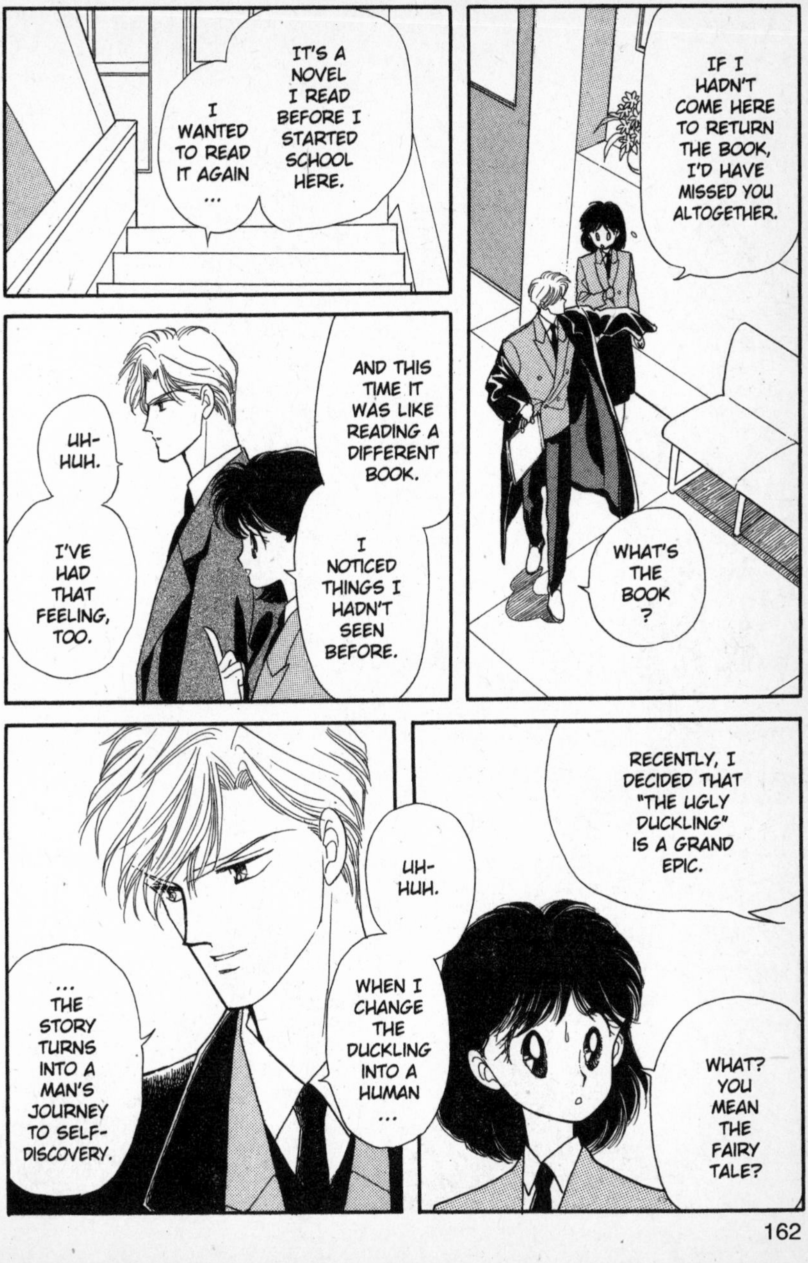
IF I HADN'T COME HERE TO RETURN THE BOOK, I'D HAVE MISSED YOU ALTOGETHER.
WHAT'S THE BOOK ?
IT'S A NOVEL I READ BEFORE I STARTED SCHOOL HERE.
I WANTED TO READ IT AGAIN ...
AND THIS TIME IT WAS LIKE READING A DIFFERENT BOOK.
UH-HUH.
I NOTICED THINGS I HADN'T SEEN BEFORE.
I'VE HAD THAT FEELING, TOO.
RECENTLY, I DECIDED THAT "THE UGLY DUCKLING" IS A GRAND EPIC.
WHAT? YOU MEAN THE FAIRY TALE?
UH-HUH.
WHEN I CHANGE THE DUCKLING INTO A HUMAN ...
... THE STORY TURNS INTO A MAN'S JOURNEY TO SELF-DISCOVERY.

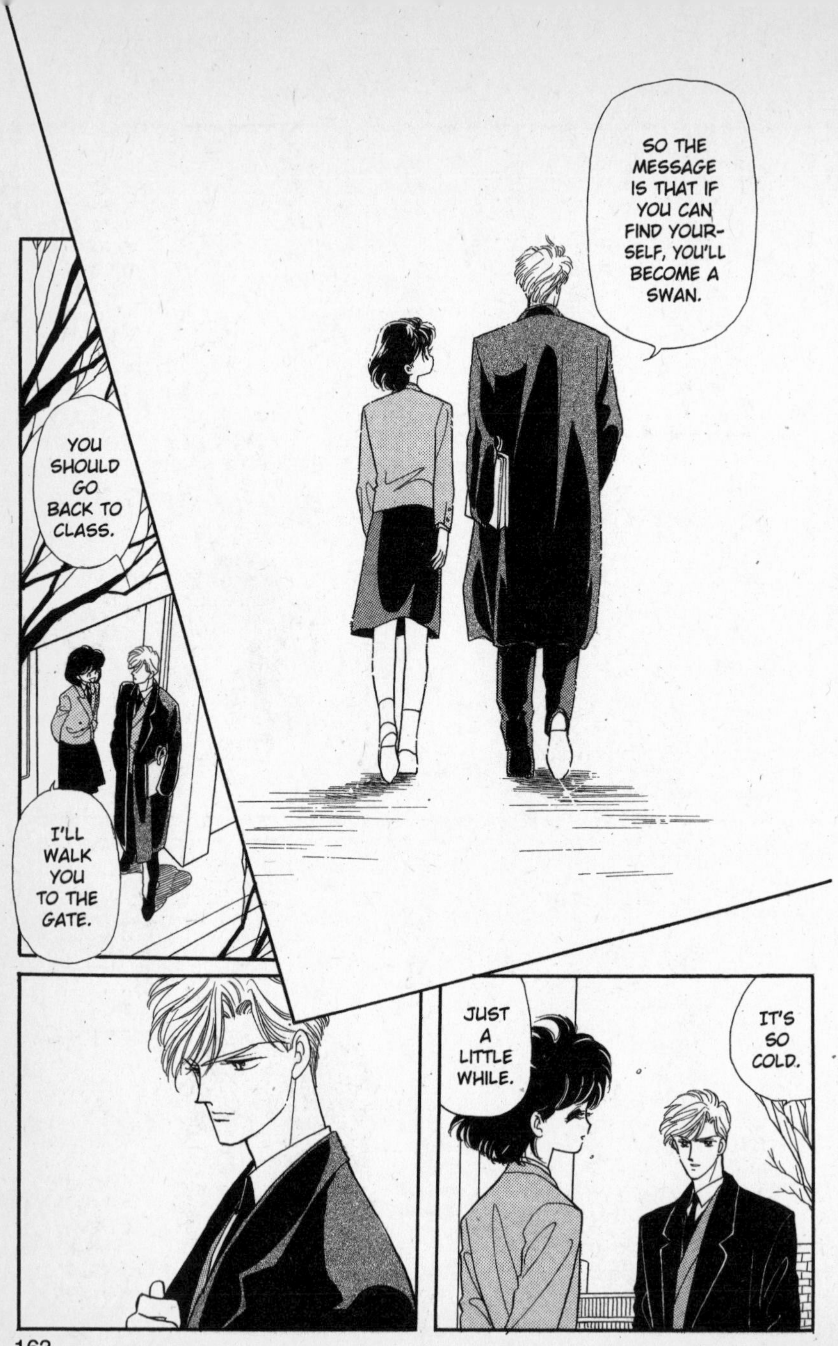
SO THE MESSAGE IS THAT IF YOU CAN FIND YOUR-SELF, YOU'LL BECOME A SWAN.
YOU SHOULD GO BACK TO CLASS.
I'LL WALK YOU TO THE GATE.
IT'S SO COLD.
JUST A LITTLE WHILE.

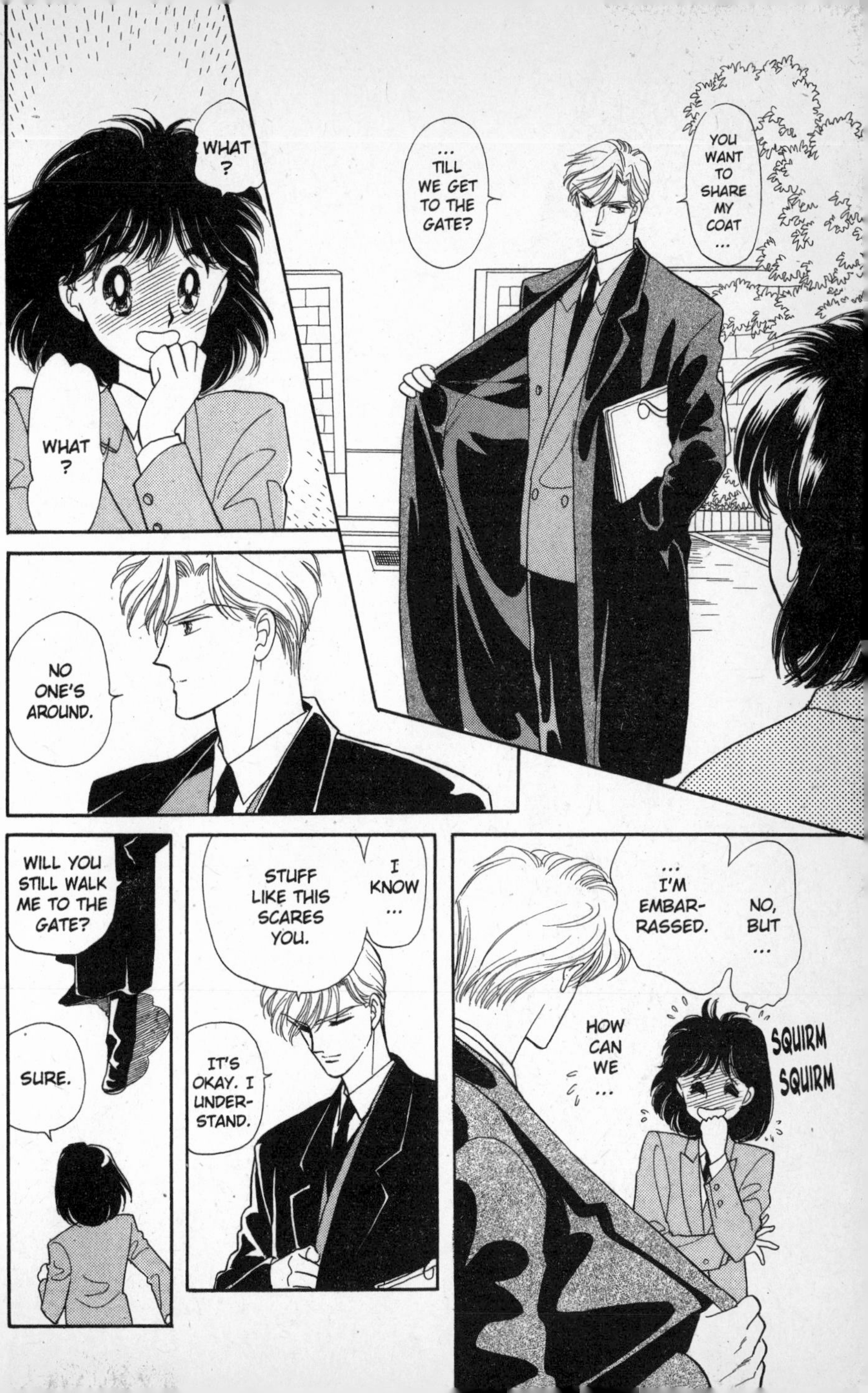
YOU WANT TO SHARE MY COAT ...
... TILL WE GET TO THE GATE?
WHAT ?
WHAT ?
NO ONE'S AROUND.
NO, BUT ...
... I'M EMBARRASSED.
HOW CAN WE ...
SQUIRM SQUIRM
I KNOW ...
STUFF LIKE THIS SCARES YOU.
IT'S OKAY. I UNDERSTAND.
WILL YOU STILL WALK ME TO THE GATE?
SURE.

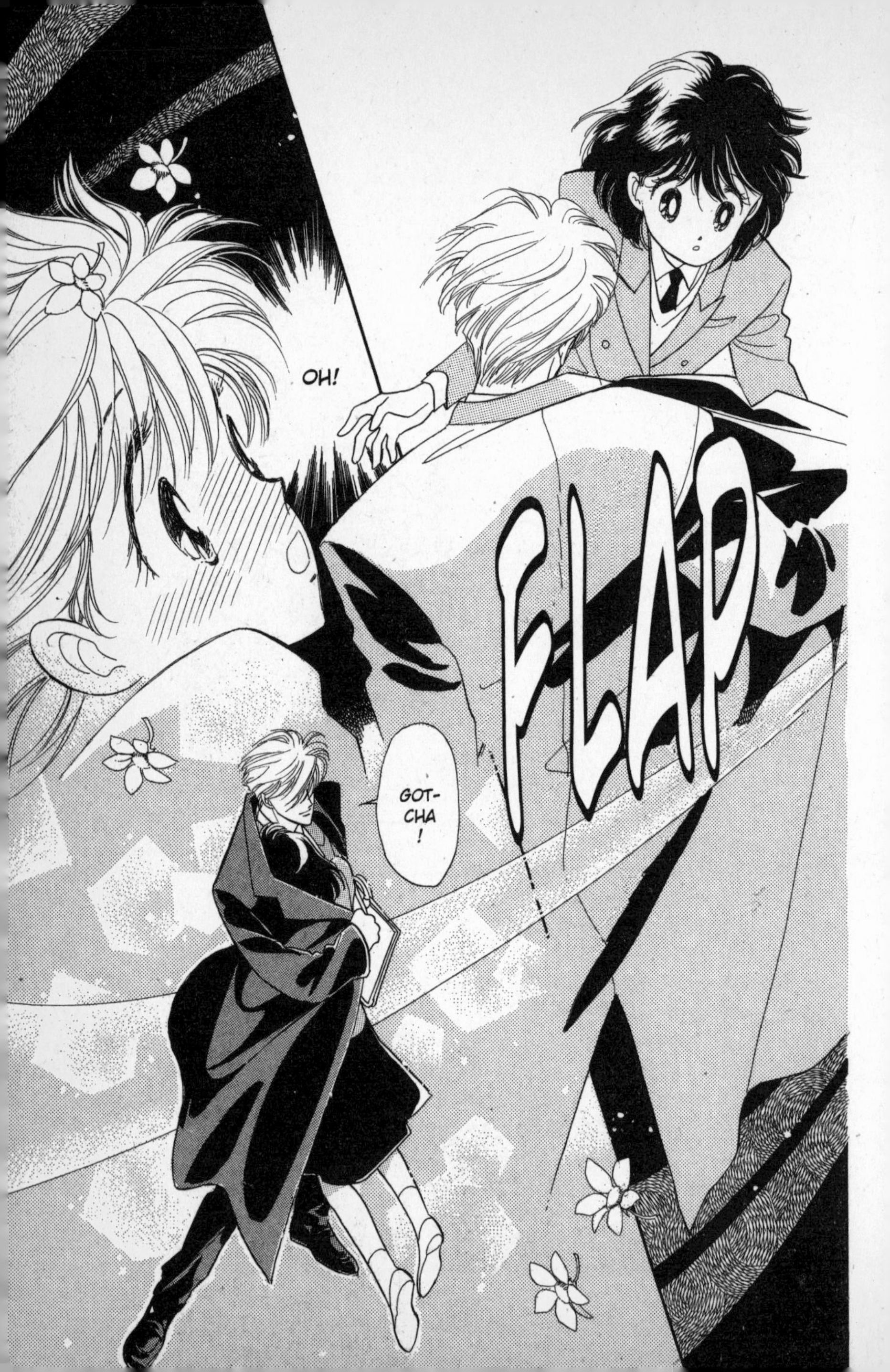
OH!
FLAP
GOT-CHA!

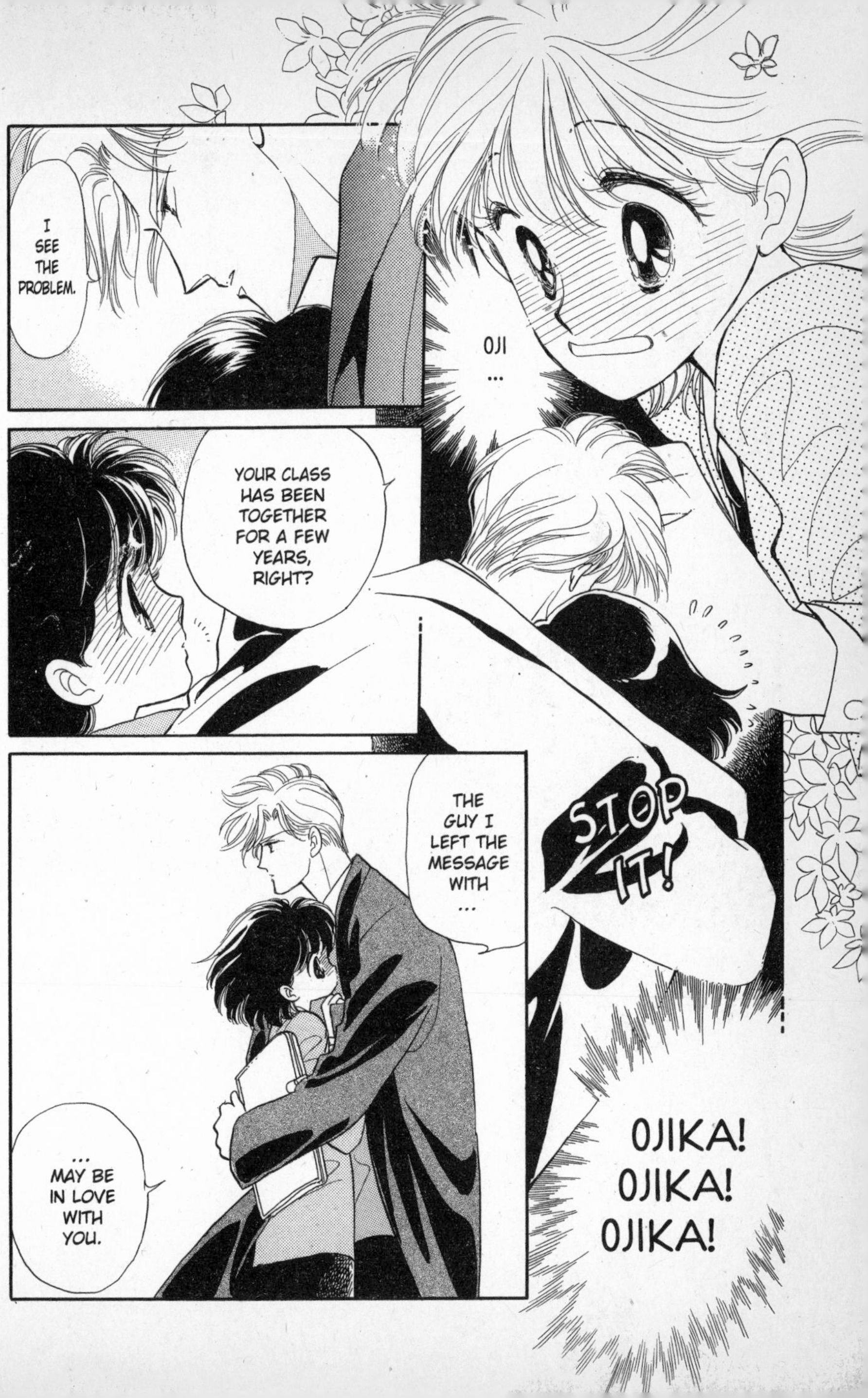
OJI ...
STOP IT!
OJIKA! OJIKA! OJIKA!
I SEE THE PROBLEM.
YOUR CLASS HAS BEEN TOGETHER FOR A FEW YEARS, RIGHT?
THE GUY I LEFT THE MESSAGE WITH ...
... MAY BE IN LOVE WITH YOU.

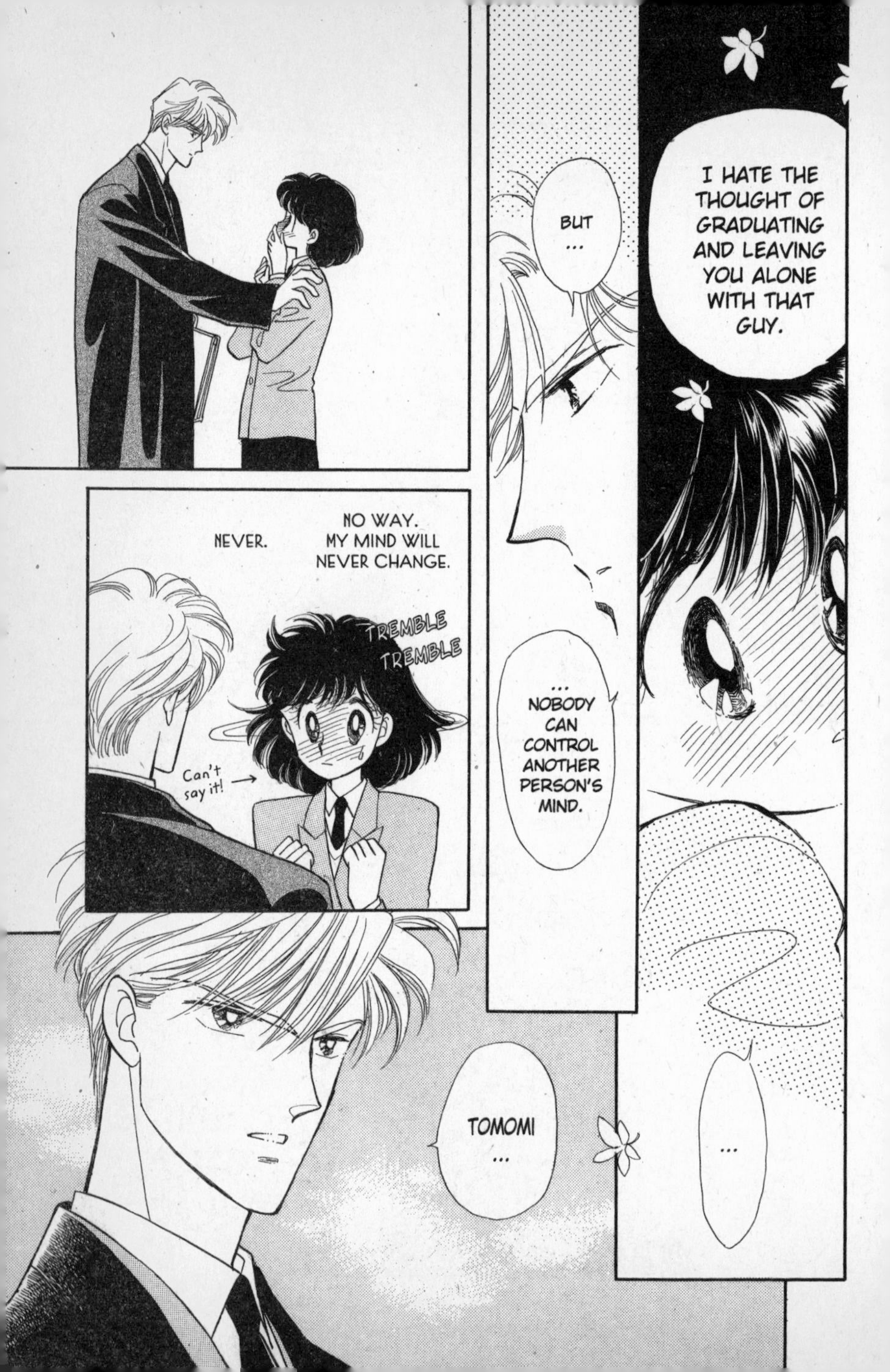
I HATE THE THOUGHT OF GRADUATING AND LEAVING YOU ALONE WITH THAT GUY.
BUT ...
... NOBODY CAN CONTROL ANOTHER PERSON'S MIND.
NO WAY. MY MIND WILL NEVER CHANGE.
NEVER.
TREMBLE TREMBLE
Can't say it!
...
TOMOMI ...

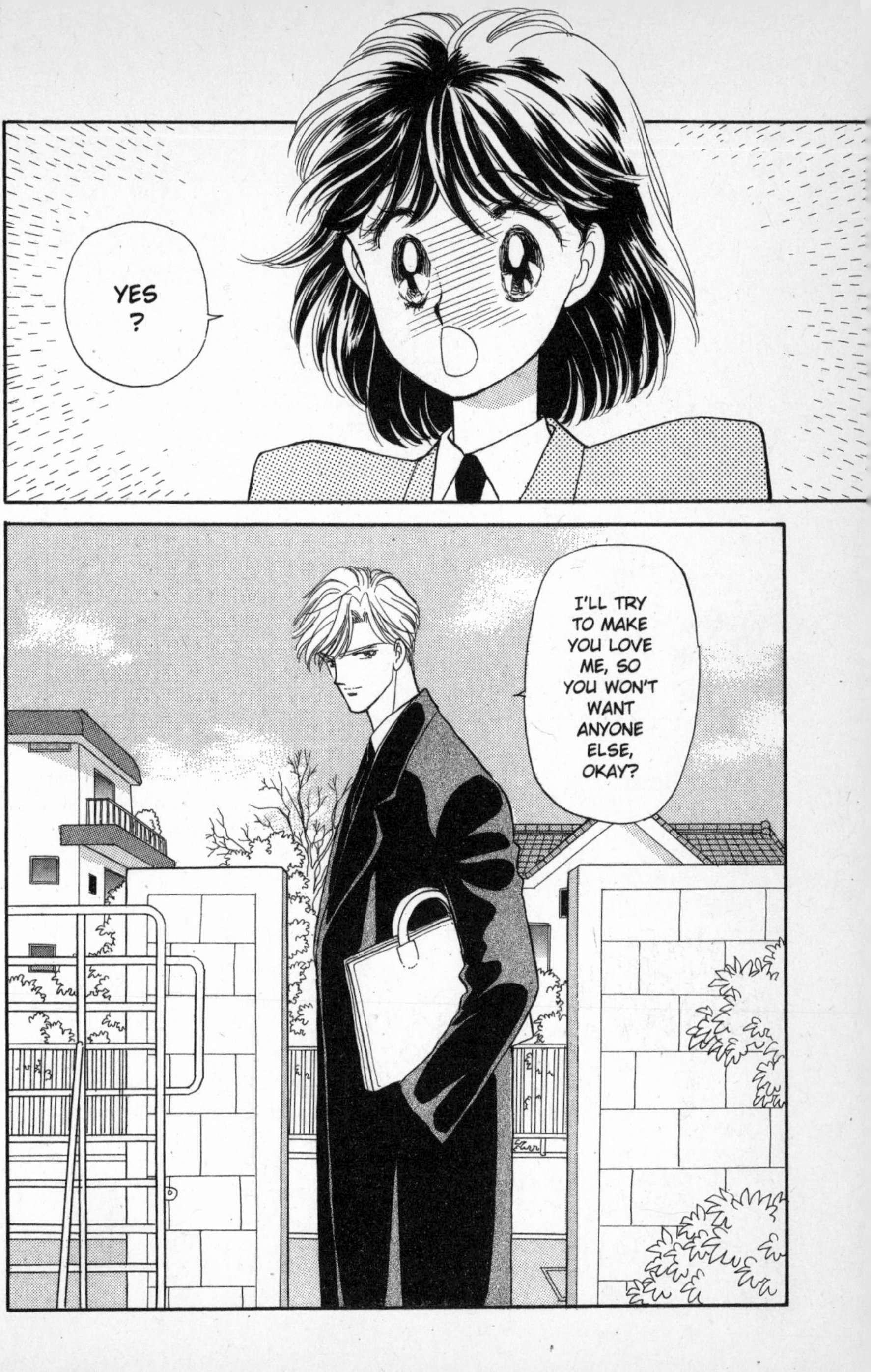
YES?
I'LL TRY TO MAKE YOU LOVE ME, SO YOU WON'T WANT ANYONE ELSE, OKAY?

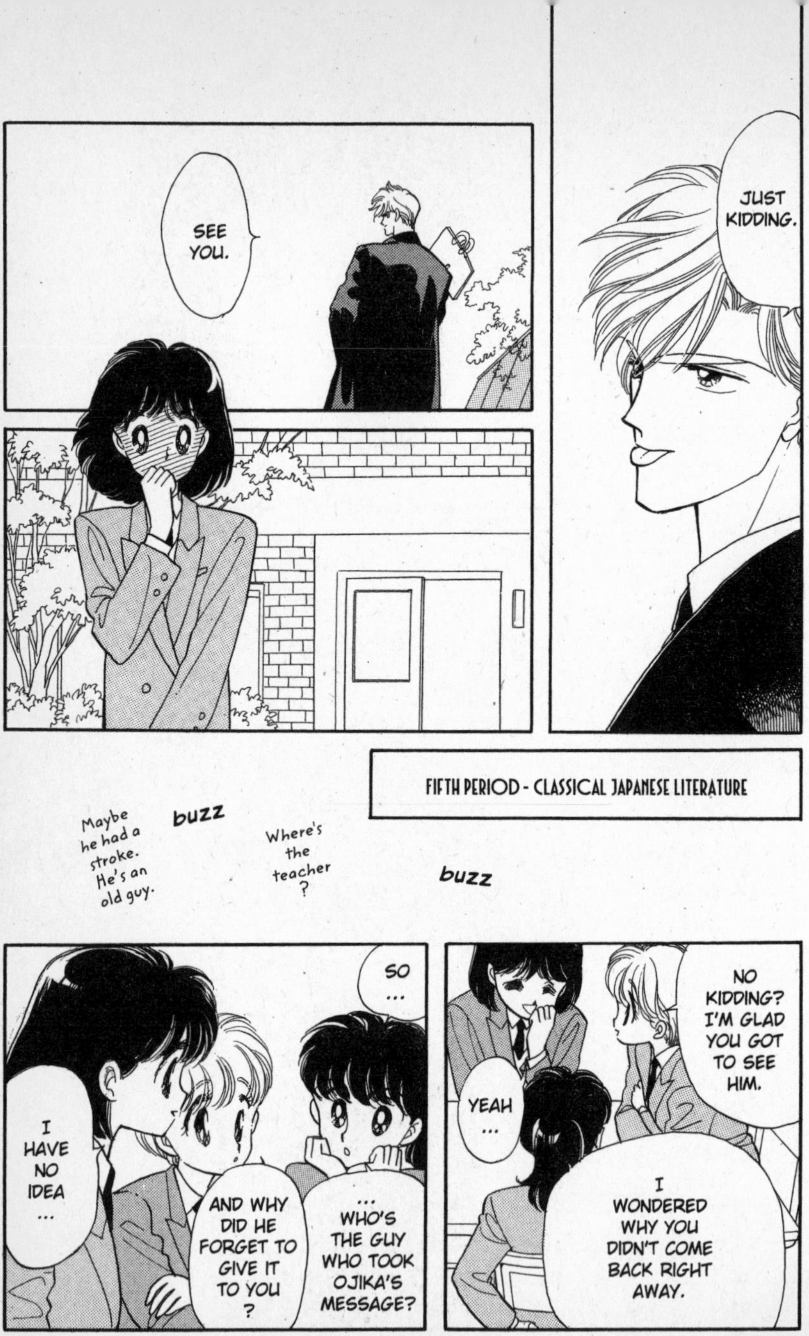
JUST KIDDING.
SEE YOU.
FIFTH PERIOD - CLASSICAL JAPANESE LITERATURE
buzz
Where's the teacher ?
buzz
Maybe he had a stroke. He's an old guy.
NO KIDDING? I'M GLAD YOU GOT TO SEE HIM.
YEAH ...
I WONDERED WHY YOU DIDN'T COME BACK RIGHT AWAY.
SO ...
... WHO'S THE GUY WHO TOOK OJIKA'S MESSAGE?
AND WHY DID HE FORGET TO GIVE IT TO YOU ?
I HAVE NO IDEA ...

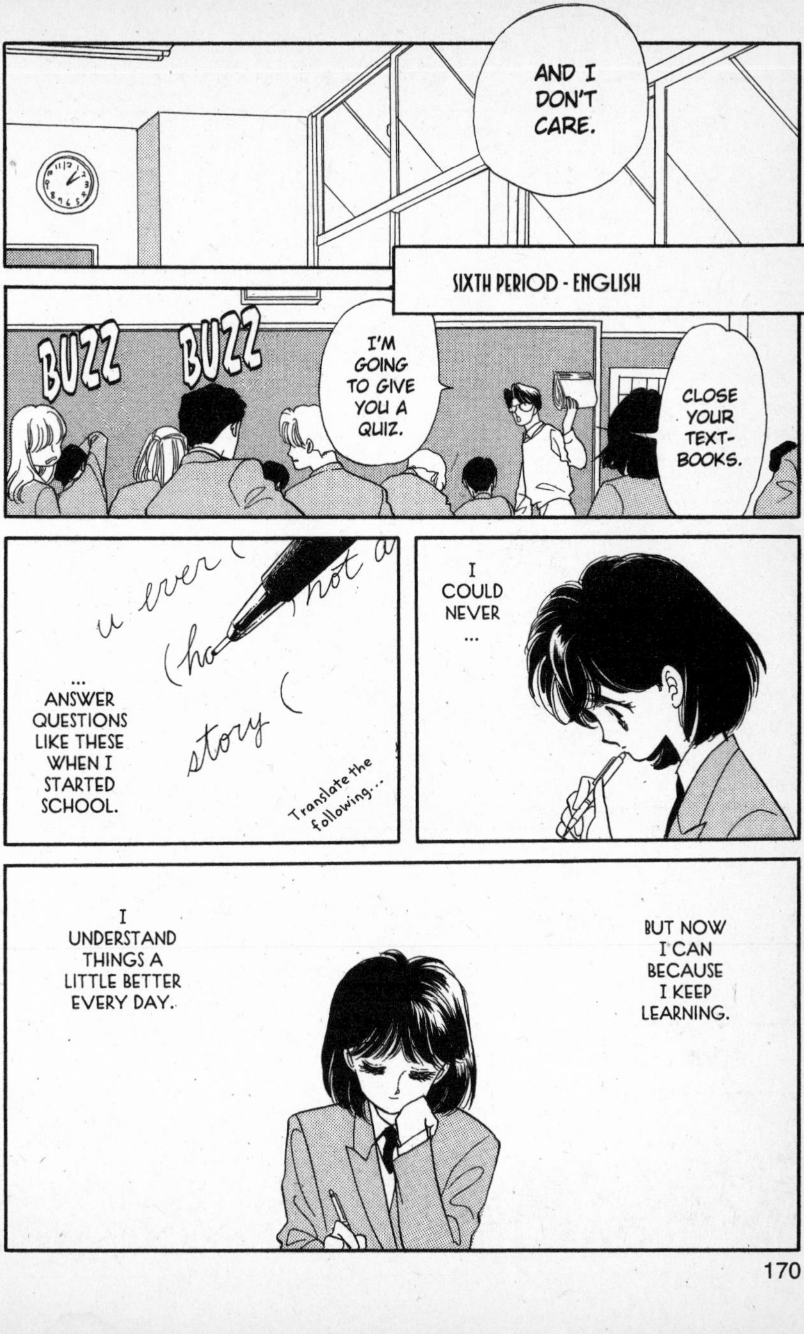
AND I DON'T CARE.
SIXTH PERIOD - ENGLISH
CLOSE YOUR TEXT-BOOKS.
I'M GOING TO GIVE YOU A QUIZ.
BUZZ BUZZ
I COULD NEVER ...
... ANSWER QUESTIONS LIKE THESE WHEN I STARTED SCHOOL.
Translate the following...
BUT NOW I CAN BECAUSE I KEEP LEARNING.
I UNDERSTAND THINGS A LITTLE BETTER EVERY DAY.

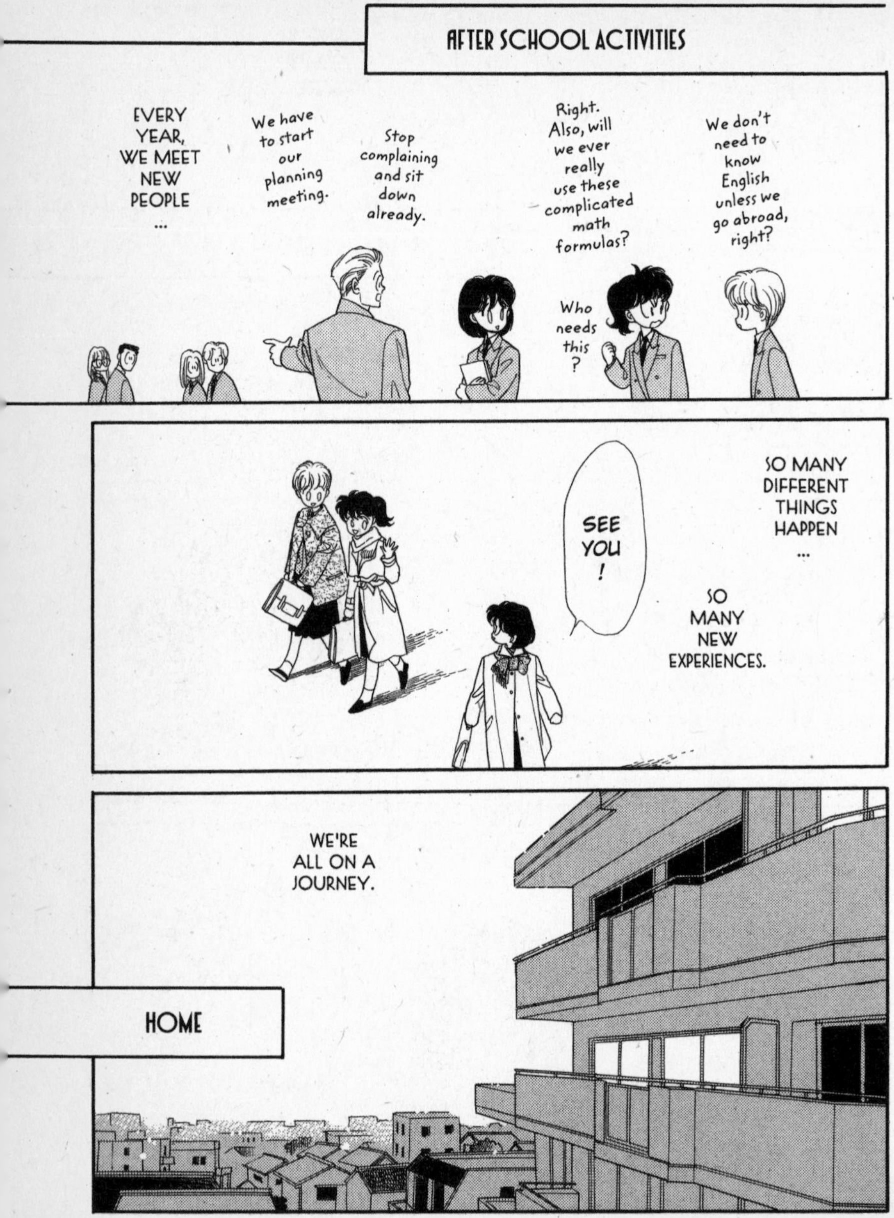
AFTER SCHOOL ACTIVITIES
We don't need to know English unless we go abroad, right?
Right. Also, will we ever really use these complicated math formulas?
Who needs this ?
Stop complaining and sit down already.
We have to start our planning meeting.
EVERY YEAR, WE MEET NEW PEOPLE ...
SO MANY DIFFERENT THINGS HAPPEN ...
SO MANY NEW EXPERIENCES.
SEE YOU !
WE'RE ALL ON A JOURNEY.
HOME

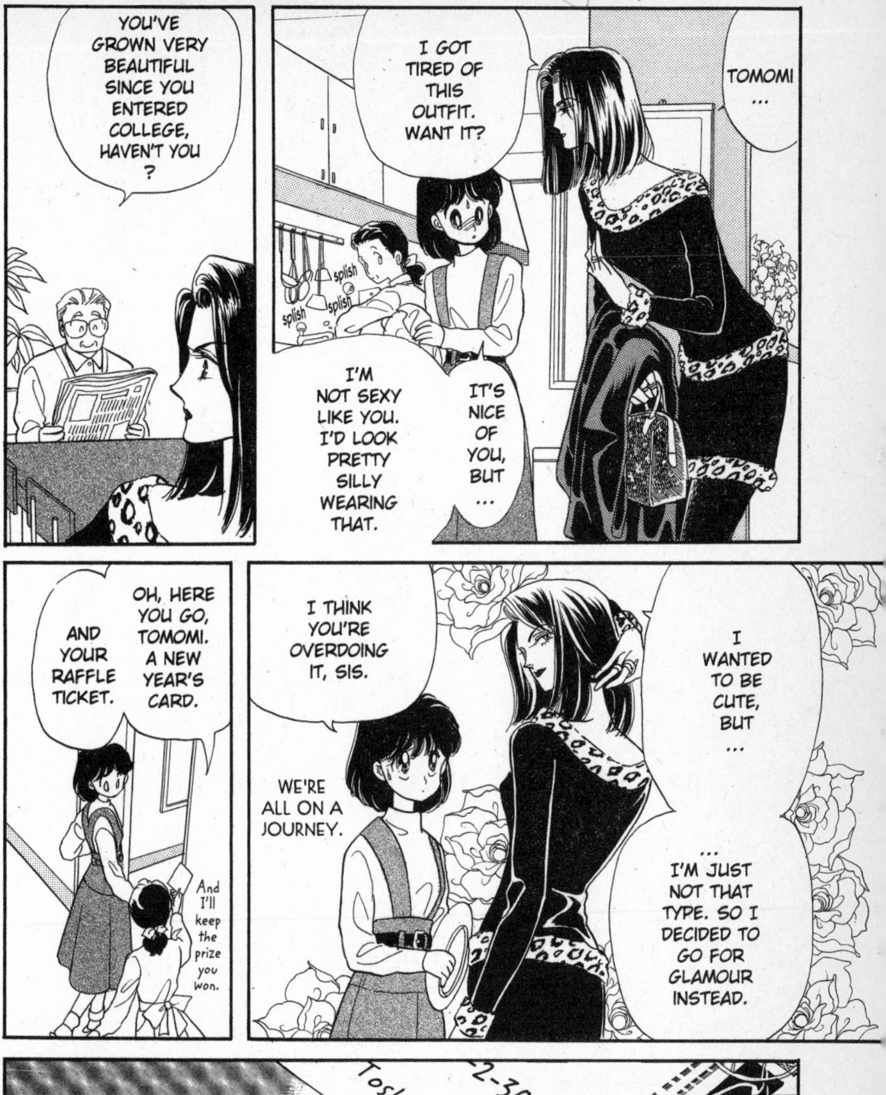
TOMOMI ...
I GOT TIRED OF THIS OUTFIT. WANT IT?
splish
splish
splish
IT'S NICE OF YOU, BUT ...
I'M NOT SEXY LIKE YOU. I'D LOOK PRETTY SILLY WEARING THAT.
YOU'VE GROWN VERY BEAUTIFUL SINCE YOU ENTERED COLLEGE, HAVEN'T YOU ?
I WANTED TO BE CUTE, BUT ...
... I'M JUST NOT THAT TYPE. SO I DECIDED TO GO FOR GLAMOUR INSTEAD.
I THINK YOU'RE OVERDOING IT, SIS.
WE'RE ALL ON A JOURNEY.
OH, HERE YOU GO, TOMOMI. A NEW YEAR'S CARD.
AND YOUR RAFFLE TICKET.
And I'll keep the prize you won.
2-301
Toshiyuki Ojika

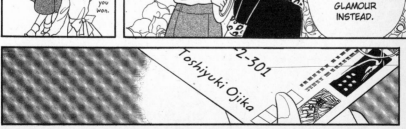

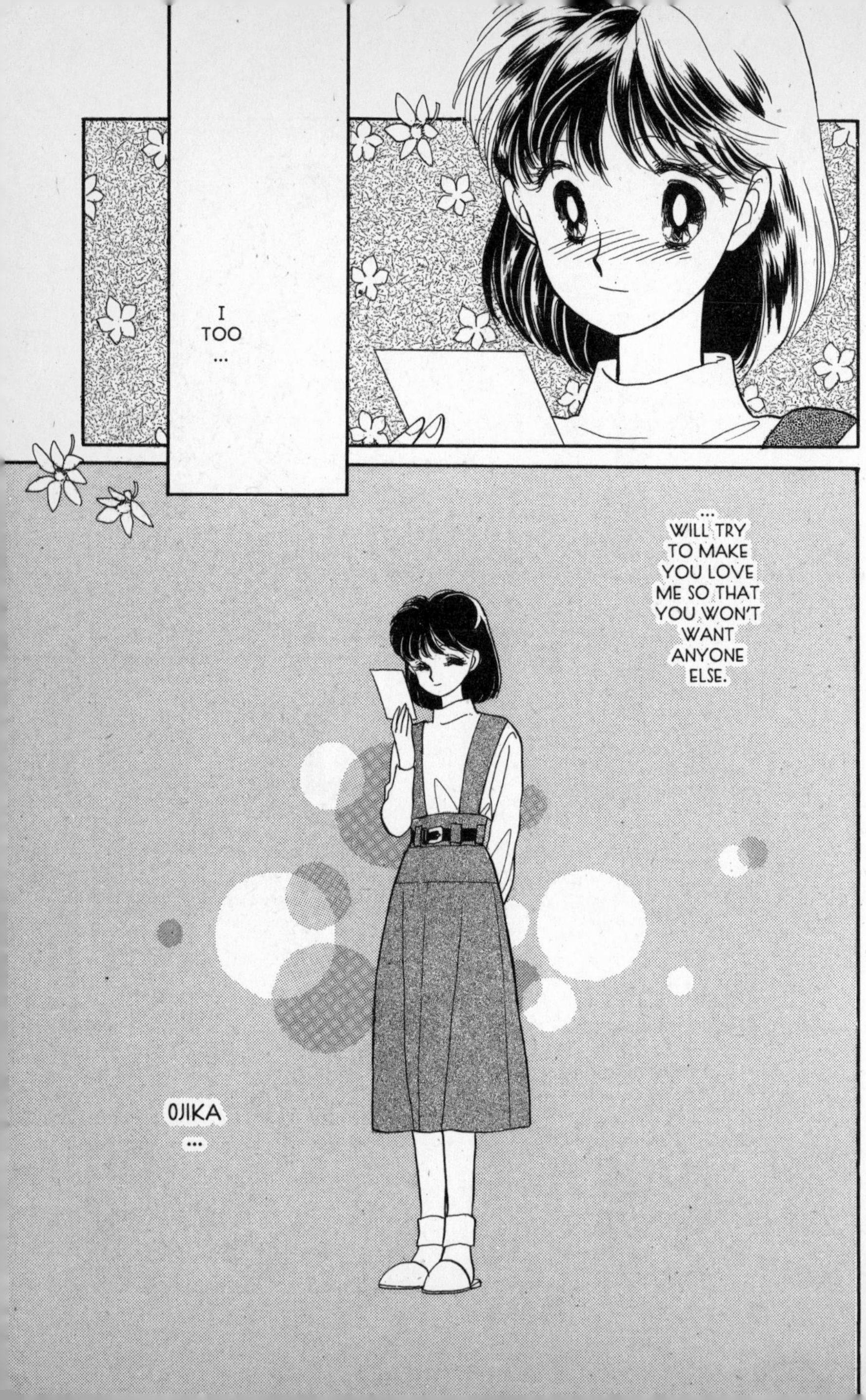
I TOO ...
... WILL TRY TO MAKE YOU LOVE ME SO THAT YOU WON'T WANT ANYONE ELSE.
OJIKA ...

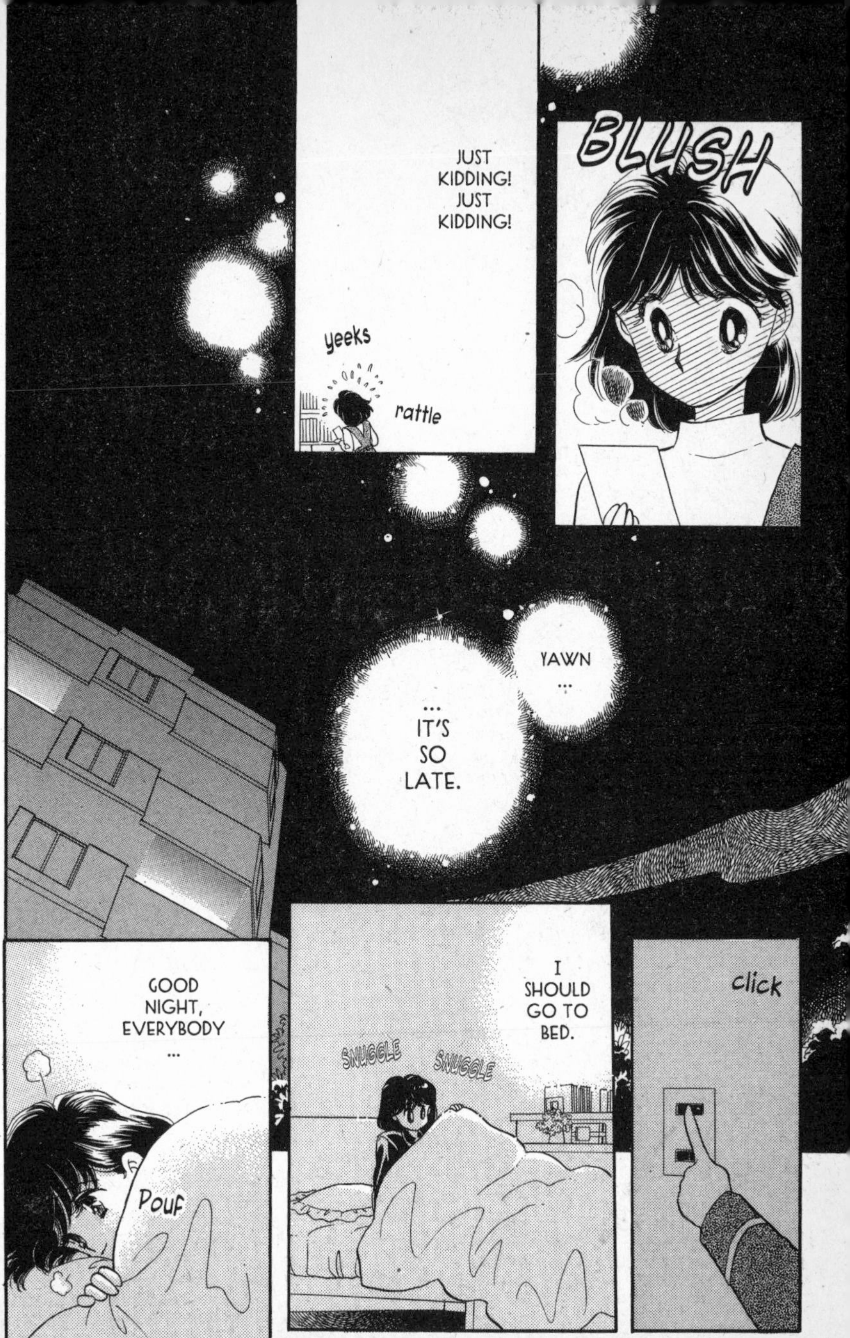
BLUSH
JUST KIDDING! JUST KIDDING!
yeeks
rattle
YAWN ...
... IT'S SO LATE.
click
I SHOULD GO TO BED.
SNUGGLE
SNUGGLE
GOOD NIGHT, EVERYBODY ...
Pouf

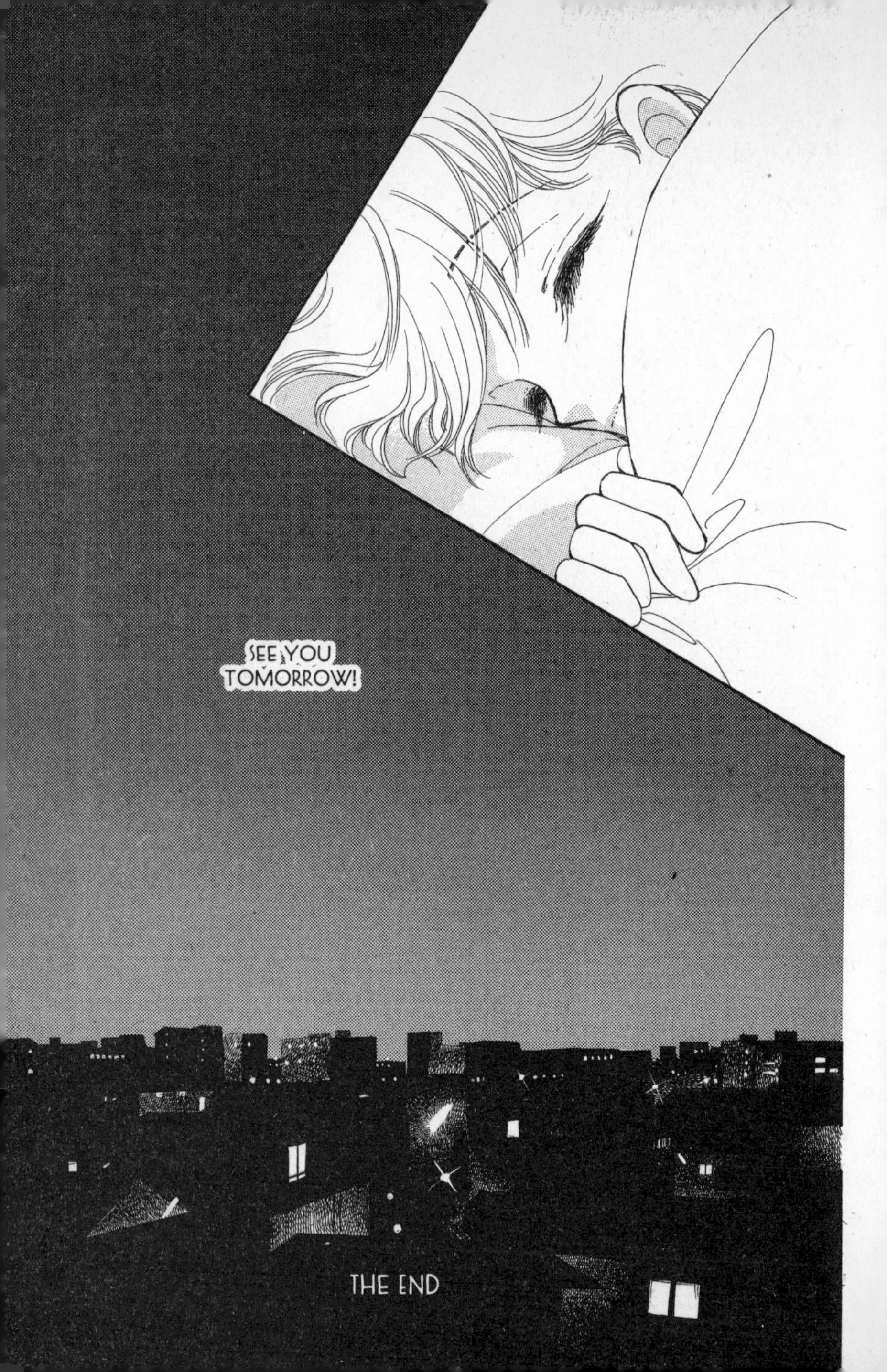
SEE YOU TOMORROW!
THE END

FROM FAR AWAY

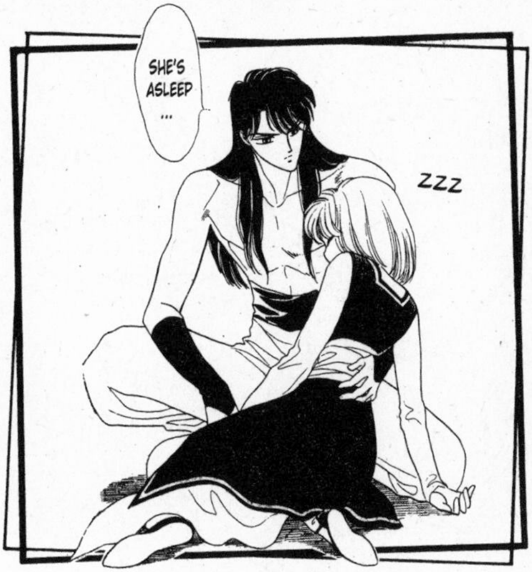
SHE'S ASLEEP ...
ZZZ

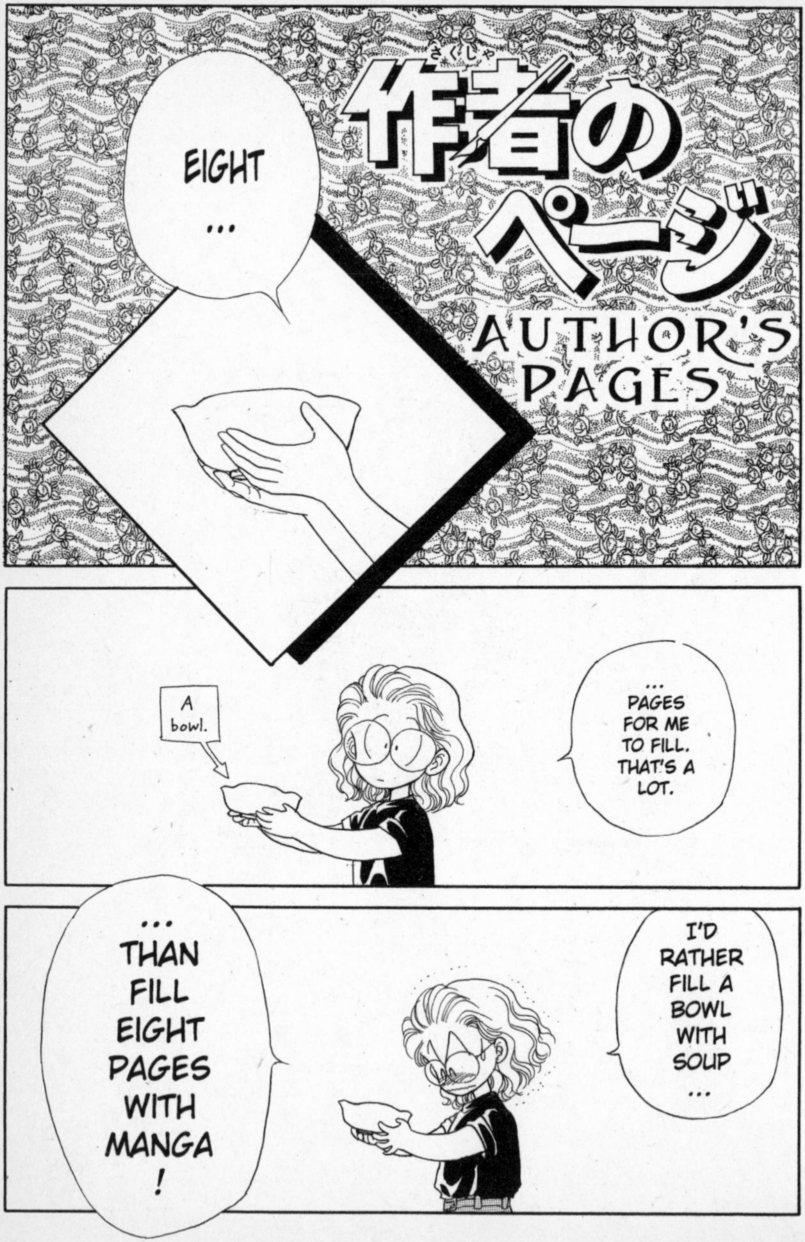
作者(さくしゃ)のページ
AUTHOR'S PAGES
EIGHT ...
... PAGES FOR ME TO FILL. THAT'S A LOT.
A bowl.
I'D RATHER FILL A BOWL WITH SOUP ...
... THAN FILL EIGHT PAGES WITH MANGA !

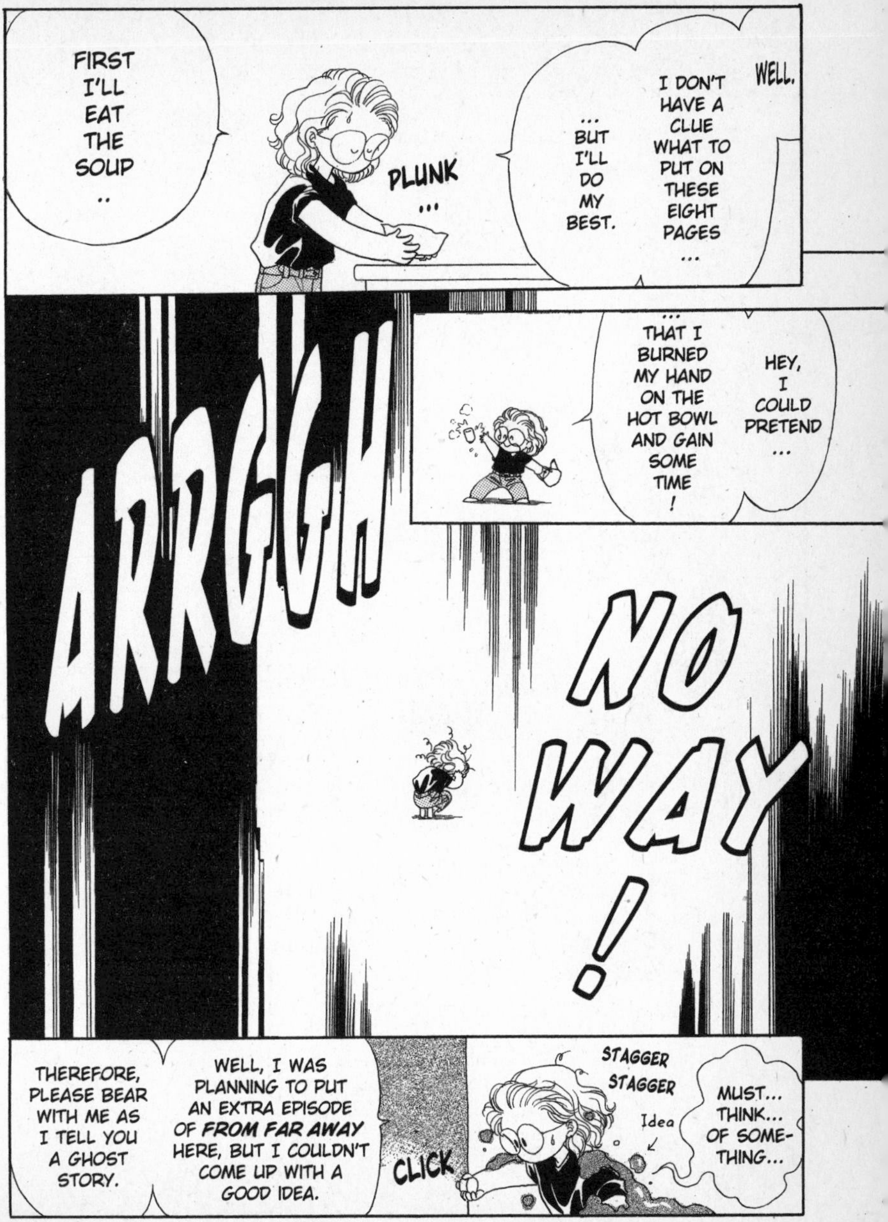

WELL.
I DON'T HAVE A CLUE WHAT TO PUT ON THESE EIGHT PAGES ...
... BUT I'LL DO MY BEST.
PLUNK ...
FIRST I'LL EAT THE SOUP ..
HEY, I COULD PRETEND ...
... THAT I BURNED MY HAND ON THE HOT BOWL AND GAIN SOME TIME !
NO WAY !
ARRGGH
STAGGER STAGGER
Idea
MUST... THINK... OF SOME-THING...
CLICK
WELL, I WAS PLANNING TO PUT AN EXTRA EPISODE OF *FROM FAR AWAY* HERE, BUT I COULDN'T COME UP WITH A GOOD IDEA.
THEREFORE, PLEASE BEAR WITH ME AS I TELL YOU A GHOST STORY.

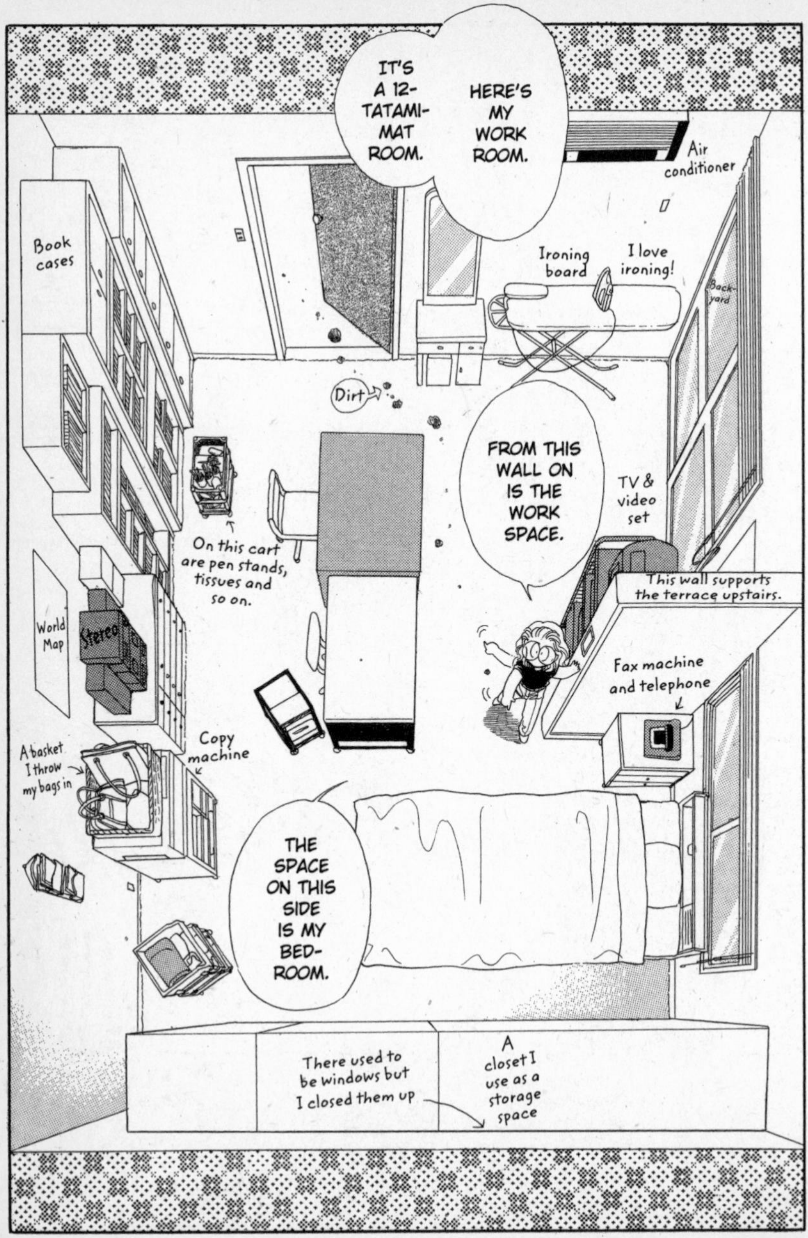

HERE'S MY WORK ROOM.
IT'S A 12-TATAMI-MAT ROOM.
Air conditioner
I love ironing!
Ironing board
Book cases
Back-yard
Dirt
TV & video set
FROM THIS WALL ON IS THE WORK SPACE.
On this cart are pen stands, tissues and so on.
This wall supports the terrace upstairs.
World Map
Stereo
Fax machine and telephone
Copy machine
A basket I throw my bags in
THE SPACE ON THIS SIDE IS MY BED-ROOM.
A closet I use as a storage space
There used to be windows but I closed them up

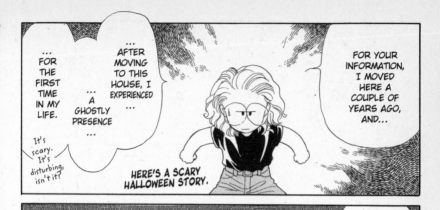

FOR YOUR INFORMATION, I MOVED HERE A COUPLE OF YEARS AGO, AND...
... AFTER MOVING TO THIS HOUSE, I EXPERIENCED ...
... A GHOSTLY PRESENCE ...
... FOR THE FIRST TIME IN MY LIFE.
HERE'S A SCARY HALLOWEEN STORY.
It's scary. It's disturbing, isn't it?
I DIDN'T SEE THE GHOST, THOUGH.
I NEVER EVER WANT TO SEE A GHOST!!
SO I DON'T OPEN MY EYES WHEN I FEEL THAT PRESENCE NO MATTER WHAT!!
LET ME TELL YOU ...
... I WAS SLEEPING LIKE THIS ...
... AND I BEGAN TO FEEL SOME-THING WEIRD.
A GHOSTLY PRESENCE FILLED THE ROOM.
I SAID TO MYSELF, "WHOA, WHAT'S THIS?"
WHOOOOOO
I try to express the feeling I have when the ghost's near me with this sound.
... IT HIT ME INTENSELY!
BIFF
Was that intense enough?
AFTER THAT, IT HAPPENED EVERY DAY.
Kyaa!

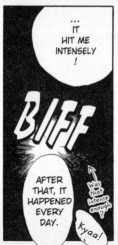

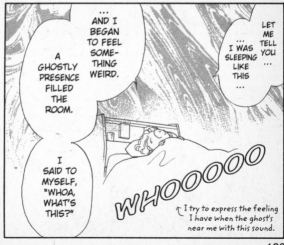

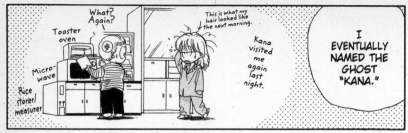

I EVENTUALLY NAMED THE GHOST "KANA."
This is what my hair looked like the next morning.
Kana visited me again last night.
What? Again?
Toaster oven
Micro-wave
Rice storer/measurer
I JOKED ABOUT IT, BUT I WAS REALLY SCARED.
Buddhist rosary
I WENT TO A BUDDHIST SCHOOL SO I RECITED BUDDHIST PRAYERS DESPERATELY.
AS SOON AS THE GHOSTLY FEELING LEFT, I WOULD JUMP UP AND TURN ON THE LIGHT.
AFTER A WHILE, I BEGAN TO FEEL THE GHOST EVEN WHEN THE LIGHT WAS ON, OR WHEN I WAS HAVING A NAP.
AS A RESULT, MY INSOMNIA ...
... GOT MUCH WORSE.
ONE DAY, I REALIZED MY WINDOW SHUTTERS ...
... HAD BEEN CLOSED ALL THE TIME.
HMMM...
Big windows
These shutters were open.
I WASN'T SURE IF THAT HAD ANYTHING TO DO WITH THE GHOST, BUT ...
I had curtains over the windows.

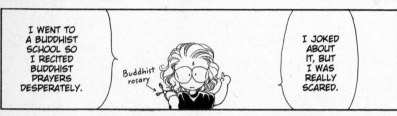

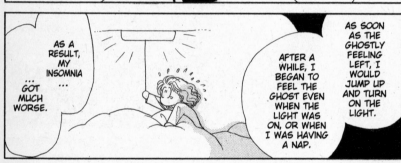

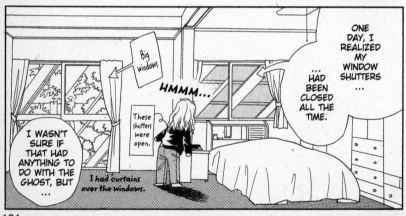

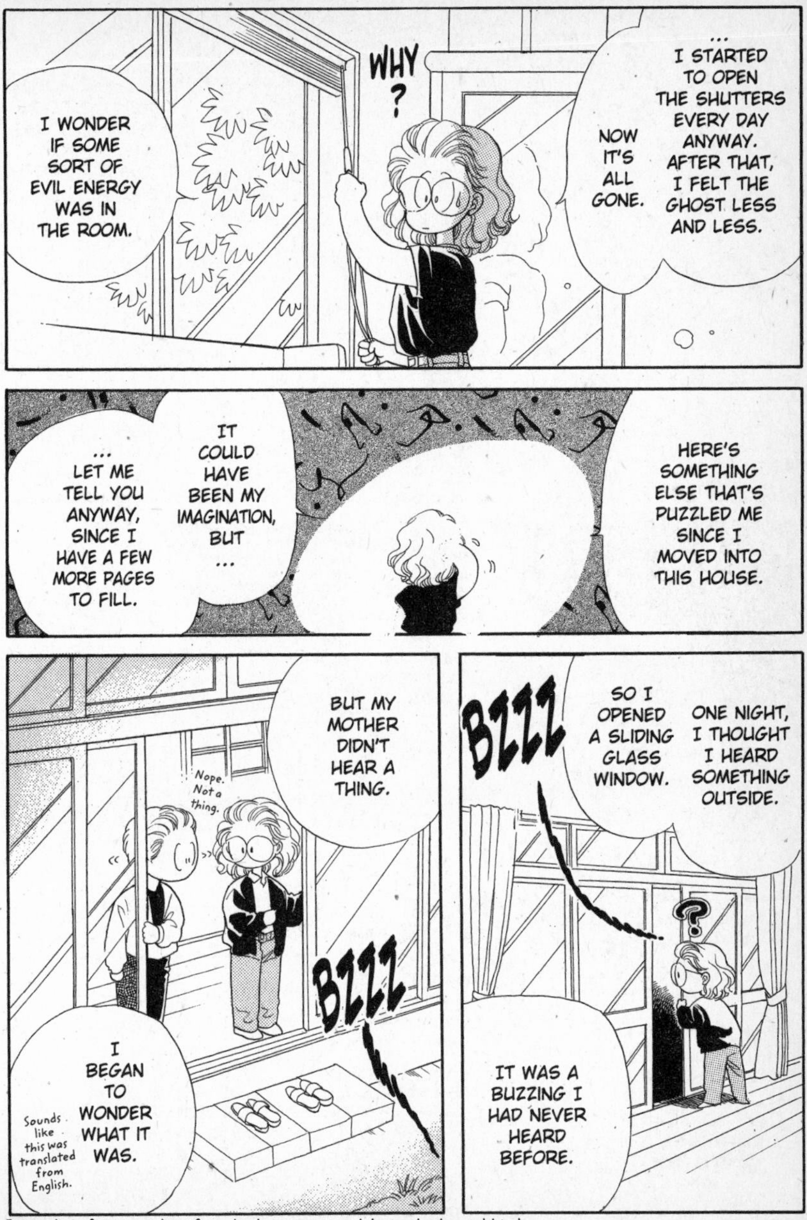
... I STARTED TO OPEN THE SHUTTERS EVERY DAY ANYWAY. AFTER THAT, I FELT THE GHOST LESS AND LESS.
NOW IT'S ALL GONE.
WHY ?
I WONDER IF SOME SORT OF EVIL ENERGY WAS IN THE ROOM.
HERE'S SOMETHING ELSE THAT'S PUZZLED ME SINCE I MOVED INTO THIS HOUSE.
IT COULD HAVE BEEN MY IMAGINATION, BUT ...
... LET ME TELL YOU ANYWAY, SINCE I HAVE A FEW MORE PAGES TO FILL.
ONE NIGHT, I THOUGHT I HEARD SOMETHING OUTSIDE.
SO I OPENED A SLIDING GLASS WINDOW.
BZZZ
IT WAS A BUZZING I HAD NEVER HEARD BEFORE.
BUT MY MOTHER DIDN'T HEAR A THING.
Nope. Not a thing.
BZZZ
I BEGAN TO WONDER WHAT IT WAS.
Sounds like this was translated from English.

I asked my father and my friends about the sound, but nobody could help.

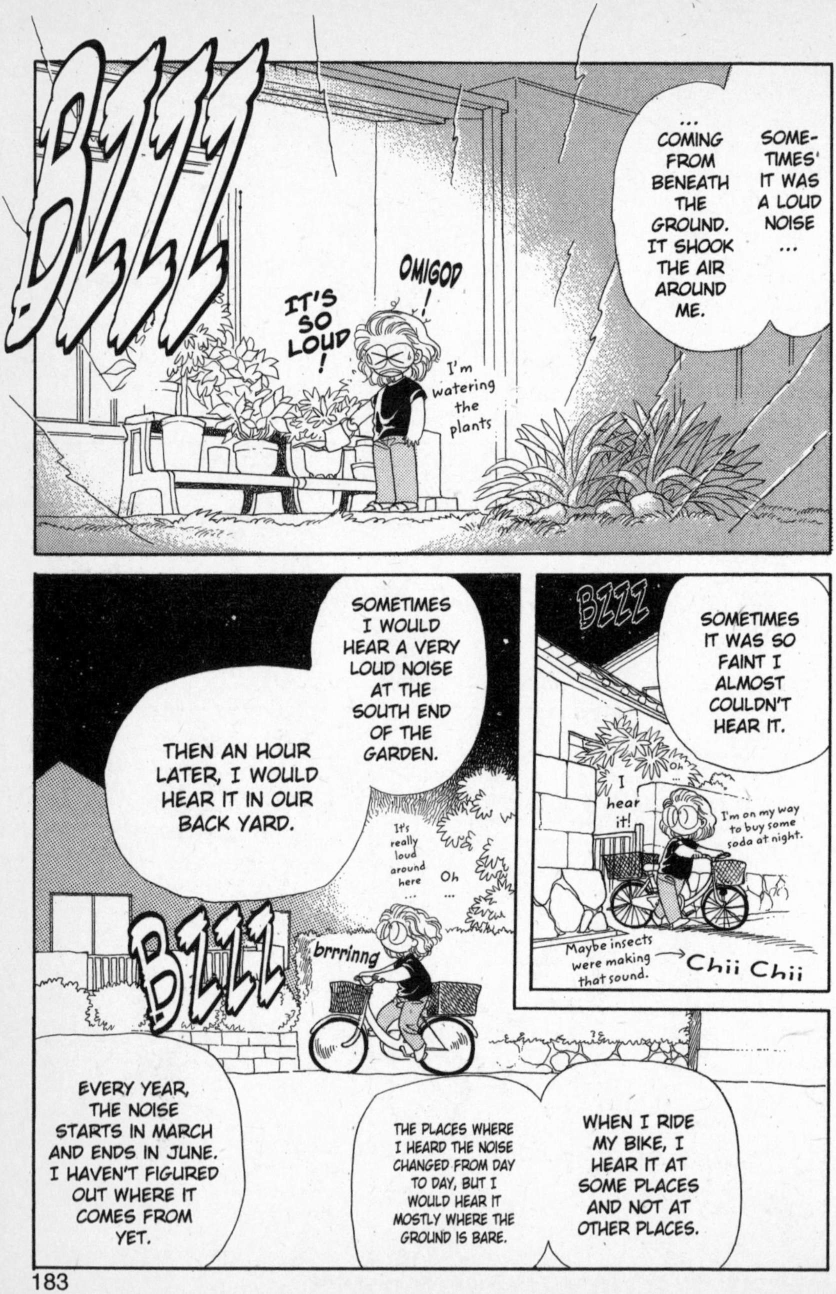
SOME-TIMES' IT WAS A LOUD NOISE ...
... COMING FROM BENEATH THE GROUND. IT SHOOK THE AIR AROUND ME.
OMIGOD !
IT'S SO LOUD !
I'm watering the plants
BZZZ
BZZZ
SOMETIMES IT WAS SO FAINT I ALMOST COULDN'T HEAR IT.
Oh ...
I hear it!
I'm on my way to buy some soda at night.
Maybe insects were making that sound.
Chii Chii
SOMETIMES I WOULD HEAR A VERY LOUD NOISE AT THE SOUTH END OF THE GARDEN.
THEN AN HOUR LATER, I WOULD HEAR IT IN OUR BACK YARD.
Oh ...
It's really loud around here ...
brrrinng
BZZZ
WHEN I RIDE MY BIKE, I HEAR IT AT SOME PLACES AND NOT AT OTHER PLACES.
THE PLACES WHERE I HEARD THE NOISE CHANGED FROM DAY TO DAY, BUT I WOULD HEAR IT MOSTLY WHERE THE GROUND IS BARE.
EVERY YEAR, THE NOISE STARTS IN MARCH AND ENDS IN JUNE. I HAVEN'T FIGURED OUT WHERE IT COMES FROM YET.

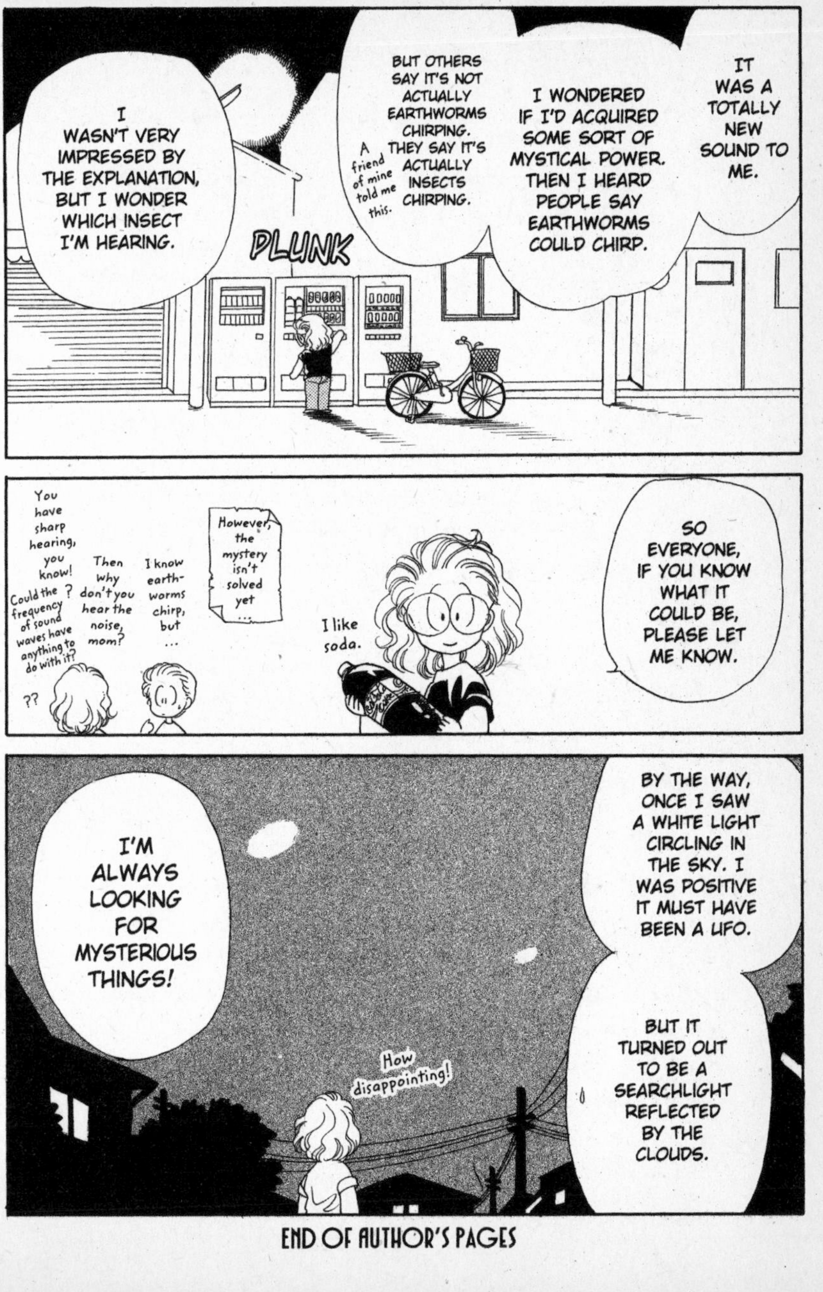
IT WAS A TOTALLY NEW SOUND TO ME.
I WONDERED IF I'D ACQUIRED SOME SORT OF MYSTICAL POWER. THEN I HEARD PEOPLE SAY EARTHWORMS COULD CHIRP.
BUT OTHERS SAY IT'S NOT ACTUALLY EARTHWORMS CHIRPING. THEY SAY IT'S ACTUALLY INSECTS CHIRPING.
A friend of mine told me this.
I WASN'T VERY IMPRESSED BY THE EXPLANATION, BUT I WONDER WHICH INSECT I'M HEARING.
PLUNK
SO EVERYONE, IF YOU KNOW WHAT IT COULD BE, PLEASE LET ME KNOW.
I like soda.
However, the mystery isn't solved yet...
I know earthworms chirp, but...
Then why don't you hear the noise, mom?
?
You have sharp hearing, you know! Could the frequency of sound waves have anything to do with it?
??
BY THE WAY, ONCE I SAW A WHITE LIGHT CIRCLING IN THE SKY. I WAS POSITIVE IT MUST HAVE BEEN A UFO.
BUT IT TURNED OUT TO BE A SEARCHLIGHT REFLECTED BY THE CLOUDS.
I'M ALWAYS LOOKING FOR MYSTERIOUS THINGS!
How disappointing!

END OF AUTHOR'S PAGES

☆ INVESTIVATION REPORT ➔ ☆

I got lots of responses to my questions on these pages.

Someone said the insect is a mole cricket.
I looked it up in an encyclopedia.

It looks like this.

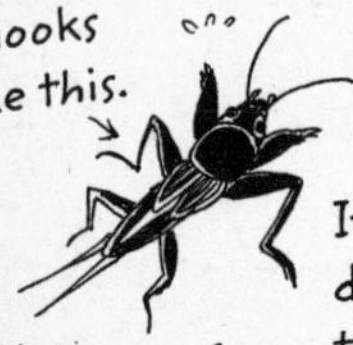

Not a very accurate drawing.

Mole Cricket (family of Gryllotalpidae (mole cricket), size: 35mm)

Some books say 30mm

It's like a cricket. Looks a bit like a mole, doesn't it? It digs a hole in the ground and lives there, but it can also climb trees, fly and swim.

Some readers wrote that if you sprinkle water on the ground at night and wait, you'll hear mole crickets chirping. When you dig where the chirping comes from, you find the insects.

Many people asked their families about this.

It was fun reading those letters because they told me about their families, too.

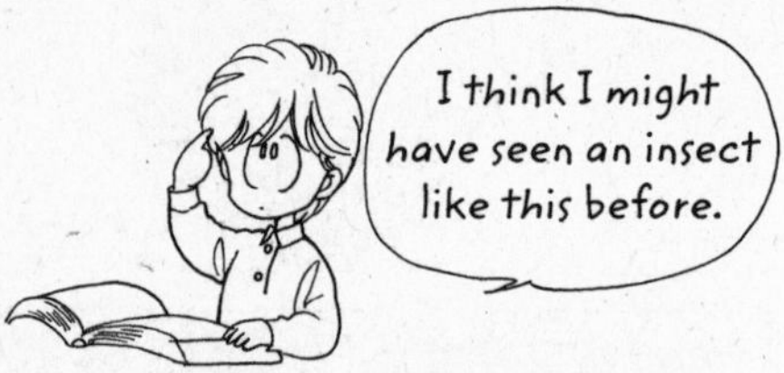
I think I might have seen an insect like this before.

☆ ☆ ☆ ☆ ☆ ☆ ☆ ☆ ☆ ☆ ☆

I also got a letter from someone who says hearing the noise means there's a ghost nearby. (She seems to encounter the supernatural so often that I felt sorry for her.) Since I love mysterious stuff, her claim was hard to ignore. Tee hee! I like her idea because it's romantic. (She said she asked her grandma, who is a medium, about this.)

Many thanks to everyone who helped me find out about the noise.

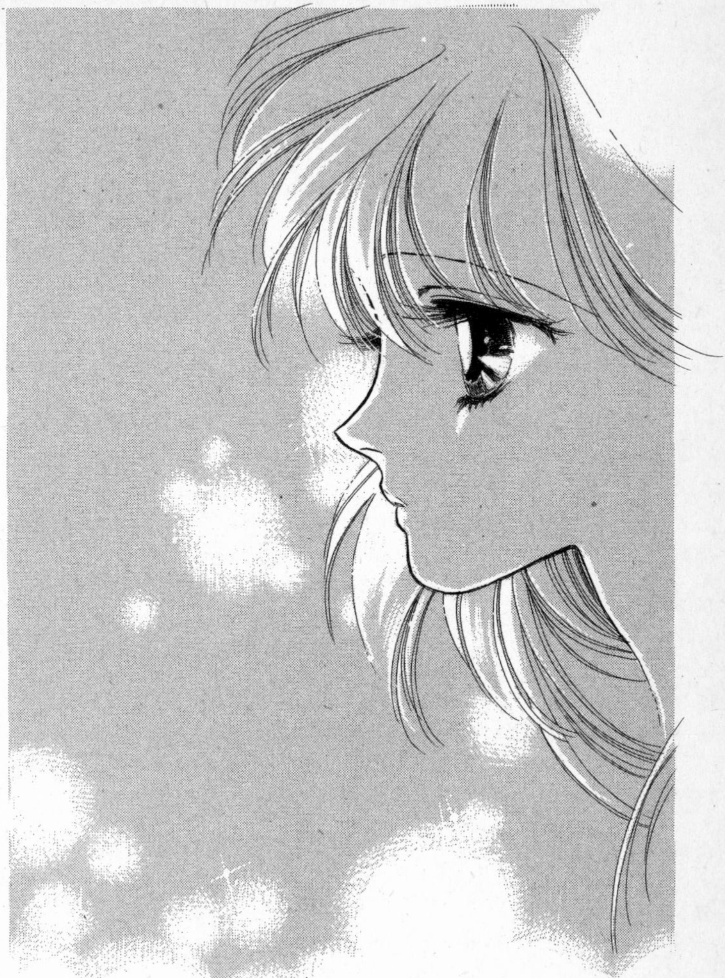

From Far Away
Vol. 3
Shôjo Edition

Story and Art by
Kyoko Hikawa

English Adaptation/Trina Robbins
Translation/Yuko Sawada
Touch-Up Art & Lettering/Walden Wong
Cover & Graphic Design/Andrea Rice
Editor/Eric Searleman

Managing Editor/Annette Roman
Director of Production/Noboru Watanabe
Editorial Director/Alvin Lu
Sr. Director of Acquisitions/Rika Inouye
Vice President of Sales & Marketing/Liza Coppola
Executive Vice President/Hyoe Narita
Publisher/Seiji Horibuchi

Printed in the U.S.A.

Published by VIZ, LLC
P.O. Box 77010
San Francisco, CA 94107

Shôjo Edition
10 9 8 7 6 5 4 3 2 1
First printing, February 2005

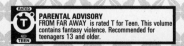

www.viz.com   store.viz.com

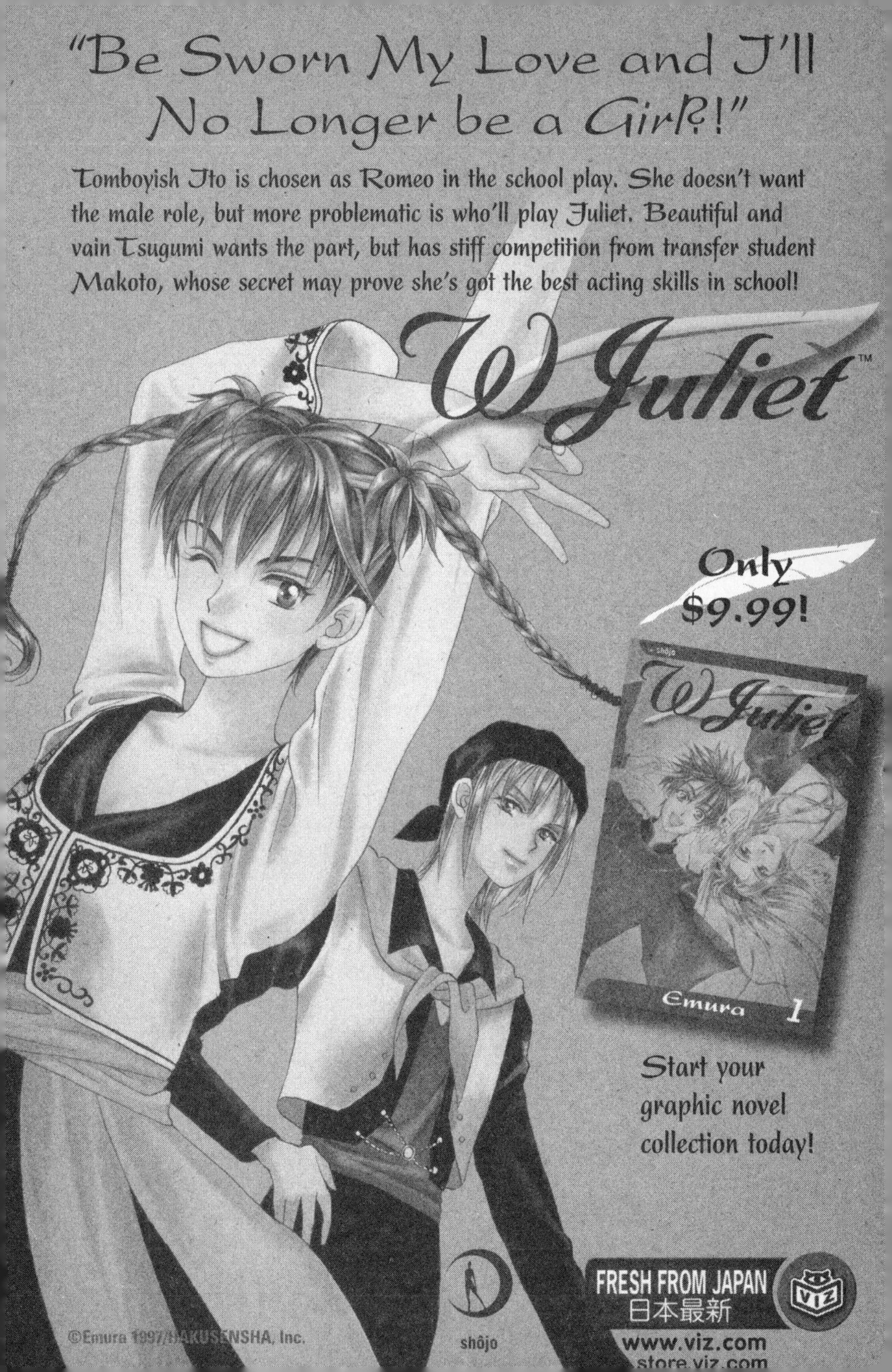
"Be Sworn My Love and I'll No Longer be a Girl?!"
Tomboyish Ito is chosen as Romeo in the school play. She doesn't want the male role, but more problematic is who'll play Juliet. Beautiful and vain Tsugumi wants the part, but has stiff competition from transfer student Makoto, whose secret may prove she's got the best acting skills in school!
W Juliet™
Only $9.99!
W Juliet
Emura 1
Start your graphic novel collection today!
©Emura 1997/HAKUSENSHA, Inc.
shôjo
FRESH FROM JAPAN
日本最新
VIZ
www.viz.com
store.viz.com

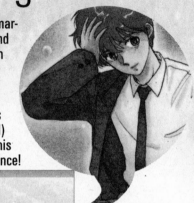

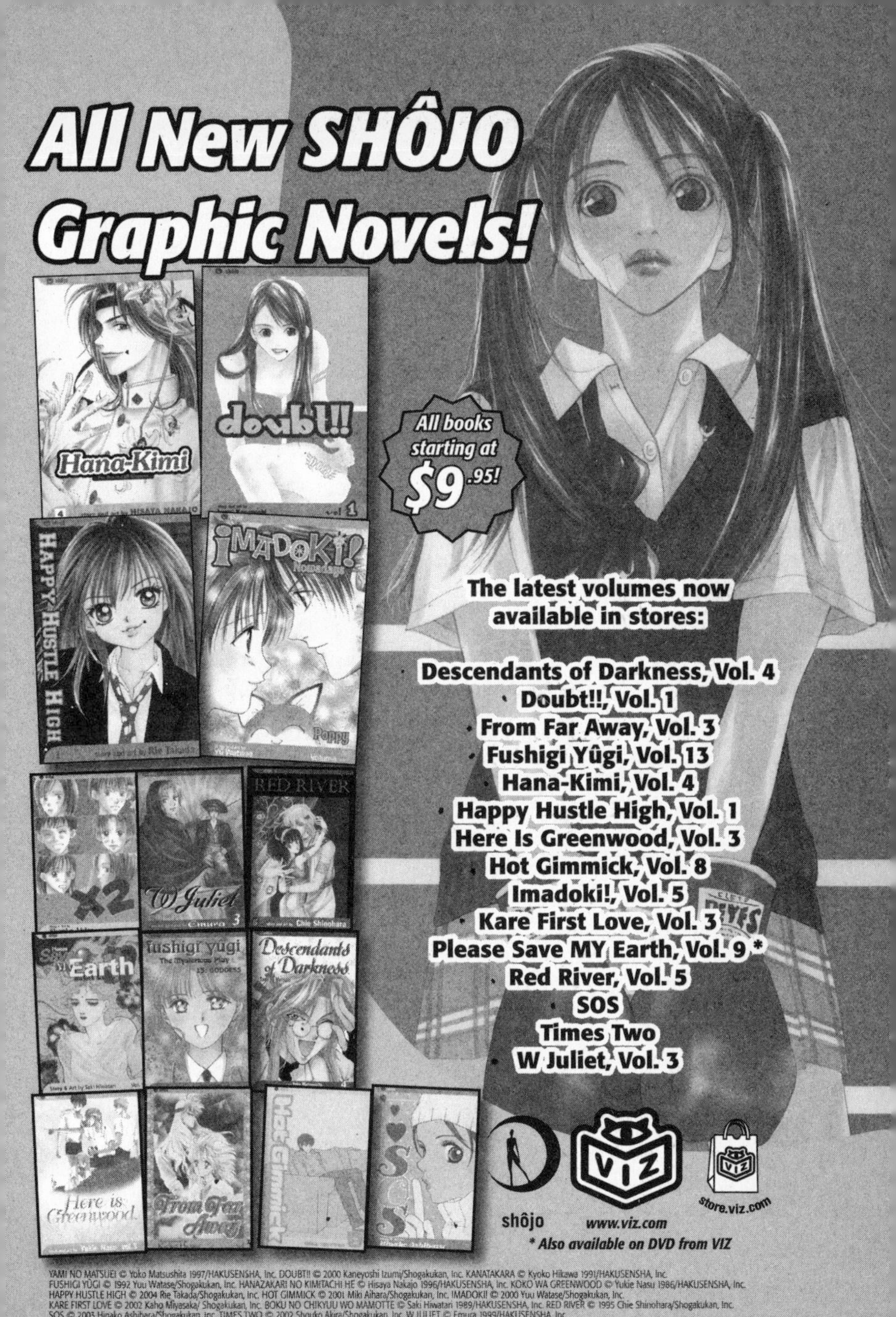
All New SHÔJO Graphic Novels!
All books starting at $9.95!
The latest volumes now available in stores:
Descendants of Darkness, Vol. 4
Doubt!!, Vol. 1
From Far Away, Vol. 3
Fushigi Yûgi, Vol. 13
Hana-Kimi, Vol. 4
Happy Hustle High, Vol. 1
Here Is Greenwood, Vol. 3
Hot Gimmick, Vol. 8
Imadoki!, Vol. 5
Kare First Love, Vol. 3
Please Save MY Earth, Vol. 9 *
Red River, Vol. 5
SOS
Times Two
W Juliet, Vol. 3
shôjo
www.viz.com
store.viz.com
* Also available on DVD from VIZ

COMPLETE OUR SURVEY AND LET
US KNOW WHAT YOU THINK!

☐ Please do NOT send me information about VIZ products, news and events, special offers, or other information.

☐ Please do NOT send me information from VIZ's trusted business partners.

Name: _____

Address: _____

City: _____ **State:** _____ **Zip:** _____

E-mail: _____

☐ **Male** ☐ **Female** **Date of Birth** (mm/dd/yyyy): ___ / ___ / ___ (Under 13? Parental consent required)

What race/ethnicity do you consider yourself? (please check one)

☐ Asian/Pacific Islander ☐ Black/African American ☐ Hispanic/Latino

☐ Native American/Alaskan Native ☐ White/Caucasian ☐ Other: _____

What VIZ product did you purchase? (check all that apply and indicate title purchased)

☐ DVD/VHS _____

☐ Graphic Novel _____

☐ Magazines _____

☐ Merchandise _____

Reason for purchase: (check all that apply)

☐ Special offer ☐ Favorite title ☐ Gift

☐ Recommendation ☐ Other _____

Where did you make your purchase? (please check one)

☐ Comic store ☐ Bookstore ☐ Mass/Grocery Store

☐ Newsstand ☐ Video/Video Game Store ☐ Other: _____

☐ Online (site: _____)

What other VIZ properties have you purchased/own? _____

_____

How many anime and/or manga titles have you pu[...]
VIZ titles? (please check one from each column)

ANIME	MANGA	V[...]
☐ None	☐ None	☐ None
☐ 1-4	☐ 1-4	☐ 1-4
☐ 5-10	☐ 5-10	☐ 5-10
☐ 11+	☐ 11+	☐ 11+

I find the pricing of VIZ products to be: (please check one)

☐ Cheap ☐ Reasonable ☐ Expensive

What genre of manga and anime would you like to see from VIZ? (please check two)

☐ Adventure ☐ Comic Strip ☐ Science Fiction ☐ Fighting

☐ Horror ☐ Romance ☐ Fantasy ☐ Sports

What do you think of VIZ's new look?

☐ Love It ☐ It's OK ☐ Hate It ☐ Didn't Notice ☐ No Opinion

Which do you prefer? (please check one)

☐ Reading right-to-left

☐ Reading left-to-right

Which do you prefer? (please check one)

☐ Sound effects in English

☐ Sound effects in Japanese with English captions

☐ Sound effects in Japanese only with a glossary at the back

THANK YOU! Please send the completed form to:

VIZ

NJW Research
42 Catharine St.
Poughkeepsie, NY 12601

All information provided will be used for internal purposes only. We promise not to sell or otherwise divulge your information.